The Pan dictionary of
synonyms and antonyms

edited by
Laurence Urdang
and
Martin Manser

Pan Books London and Sydney

First published 1978 by The New American Library Inc.
This revised edition published 1980 by Pan Books Ltd,
Cavaye Place, London SW10 9PG
©Laurence Urdang Inc. 1978, 1980
ISBN 0 330 26150 9
This edition produced by Laurence Urdang Associates Ltd,
Aylesbury
Typesetting by Tradespools Ltd, Frome
Printed in Great Britain
by Richard Clay (The Chaucer Press) Ltd,
Bungay Suffolk

Introduction

A synonym is a word that has a meaning similar to that of another word. This dictionary gives a list of synonyms for common words in English. It can be used when you cannot think of a word to express your exact meaning, or when you want to add variety to your speech or writing.

how to use this book

Look up the word for which you want to find a synonym, as in a normal dictionary; all the entries are in alphabetical order. Each entry indicates the part of speech of the word – noun, verb, etc. – followed by the list of synonyms. Where the word has more than one meaning, different meanings are numbered, and an example of the use of the word is given. For example:

angle *n.* **1** corner, edge; branch fork: *A triangle has three angles.* **2** viewpoint, point of view, position, standpoint: *Let's look at this question from a different angle.*

The first meaning has the synonyms *corner, edge,* . . . and an example of the use of the meaning is given. The second meaning has the synonyms *viewpoint, point of view,* . . . with a different example. Sometimes more than one example is given to explain the use of the word in more detail.

Not all the words given in the list of synonyms have exactly the same meaning: in fact there are no such things as exact synonyms; words are never completely substitutable for each other. For example:

dislike *vb.* disapprove of; hate, detest, loathe.

The words *hate, detest, loathe* are stronger than *disapprove of,* and this difference is shown by dividing the groups by a semicolon. Furthermore, the synonyms given may also combine with other words in different ways. For example:

favour ... *vb.* prefer, support, want to: *We favour going to Germany for our holiday.*

The words *prefer, support* can replace *favour*, but if *want to* is chosen, the sentence has to be rephrased to give something like *We want to go to Germany for our holiday.* The list of synonyms given should therefore be used with care. If you are in doubt, check first how the word is used by asking someone or by looking it up in a good dictionary.

antonyms —

An antonym is a word that has a meaning opposite to that of another word. At the end of many entries there is a list of antonyms, shown after the word ANT. Where there is more than one part of speech, the part of speech that the antonyms refer to is given. Similarly, when there is more than one numbered meaning, the number of the meaning referred to in the list of antonyms is shown in brackets. For example:

attack *vb.* **1** assault, set upon, assail, charge, storm: *The army attacked the fort, and it was soon captured.* **2** criticize, blame, abuse: *The newspapers attacked the local council for refusing to collect the rubbish.* *n.* assault, charge, on-slaught, encounter: *The robber was accused of an armed attack outside the bank.* ANT. *vb.* (**1**) withdraw, retreat. (**2**) praise, endorse. *n.* withdrawal, retreat.

The antonyms *withdraw, retreat* refer to the first meaning of the verb part of the entry: *assault, set upon* ...; the antonyms *praise, endorse* to the second meaning of the verb part of the entry; and *withdrawal, retreat* to the noun part of the entry. Occasionally, the same list of synonyms may refer to more than one numbered part of the entry or more than one part of speech, and this is also shown.

levels of usage

Some words are used informally, that is they are used widely in conversation but would not be used in writing a formal letter or composition. This is shown by placing the word *Informal* before the list of synonyms. For example:

cranky *adj.* *Informal:* eccentric, odd, strange, peculiar.

This means that the word *cranky* is informal. The label *Slang* is used in a similar way, to show words that are very informal and are to be used in fewer contexts than informal words. They are not suitable for use in most kinds of writing. If you are uncertain about how to use a particular word, look it up in a dictionary.

Some of the words that are given in the list of synonyms itself may also be either informal or slang. In this case the label is put in front of the particular word in brackets. For example:

mislead *vb.*   deceive, delude, (*informal*) take in; trick.

cross-references

Occasionally a cross-reference is used to show that the list of synonyms of a word is in a different part of the book. For example:

lethal *see* **fatal.**

This means that a list of synonyms for the word *lethal* is given at the entry *fatal*.

list of abbreviations

adj.	adjective	*n.*	noun
adj. phr.	adjectival phrase	*n. phr.*	noun phrase
adv.	adverb	*pl.*	plural
adv. phr.	adverbial phrase	*prep.*	preposition
ANT.	antonym	*prep. phr.*	prepositional phrase
conj.	conjunction	*v.*	verb
foll.	followed	*vb. phr.*	phrasal verb

a

abandon *vb.* **1** leave; desert, forsake: *The captain was the last to abandon the sinking ship.* **2** give up, surrender: *The castaways never abandoned hope that they would be found.* *adv. phr.* **with abandon** freely, unrestrainedly, without restraint, control, inhibition, *or* constraint: *Whenever his parents were not at home, he behaved with wild abandon.* ANT. *adv.* join, engage, unite, embrace, retain.

abbey *n.* church, minster; priory, monastery, friary, nunnery.

abbot *n.* prior, monk, friar.

abbreviate *vb.* shorten, abridge, cut, reduce, condense. ANT. lengthen, extend, augment.

abbreviation *n.* shortening, abridgment, condensation.

abdicate *vb.* give up, relinquish, resign, renounce.

abide (by) *vb.* tolerate, endure, put up with, accept.

ability *n.* capability, skill, competence; power.

able *adj.* **1** capable, qualified, fit, competent: *People are able to speak a language.* **2** talented, skilled, clever, skilful: *She is an able mathematician.* ANT. unable, incompetent; incapable.

abnormal *adj.* unusual, uncommon, odd, peculiar, queer; strange, weird. ANT. normal, average, usual.

abolish *vb.* end, obliterate, erase, put out, eliminate. ANT. establish; keep, retain.

abominable *adj.* bad, terrible, awful, nasty, unpleasant. ANT. admirable, fine, noble.

about *prep.* **1** concerning, relating to, involving: *The book was about pirates.* **2** near, close to, around, almost, approximately: *The blouse is about my size.* *adv.* **1** nearby, around, close, close by: *There's a ghost about at midnight!* **2** nearly, almost: *It is about four o'clock.*

above *prep.* over, higher than, superior to. ANT. below, under, beneath.

abreast *adv.* alongside, beside, side by side.

abridge *vb.* shorten, cut, abbreviate, abstract. ANT. expand, extend, increase.

abroad *adv.* **1** overseas: *She studied abroad last year.* **2** publicly, widely, at large; in all directions, in all places: *The news was made known abroad that they were to be married.* ANT. (2) privately, secretly.

abrupt *adj.* 1 sudden, hasty: *He came to an abrupt stop at the door.* 2 short, curt, blunt, brusque, rude: *When I asked where she had been, she became very abrupt and asked me to leave.* 3 steep, precipitous: *The road made an abrupt descent to the valley.* ANT. (1, 3) gradual.

abscess *n.* sore, inflammation, boil.

absence *n.* want, need, lack. ANT. presence, existence.

absent *adj.* 1 away, not present, off: *I was absent from school on Monday.* 2 missing, lacking, nonexistent: *Common sense was clearly absent from their decision.* ANT. present.

absent-minded *adj.* forgetful; inattentive, day-dreaming, preoccupied. ANT. alert, attentive, observant; aware.

absolute *adj.* 1 real, undoubted; perfect: *The court had absolute proof that he had committed the crime.* 2 total, complete, unlimited, limitless, unrestricted; tyrannical, dictatorial: *The dictator assumed absolute power.* ANT. partial, limited, fragmentary, incomplete.

absolutely *adv.* definitely, positively, really, doubtlessly. ANT. doubtfully, questionably.

absolve *vb.* acquit, exonerate, excuse, forgive, pardon, clear, cleanse, discharge. ANT. blame; accuse, charge.

absorb *vb.* 1 consume, occupy, engage: *The film absorbed their attention completely.* 2 suck up, sop up, take in *or* up: *A sponge absorbs water.* ANT. (2) leak, drain.

abstain *vb.* do without, give up, deny oneself, renounce.

abstract *adj.* theoretical, hypothetical; unreal. ANT. concrete, real, substantial.

absurd *adj.* foolish, ridiculous, preposterous, laughable, silly. ANT. sensible, sound, reasonable.

abundance *n.* plenty, copiousness, ampleness, profusion. ANT. scarcity, want, dearth, absence.

abundant *adj.* plentiful, abounding, copious, profuse, ample. ANT. scarce, scant, poor, insufficient.

abuse *vb.* 1 misuse, misapply: *The king abused his power by making the people pay high taxes.* 2 maltreat, hurt, harm, injure: *It was cruel of the children to abuse their kitten by keeping it in a cage.* 3 insult, malign, revile: *The politicians abused each other in the election campaign.* *n.* misuse, mistreatment, maltreatment: *The puppy suffered the boys' abuse without whimpering.*

accelerate *vb.* speed up, quicken, hasten. ANT. slow down.

accent *n.* 1 stress, accentuation: *The accent in the word "college" comes on the first syllable.* 2 emphasis, importance, weight: *The preacher put a great stress on discipline in his sermon.*

accept *vb.* **1** receive, take: *She accepted the gift with thanks.* **2** admit, allow, consent to: *He accepts criticism from anyone but his father.* **3** believe, think, hold, trust: *Few people find it easy to accept that they will die one day.* ANT. **(1, 2)** refuse, reject, ignore.

access *n.* approach, entrance; way, passage.

accessory *n.* addition, extra, supplement.

accident *n.* mishap, misadventure, misfortune, disaster, calamity, catastrophe: *Three men were knocked unconscious in the accident at the factory.* *n. phr.* **by accident** unintentionally, accidentally: *I spilt the sugar by accident.*

acclaim *vb.* praise, applaud; welcome.

accommodate *vb.* provide for, house, serve; hold.

accompany *vb.* escort, go with, join, attend. ANT. abandon, leave, forsake.

accomplice *n.* confederate, accessory, assistant, associate, partner (in crime).

accomplish *vb.* do, complete, achieve, fulfil, perform, finish. ANT. fail.

accord *vb.* **1** agree, correspond, concur: *The description that the witness gave of the attack accorded with that of the victim.* **2** award, grant, reward with, give: *When the sergeant was killed in action, he was accorded an officer's burial.* *n.* agreement, concord: *The governments reached accord regarding offshore fishing rights.* ANT. *n.* disagreement, difference, quarrel.

account *n.* **1** explanation, report, description: *John gave an account of what had happened to him over the weekend.* **2** story, tale, anecdote, narration, narrative: *We were frightened by the old man's strange account of the cave.* **3** record, balance sheet, ledger, book: *According to the store's account, we owe them £52.* *vb.* explain, make *or* give excuses for: *The teacher asked Maria to account for her absence from school.*

accumulate *vb.* gather, store up, amass.

accurate *adj.* precise, correct, exact, right, true. ANT. inaccurate, inexact, mistaken, wrong.

accuse *vb.* blame, charge, incriminate. ANT. absolve, clear, discharge, acquit.

accustomed (to) *adj.* used to, in the habit of, wont to.

ache *vb.* hurt; be sore; throb, sting.

achieve *vb.* **1** do, perform, complete, accomplish, reach, realize: *Only after much hard work are most of us able to achieve our goals.* **2** attain, gain, acquire, secure, procure: *The candidate achieved victory in the election after a hard campaign.* ANT. fail.

acid *adj.* **1** sour, tart, vinegary: *Lemons have an acid taste.* **2** sardonic, sarcastic, bitter, biting: *Because of his acid wit, few people would associate with him.* ANT. (1) sweet, bland, mild.

acknowledge *vb.* **1** agree to, admit, allow, concede, accept, grant: *After a fierce battle, the general finally acknowledged defeat.* **2** accept, receive, thank for: *The prizewinner gratefully acknowledged the award.* ANT. deny, refuse, reject.

acquaintance *n.* associate, colleague, companion.

acquire *vb.* obtain, procure, secure, get, gain, appropriate. ANT. lose, forfeit.

acquit *vb.* excuse, forgive, exonerate, discharge. ANT. condemn, sentence.

act *n.* **1** deed, achievement, action, accomplishment, feat, exploit: *He received a medal for an act of bravery.* **2** law, decree, statute, judgment: *Parliament voted on the crime-prevention act.* **3** performance: *We saw the balancing act at the circus.* *vb.* **1** do, operate, function: *The crowbar acts as a lever.* **2** perform, play, impersonate: *She acts the part of the vampire in the film.*

action *n.* **1** movement: *His actions are not graceful.* **2** battle, fight, fighting, combat: *He saw action on the western front.*

active *adj.* **1** energetic, vigorous, agile: *He's 80 but still active.* **2** busy, occupied, engaged, committed: *Mrs. Robinson is active in many charitable organizations.* ANT. (1) lazy, lethargic, inactive. (2) apathetic.

activity *n.* action, motion, movement.

actor *n.* performer, entertainer, player; star.

actual *adj.* real, true, genuine, certain. ANT. unreal, pretended, fake, bogus, false.

actually *adv.* really, in fact, truly.

acute *adj.* **1** severe, piercing, intense: *I have an acute pain in my toe.* **2** sharp, keen, quick, perceptive, discerning, intelligent: *A human's eyesight is not as acute as that of an eagle.* ANT. (2) insensitive, dull, blind, deaf.

adapt *vb.* conform, suit, modify, adjust, fit.

add *vb.* **1** combine, put together, join, unite: *Add this painting to your collection.* **2** total: *Adding the numbers in this column gives exactly 312.* ANT. subtract, remove, withdraw.

additional *adj.* new, extra, further, supplementary.

address *n.* 1 location; residence, home; office: *Please let me have your address so that I can write to you.* 2 speech, lecture, oration, presentation: *The president's address lasted three hours.* *vb.* 1 speak to, talk to: *Don't ever address me in that way in public.* 2 apply oneself to, concentrate on, pay attention to: *You should address yourself to the problem in hand and avoid rambling.*

adequate *adj.* sufficient, enough; satisfactory, fit, suitable. ANT. inadequate, insufficient.

adhere *vb.* 1 cling, stick, hold; cleave: *The new tape will adhere to anything.* 2 be attached, be faithful, be devoted: *She adheres to the ideas she had as a child.* ANT. (1) separate, loosen.

adherent *n.* supporter, follower. ANT. defector, renegade, drop-out.

adjacent *adj.* near, next (to), close (to), neighbouring, nearby. ANT. apart, separate, distant.

adjoining *adj.* next (to), near (to), touching, bordering. ANT. separate, distant, remote.

adjourn *vb.* suspend, postpone, put off; defer, delay. ANT. assemble, convene, begin.

adjust *vb.* 1 set, regulate; change, alter; repair, fix: *I adjusted the clock so that it would run on time.* 2 arrange, settle: *We adjusted our spending to our income.* 3 adapt, acclimatize; accustom oneself, get used to: *Betty quickly adjusted to her new school.*

adjustable *adj.* adaptable, variable, changeable; flexible, pliable.

administer *vb.* 1 manage, direct, supervise, oversee; rule, govern; conduct, control, superintend; administrate: *The general manager administers the work schedules in the company.* 2 dispense, mete out, deal out, give out, distribute: *The magistrate administers justice in a court.* 3 give, provide, contribute, distribute: *The doctor administered the vaccine to the villagers.*

administration *n.* management, direction, conduct, supervision.

admirable *adj.* excellent, fine, worthy, praiseworthy. ANT. contemptible, despicable, sorry.

admiration *n.* wonder, awe, pleasure, approval, esteem. ANT. contempt, disdain, disrespect.

admire *vb.* revere, esteem, venerate; like; honour, praise. ANT. dislike, loathe, detest, hate.

admissible *adj.* permissible, lawful; proper, fair, just.

admission *n.* 1 entrance, access, admittance; ticket, pass: *The authorities charged for admission to the hockey game.* 2 confession, acknowledgment: *Her admission of guilt resulted in a suspension of two days from school.*

admit *vb.* 1 confess, acknowledge, own: *Bob admits that he ate all the cake.* 2 let in, allow to enter: *When we paid the entrance charge, we were admitted into the stadium.* ANT. (1) deny. (2) obstruct, reject.

admittance *n.* entrance, access, admission.

admonish *vb.* 1 urge; warn, caution, advise against: *The teacher admonished Jimmy to stop talking in class.* 2 scold, reprimand, rebuke, censure, reprove: *Afterwards the teacher had to admonish him for making faces.* ANT. praise, commend, extol.

ado *n.* fuss, trouble, bother, to-do, bustle, flurry, activity, commotion, stir, excitement, upset, hubbub, confusion, tumult, turmoil. ANT. quietness, composure, tranquillity.

adolescent *adj.* teenage, young, youthful; immature: *Why do so many adults act in such an adolescent way?* *n.* teenager, youth, young person: *Many adolescents have difficulties growing into adults.* ANT. *adj.* adult, grown, mature.

adopt *vb.* 1 foster, take in, take care of: *The family adopted a little girl named Rachel.* 2 take up, choose, select: *The director adopted the committee's plans.*

adorable *adj.* delightful, lovely, charming, wonderful.

adore *vb.* love, idolize, worship, revere, venerate; respect, honour, esteem. ANT. hate, despise, loathe.

adorn *vb.* decorate, ornament, beautify, enhance, embellish. ANT. strip, bare, denude.

adrift *adj.* drifting, floating, afloat.

adroit *adj.* skilful, clever, adept, dexterous, ingenious, expert. ANT. clumsy, awkward, graceless.

adult *adj.* mature, developed, full-grown; of age: *"Please act in a more adult way," the teacher reminded her pupils.* *n.* man, woman, grown-up: *This ticket admits one adult and one child.* ANT. *adj.* immature, infantile.

adulterate *vb.* contaminate, defile, pollute, debase.

adultery *n.* unfaithfulness, infidelity, unchastity.

advance *vb.* 1 proceed, progress, move, bring, *or* go forward: *The armies advanced towards one another.* 2 further, promote: *These treaties will advance the cause of peace.* *n.* progress, advancement, improvement, promotion: *Progress* *in many industries has been brought about by advances in technology.* ANT. *vb.* (1) retreat, withdraw, flee. (2) retard, obstruct. *n.* decline, deterioration; retreat, withdrawal.

advantage *n.* 1 benefit, gain, profit: *Driving a car has some advantages over travelling by train.* 2 favour, help, (*informal*) edge: *Because of his height, Mark·has the advantage in the long jump.* ANT. (1) disadvantage, drawback. (2) obstacle, hindrance.

adventure *n.* exploit, experience; event, undertaking, incident.

adventurous *adj.* daring, bold, brave; enterprising.

adversary *n.* opponent, antagonist, foe, enemy, contestant. ANT. friend, ally.

adverse *adj.* 1 unlucky, unfortunate, unfavourable: *Adverse business conditions made him decide to close the shop.* 2 contrary, opposite, opposing, opposed: *Adverse winds delayed the plane by two hours.* ANT. (1) beneficial, favourable.

adversity *n.* trouble, misfortune; distress, calamity, disaster, catastrophe. ANT. fortune; happiness, benefit.

advertise *vb.* publicize, (*informal*) plug; make known, propagate.

advertisement *n.* commercial, poster, billboard; brochure, bill, handbill.

advice *n.* counsel, recommendation, guidance, suggestion.

advisable *adj.* prudent, sensible, wise; proper, suitable, fit, fitting. ANT. inadvisable, ill-considered, imprudent.

advise *vb.* 1 counsel, recommend, suggest: *Her father advised her to go out with friends of her own age.* 2 inform, notify, acquaint: *The premier was advised of the treachery of the generals.*

advocate *vb.* support, recommend, defend, argue for, plead for: *The ecologists advocate preservation of forests.* *n.* supporter, promoter, upholder: *Advocates of spelling reform in English have a long fight ahead of them.* ANT. *vb.* oppose, withstand, resist. *n.* opponent, foe, adversary.

affair *n.* business, concern; matter, thing.

affect *vb.* 1 influence, determine, modify, alter, change: *A change in the speed limit affects everyone's driving habits.* 2 impress, stir, move, touch: *The death of Jennie's kitten affected her deeply.*

affection *n.* liking, fondness, attachment, friendliness, tenderness, warmth.   ANT. dislike, aversion, antipathy.

affectionate *adj.*   fond, tender, attached, warm, loving.   ANT. cold, distant, unfeeling.

affirm *vb.*   1 declare, state, assert: *The defendant affirmed that he was at home on the night of the murder.*   2 confirm, establish, ratify: *Parliament affirmed the minister's plans.*   ANT. (1) deny, contradict, repudiate, disclaim.

afflict *vb.*   hurt, trouble, distress; disturb, torment, harass.

affliction *n.*   1 trouble, distress, grief, misfortune: *Poverty is the affliction of millions of people.*   2 pain, suffering, misery; illness, sickness, ailment: *In his old age, headaches became a serious affliction.*   ANT. (1) benefit, gain.   (2) relief, comfort.

afford *vb.*   be able to pay; spare; manage, support, provide for.

afraid *adj.*   frightened, fearful, scared, terrified.   ANT. courageous, bold, daring.

age *n.*   era, time, period, epoch: *The last ice age ended about 20 000 years ago.*   *n. phr.* **of age** mature, grown-up: *When you become of age, you will have the right to vote.*   *vb.* 1 grow old, get on; decline: *My grandmother began to age in her early seventies.*   2 mature, develop, ripen: *I think this wine has aged long enough.*

aged *adj.*   old, elderly, ancient.   ANT. young, youthful.

agent *n.*   1 representative, delegate, deputy; operator: *John is an agent for a plastics firm.*   2 instrument, means, cause: *The sun is an agent in the growth of plants.*

aggravate *vb.*   1 intensify, worsen, heighten: *His illness was aggravated by the lack of heat in the room.*   2 *Informal:* irritate, exasperate, annoy: *"Stop aggravating your sister!" shouted Jean.*   ANT. (1) ease, relieve, soothe.

aggressive *adj.*   1 attacking, pugnacious, ready to fight, offensive: *Her aggressive manner irritated so many people that no one wanted to spend time with her.*   2 assertive, vigorous, energetic, enterprising, determined: *We need an aggressive chairman, not one who is too shy to act for us.*   ANT. (1) peaceful, friendly, amicable.   (2) passive, shy, timid, withdrawn.

agile *adj.*   active, nimble, graceful, lively, spry.   ANT. clumsy, awkward, inept.

agitate *vb.*   stir up, excite, disturb.   ANT. calm, soothe.

agony *n.*   pain, suffering, torment, torture.

agree *vb.*   1 settle, concur, harmonize, unite: *The members of the committee could not agree on where the party should be held.*   2 assent, consent, yield, concede: *He agreed to leave* *the room so that his parents could talk in private.* ANT. (1) differ, disagree, argue. (2) refuse.

agreeable *adj.* friendly, cooperative, pleasing, pleasant. ANT. disagreeable, quarrelsome, contentious, touchy.

agreement *n.* 1 treaty, pact; deal, bargain, contract, understanding, arrangement: *An agreement was reached between the union and the company.* 2 settlement, accord, harmony, concord: *There was basic agreement on the terms of the pension contribution.* ANT. disagreement, discord, misunderstanding.

agriculture *n.* farming, husbandry; cultivation, growth.

aid *vb.* help, assist, support, back: *Unless you all aid me, I cannot win.* *n.* help, assistance, support, backing: *Without his aid I couldn't have climbed to the top of the mountain.* ANT. *vb.* impede, obstruct, hinder. *n.* obstacle, hindrance.

ailing *adj.* sick, ill, unwell. ANT. well, hearty, hale.

ailment *n.* sickness, illness, affliction, disease.

aim *vb.* 1 point, direct: *Aim a little below the bull's eye when firing a rifle at a target.* 2 try *or* strive for: *Some of us aim at perfection, but only a few ever achieve it.* *n.* 1 purpose, goal, target, object, objective: *My aim in life is to be a really good doctor.* 2 direction, sight, sighting: *His aim was so poor that he missed the target completely.*

air *n.* 1 atmosphere: *The envelope of air is kept close to earth by gravity.* 2 manner, appearance, character, look, attitude: *He has an air about him that gives everyone the impression that he thinks he's just wonderful.* *vb.* 1 ventilate: *We really ought to air the room to get rid of the smell.* 2 display, publicize, expose, reveal: *The headmaster gave the students the chance to air their complaints against the teacher.* ANT. *vb.* (2) hide, conceal, cover up.

aisle *n.* passage, opening; corridor; path.

alarm *n.* 1 fright, fear, dismay: *They greeted the news of the accident with alarm.* 2 siren, bell, gong: *The fire alarm could be heard far away.* *vb.* frighten, scare, terrify, startle: *The nurse was alarmed by Jane's temperature.* ANT. *vb.* calm, soothe, comfort.

alarming *adj.* frightening, disturbing, shocking, appalling, daunting.

album *n.* book, scrapbook, notebook; collection, record.

alcohol *n.* spirits, intoxicants, (strong) drink, liquor.

alert *adj.* 1 watchful, attentive, wide-awake, vigilant, keen, observant: *The alert watchman gave the alarm when he found the broken window.* 2 quick, lively, active, spirited, bright:

Dick's alert mind understood at once where the error was in the calculation. n. alarm, warning: *When they smelled smoke, they sounded the alert.* ANT. *adj.* listless, dulled, sluggish, lethargic.

alien *n.* foreigner, immigrant; stranger: *In some countries, aliens become eligible for citizenship after one year.* *adj.* foreign, strange; non-native: *The spacemen landed on an alien planet.* ANT. *adj.* familiar, commonplace, accustomed.

alike *adj.* like, same, identical; similar.

alive *adj.* live, living, existing, breathing; lively.

allay *vb.* quiet, soothe, calm, lessen, lighten, soften, moderate. ANT. arouse, worsen, intensify.

allege *vb.* delcare, affirm, state, assert. ANT. deny, refute, contradict.

allegiance *n.* loyalty, faithfulness, duty, obligation. ANT. disloyalty, treachery, infidelity.

alley *n.* lane, alleyway, way; path, footpath.

alliance *n.* **1** agreement, treaty, pact; union, league: *The Triple Alliance was between Germany, Austria-Hungary, and Italy.* **2** association, connection, combination; affinity, correspondence: *The alliance between biology and psychology is well established.*

allot *vb.* distribute, divide, deal out.

allow *vb.* **1** permit, let: *My mother won't allow me to go out until my cold is better.* **2** grant, let have, concede: *Allow me one more chance to prove I can run faster than Jim.* **3** set aside *or* apart, provide for: *We didn't allow enough time to drive to the station and missed the train.* ANT. **(1)** forbid, prohibit.

ally *n.* associate, friend, partner: *Britain and America were allies against Germany in the Second World War.* *vb.* **1** associate, join, unite: *The countries were allied by the treaty.* **2** unite, unify, combine, connect, join: *If we ally ourselves with them, we could be much stronger than if we remain alone.* ANT. *n.* enemy, foe, adversary.

almost *adv.* nearly, somewhat.

alone *adj.* isolated, solitary; deserted: *Robinson Crusoe was alone until he found Friday.* *adv.* solo, solitarily; solely, exclusively: *She sang alone at the concert.* ANT. *adv.* accompanied, together.

aloof *adj.* distant, uninvolved, uninterested, withdrawn, separate; disdainful. ANT. friendly, outgoing, cordial, warm.

aloud *adv.* audibly, out loud; articulately, clearly, plainly, distinctly.

already *adv.* now, by this time, before now; yet.

also *adv.* too, as well, besides, furthermore, moreover, further.

alter *vb.* change, modify; vary; adjust. ANT. keep, preserve, maintain.

alteration *n.* change, modification, difference, adjustment. ANT. preservation, maintenance.

alternate *vb.* substitute, interchange, rotate: *In order to be fair, the teacher alternated the children at the head of the line.* *adj.* successive, consecutive, in rotation: *The guards stood watch outside the palace for alternate hours.*

alternative *n.* choice, selection, option; possibility.

although *conj.* even though, though, even if, in spite of (the fact that), despite, notwithstanding.

altitude *n.* height, elevation. ANT. depth, deepness, profundity.

altogether *adv.* entirely, completely, wholly, quite: *He was altogether too rude to his father.* *n. phr.* **in the altogether** *Informal:* nude, naked, stripped: *After the night football game, the whole team went swimming in the altogether.*

always *adv.* forever; everlastingly, eternally, forevermore. ANT. never, rarely.

amateur *n.* novice, nonprofessional, beginner, tiro: *When it came to repairing watches, Jimmy was obviously an amateur.* *adj.* unprofessional, nonprofessional: *The amateur theatre group put on an excellent performance.* ANT. professional.

amaze *vb.* astonish, astound, surprise, stun, dumbfound. ANT. bore, tire, weary.

amazement *n.* astonishment, wonder, surprise, bewilderment.

ambassador *n.* diplomat, envoy, representative; minister.

ambiguous *adj.* unclear, uncertain, vague, deceptive. ANT. clear, unmistakable, certain.

ambition *n.* drive, initiative; eagerness, enthusiasm.

ambitious *adj.* aspiring, zealous, (*informal*) pushing, (*informal*) high-flying.

ambush *vb.* ensnare, trap, lure, trick; lie in wait for: *Twelve o'clock struck and the thugs knew it was time to ambush the patrol.* *n.* trap, snare, lure, pitfall: *The highwaymen planned the ambush of the mail coach.*

amend *vb.* improve, better. ANT. worsen.

amiable *adj.* friendly, amicable, good-natured, outgoing, agreeable, kindhearted, kind, pleasant. ANT. disagreeable, ill-tempered, cross, touchy.

amid *prep.* amidst, surrounded by, among, amongst, in the middle of.

amiss *adv.* improperly, wrongly, astray, awry: *We knew that something had gone amiss when Barbara didn't come to school for three days.* *adj.* improper, wrong, faulty: *Something is amiss in the wiring of this house—the lights always flicker.* ANT. *adv.* properly, correctly, rightly. *adj.* right, correct.

among *prep.* amid, in the middle *or* midst of, surrounded by.

amount *n.* quantity, measure: *There was only a small amount of sugar in the box.* *vb.* add up, total, come: *At the last count, those opposed to the plan amounted to less than a majority.*

ample *adj.* abundant, plentiful, generous, liberal. ANT. insufficient, inadequate.

amplify *vb.* enlarge, extend, broaden, develop, expand. ANT. restrict, confine, narrow, shorten, condense.

amuse *vb.* entertain, please, interest, divert. ANT. bore, tire.

amusement *n.* entertainment, pastime; diversion; enjoyment, recreation, pleasure. ANT. boredom, tedium.

amusing *adj.* entertaining, diverting, pleasing, pleasant; funny, comical. ANT. boring, tiring, tedious.

analyse *vb.* examine, investigate, study, scrutinize; explain.

analysis *n.* examination, investigation, study.

ancestor *n.* forefather; predecessor.

ancestral *adj.* inherited, hereditary.

ancestry *n.* lineage, descent, line, family, house. ANT. posterity, descendants.

anchor *n.* stay, mooring: *The anchor was thrown overboard as the ship docked.* *vb.* **1** moor, berth, tie up: *The ship anchored offshore.* **2** fasten, tie, secure, attach, fix: *We anchored the rope to the rock.* ANT. *vb.* (1) set sail. (2) loosen, free, detach.

ancient *adj.* antique, old, aged, old-fashioned, primitive. ANT. new, fresh, recent, current.

anecdote *n.* story, tale, narrative, account.

angel *n.* seraph, cherub, archangel. ANT. devil, demon.

anger *n.* fury, rage, indignation, wrath; displeasure, exasperation: *We felt anger at the unfair way that Sue had been treated.*

vb. enrage, infuriate, arouse, nettle, exasperate, inflame, madden: *Jean's mother was angered at her refusal to help with the housework.*

angle *n.* 1 corner, edge; branch, fork: *A triangle has three angles.* 2 viewpoint, point of view, position, standpoint: *Let's look at this question from a different angle.*

angry *adj.* furious, mad, inflamed, irate. ANT. happy, content, peaceful, tranquil.

anguish *n.* pain, suffering, misery, distress, torment, agony.

animal *n.* creature, beast.

animate *vb.* enliven, vitalize, invigorate, stimulate: *Her animated conversation made Amy a welcome guest at parties. adj.* alive, lively, vital, vigorous: *Rocks are not animate beings, but mice are.* ANT. *adj.* inanimate, dead.

annex *vb.* add, attach, join, append.

annexe *n.* extension, wing.

announce *vb.* proclaim, declare, report, publish, publicize. ANT. suppress, stifle; censor.

announcement *n.* notice, declaration, report, statement, message.

annoy *vb.* bother, irritate, irk, pester, harass, disturb. ANT. comfort, soothe, please.

annual *adj.* yearly, every year, once a year.

annul *vb.* cancel, repeal, invalidate, revoke.

answer *n.* reply, response; retort, rejoinder: *His answer to her question was a nod. vb.* reply, respond: *She answered him with a shake of the head.* ANT. *n.* question, query, inquiry. *vb.* ask, question, inquire.

antagonism *n.* hostility, enmity, opposition, conflict, animosity. ANT. friendliness, geniality, cordiality.

antagonist *n.* adversary, opponent, rival; enemy, foe. ANT. friend, ally.

anticipate *vb.* 1 expect, foresee, forecast: *Because we had anticipated our parents' permission, we got ready to go.* 2 forestall, provide against, prevent: *He anticipated the attack by altering his route home.*

antique *n.* objet d'art, rarity, curio: *The auctioneer sold the antiques to the collector for a huge sum. adj.* old, ancient, early; antiquated, old-fashioned, out-of-date: *They sold the antique furniture at the auction.* ANT. *adj.* new, fresh, recent.

anxiety *n.* uneasiness, distress, worry, foreboding, apprehension. ANT. peacefulness, placidity, calmness, tranquillity.

anxious *adj.* worried, troubled, concerned, uneasy, apprehensive. ANT. calm, composed.

anyway *adv.* anyhow, nevertheless, in any case.

apathetic *adj.* indifferent, unconcerned; uncaring. ANT. interested, concerned; excited.

apologetic *adj.* regretful, sorry. ANT. unrepentant; stubborn, obstinate.

apologize *vb.* say sorry, confess; be sorry, regret.

apology *n.* explanation, plea, excuse, justification.

appal *vb.* horrify, shock, dismay; frighten. ANT. please, edify, comfort.

appalling *adj.* awful, frightful, shocking, dreadful.

apparatus *n.* machinery, equipment, materials; mechanism, device.

apparel *n.* clothing, clothes, attire, garb, garments, robes, dress.

apparent *adj.* 1 plain, evident, clear, obvious; transparent: *When we found the book in Cora's desk, it was apparent who had taken it.* 2 seeming: *Although the grey mare had been the apparent winner of the race, the photo showed the real winner to be the brown one.* ANT. (2) real, actual.

appeal *n.* 1 request, plea, petition, entreaty: *The annual appeal for contributions resulted in huge donations this year.* 2 attractiveness, glamour, charm: *The cartoon has much more appeal than the main feature film.* *vb.* 1 request, plead, petition, entreat, beseech: *The charity appealed to the millionaire for financial support.* 2 attract, interest; captivate, fascinate: *Frankly, that colour doesn't appeal to me at all.* ANT. *vb.* (2) repel, repulse.

appear *vb.* 1 seem, look: *Although that person may appear wise, he is really very stupid.* 2 emerge; arise; turn up, arrive: *Just when we were sure he wouldn't come, he appeared.* ANT. (2) disappear, vanish, evaporate.

appearance *n.* 1 look, condition, expression; attitude, bearing: *From his appearance, I'd say he hasn't slept for days.* 2 arrival, presence: *Her appearance at the party wearing a long dress was a surprise to us all.* ANT. (2) departure, going; disappearance, vanishing.

append *vb.* add, attach, supplement.

appetite *n.* hunger, craving, thirst, desire.

applaud *vb.* praise, approve of, acclaim. ANT. disapprove of, criticize, condemn, denounce.

appliance *n.* apparatus, machine; instrument, device, contrivance.

applicable *adj.* usable, fitting, suitable, proper, fit, appropriate, suited. ANT. inapplicable, inappropriate.

application *n.* **1** use, utilization, employment; relevance, value: *The professor's ideas had application in the field of technology.* **2** form, request; statement, paper: *She filled in an application for a new job.*

apply *vb.* use, utilize, employ, make use of, put to use. ANT. neglect, ignore.

appoint *vb.* assign, nominate, name, designate, elect, establish, place. ANT. dismiss, discharge, (*informal*) fire.

appointment *n.* **1** engagement, meeting: *I made two appointments for ten o'clock, so please change one of them.* **2** selection, choice; installation: *Her appointment as head of the school board was widely applauded.* ANT. (**2**) dismissal, discharge.

appreciate *vb.* **1** prize, value, acknowledge; thank, be grateful for: *What child really appreciates what his parents do for him?* **2** recognize, understand: *I don't think that Martin fully appreciates the dangers of swimming alone.* ANT. (**1**) take for granted; scorn, depreciate, undervalue.

apprehend *vb.* **1** arrest, catch, seize, capture: *The police apprehended the burglar while he was trying to pick the lock on the door.* **2** understand, perceive, grasp: *He had difficulty apprehending all that the company director said in his statement.*

apprehension *n.* **1** uneasiness, worry, fear, fearfulness, misgiving, dread, anxiety: *When the police officer asked to speak to his father, Philip was filled with apprehension.* **2** arrest, capture, seizure: *The apprehension of the fugitive at the top of the tower was dramatic.* ANT. (**1**) composure, self-assuredness, confidence.

apprehensive *adj.* troubled, worried, uneasy, fearful. ANT. calm, composed.

apprentice *n.* learner, beginner; amateur; recruit. ANT. master, professional.

approach *vb.* come near, draw near, progress. ANT. recede, go away.

appropriate *adj.* fitting, proper, suitable: *Her blue jeans were not appropriate clothing for school.* *vb.* take posesssion of, seize; take up: *The treasurer appropriated the society's funds for his own use.* ANT. *adj.* inappropriate, unfit, inapt.

approve (of) *vb.* **1** praise, commend; favour, support; appreciate: *I approve neither of borrowing nor of lending money.* **2** authorize, sanction, endorse, confirm: *The committee approved plans for an increase in teachers' salaries.* ANT. (2) disapprove, oppose.

approximate *adj.* rough, loose, inexact, imprecise; close. ANT. exact, precise; perfect.

apt *adj.* **1** proper, suitable, fitting, appropriate, fit, suited: *Before dinner, the speaker offered some apt comments on the undernourished peoples of the world.* **2** likely, disposed, liable, prone, inclined: *If you criticize him, he's apt to tell you to jump in the lake!* ANT. (1) unfit, ill-becoming, unsuitable. (2) unlikely.

aptitude *n.* gift, talent, knack, faculty; ability.

arch *n.* curve, bend, vault.

architect *n.* designer, planner; draughtsman.

ardent *adj.* passionate, fervent, intense. ANT. cold, unemotional, unfeeling; feeble.

area *n.* **1** district, region, locality: *James lives in a new area of the town.* **2** part, section: *Tony kicked the ball into the goal area.* **3** expanse, space; range, field: *The area covered by the sky is enormous.*

arena *n.* ground, field, pitch.

argue *vb.* **1** debate, discuss: *We argued for an increase in time for lunch, and we won.* **2** dispute, disagree: *My parents never argued about what they wanted to do.* ANT. (2) agree, concur.

argument *n.* **1** quarrel, dispute, controversy; disagreement: *There was a big argument at the restaurant about whether chocolate ice cream was more fattening than vanilla.* **2** reason, ground, grounds, proof: *José's argument was that Cuba was still better off under Castro than it had been under Batista.* ANT. (1) agreement, harmony, accord.

arise *vb.* emerge, originate, appear, spring up.

aristocrat *n.* nobleman, noble, peer, lord. ANT. commoner, peasant.

arm *n.* forearm: *Anne held her handbag over her arm.* *vb.* provide, supply, furnish, fit out: *The navy will be armed with new types of missiles.*

arouse *vb.* awaken, stir, activate, animate, excite, stimulate, fire. ANT. calm, settle, soothe; dull.

arrange *vb.* **1** place, order, put in order, group, distribute; array: *Before we arranged the furniture in the bedroom, we laid down the rug.* **2** organize, plan, prepare: *The travel* *agent arranged all of my hotel reservations.* ANT. (1) disarrange, disturb, disorder.

arrangements *n.pl.* plans, preparations.

array *vb.* 1 clothe, dress, attire; adorn: *Penny came into the room arrayed in her best clothes.* 2 arrange, order, line up, distribute: *The soldiers were arrayed along the front line in full battle dress.* *n.* 1 order, arrangement, line up: *The troops are in battle array.* 2 display, arrangement, exhibit: *The array of diamonds in the jeweller's window took her breath away.* ANT. *n.* (1) disarray, disorder, disorganization.

arrest *vb.* 1 take into custody, seize, apprehend, catch, capture, take prisoner: *The police arrested the burglar as he was trying to escape through the window.* 2 stop, restrain, curb, delay, hinder, slow: *We arrested the growth of the plant by withholding water.* 3 attract, engage, capture: *A small scratch near the lock arrested the detective's attention.* *n.* 1 seizure, capture, detention, custody, apprehension: *The arrest of the judge was reported on the front page.* 2 restraint, obstruction, delay, hindrance; halt, stoppage: *Any arrest in the development of a child can have serious results.* *n. phr.* **under arrest** in custody, imprisoned, incarcerated: *The Queen placed Sir Walter Raleigh under arrest.* ANT. *vb.* (1) release, free. (2) activate, encourage, stimulate.

arrival *n.* coming, advent; appearance. ANT. departure, going, leaving.

arrive *vb.* 1 come, reach: *We arrived in Rome at six-thirty in the morning. He arrived at the right decision.* 2 *Informal:* succeed, attain success: *Donald finally felt he had arrived when they presented him with the medal.* ANT. (1) leave, depart.

arrogance *n.* insolence, pride, haughtiness. ANT. humility, humbleness, modesty.

arrogant *adj.* proud, haughty, insolent; scornful. ANT. humble, modest.

arrow *n.* shaft, dart, missile; sign, pointer.

art *n.* skill, aptitude, craft, dexterity, ingenuity.

artful *adj.* tricky, cunning, clever, deceitful. ANT. artless, simple, naive.

article *n.* 1 thing, object, item, commodity: *"Articles for sale" said the notice in the shop window.* 2 essay, commentary; review; column: *Phil writes a weekly article for the local paper.*

artificial *adj.* 1 unnatural, synthetic, man-made, manufactured, unreal: *Can't you tell artificial flowers from real* *ones?* **2** false, pretended, unnatural, feigned, fake, faked, fraudulent: *Betty's sympathy for my problem was entirely artificial—she really didn't care.* ANT. real, genuine, authentic.

artist *n.* painter, sculptor; creator, composer.

artistic *adj.* imaginative, creative; tasteful. ANT. tasteless, dull, flat.

artless *adj.* simple, naive, innocent, natural, open, frank, honest, sincere; candid, truthful. ANT. artful.

ascend *vb.* rise, mount, climb *or* go upward. ANT. descend, go down.

ascent *n.* rise, climb; slope, incline, gradient. ANT. descent, fall.

ashamed *adj.* embarrassed, shamefaced, abashed, humiliated. ANT. proud; self-respecting.

ask *vb.* **1** question, inquire (of), seek information (from), put a question (to): *Della asked people on the street if they knew where the bus stopped.* **2** demand, request, charge, expect: *Alan complained that the shop was asking too much for the pair of sandals.* **3** invite, call in: *Marie asked all of her friends to her party.* ANT. (**1**) answer, reply.

asleep *adj.* sleeping; inactive, resting, dormant. ANT. awake, alert.

aspect *n.* **1** look, appearance: *The gloomy aspect of the mountains through the fog depressed the hikers.* **2** point of view, viewpoint, attitude, view, outlook: *If you look at the problem from another aspect, you might understand what I mean.* **3** phase, side, part, feature: *But I haven't considered that aspect of the situation.*

aspire *vb.* yearn for, wish for, hope for, desire.

assail *vb.* attack, assault, set upon.

assault *n.* attack, onslaught: *The cavalry could not withstand the assault of the trained mountain troops.* *vb.* attack, assail; rape: *The woman told the police that the tall man had assaulted her.*

assemble *vb.* **1** meet, convene, collect, gather: *The class assembled in the hall to listen to the teacher.* **2** put together, connect, manufacture: *The manager told us that they could assemble an entire car in 30 minutes.* ANT. (**1**) scatter, disperse. (**2**) disassemble, undo.

assembly *n.* parliament, legislature, congress, council.

assent (to) *vb.* agree, consent; allow, concede, accede: *When Janet asked her father if she could go on the summer camp, he* *assented.* *n.* consent, agreement, approval, permission: *I'll have to ask the headmaster's assent if I want to go on holiday during term.* ANT. *vb.* refuse, dissent; disapprove. *n.* refusal; disapproval, opposition.

assert *vb.* **1** declare, state, affirm: *The judge asserted that the suspect had been in jail at the time of the murder.* **2** insist (on), emphasize, claim, support, uphold, maintain: *These days, women are very firm about asserting their rights.* ANT. (1) deny, contradict. (2) decline, reject.

assertion *n.* declaration, statement, affirmation. ANT. denial, contradiction.

assess *vb.* estimate, evaluate, appraise; value.

assign *vb.* **1** appoint, designate: *The minister assigned an expert to the new post.* **2** give, distribute, allot, apportion: *The English teachers always assign too much homework.* **3** fix, pinpoint, arrange: *Please don't assign Friday as the day for the meeting because I want to leave early.*

assimilate *vb.* absorb, digest, take in; incorporate, embody.

assist *vb.* aid, help, support, back. ANT. hinder, obstruct, impede, thwart.

assistance *n.* help, aid, support. ANT. obstruction, interference.

assistant *n.* helper, supporter, aide.

associate (with) *vb.* **1** connect, relate, link: *I notice that cream always seems to be associated with jelly in your mind.* **2** join, ally, team up; keep company, go around: *Jim's father didn't think he associated with the right sort of people.* *n.* colleague, fellow-worker, partner, ally; companion; accomplice: *Greg's associate in the deal provided all of the money.* ANT. *vb.* dissociate, disassociate, disconnect.

association *n.* **1** society, organization, club, union, group: *Some joined the association in order to meet people with common interests.* **2** friendship, companionship: *My mother disapproves of my continued association with you because she thinks you're a bad influence.*

assorted *adj.* various, varied, miscellaneous. ANT. same, alike.

assortment *n.* mixture, variety, collection; ragbag, conglomeration.

assume *vb.* **1** suppose, presume, postulate: *I assume that you will arrive an hour before the party.* **2** take on, undertake: *At the age of 16, he had to assume responsibility for his sister's care.* **3** pretend, affect, feign; acquire: *Although Ezra was* *really very upset, his face assumed a calm expression.*

assumption *n.* supposition, presumption; guess, theory, conjecture, postulate.

assurance *n.* **1** pledge, guarantee, warranty, promise, oath: *Despite the assurance Pedro had given the teacher, he continued to miss school.* **2** confidence, self-confidence, self-reliance; courage, boldness: *Dr. Gorman examines his patients with an assurance that comes with years of experience.*

assure *vb.* pledge, promise, warrant, guarantee. ANT. deny, equivocate.

astonish *vb.* surprise, amaze, astound; startle, shock, stupefy, stun. ANT. bore, tire.

astonishment *n.* surprise, amazement, wonder; bewilderment.

astute *adj.* perceptive, shrewd, keen. ANT. slow, dull, dim-witted.

atmosphere *n.* **1** air, wind; climate: *The atmosphere in many of our cities is not very clean.* **2** mood, feeling, tone, character; impression, sense: *As the play reached its climax, you could really feel the atmosphere in the theatre.*

attach *vb.* **1** fasten, affix, fix, connect: *The panel was attached to the wall with nails.* **2** bind, tie: *Carolyn is attached to her father.* ANT. (1) detach, unfasten, loosen, loose.

attachment *n.* **1** devotion, regard, affection, fondness, liking: *Dennis showed a close attachment to his teacher.* **2** accessory, addition; extension: *Tom's father bought a new set of attachments for his skis.* ANT. (1) detachment.

attack *vb.* **1** assault, set upon, assail, charge, storm: *The army attacked the fort, and it was soon captured.* **2** criticize, blame, abuse: *The newspapers attacked the local council for refusing to collect the rubbish.* *n.* assault, charge, onslaught, encounter: *The robber was accused of an armed attack outside the bank.* ANT. *vb.* (1) withdraw, retreat. (2) praise, endorse. *n.* withdrawal, retreat.

attain *vb.* accomplish, reach, achieve, gain, win, obtain, secure, procure, acquire, get. ANT. fail.

attainment *n.* achievement, accomplishment. ANT. failure.

attempt *vb.* try, seek: *The football team attempted to win every game.* *n.* try, effort, undertaking, endeavour, trial: *After three attempts, Jonathan finally jumped over the fence.* ANT. *vb.* achieve, accomplish. *n.* achievement, accomplishment.

attend *vb.* **1** go to, frequent, be present at: *The entire family attends church.* **2** care for, serve, tend, wait on, minister to: *The waitress attended to our order first.*

attendant *n.* servant, waiter, valet, footman.

attention *n.* observation, heed, alertness, care, consideration. ANT. inattention, absent-mindedness, preoccupation.

attentive *adj.* **1** observant, alert, heedful: *Unless you agree to be more attentive when I speak, I shall ask you to leave.* **2** thoughtful, kind, polite, considerate, courteous: *Michael was always a very attentive father and husband.* ANT. inattentive, absent-minded, preoccupied.

attire *vb.* dress, clothe, apparel: *The beggar was attired in rags.* *n.* dress, clothing, clothes, apparel: *Blue jeans are not appropriate attire for a dinner dance.*

attitude *n.* view, regard, position, manner, disposition, demeanour.

attract *vb.* draw, invite, win; fascinate, captivate. ANT. repel, repulse.

attraction *n.* allurement, captivation; (*informal*) pull; tendency; affinity.

attractive *adj.* appealing, alluring, pleasing, charming. ANT. unattractive, plain, ugly.

attribute *vb.* assign, credit, ascribe: *She attributed her nervousness to the importance of the interview.* *n.* characteristic, quality, property: *One of Beth's chief attributes is her patience.*

audible *adj.* distinct; perceptible, discernible. ANT. inaudible; imperceptible; indistinct.

audience *n.* spectators, viewers; hearers; turn-out, patrons.

austere *adj.* **1** stern, severe, hard, harsh, firm, strict, stiff, inflexible: *The austere look on the teacher's face told the children that he would tolerate no nonsense.* **2** plain, simple, unadorned, severe: *For the first few years, the lives of the emigrants were very austere.* ANT. (1) lenient, permissive, soft. (2) luxurious, fancy, opulent.

austerity *n.* severity, harshness, strictness. ANT. comfort, luxury.

authentic *adj.* **1** genuine, real: *Unless it is at least 100 years old, it isn't an authentic antique.* **2** true, reliable, trustworthy, accurate, authoritative: *The witness testified that the signature on the wall was authentic.* ANT. fake, bogus; imitation; counterfeit.

author *n.* writer, creator, originator; (of a play) playwright, dramatist; (of a poem) poet; (of a novel) novelist; (of a musical composition) composer; (of words to a song) lyricist, songwriter; (of a biography) biographer.

authority *n.* **1** jurisdiction, authorization; permission, sanction, approval: *You have no right to go into that room without* *the proper authority.* **2** command, rule, order, control, power: *The library is under the authority of the librarian.*

authorize *vb.* **1** empower; commission, charge, entrust: *She wasn't authorized to use that typewriter.* **2** allow, permit, sanction, approve: *The committee authorized the purchase of new playground equipment.* ANT. (2) prohibit, forbid.

automatic *adj.* **1** self-moving, self-regulating; programmed: *The spinning cycle on this washing machine is automatic.* **2** uncontrolled, uncontrollable, involuntary, unconscious: *The circulation of the blood is automatic.* ANT. (1) manual, hand-operated. (2) deliberate, intentional.

auxiliary *adj.* secondary, supplementary, supporting, subordinate.

avail *vb.* benefit, help, serve; profit.

available *adj.* obtainable, accessible, at hand, ready, handy. ANT. unavailable, unobtainable.

average *adj.* normal, common, typical, ordinary: *I never understood why "C" was considered an average mark for school work.* *n.* mean; median: *Prices rose by an average of 10 per cent last year.* ANT. *adj.* atypical, abnormal.

aversion *n.* dislike, distaste; abhorrence, disgust, loathing, hatred. ANT. liking, affinity, attraction.

avoid *vb.* elude, evade, dodge; shun. ANT. meet, confront, encounter, face.

await *vb.* wait for, expect, anticipate.

awake *vb.* wake up, arouse: *He awoke his children very early the day they went on holiday.* *adj.* **1** conscious, not asleep; up and about: *The young boys stayed awake and told each other stories for hours.* **2** aware (of); vigilant, attentive, alert; lively: *Those who are in high positions in society must be awake to the problems of pride.*

award *vb.* bestow, give: *She was awarded first prize in the essay contest. The father was awarded custody of the children.* *n.* prize, reward, payment, medal: *An award will be given to the employee who offers the best idea.*

aware (of) *adj.* conscious, informed, mindful. ANT. unaware, unconscious.

awe *n.* respect, wonder, fear, admiration. ANT. scorn, contempt.

awesome *adj.* awe-inspiring, moving, overwhelming, formidable.

awful *adj.* dreadful, terrible, abominable, bad, poor, unpleasant. ANT. wonderful, delightful.

awkward *adj.* **1** clumsy, graceless, unskilful, sloppy, ungraceful, ungainly, crude: *In an awkward attempt to reach the sugar, Eve spilled the milk.* **2** inconvenient, unwieldy, unmanageable: *From that awkward position, I was unable to turn the bolt.* ANT. (1) graceful, deft, elegant, skilled, skilful.

b

baby *n.* toddler, suckling, child; youngest.

back *adj.* rear, hind: *The back door was open so I went in.* *vb.* support, help, assist; endorse, ratify, stand by, approve; finance: *The investors agreed to back the new company with £1 million.* *vb. phr.* **back out** withdraw, retreat, escape: *Nigel backed out of the deal when he realized he wasn't going to make any profit.*

backbone *n.* **1** spine: *The backbone is part of the skeleton.* **2** determination, persistence, resolution, courage, tenacity: *To be a leading politician you have to have a lot of backbone.*

background *n.* **1** context, setting; framework, perspective; circumstances: *Let me tell you the background to this problem.* **2** training, experience, education, knowledge, qualifications: *At only 18, Peter doesn't have the background needed for this job.* *prep. phr.* **in the background** unobtrusive, inconspicuous: *Millie always kept her personal feelings in the background.*

backward *adj.* **1** rearward: *Looking over her shoulder, Suzanne gave him a final, backward glance.* **2** slow, underdeveloped, retarded: *Some of the students were backward in their physical skills.* ANT. *adv.* forward. *adj.* (**1**) forward. (**2**) advanced; precocious.

bad *adj.* **1** evil, immoral, wicked, corrupt, sinful, depraved: *The people considered the dictator to be a totally bad man.* **2** rotten, contaminated, spoiled, tainted: *Eight people were poisoned by the bad meat at that restaurant.* **3** harmful, injurious; unfavourable: *Eating too many sweets is bad for your teeth.* **4** poor, defective, inferior, imperfect, substandard, faulty: *The picture tube is bad in this TV set.* **5** improper, inappropriate, unsuited, unsuitable: *The paintings by amateurs are usually bad examples of art.* **6** upset, sorry: *We all feel bad when a pet dies.* **7** sick, ill, out of sorts; suffering: *I felt bad after eating all that chocolate.* **8** disagreeable, unpleasant, uncomfortable: *Because of the storm, we had a bad crossing from Dover.* **9** cross, nasty, unpleasant, unfriendly, irritable, disagreeable, short-tempered: *When Sam heard about who was coming for dinner, it put him into a bad mood for the rest of the day.* ANT. good.

badge *n.* symbol, emblem, crest, decoration; star; shield; medal.

baffle *vb.* mystify, puzzle, confuse, frustrate, bewilder. ANT. enlighten, inform.

bag *n.* basket, carrier bag; handbag; purse; case; sack.

baggage *see* luggage.

bait *n.* lure, enticement: *Many fishermèn use worms for bait.* *vb.* 1 lure, entice, entrap, captivate, ensnare: *Enid baited her boyfriend with her good cooking.* 2 tease, torment, worry, pester, badger, heckle: *The audience baited the politician by asking him about his record.*

bake *vb.* 1 cook; toast, dry, roast: *We baked some cakes in the oven.* 2 harden, temper: *The sun baked their skins as they lay on the beach.*

balance *n.* equilibrium: *The acrobat was able to keep his balance easily on the wire.* *vb.* 1 weigh, evaluate, compare: *When you balance the advantages against the disadvantages, I'd say we ought to go.* 2 offset, counterbalance, make up for: *My reasons for staying balance my reasons for going, so I don't know what to do.*

balk (at) *vb.* hesitate, stop.

ball[1] *n.* sphère, globe, spheroid: *The centre-forward kicked the ball into the goal.*

ball[2] *n.* dance, social, party: *We were invited to the ball given to raise money for charity.*

balloon *n.* ball, sphere, globe; bag, bubble.

balmy *adj.* mild, gentle, soothing, pleasant. ANT. stormy, tempestuous.

ban *vb.* forbid, prohibit, disallow, outlaw: *Smoking is banned in the buses.* *n.* prohibition, taboo: *In some countries there is a ban on staying out in the streets after nine o'clock.* ANT. *vb.* permit, allow.

band[1] *n.* group, company, society, association, body, crew, gang: *The band of robbers met secretly in a hut in the forest.* *vb.* unite, group, join forces: *We had to band together for our own protection.*

band[2] *n.* strip, belt: *There was a narrow band of carvings around the base of the column.*

bandit *n.* outlaw, thief, robber, highwayman, hijacker, marauder, brigand.

bang *vb.,n.* boom, crash, shot, blast: *The guns banged loudly in the distance and we knew the enemy was coming nearer. We heard a huge bang at the end of the street and found out later that a bomb had gone off.*

banish *vb.* exile, deport, expel; dismiss. ANT. receive, admit, welcome.

bank *n.* **1** savings bank; building society: *My father is the manager of the local bank.* **2** embankment, shore, ridge, mound: *I swam to the edge of the lake and climbed out onto the bank.*

bar *n.* **1** barrier, obstacle, barricade, obstruction, hindrance, impediment: *Peace should not be a bar to progress in science or business.* **2** counter; saloon, cocktail lounge, café: *The businessmen met at the bar before going in for dinner.* *vb.* prevent, obstruct, hinder, impede, stop, deter, prohibit, block: *All those who were not members of the club were barred from entering.* ANT. *n.* (1) encouragement, aid. *vb.* permit, allow; welcome, encourage.

barbarian *n.* savage, brute, boor, ruffian: *The manager of the football stadium called the police because the boys were acting like barbarians.* *adj.* savage, rude, primitive, uncivilized, uncultured, cruel, barbaric, barbarous: *A barbarian tribe never before seen was discovered in the Philippines.* ANT. *adj.* cultivated, civilized, tasteful.

barber *n.* hairdresser, hair stylist, coiffeur.

bare *adj.* **1** nude, naked, unclothed, uncovered, undressed: *In many European countries, small children run about bare on the beaches.* **2** plain, unfurnished, empty, barren: *The room was entirely bare.* **3** mere, scarce: *Robinson Crusoe was marooned with just the bare necessities of life.* *vb.* reveal, disclose, expose, publicize: *The newspaper reporter bared the details of the political scandal.* ANT. *adj.* (1) clothed, dressed. *vb.* hide, conceal, disguise.

barely *adv.* scarcely, hardly, just.

bargain *n.* deal, agreement, arrangement, contract: *I'll make a bargain with you. I'll let you use my bicycle if you let me use your car.* *vb.* agree, contract, arrange: *The two farmers bargained until a fair agreement was reached.* *vb. phr.* **bargain for** expect, anticipate, foresee: *He got more than he bargained for when the bull suddenly turned nasty.*

barren *adj.* sterile, unproductive, unfruitful, bare, childless. ANT. fertile, fruitful.

barricade *n.* barrier, obstruction, fence, enclosure: *The barricade prevented the horses from leaving the pen.* *vb.* shut in, obstruct, block, bar: *The hunters barricaded themselves in the cabin for protection against the wolves.* ANT. *vb.* release, free, open.

barrier *n.* **1** bar, barricade, fence, wall, railing, obstacle: *The* *barrier was opened to allow passengers through.* 2 obstruction, hindrance, impediment, restraint, obstacle; limit: *Neither the mountains nor love of home was a barrier to the tribe's travelling great distances.* ANT. (2) encouragement, aid, assistance.

barrister *n.* lawyer, counsel, advocate; solicitor.

barter *vb.* trade, exchange.

base[1] *n.* bottom, support, stand, rest, foundation: *The base of this column is carved from marble.* *vb.* found, establish: *A careful scholar bases his theory on sound examination of the evidence.* ANT. *n.* top, peak, pinnacle.

base[2] *adj.* 1 low, immoral, bad, evil, depraved, wicked, mean, selfish: *Anyone who would allow a kitten to starve is really base.* 2 cheap, tawdry, worthless, poor, debased, alloyed, (of coin) counterfeit: *The clasp on your brooch didn't last long because it was made of base material.* ANT. (1) noble, exalted, virtuous. (2) refined, valuable.

bashful *adj.* shy, timid, sheepish, modest, coy, shamefaced, ashamed. ANT. self-assured; immodest, arrogant.

basic *adj.* main, chief, essential, fundamental. ANT. subordinate, subsidiary.

basis *n.* foundation, ground, reason, justification.

batter *vb.* beat, pound, hit, strike.

battle *n.* fight, combat; war, warfare; conflict, action, campaign: *After the battle, each side looked after its wounded and buried its dead.* *vb.* fight, struggle against, strive against: *Battling against great odds, the team finally won.*

bay *n.* gulf, inlet, estuary, lagoon.

be *vb.* 1 exist, live; survive, breathe; continue, remain: *Descartes said, "I think, therefore I am."* 2 occur, take place, happen: *The party is at eight o'clock tonight.*

beach *n.* strand, sands, shore, seashore, coast.

bead *n.* 1 ball, sphere, globule: *Her necklace was made of blue and red beads.* 2 drop, droplet: *Because of the intense heat, there were beads of sweat on his face.*

beam *n.* 1 rafter, support, girder: *The main beams of the roof are being eaten by termites.* 2 ray, pencil, gleam: *The beam shone through the slit to light up the golden statue in the crypt.* *vb.* shine, gleam, glisten, glitter: *When the moon beams on the water it looks like a silvery path.*

bear *vb.* 1 carry, support, hold up: *The columns bear the weight of the roof.* 2 carry, transport, convey: *Beware the Greeks bearing gifts!* 3 endure, stand, suffer, abide, tolerate: *I cannot bear to hear a baby crying.* 4 give birth to, produce, beget: *The mother bore six children.* vb. phr. **bear on** relate to, affect, be relevant to, be connected with: *Whether you work hard at school bears very much on your exam results.* **bear out** substantiate, confirm, prove: *My prediction was borne out by your losing the key on the first day.* **bear up** endure, carry on, keep up: *I just don't see how Martha can bear up under the strain of caring for 15 children.* **bear with** be patient with; tolerate: *Please bear with me until I can straighten the problem out.*

bearing n. **1** posture, carriage; manner, behaviour, deportment, conduct: *The girl's regal bearing made everyone notice her when she walked into the room.* **2** reference, relation, application, connection: *What you think has no bearing on what we ought to do.* **3** direction, course, position: *It took a few minutes with the chart to get our bearings.*

beast n. animal; brute, monster.

beat vb. **1** hit, strike, pound, batter, thrash: *When we came into the garden, Jan's mother was beating the carpet.* **2** throb, pound, pulse, pulsate: *I can feel my heart beating if I put my hand here.* **3** defeat, conquer, overcome: *The home team beat the visitors 3–2.* n. stroke, blow; throb, pulse, pulsation: *The beat of the jungle drums could be heard for miles.*

beautiful adj. pretty, lovely, handsome, attractive. ANT. unattractive, plain, ugly, hideous.

beauty n. loveliness, comeliness, attractiveness. ANT. plainness, ugliness, unsightliness.

because conj. since, as, for, for the reason that.

become vb. **1** grow, change, come to be: *When I told him what his friend had said, he became angry.* **2** suit, befit, be appropriate *or* attractive to: *The green dress becomes you, but I don't care for the red one.*

becoming adj. attractive, pleasing, seemly, graceful.

before adv. earlier, previously: *The couple had been doctors in Africa many years before.* prep. in front of, ahead of: *He knelt before the altar and prayed for mercy.* ANT. adv. later, afterwards. prep. behind.

beg vb. **1** ask, request, entreat, beseech, petition, solicit, implore: *Kathy begged her mother to be allowed to go to the party.* **2** cadge, (*slang*) scrounge, ask alms, ask charity: *He was so poor he had to beg for something to eat.*

beggar n. pauper; tramp, loafer.

begin vb. **1** start, commence; initiate; inaugurate: *Don't begin until everyone is ready.* **2** originate, create, arise, come into being: *The practice of working five days a week didn't begin until fairly recently.* ANT. stop, end, finish, terminate.

beginner *n.* amateur, nonprofessional, apprentice. ANT. professional.

beginning *n.* **1** start, outset, commencement, emergence, initiation, inauguration: *At the beginning of a new enterprise everyone works very hard.* **2** origin, source, rise, birth, creation: *The beginning of modern scientific thought can be traced to the 16th century.* ANT. ending, finish, termination.

behalf *n.* part, support, interest, aid.

behave *vb.* act, conduct oneself, deport oneself. ANT. misbehave, rebel.

behaviour *n.* conduct, deportment, manners. ANT. misbehaviour, misconduct, mischief, rebelliousness.

behind *prep.* at the back *or* rear of. ANT. in front of, before.

belief *n.* **1** view, opinion, conviction, creed, credo: *His belief is that all men are equal.* **2** faith, trust, confidence, assurance: *Nothing could shake his belief that his parents were the most wonderful people.*

believe *vb.* **1** accept, be convinced; hold, think, trust: *He believed in God.* **2** think, suppose, assume, gather: *I believe he's coming to dinner, but I'm not sure.*

belong (to) *vb.* **1** be owned *or* possessed by: *This book belongs to me.* **2** be a member of, be a part of: *Which sports club do you belong to?*

belt *n.* band, stripe, tape, girdle, strap, strip.

bench *n.* **1** seat; bank: *The benches in the hall are most uncomfortable.* **2** table, trestle, board: *The carpenter worked away at his bench for hours making the fine carvings.*

bend *vb.* **1** curve, bow, deflect: *You could never bend that steel bar with your bare hands.* **2** stoop, kneel, crouch, bow: *Martin bent to look through the keyhole in the door.* **3** submit, yield, bow, stoop, agree: *The foreman had to bend under the pressure from the board of directors.* **4** subdue, suppress, oppress, influence, cause to yield: *The president was accustomed to bending all his people to suit his will.* ANT. (1) straighten.

beneficial *adj.* good, advantageous, helpful, useful, profitable, wholesome. ANT. unwholesome, disadvantageous.

benefit *n.* good, profit, advantage; service, favour, help, support: *Dick won't do anything unless it's for his own benefit.* *vb.* help, aid, support, profit, serve: *Every time you help someone else you benefit yourself.*

benevolent *adj.* good, kind, well-wishing, kindly, kindhearted, humane, well-disposed; generous, open-hearted, liberal, charitable.   ANT. malevolent, mean, cruel, evil.

bent *adj.*   **1** crooked, curved: *The lock was so crude we could open it with a bent nail.*   **2** determined, resolved, set, decided, firm: *Although I tried to discourage him, Jim was bent on sailing across the ocean alone.*   ANT. (**1**) straight.

bereavement *n.*   loss; sense of loss, affliction; death.

beseech *vb.*   beg, implore, ask, entreat.

besides *adv.*   furthermore, moreover, in addition, further: *You can't go out to play because it's raining and, besides, you haven't finished your homework.*   *prep.* in addition to, except for, other than: *Besides me, there's no one else who cares about winning the game.*

besiege *vb.*   blockade, lay siege to, surround.

best *adj.*   finest, highest, supreme, excellent.   ANT. worst.

bestow *vb.*   give, confer, present, award.   ANT. withhold, withdraw.

bet *vb.*   wager, lay *or* put (money), gamble: *I have never bet on a horse race in my life.*   *n.* wager, stake, ante, pledge: *Madame DeTour placed a bet at roulette and won.*

betray *vb.*   **1** deliver, be treacherous *or* disloyal: *The traitor betrayed the location of the arsenal to the enemy.*   **2** reveal, expose; display, show, exhibit: *Although she seemed very angry, her smile betrayed her real feelings.*   ANT. safeguard, protect, shelter.

better *adj.*   **1** greater, superior: *My school is better than yours.*   **2** recovering, improving; well, healthy: *"How are you today?" she asked her child. "Better, mummy."*   *vb.* improve, ameliorate; amend, polish up: *I could better my tennis game if I practised more.*   ANT. *adj.* (**1**) worse, inferior. (**2**) worse; ill.   *vb.* worsen.

bewilder *vb.*   confuse, puzzle, perplex, mystify, overwhelm.   ANT. enlighten, clarify.

bewitch *vb.*   enchant, charm, captivate.

bias *n.*   prejudice, tendency, inclination: *The executive has a bias in favour of employing only friends.*   *vb.* influence, prejudice, bend, warp: *The politician's opinion was biased because he had received gifts from the manufacturers.*   ANT. *n.* impartiality, fairness.

bid *vb.*   **1** command, order, direct: *When the chairman bids you to stand, you are expected to immediately get up.*   **2** greet, say, wish: *I bid you good day, sir.*   **3** offer, tender, propose: *Mother bid only three pounds for the chair at the auction, but* *she got it.* *n.* offer, proposal: *I made an unsuccessful bid of two pounds for the lamp.*

bide *vb. phr.* **bide one's time** wait, remain, delay.

big *adj.* **1** large, great, huge, immense, enormous, gigantic, tremendous: *If it has 37 rooms, I'd certainly agree that it's a big house.* **2** important, significant, prominent: *The big event of the year was the Christmas party.* **3** generous, kind, outgoing, bighearted: *It was very big of you to let us use your pool.* ANT. (1) small, little; tiny.

bill *n.* invoice, statement, charge, account.

bin *n.* container, store; rubbish bin, dustbin.

bind *vb.* **1** tie, fasten, band: *Don't bind that bundle of clothes too tight because they'll tear.* **2** oblige, require, command, obligate: *He was bound by the contract.* ANT. (1) loosen, free, untie.

birth *n.* coming, creation, appearance; beginning, start, foundation. ANT. death, passing.

bit *n.* scrap, particle, fragment, speck, drop: *May I have just a bit more sugar in my coffee?* *n. phr.* **bit by bit** gradually, slowly: *Bit by bit, Jim saved enough money to buy a bicycle.*

bite *vb.* nip; gnaw, chew: *They say that barking dogs don't bite, but let someone else prove it.* *n.* **1** nip, sting: *A dog bite is more serious than a mosquito bite.* **2** *Informal:* morsel, mouthful; snack: *May I have a bite of that hot dog?*

biting *adj.* **1** piercing, sharp, keen, stinging: *The wind was biting as they walked along the cliffs.* **2** penetrating, sarcastic, incisive: *Her biting comments hurt him deeply and he wept for hours.*

bitter *adj.* **1** acrid, harsh, biting: *If you chew aspirin instead of swallowing it whole, it leaves a bitter taste in your mouth.* **2** distressing, distressful, painful, grievous: *I had the bitter experience of studying hard but failing the examination.* **3** stinging, piercing, biting: *The day was bitter cold.* **4** hostile, hated, severe, vicious: *The citizens of the two countries were bitter enemies.* ANT. (1) sweet, bland.

black *adj.* **1** dark, sooty, inky, swarthy: *The black man stood in the doorway.* **2** soiled, dirty, filthy, stained: *When he finished repairing the car, he was black from head to toe.* **3** gloomy, dismal, sad, depressing, dark, sombre: *It was a black day for the country when our party lost the election.* ANT. (1) white, light-skinned. (2) clean, pure, pristine. (3) bright, cheerful.

blame *vb.* reproach, condemn, criticize: *The taxi driver was* *blamed for causing the accident.* n. responsibility, guilt, fault: *Before you place the blame on me, you'd better find out the facts.* ANT. n. honour, credit.

blank adj. 1 empty, unmarked: *The application was blank except for where Michael had filled in his name.* 2 uninterested, expressionless: *A sea of blank faces greeted the teacher on the first day of school.* n. void, area, form, vacancy: *Just fill in the blanks with the correct information, please.* ANT. adj. (1) filled. (2) animated, alert; excited.

blast n. explosion, detonation, eruption; noise, bang: *The blast from the quarry was heard far away.* vb. detonate, explode, blow up: *The explosion blasted the house sky-high.*

blaze n. flame, fire; holocaust, inferno: *The firemen fought the blaze at the department store in the High Street.* vb. burn, flare, flare up, flame, shine: *The fire was blazing in the hearth when we arrived for the Christmas party.* ANT. vb. dwindle, die.

bleach vb. whiten, blanch; pale: *The blue jeans were bleached pale blue by the sun.* n. whitener: *Don't use so much bleach in the wash.* ANT. vb. darken, blacken.

bleak adj. 1 bare, desolate, barren, windswept: *The bleak landscape offered no shelter.* 2 depressing, cheerless, gloomy, dreary: *The financial future of the company was bleak after the fire.* ANT. (2) hopeful, cheerful, promising.

bleed vb. lose or shed blood; flow, spurt, gush, issue.

blemish n. flaw, stain, tarnish, blotch, defect.

blend vb. mix, intermingle, mingle, combine: *Before pouring the batter into the baking dish, you should blend all the ingredients thoroughly.* n. mixture, combination, compound: *That pipe tobacco smells like a mild blend.* ANT. vb. separate, divide.

blight n. epidemic, disease, sickness, affliction: *The blight killed off the entire crop.* vb. damage, ruin, harm, spoil, destroy: *His career was blighted by his poor school record.*

blind adj. 1 sightless, unseeing, purblind: *A blind person's hearing is often very acute.* 2 unaware, unknowing, unconscious, ignorant, thoughtless, unthinking: *Irena was blind to the fact that no one really liked her.* n. screen, shade, curtain, cover: *The sun is in my eyes; please pull down the blind.* ANT. adj. (1) sighted, seeing. (2) clearsighted, knowing, discerning, aware.

blink vb. 1 wink: *She blinked when you shone the light in her eyes.* 2 flicker, twinkle: *The stars are blinking in the black sky.*

bliss *n.* happiness, joy, gladness, ecstasy, rapture. ANT. misery, unhappiness, torment.

block *n.* obstacle, obstruction, impediment, hindrance, blockade: *The police stopped every car at the road block, looking for the escaped men.* *vb.* stop, obstruct, impede, retard, hinder, blockade, check: *The fallen trees blocked our passage to freedom from the wood.* ANT. *n.* aid, advantage. *vb.* aid, assist, forward, promote.

blood *n.* **1** gore, bloodshed, murder, slaughter: *Cain had his brother's blood on his hands.* **2** lineage, heritage, ancestry: *The Prince of Wales is of royal blood.*

bloody *adj.* bloodthirsty, cruel, inhuman, pitiless, ruthless, murderous, ferocious. ANT. gentle, kind.

bloom *n.* flower, blossom: *My new roses are growing with huge blooms.* *vb.* flourish, blossom, flower: *Rose of Sharon blooms in September in this part of the country.* ANT. *vb.* wither, shrivel.

blossom *n.* flower, bloom: *The cherry blossoms are beautiful in the spring.* *vb.* bloom, flower, flourish: *The century plant is so called because it is said to blossom only once every 100 years.* ANT. *vb.* wither, shrink, dwindle, fade.

blot *n.* **1** spot, stain, inkstain, inkblot: *I got that awful blot on my skirt when Ronnie spilled ink on me.* **2** blemish, taint, disgrace, dishonour: *The blot on his record harmed his career.* *vb.* **1** spot, stain, spatter, soil: *You've blotted my book with your leaky pen!* **2** dry, soak up, sponge up: *If you blot the ink it won't smear when you turn the page.* *vb. phr.* **blot out** eliminate, destroy, obliterate, erase, rub out, cancel: *I've blotted that terrible experience from my mind.*

blow[1] *n.* **1** thump, hit, slap, rap, cuff, box, knock, stroke: *The boxer knocked his challenger out with a blow to the stomach.* **2** shock, tragedy, calamity: *The news of the death of her turtle was a terrible blow to Joanne.*

blow[2] *vb.* **1** move, spread, drive: *The leaves started to blow down the street in the breeze.* **2** whistle: *The siren blew at noon each day.* *vb. phr.* **blow up 1** explode, detonate: *The spies blew up the bridge.* **2** enlarge, inflate: *Blow up that balloon.*

blue *n.* azure, sapphire, turquoise: *On a clear day, blue is the colour of the sky.* *adj.* sad, gloomy, depressed, unhappy, dejected, melancholy: *I felt blue at the thought of leaving home.* ANT. *adj.* happy, cheerful, optimistic.

bluff *vb.* mislead, deceive, fool, pretend: *The gambler bluffed the others into thinking he had a good hand.* *n.* pretence, lie, fraud, fake, deceit: *Bill's tough manner is just a bluff—he's really soft inside.*

blunder *n.* mistake, error: *Telling Kitty about the party when she hadn't been invited was a stupid blunder.* *vb.* stumble: *I blundered into the lamp and knocked it over in the dark.*

blunt *adj.* **1** dull, unsharpened, rounded, worn: *That blunt knife could hardly cut butter.* **2** rude, crude, direct, impolite, abrupt, short, curt, brusque, gruff: *I don't invite Walter any more because his manner is too blunt.* *vb.* dull: *He blunted the axe on the rock.* ANT. *adj.* (1) sharp, keen, pointed. (2) diplomatic, tactful.

blur *vb.* stain, sully, obscure, dim, dull; confuse. ANT. clarify, clear.

blush *vb.* glow, redden, go red, colour.

board *n.* **1** plank, slat; frame; cover: *He put a board over the hole so that people wouldn't fall in.* **2** committee, council, body, group: *Robert has joined the board to help with the company's finances.*

boast *vb.* brag, crow, exaggerate: *Nobody could stand being with Bill because he was always boasting about how great he was.* *n.* bragging, braggadocio: *Despite his boast, Bill was unable to jump across the stream.*

boat *n.* ship, vessel, craft; launch, canoe; dinghy.

body *n.* **1** corpse, cadaver, carcass: *The body of the dead man was taken away. The body of the wolf was buried in the snow.* **2** trunk, torso: *He had spots all over his body but none on his arms, legs, or head.* **3** group, party, company, band: *We walked out of the meeting in a body.*

boil *vb.* seethe, foam, bubble, simmer, stew.

boisterous *adj.* noisy, lively, unruly; rude; stormy, turbulent. ANT. quiet, calm, composed.

bold *adj.* **1** brave, unafraid, fearless, intrepid, courageous, daring, valiant, heroic, gallant: *The four bold men stormed the machine-gun and captured it.* **2** rude, disrespectful, insolent, impudent, shameless: *Richard was bold enough to answer back to the teacher.* ANT. (1) afraid, cowardly, fearful, timid, timorous. (2) courteous, polite, deferential.

bolt *n.* bar, rod: *The bar on this lock is worn so that it doesn't work properly.* *vb.* lock, secure, close, shut: *Everyone should bolt their door at night to stop burglars breaking in.*

bomb *n.* explosive; grenade, mine, torpedo, incendiary.

bond *n.* **1** fastening, fastener, rope, tie, cord, band: *The prisoner was unable to release the bonds on his wrists.* **2** connection, tie, attachment, link: *The bonds of friendship* *prevented me from telling the supervisor about Alice's taking three hours for lunch.* **3** promise, promissory note, obligation, I.O.U.: *My word is my bond and everyone knows that I pay all my debts.*

bone *n.* tissue; spine, rib.

bonus *n.* reward, premium, gift, bounty.

book *n.* volume, tome, publication, work; hardback, paperback; novel, text.

boom[1] *vb.* **1** reverberate, thunder, roar: *The huge guns boomed in the distance.* **2** prosper, flourish: *The late 1960s was a time of booming prosperity: business was booming.* *n.* **1** blast, roar, thunder: *I couldn't hear the music over the boom of the aeroplanes.* **2** prosperity, rush: *Just before Christmas there is always a big boom in toy sales.* ANT. *n.* (2) recession.

boom[2] *n.* spar, pole: *The wind changed suddenly, causing the boom to swing around and hit me.*

boon *n.* blessing, benefit, help.

boost *n.* support, help; improvement, rise, increase: *The pay increase was a real boost to morale.* *vb.* promote, encourage, assist, increase, expand: *The government's plans will boost exports in a big way.*

boot *n.* shoe; Wellington boot.

booth *n.* stall, stand; compartment, enclosure, cubicle.

border *n.* **1** frontier, boundary, limit: *We crossed the border between France and Italy.* **2** edge, margin: *There was a border of blue flowers around the tablecloth.* *vb.* join, adjoin, edge, abut: *Scotland is bordered by England.* ANT. *n.* (2) centre, middle.

bore *vb.* **1** weary, tire: *We were all so bored by the film that we almost fell asleep.* **2** drill, hole, perforate: *This machine bores into the steel plate in 36 places at the same time.* ANT. (1) interest, excite, arouse, captivate.

borrow *vb.* hire; take, receive; adopt, appropriate. ANT. lend.

bosom *n.* breast, chest; heart, feelings, mind, thoughts.

boss *n.* manager, director, supervisor, employer, foreman. ANT. employee, worker.

botch *vb.* spoil, mess up, bungle, mishandle, mar.

bother *vb.* irritate, trouble, worry, disturb, annoy, vex, pester, upset, inconvenience: *It bothered me that I couldn't recall the name of the last prime minister.* *n.* trouble, inconvenience, upset, distress, anxiety: *I never wanted to cause any bother—I only tried to help.* ANT. *n.* comfort, solace.

bottle *n.* jug, jar, flask; carafe.

bottom *n.* **1** base, foot, depths: *I heard the bucket strike the ground at the bottom of the dried-out well.* **2** underside: *The mark on the bottom of the cup shows the maker's name.* **3** seat, buttocks, behind, rear: *Billy's mother gave him a sharp slap on his bottom for breaking the window.* ANT. (**1, 2**) top, topside.

bough *n.* branch, arm, limb.

bounce *vb.* rebound, recoil, spring (back).

bound[1] *vb.,n.* leap, jump, spring, bounce, skip: *The dog bounded along next to the car. With one bound Barbara had crossed the stream.*

bound[2] *adj.* **1** tied, trussed; shackled, fettered: *The prisoner was bound hand and foot.* **2** sure, certain, destined; required, compelled: *Suzanne knew that her father was bound to say no when she asked him if she could go.* ANT. (**1**) unfettered, free.

bound[3] (**for**) *adj.* on the way to, destined for: *The train is bound for Edinburgh.*

bound[4] *n.* (usually **bounds**) boundary, limit: *Within the bounds of reason, there is no limit to how far you can push your imagination.*

boundary *n.* limit, bound, border, outline, margin, circumference, perimeter, edge, frontier.

bounty *n.* **1** generosity, liberality; gift: *The early settlers in America were grateful for the bounty from the earth.* **2** reward, award, bonus, prize, premium: *The farmers offered a bounty of 30p for every dead mole.*

bouquet *n.* bunch, garland, spray, nosegay, wreath.

bourgeois *adj.* middle-class, common, conventional. ANT. aristocratic, upper-class.

bout *n.* match, round, fight, contest; conflict.

bow *vb.* **1** stoop, bend: *The porter was bowed down under the weight of the trunk.* **2** yield, submit: *You ought to bow to the force of a stronger argument.* **3** curtsy, salaam, kowtow, kneel: *Everyone bowed when the king came into the room.*

bowl *n.* dish, plate; basin, vessel; pot.

box *n.* case, carton; coffer, trunk; bin; container, receptacle.

boy *n.* lad, youth, youngster; (*informal*) kid. ANT. man; girl.

brace *n.* support, prop, stay, strut, bracket, crutch: *This wall ought to have a steel brace to hold it in place.* *vb.* support, prop, steady: *Brace yourself for some bad news.*

bracelet *n.* bangle, circlet, armband.

brag *vb.* boast, gloat, swagger. ANT. deprecate, depreciate.

braid *vb.* plait, wreath, weave, twine.

brain *n.* (usually **brains**) intelligence, sense, common sense, intellect, reason, understanding. ANT. stupidity, dullness, imbecility.

brake *n.* restraint, fetter; curb, hindrance, discouragement: *You must release the brake before you drive off.* *vb.* slow down, decelerate, retard, curb: *The car braked as it came near to the corner.*

branch *n.* **1** limb, bough, shoot: *The branches on this tree grow very close to the ground.* **2** offshoot, tributary: *The two branches of the stream join here.* **3** division, part, subdivision, department: *The restaurant opened a new branch on the main road.*

brand *n.* **1** kind, make, manufacture, trademark, label, trade name: *What brand of shampoo do you use?* **2** stamp, mark, blaze: *The stolen cattle bore the brand of our farm.* *vb.* mark, label; burn; stamp: *He branded the sheep with a red dye.*

brandish *vb.* flourish, flaunt, swing, wave.

brave *adj.* courageous, gallant, fearless, daring, valiant, intrepid, unafraid, heroic, bold. ANT. timid, cowardly, fearful, craven.

bravery *n.* courage, daring, valour, fearlessness, heroism, boldness. ANT. cowardice, timidity, fearfulness.

brawl *n.* fight, melee, fray, fracas, riot, disturbance, dispute, disagreement.

brazen *adj.* bold, shameless, impudent, insolent, rude, immodest. ANT. modest, retiring, shy, self-effacing.

breach *n.* **1** break, rift, rupture, fracture, crack, opening, gap: *The explosion tore a breach in the wall big enough for the tank to pass through.* **2** violation, breaking: *Her failure to deliver the merchandise by Monday was a breach of our agreement.* ANT. (2) keeping, observation.

breadth *see* **width.**

break *vb.* **1** fracture, rupture, shatter, smash, wreck, crash, atomize, demolish: *When Jack sat on the antique chair he broke it into a hundred pieces.* **2** violate, disobey: *I have no respect for those who break the law.* **3** disintegrate, fall apart, collapse, splinter, smash, shatter: *The old vase might break if you looked at it!* *n.* **1** crack, gap, opening, breach, rupture: *The water poured through the break in the dike.* **2** suspension, stop, hesitation, interruption: *We all took a ten-minute break and then went back to work.* *vb. phr.* **break down** fail, falter, stop: *Our car broke down on the steep hill.* **break in 1** educate, train, initiate, prepare, instruct:

The foreman had to break in the new machinist. **2** invade, trespass: *The burglars broke in and stole goods worth hundreds of pounds.* **break off** interrupt, discontinue, stop, cease: *Roger broke off when Marie entered the room and didn't continue until after she had left.* **break out** **1** start, initiate, begin, commence: *A riot broke out among the strikers.* **2** escape, flee, depart, leave: *Three prisoners broke out of the local prison last night.* **3** erupt: *Her face broke out in a rash.* **break through** penetrate, invade: *The platoon finally broke through the enemy lines.* **break up** **1** divide, separate, split: *I see Ellie has broken up with her boyfriend again.* **2** disassemble, separate, divide, dismantle, take apart: *The boss insisted that the clique be broken up at once.* ANT. *vb.* (1) mend, repair. (2) obey, keep.

breathe *vb.* inhale, exhale; gasp, sigh; pant; blow.

breed *vb.* **1** bear, conceive, beget, father, mother; create, produce, originate, generate: *The farmer bred prize cattle from stock he had imported.* **2** rear, raise, nurture, bring up; educate, train, teach: *The Forster's children are very well bred.* *n.* kind, sort, variety, species, strain: *The dogs on the farm were of mixed breed.*

breeze *n.* wind, breath, air, flurry, zephyr.

bribe *vb.* tempt, entice, lure; influence, pervert, corrupt.

bridle *n.* curb, check, restraint, control, halter: *The leather bridle for his favourite horse was studded with brass.* *vb.* curb, control, check, restrain, govern: *Walter would get along better with people if he could learn to bridle his temper.* ANT. *vb.* loose, free, release.

brief *adj.* **1** short, temporary, fleeting: *The life of some insects is so brief that it lasts only a day.* **2** short, terse, concise, condensed, compact: *The brief reports did not leave time for any details.* *vb.* advise, teach, instruct: *The men were briefed before going into the meeting.* ANT. *adj.* (1) long, extended, protracted. (2) extensive, comprehensive, exhaustive.

bright *adj.* **1** shining, shiny, gleaming, brilliant, sparkling, shimmering, radiant: *The seaman had bright brass buttons on his uniform.* **2** lively, cheerful, happy, lighthearted: *Her bright personality makes her a pleasure to be with.* **3** vivid, intense, brilliant: *That bright green dress becomes you very well.* **4** intelligent, quick-witted, clever, keen: *The bright children were mixed with the average ones to stimulate them.* **5** promising, encouraging, favourable: *Bob seems to have a bright future in that new job.* ANT. (1) dull, dim, lustreless. (2) boring, dull, colourless. (4) stupid, slow, backward.

brilliant *adj.* 1 bright, splendid, radiant, shining, sparkling, glittering: *Mrs. Van Patten was wearing a brilliant diamond necklace.* 2 talented, intelligent, gifted, ingenious: *That fellow George is a brilliant engineer.* ANT. (1) dull, lustreless. (2) mediocre, second-rate.

brim *n.* edge, lip, rim, margin, border. ANT. centre, middle.

bring *vb.* carry, take, fetch: *Please bring that chair over here.* *vb. phr.* **bring about** cause, accomplish, effect: *The judge brought about a compromise between the two parties.* **bring round** convince, persuade: *If you argue enough, you can bring him round to your way of thinking.* **bring to** or **round** revive, restore: *It took 20 minutes to bring Vickie round after she had been knocked unconscious.* **bring up** 1 rear, raise, nurture, educate, train, teach: *Anita's parents were away a great deal, so she was brought up by her aunt.* 2 introduce, raise, propose: *Why did he bring up the question of her honesty?* ANT. *vb.* withdraw, remove.

brink *n.* edge, rim, verge, margin, limit.

brisk *adj.* 1 lively, active, animated, energetic, nimble, quick, agile, spry: *Every morning Harry would take a brisk walk in the park.* 2 sharp, cool, stimulating, keen, invigorating: *On these November mornings the air can be very brisk.* ANT. (1) slow, sluggish, lethargic. (2) heavy, still, oppressive.

brittle *adj.* frail, fragile, breakable, weak. ANT. flexible, elastic, supple.

broad *adj.* 1 wide; large, expansive, extended, roomy: *The broad plain stretched out before them.* 2 general: *In a broad sense, intolerance should be against the law.* 3 extensive, wide, full: *He was appointed a judge because of his broad knowledge of the law.* ANT. (1) narrow, constricted. (2) detailed. (3) limited, negligible.

broadcast *vb.* spread, distribute, send, transmit, announce, relay.

broaden *vb.* extend, widen, expand, grow, increase. ANT. narrow.

broad-minded *adj.* tolerant, open-minded, unprejudiced, liberal. ANT. narrow-minded, prejudiced, bigoted, petty.

brood *n.* litter, young, offspring: *The mother hen defended her brood of chicks from the kitten.* *vb.* ponder, think about, meditate on *or* about, consider, reflect on, deliberate on: *The old man was brooding over the unfriendly things he had done in his youth.*

brook *n*. stream, rivulet, branch, run, rill, creek.

brother *n*. **1** sibling: *Any son of my parents is my brother.* **2** fellow man, kinsman; comrade: *All men are brothers.* ANT. (1) sister.

brow *n*. forehead, front, face.

brown *adj*. copper, rust, bronze, chestnut, russet.

browse *vb*. glance, scan, skim, thumb through, peruse.

bruise *vb*. injure, hurt, wound, damage: *Alan was bruised on his arm when the mast fell against him.* *n*. abrasion, injury, wound, damage, harm: *Beth suffered multiple bruises when she fell off her bicycle.*

brush *n*. **1** hairbrush; broom; whisk; paintbrush: *I keep my brush alongside my comb.* **2** bush, bushes, scrub, thicket: *We lost sight of the fox when he ran into the brush.* **3** encounter, meeting, affair, contact, skirmish: *After he was released from prison, he never again had a brush with the law.*

brutal *adj*. cruel, mean, savage, pitiless, inhuman, barbaric, ferocious. ANT. kind, kindhearted, gentle, mild.

brute *n*. beast, monster; savage, barbarian: *We caught the brute and put him into a cage.* *adj*. physical; savage, wild: *He picked up the two men using just brute strength and flung them away.*

bubble *n*. foam, froth, lather, effervescence: *Soap makes the water full of bubbles.* *vb*. froth, foam, seethe, boil: *The oil bubbled on the stove when we dropped in the potatoes for frying.*

bucket *n*. pail; container, can, canister, pot.

buckle *n*. fastening, fastener, clasp: *He wears a gold buckle on his belt.* *vb*. **1** fasten, clasp: *Don't buckle your belt too tightly.* **2** bend, collapse, warp, yield, fail, give way: *The bridge buckled under the weight of the huge lorry.*

budge *vb*. move, stir, shift.

buffet[1] *vb*. strike, beat, hit, slap: *The winds buffeted the house for three days.* *n*. blow, hit: *A quick buffet to the side of the head brought him to his senses.*

buffet[2] *n*. **1** sideboard, cabinet, counter: *The food was set out on the buffet so that each person could help himself.* **2** meal, snack: *Come round for a buffet tonight.*

build *vb*. construct, erect, put together, assemble: *In their spare time the children built kennels and sold them to neighbours.* *vb. phr.* **build up** increase, strengthen, expand, develop: *Over the years he built up the size of his record library considerably.* *n*. physique, form, figure: *Kathy has* *the build of a child.* ANT. *vb.* demolish, pull down, raze.

building *n.* structure, edifice; residence, house.

bulge *n.* swelling, lump, protrusion, protuberance, bump: *The bulge at the side of the building looked dangerous.* *vb.* swell, protrude, extend: *As he blew air into the balloon, it began to bulge.* ANT. *n.* depression, hollow.

bulk *n.* 1 size, volume, magnitude: *The package wasn't heavy but its huge bulk made it difficult to carry.* 2 majority, most, main part: *The bulk of my income comes from my salary.*

bulky *adj.* large, big, huge, clumsy, unwieldy, cumbersome, massive. ANT. delicate, small, handy.

bully *n.* rowdy, ruffian, rascal, scamp: *The village bully used to set upon the young lads.* *vb.* domineer, harass, intimidate: *You could tell that he was a coward because he was always bullying the smaller children.*

bump *vb.* knock, bang, collide with, hit, strike: *The first day he took out his new bicycle Alan bumped into a car.* *n.* knock, bang; collision, blow: *For trying to help the shop-keeper, Jim was given a bump on the head by the thief.*

bun *n.* roll, bread, scone, cake, pastry.

bunch *n.* cluster, group, batch, bundle, collection.

bundle *n.* bunch; package, parcel, packet.

bungle *vb.* mess up, spoil, blunder; fumble.

burden *n.* load, weight; worry, trial; trouble: *The donkey is a beast of burden. Concern about his father's health was too much of a burden for a child to manage.* *vb.* load, weigh down, overload, oppress: *I don't want to burden you with my troubles.* ANT. *vb.* disburden.

bureau *n.* 1 desk: *You'll find the keys in the top drawer of my bureau.* 2 office, agency: *Let's go down to the travel bureau to see about our tickets.*

burglar *n.* thief, robber, housebreaker.

burial *n.* funeral, interment.

burn *vb.* 1 blaze, flame: *The fire burned for three days in the forest.* 2 scorch, sear, char, set on fire, consume: *The wooden carving was burned beyond recognition.* *n.* scorch, injury, singe, scald: *There were some burns on her arms where the boiling water had accidentally been poured.*

burrow *n.* lair, den, hole, tunnel.

burst *vb.* explode, blow up, erupt: *The electric light bulb burst into lots of pieces when I dropped it.* *n.* explosion; breach, rapture; outburst, outbreak: *A sudden burst of firing broke the silence of the prison.* ANT. implode.

bury *vb.* **1** inter, entomb: *The men were buried for two hours by the avalanche.* **2** hide, conceal, cover, secrete: *The book I was looking for was buried under the pile of magazines.* ANT. (1) disinter, raise.

bus *n.* coach, minibus; tram.

bush *n.* shrub, plant; thicket, woodland, forest.

business *n.* **1** trade, occupation, commerce: *What business is your father in?* **2** company, firm, concern; partnership: *After graduating from college, Victor went into his father's business.* **3** affair, concern: *My personal life is none of your business.*

bustle *vb.* hurry, rush, hasten.

busy *adj.* active, occupied, engaged, employed, industrious, hardworking. ANT. inactive, unemployed, indolent, lazy.

but *conj.* however, nevertheless, yet; on the other hand, though, still, although.

buy *vb.* purchase; procure, obtain, get. ANT. sell.

by *prep.* near, at, close to, next to.

C

cab *n.* taxi, taxicab, minicab.

cabin *n.* **1** compartment, berth, stateroom: *Our cabin on the ship was on the lower deck.* **2** hut, shack: *The hermit lived in a cabin in the woods.*

cabinet *n.* **1** council, committee, ministry: *The prime minister depends on the members of his cabinet for advice.* **2** cupboard, wardrobe, chest: *We bought a fine nineteenth-century cabinet from an auction.*

cable *n.* wire, rope, string, cord, line.

cackle *vb.* cluck, quack; laugh, giggle, chortle, chuckle.

café *n.* snack-bar; cafeteria, restaurant.

cagey *adj.* evasive, secretive, uncommunicative. ANT. frank, open, straightforward.

cajole *vb.* persuade, coax, flatter.

cake *n.* pastry, roll, bun, patisserie, tart.

calamity *n.* disaster, bad luck, misfortune, distress, trouble, hardship, catastrophe. ANT. boon, blessing, godsend, windfall.

calculate *vb.* work out, reckon, compute, measure; add, multiply, divide.

calculating *adj.* scheming, crafty, cunning, shrewd. ANT. ingenuous, simple, direct, guileless.

calculation *n.* reckoning, working out, computation. ANT. guess, estimate.

call *vb.* **1** call out, cry out, exclaim, shout: *I hear my name being called.* **2** name, designate, dub, label: *Her name is Catherine but they call her Sophie.* **3** telephone, phone, ring, ring up: *Please call me when you arrive at the hotel.* **4** collect, assemble, convene: *The directors called a meeting.* **5** wake up, awaken, waken, wake, rouse, arouse: *They called us at five o'clock to start on the hike.* *n.* **1** cry, shout, yell, exclamation: *I heard the call of the hunters trying to find me in the forest.* **2** demand, need, occasion, claim: *There isn't much call for fountain pens these days.* *vb. phr.* **call off** cancel, postpone: *The match was called off at the last moment.* **call on** visit: *I called on our new neighbours yesterday.*

callous *adj.* hardened, insensitive, unfeeling. ANT. tender; merciful.

calm *adj.* 1 quiet, peaceful, still, tranquil, mild, serene, smooth: *The sea became calm towards sunset.* 2 composed, collected, unruffled, levelheaded, cool, unexcited; detached, aloof: *Nell remained quite calm after I told her the bad news.* *n.* calmness, stillness, serenity, quiet; composure: *The wind and rain stopped suddenly in the calm before the storm struck.* *vb.* pacify, soothe: *When he learned that it had not been his son who had been in the accident, Bill calmed down.* ANT. *adj.* (1) tempestuous, stormy. (2) emotional, disturbed, excited. *n.* turmoil, upheaval, disturbance. *vb.* upset, excite, disturb.

camouflage *n.* disguise, covering; mask, blind, veil; deception.

campaign *n.* operation, exercise, task; fight, crusade, offensive.

cancel *vb.* 1 call off, rescind, set aside: *I'm sorry but I have to cancel our appointment for dinner tonight.* 2 delete, cross out *or* off, erase: *She cancelled his name and substituted hers on the list.*

candid *adj.* frank, open, straightforward, honest. ANT. devious, dishonest; cagey.

candidate *n.* nominee, aspirant, applicant.

capable *adj.* able, skilled, fit, skilful, accomplished, competent. ANT. inept, incompetent, unskilled.

capacity *n.* 1 volume, content: *This tank has a capacity of 40 litres.* 2 ability, capability, aptitude, talent, faculty: *If he would only study harder, John has the capacity to be a first-class student.* ANT. (2) incapacity, inability.

capital *n.* cash, money, assets, property, wealth, principal, resources: *My father started his business with capital of £2000.* *adj.* major, chief, first, primary, leading, important, principal: *St. Peter's Church is of capital interest to visitors to Rome.* ANT. *adj.* trivial, unimportant, secondary.

capsize *vb.* turn over, tip up, overturn.

captain *n.* 1 supervisor, commander, director, authority, leader: *The teacher appointed Eugene to be the captain of the group.* 2 (of a ship) skipper, commander, commanding officer, master: *The captain ordered the lifeboats to be lowered over the side.*

captivate *vb.* fascinate, charm, enchant, delight.

captive *n.* prisoner, convict, hostage.

captivity *n.* imprisonment, confinement, detention, custody; slavery, bondage. ANT. freedom, liberty.

capture *vb.* seize, take prisoner, trap, grab, catch, arrest: *We set the trap to capture rabbits, but not one fell into it.* *n.* seizure, catching; recovery: *The escaped tiger avoided capture for three hours.* ANT. *vb.* release, free, liberate.

car *n.* automobile, vehicle, motorcar.

carcass *n.* body, corpse, remains, cadaver.

card *n.* paper, cardboard, sheet; board; poster, ticket, voucher.

cardinal *adj.* important, chief, principal, primary, prime, major, leading, essential. ANT. secondary, subordinate, auxiliary.

care *n.* **1** worry, concern, anxiety, trouble: *Although his business was very bad, my father acted as though he didn't have a care in the world.* **2** carefulness, attention, regard, concern, consideration: *Like many parents, Bob and Diane treated their first child with much more care than the later children.* **3** charge, custody, protection, keeping, supervision, guardianship: *We left our dog in the care of the vet when we went away for a holiday.* *vb.* **1** mind; attend, consider: *I don't care what you do with that eggshell.* **2** look after, keep; watch, guard, supervise: *Who's going to care for me when I'm old?* ANT. *n.* (2) indifference, unconcern, apathy.

career *n.* profession, occupation, job, vocation.

careful *adj.* **1** cautious, watchful, wary, guarded, vigilant: *You have to be careful of what you say when you're talking to the headmaster.* **2** thorough, concerned, painstaking, meticulous: *I thought that Tim did a very careful job when he painted the railings.* ANT. (1) incautious, heedless. (2) careless, messy, sloppy.

careless *adj.* messy, sloppy, unthoughtful, unconcerned, negligent, reckless, thoughtless, uncaring. ANT. careful, cautious, prudent, painstaking.

caress *n.* embrace, pat, kiss: *Under his mother's gentle caress, Billy was soothed enough to stop crying.* *vb.* pat, pet, stroke, fondle, cuddle: *Dad took the photograph of Jennie while she caressed her kitten.*

cargo *n.* load, freight, baggage.

carriage *n.* vehicle, coach; cart, wagon, chariot.

carry *vb.* bear, transport, move, transfer; take, bring: *The porter will help carry your luggage to the train.* *vb. phr.* **carry off** abduct, seize, kidnap, capture: *When the bandits attacked a village, they would often carry off all the girls.* **carry on** **1** continue, go on, proceed: *Please excuse the interruption: you may carry on with your conversation now.*

2 fuss, misbehave: *Victor carried on so about being left behind that he was finally allowed to go.* **carry out** fulfil, complete, succeed, accomplish, win, effect: *The plan sounds good, but will they be able to carry it out?*

cart *n.* barrow, wagon, carriage.

carton *n.* box, case, container, can, canister.

carve *vb.* cut, chisel, sculpt, hew, whittle, shape.

case[1] *n.* **1** instance, occurrence, example, happening; sample, illustration: *The detectives were investigating a case of murder.* **2** action, suit, lawsuit, claim: *The prosecution opened the case at the Old Bailey.*

case[2] *n.* container, crate, box, carton, chest; receptacle: *When he opened the case of wine, it contained only eight bottles, not twelve.*

cash *n.* money, currency; banknotes, coins, change.

cast *vb.* **1** throw, hurl, fling, toss, pitch, sling: *To avoid being caught with the stolen papers, Ezra cast them into the deep well.* **2** direct, shed, impart: *The lamp cast a strange yellow glow about the room.* **3** direct, turn: *Whenever her name was mentioned, Elizabeth cast her eyes downward in embarrassment.* **4** mould, shape, form: *I cast this bronze statue in my own shop.* *n.* players, actors, performers: *There was a party for the entire cast after the first performance of the play.*

castle *n.* palace, mansion, chateau.

casual *adj.* **1** chance, accidental, unintentional, unexpected, offhand, unplanned, spontaneous: *The whole trouble can be traced to their casual meeting in the garden.* **2** informal, sporty: *At weekends we wear casual clothes unless we expect company or go out.* ANT. (1) planned, calculated, deliberate, premeditated. (2) formal, dressy.

catalogue *n.* list, roll, inventory, record, directory; file; index.

catastrophe *n.* disaster, calamity, accident, misfortune, mishap. ANT. boon, blessing, triumph.

catch *vb.* **1** seize, capture, take, grasp, grab, nab: *Did they catch the thief who stole the car?* **2** trap, snare, entrap, ensnare: *We caught two rabbits in the trap but let them go after a while.* **3** go down with, contract, succumb to: *You'll catch a cold if you don't wear your hat.* *vb. phr.* **catch on** become popular, become fashionable: *That new style of dress has really caught on these last few months.* **catch out** trap, trick, trip up: *Jane tried to catch her brother out by asking him a trick question.* **catch up** reach, pass: *Your brother has just left, so if you go now you'll soon catch him up.* *n.* **1** seizure; capture, arrest, apprehension: *The fishermen made a great* *catch of fish.* **2** bolt, latch: *The catch on the door is broken again.* ANT. *vb.* **(1, 2)** release, free, let go.

cattle *n.* animals, stock, herd; cows, bulls.

cause *n.* **1** reason, origin, creation, occasion, ground: *The cause of the accident was a broken brake lever.* **2** aim, purpose, object: *We managed to raise £20 for the cause of orphans.* *vb.* occasion, give rise to, bring about, originate, effect: *According to the report, the breakdown caused the accident.*

caution *n.* **1** wariness, watchfulness, vigilance, heed, care: *Exercise caution when you approach that dog—he may be unfriendly.* **2** warning, advice: *She gave me a caution about the broken stair.* *vb.* warn, admonish, forewarn: *The lifeguard cautioned us about the strong undercurrent.* ANT. *n.* **(1)** heedlessness, carelessness, incaution.

cautious *adj.* careful, watchful, wary; vigilant. ANT. heedless, headstrong, indiscreet, foolish.

cave *n.* grotto, cavern, hole: *Bears hibernate in a cave during the winter.* *vb. phr.* **cave in** collapse, fall in: *Just as we were about to leave, the roof caved in and trapped us.*

cease *vb.* stop, end, put a stop *or* an end to, terminate. ANT. begin, start.

celebrate *vb.* honour, observe, keep, commemorate. ANT. ignore, disregard.

celebrated *adj.* famous, renowned, famed, well-known, noted, illustrious, eminent; popular. ANT. unheard of, unknown.

celebrity *n.* notable, dignitary; hero, heroine.

cell *n.* room, cubicle, compartment, recess, den.

cellar *n.* basement, vault, crypt.

censor *n.* examiner, inquisitor; snoop.

censure *n.* disapproval, criticism, reproach: *The commission's vote for censure of the judge was unanimous.* *vb.* disapprove, criticize, condemn, reproach: *After the dishonest things the mayor did, the town council had to censure him.* ANT. *n.* approval, praise. *vb.* praise, approve, applaud.

central *adj.* **1** middle, mid, focal, inner, halfway: *The chief's hut was central in the arrangement of the village.* **2** principal, chief, dominant, basic, fundamental, necessary: *The central issue for the workers was more pay; increased pensions were secondary.* ANT. **(2)** secondary, auxiliary, side, incidental.

centre *n.* **1** middle, midst, inside, midpoint: *The centre of the earth is said to be a sphere of molten iron.* **2** focus, hub, heart, core: *The monument is at the centre of the city.* *vb.* focus, direct, concentrate: *The attention of the crowd centred* *on the clown in the red costume.* ANT. *n.* (1) edge, brim.

ceremony *n.*   ritual, rite, service, formality.

certain *adj.*   **1** confident, sure, positive, assured: *After all he'd done for the town, his election as mayor was certain.*   **2** definite, particular, special: *It would not be wise for me to name certain people who were seen together at the party.* ANT. (1) doubtful, uncertain, questionable.

certainly *adv.*   surely, absolutely, definitely.   ANT. doubtfully, dubiously, questionably.

certificate *n.*   document, credential(s), declaration, affidavit.

chain *n.*   string, link; set, series.

chair *n.*   seat, bench, stool.

challenge *n.*   dare, threat: *The supermarket met the challenge of competition by reducing prices.*   *vb.* dare, threaten: *John challenged Peter to a duel.*

chamber *n.*   room, salon; cell.

champion *n.*   hero, winner, victor: *The champion of the heavyweight boxers was Joe.*   *vb.* defend, support: *The housewives championed the cause of the poor in their area.*

chance *n.*   **1** opportunity, possibility, prospect: *I'll tell you what you want to know if you'll stop talking and give me a chance.*   **2** luck, accident, fate: *You ought to make absolutely certain that he's coming and leave nothing to chance.*   *adj.* accidental, casual: *A chance meeting at the club resulted in my getting the job.*   ANT. *n.* (2) certainty, inevitability.

change *vb.*   **1** exchange, substitute, replace: *We changed our clothes before going out.*   **2** vary; modify, alter: *I wish you would change your mind and let us go swimming.*   **3** exchange, trade: *I have to change this pound note into coins to use in the telephone.*   *n.* variation, modification, alteration: *Ellie had a change of heart and came with us.*   ANT. *vb.* endure, remain.   *n.* endurance, steadfastness, immutability.

channel *n.*   canal, duct, trough, way, runway, groove.

chant *n.*   song, singing, hymn, incantation: *Certain kinds of chants have been used in church music for centuries.*   *vb.* sing, recite, intone: *The children started to chant, "Kitty is a baby! Kitty is a baby!"*

chaos *n.*   disorder, confusion, turmoil.   ANT. tranquillity, order, organization, tidiness.

chaotic *adj.*   disordered, confused, messy, disorganized.   ANT. ordered, organized, neat, tidy, systematic.

character *n.*   **1** qualities, features, characteristics: *The judge is a man of outstanding character.*   **2** person, role: *The characters* *in the play were all very well acted.* **3** *Informal:* individual, eccentric: *That fellow is quite a character.*

characteristic *adj.* typical, distinctive, distinguishing, special: *Dictionaries often give examples of characteristic uses of words.* *n.* character, feature, quality, trait: *A characteristic of the Pygmy people is their short stature.*

charge *vb.* **1** price at, sell for: *They charge too much for a service at that garage.* **2** attack, assault, assail: *The cavalry charged up the hill.* **3** accuse, indict, blame: *Even though he had a perfect alibi, they charged Evans with robbery.* *n.* **1** accusation, blame, indictment, allegation: *The charge against us was trespassing on private property.* **2** care, management, custody: *The teacher left a student in charge of the class.* **3** price, cost: *The charge for making a phone call increased again this year.* ANT. *vb.* (2) retreat, flee. (3) absolve, excuse, pardon.

charitable *adj.* kind, generous, liberal; considerate. ANT. mean, petty, stingy, narrow-minded.

charm *n.* **1** attractiveness, allure, enchantment; spell, magic witchery: *When she used her charm on Rudolf, she could make him do anything she wanted.* **2** amulet, good-luck piece, talisman: *The bearded pirate wore a strange charm on a chain around his neck.* *vb.* attract, enchant, lure, fascinate, captivate, bewitch: *When you were in India, did you see any men charming snakes?*

chart *n.* plan, map; diagram.

chase *vb.* pursue, run after, follow, hunt: *The farmer chased us out of the field.* *n.* pursuit, hunt: *At first, I ran after the thief alone, but two other people later joined in the chase.*

chaste *adj.* virtuous, pure, innocent, decent; virginal. ANT. impure, worldly, sinful.

chasten *vb.* discipline, rebuke, reprove.

chat *vb.* talk, converse: *I chatted for a while with Mrs. Philbey about where she was going for her holiday.* *n.* conversation, talk: *During our chat, she told me she loved to go to the mountains.*

chatter *vb.* talk, chat; prattle, gossip, gabble.

cheap *adj.* **1** inexpensive, low-priced, low-cost: *Fresh fruit is cheaper when it's in season.* **2** shoddy, inferior, poor: *If you buy cheap clothes, you rarely get good value.* ANT. (1) costly, expensive, dear. (2) well-made.

cheat *n.* swindler, fraud, phoney, charlatan; crook, thief, confidence trickster, con man: *The man who offered to sell*

Tower Bridge was nothing but a cheat. *vb.* swindle, trick, defraud, deceive, victimize, dupe, hoax: *The crook cheated me out of my life savings.*

check *vb.* 1 stop, halt, arrest, block: *The tanks checked the advance of the enemy's soldiers.* 2 restrain, control, curb; hinder: *This valve checks the flow of gas.* 3 review, investigate, test, examine, compare: *Please check the inventory against the list.* *n.* control, curb; hindrance, barrier, bar, obstacle, restriction: *When running a household you have to keep a check on the amount of money you spend. Bill doesn't seem able to keep a check on his temper.* ANT. *vb.* (1, 2) advance, continue, foster, promote.

checkup *n.* examination, medical *or* physical (examination).

cheek *n.* impudence, impertinence, nerve, gall, effrontery.

cheer *n.* 1 approval, applause, encouragement: *A large cheer went up from the crowd as Bob won the race.* 2 glee, joy, mirth, gaiety, cheerfulness: *Be of good cheer: happiness is just around the corner.* *vb.* 1 encourage, comfort: *The coach's words cheered us, and we won.* 2 shout, yell, applaud: *The crowd cheered for the new champion.* ANT. *n.* (1) discouragement, derision. *vb.* (1) discourage, sadden. (2) boo, hiss.

cheerful *adj.* cheery, happy, joyous, joyful, merry. ANT. sad, gloomy, morose, downhearted.

cherish *vb.* 1 treasure, hold dear, value, prize: *She cherished the memories of her days at summer camp.* 2 nurse, comfort, nurture: *I cherish the relationship I have with my brothers and sisters.* ANT. (1) scorn, undervalue, deprecate, disparage.

chest *n.* 1 breast, bosom: *The little girl clasped the puppy to her chest.* 2 box, trunk, coffer, case, casket: *The treasure chest contained rubies, pearls, diamonds, and gold.* 3 (of drawers) dresser, cabinet, commode, chiffonier, bureau: *My father's cufflinks were on the chest.*

chew *vb.* bite, munch, gnaw; nibble.

chide *vb.* scold, criticize, admonish, reprimand, rebuke, reprove. ANT. praise, extol, commend.

chief *n.* leader, ruler, commander, boss, head: *The chief of the robber band was masked.* *adj.* leading, principal, main; head: *The chief reason for going to school is to learn something.* ANT. *adj.* secondary, incidental.

chiefly *adv.* mostly, mainly, principally, especially.

child *n.* infant, youth, youngster, boy, girl. ANT. adult, grown-up.

childish *adj.* childlike, immature, babyish, infantile. ANT. adult, grown-up, mature, seasoned.

chill *n.* cold, coldness, coolness, cool. ANT. warmth, heat.

chilly *adj.* cool, brisk, frosty. ANT. warm, heated, hot.

chip *n.* bit, fragment; flake, slice, wedge: *Chips of wood were thrown up by the lathe.* *vb.* break, cut, hew, splinter, crumble: *The paint is beginning to chip because of the weather.*

chirp *vb.,n.* twitter, peep, tweet, warble, cheep, chirrup: *The birds were chirping happily in the trees. The chirps of the crickets and the birds woke me up.*

chivalrous *adj.* brave, noble; polite, courteous, gallant, gentlemanly. ANT. rude, impolite, crude, uncivil.

chivalry *n.* nobility, knighthood; courtesy, gallantry.

choice *n.* selection, option, pick: *The saleslady offered us a choice of styles and colours.* *adj.* select, fine, rare, uncommon, valuable, precious: *The mare in the pasture is a choice example of the best horsebreeding.*

choke *vb.* strangle, throttle; gag, gasp, suffocate.

choose *vb.* select, pick, decide between *or* on, settle on *or* for.

chop *vb.* cut; hew, fell.

chorus *n.* refrain, song, melody, tune.

chronic *adj.* continuing, persistent, continuous, lingering, sustained, constant, lifelong, permanent, unending, eternal, everlasting. ANT. fleeting, temporary; acute.

chuckle *vb.,n.* giggle, titter, laugh: *The teacher chuckled over the story that Marjorie had written. Every few minutes, he gave a little chuckle.*

church *n.* **1** congregation; denomination, faith, tradition: *The church was learning to respond to the Word of God more.* **2** chapel, cathedral, abbey, sanctuary: *Our church is full at Harvest, Christmas, and Easter.*

circle *n.* **1** ring; loop, disc: *The magician drew a circle in in the sand.* **2** group, set, class, club: *In her circle of friends, everyone now buys Elvis records.* *vb.* encircle, surround, round, enclose: *The road circled our farm.*

circuit *n.* orbit, circle, revolution; course, tour, journey.

circular *adj.* round, ringlike, dislike: *Most drinking glasses are circular.* *n.* advertisement, handbill, leaflet: *We received a circular advertising the sale at the department store.* ANT. *adj.* straight.

circulate *vb.* distribute, send round, diffuse.

circumference *n.* periphery, border, edge, perimeter.

circumstances *n.pl.* situation, conditions, facts, factors, grounds, background.

cite *vb.* quote, mention, refer to.

citizen *n.* inhabitant, native, national, subject, denizen, dweller, resident.

city *n.* town, conurbation, capital, metropolis.

civil *adj.* 1 municipal, public: *Every citizen has his civil rights.* 2 polite, courteous, gracious, well-mannered, respectful: *Roger has always been very civil to me.* ANT. (2) impolite, rude, crude.

civilization *n.* culture, society.

civilize *vb.* cultivate, refine, polish, tame, teach, instruct.

claim *vb.* 1 demand, require, request, ask for: *After my grandfather died, my father claimed for himself all his property.* 2 assert, state, maintain, insist, declare: *Donald claimed that he knew nothing about the theft of the statue.* *n.* 1 demand, request, requirement: *The court ruled that the miner's claim was invalid.* 2 title, right, interest: *I told you that Kitty has no claim to the brooch.*

clairvoyance *n.* premonition, precognition, foreknowledge; insight, discernment; intuition.

clamour *n.* din, noise, shouting, uproar: *When the teacher announced another exam, there was such a clamour from the students that he cancelled it.* *vb.* demand, shout: *The girls in the audience clamoured for the guitar player to come back on stage.* ANT. *n.* quiet, serenity, tranquillity.

clan *n.* family, set, group.

clang *vb.,n.* jangle, jingle, ring: *The metals clanged as the tins fell on the scrap heap. The clang of the alarm could be heard all over the building.*

clap *vb.* applaud, acclaim, praise, cheer.

clarify *vb.* explain, clear, define. ANT. confuse, muddle, obscure.

clarity *n.* clearness, lucidity; precision; distinctiveness.

clash *n.* 1 clang, crash, clank: *The clash of armour could be heard far away as the knights fought.* 2 conflict, opposition, struggle, disagreement; collision: *There was a clash between those in office and those who sought to replace them.* *vb.* 1 contrast, mismatch, jar: *Your tie clashes with your shirt.* 2 conflict, disagree, interfere; collide: *We always clash over our different points of view.* ANT. *n.* (2) harmony, agreement, accord. *vb.* (1) harmonize, blend. (2) agree, match, coincide.

clasp *vb.* grasp, embrace, hug, clutch, hold: *Her father was so* *happy to find her safe and sound that he wept as he clasped her to him.*   *n.* hook, catch, pin, fastening, brooch, buckle: *These two parts of the dress are held together by a silver clasp.*

class *n.*   **1** classification, rank, order, grade, division, subdivision, family, sort, kind, set, species, group: *I don't know whether this animal belongs to the fish or reptile class.*   **2** form, group, set, year: *I'm in Miss Clarendon's class next year.*   *vb.* classify, rank, grade: *I wouldn't class you in the same category as your sister.*

classic *n.*   masterpiece: *Paradise Lost is considered one of the greatest classics in the English language.*   *adj.* model, definitive, standard; highest: *California is the classic haven for tax exiles.*

classification *n.*   **1** category, order, class: *Into which classification should I put this book, science or philosophy?*   **2** arrangement, grouping, ordering, organization: *The librarian's classification of new books takes a great deal of time.*

classify *vb.*   class, arrange, sort, order, organize, group, grade, index.

clause *n.*   paragraph, article, condition, limitation.

claw *n.*   nail, talon, hook: *The cat's claw caught in the curtain and tore it.*   *vb.* scratch, tear; rip: *The dog kept clawing at the door, trying to get in.*

clean *adj.*   **1** clear, dustless, immaculate, unsoiled, unstained: *My mother made me scrub the floor till it was clean.*   **2** pure, untainted, uncontaminated, purified: *Don't drink from a glass that isn't clean.*   *vb.* **1** dust, mop, vacuum, scour, scrub, sweep, wipe, wash, rinse, cleanse: *If you don't clean your room, you can't go out to play.*   **2** purify, decontaminate; sterilize: *All surgical instruments must be cleaned after every use.*   ANT. *adj.* dirty, soiled, impure, contaminated. *vb.* soil, dirty, pollute.

cleanse *see* **clean**.

clear *adj.*   **1** plain, understandable, distinct, lucid, obvious: *I want to make the entire matter as clear as possible.*   **2** uncloudy, unclouded, bright, light; sunny, fair: *Water is a clear liquid. Saturday was such a clear day you could see the mountains in the distance.*   **3** certain, sure, doubtless, obvious: *Alan's innocence was clear.*   **4** open, free, unobstructed, unblocked: *The road was clear early in the morning.*   *vb.* **1** empty: *Please clear the room so that it can be painted.*   **2** acquit, free, release, emancipate, let go: *The statements the murderer made about his other crimes cleared two men who had been arrested for them.*   **3** rid, free, remove: *If they clear* *the channel of debris, we shall be able to sail the boat through it.* ANT. *adj.* **(1)** confused, muddled. **(2)** overcast, cloudy, dark. **(3)** dubious, questionable. **(4)** obstructed, blocked, blockaded. *vb.* **(1)** fill, clutter. **(2)** implicate, involve. **(3)** obstruct, block, blockade.

clearly *adv.* obviously, definitely, plainly, evidently, unmistakably, certainly, surely. ANT. dubiously, questionably.

cleave¹ *vb.* split, cut, sever, divide: *The thunderstorm cleft the tree trunk in two.*

cleave² (to) *vb.* stick, cling, adhere: *The Bible says a man cleaves to his wife when he marries her.*

clergy *n.* ministers, ministry, priesthood.

clergyman *n.* minister, parson, priest, vicar, pastor, preacher.

clerical *adj.* **1** priestly, ministerial, churchly, pastoral, ecclesiastical; sacred, holy: *The bishop's other clerical duties did not prevent him from conducting services.* **2** stenographic, secretarial: *After leaving school, Anne was lucky to get a clerical job in town.*

clerk *n.* office worker; office girl, office boy, junior, typist

clever *adj.* **1** bright, intelligent, shrewd, quick, talented, expert, gifted, smart: *A clever person could move ahead in that company.* **2** skilful, adroit, dexterous, handy: *My brother is so clever with his hands that he finished a model aeroplane in two hours.* ANT. **(1)** stupid, slow, backward, dull. **(2)** clumsy, maladroit, inept.

client *n.* customer, patron.

cliff *n.* rock, hill, precipice.

climb *vb.* go up, scale, ascend, mount. ANT. go down, descend.

cling *vb.* stick, adhere, hold fast, cleave.

clinic *n.* hospital, infirmary, sick bay.

clip¹ *vb.* cut, mow, crop, snip: *They clipped my lawn too short.*

clip² *n.* fastener, paper clip, clasp: *Please put a clip on those papers to keep them together.*

clique *n.* coterie, faction, group, party; splinter group.

cloak *n.* cape, mantle, wrap, shawl: *You'd better take your cloak—it's cold outside.* *vb.* conceal, hide, cover, mask: *Her smile cloaked her real feelings about him.* ANT. *vb.* reveal, show, display.

clock *n.* timepiece; watch; chronometer.

close¹ *vb.* **1** shut, fasten, bolt, lock: *Be careful and make sure to close your doors at night.* **2** end, terminate, conclude: *The speaker closed his remarks with a few compliments to the mayor.* ANT. **(1)** open, unlock. **(2)** begin, start.

close² *adj.* **1** near, nearby: *If the supermarket were closer to the house, I wouldn't have to walk so far to shop.* **2** stuffy, unventilated, oppressive: *With the windows closed and the heater on, it feels very close in this room.* **3** stingy, mean, (*informal*) mingy, tight: *Scrooge was certainly a close man with his money.* ANT. (**1**) far, distant. (**2**) fresh, clear. (**3**) generous, open-handed, charitable.

cloth *n.* material, fabric, textile; tablecloth.

clothe *vb.* dress, apparel, garb. ANT. undress, strip.

clothes *n.pl.* garments, clothing, dress; garb, attire, apparel, costume.

cloud *n.* **1** haze, mist, fog: *The clouds made it a gloomy day for our picnic.* **2** collection, mass: *The stagecoach rattled into town in a cloud of dust.* *vb.* dim, obscure, shadow: *The politician clouded the issue with his evasive answers.*

cloudy *adj.* **1** dim, obscure, vague, indefinite, blurred, unclear, confused: *If your thinking is cloudy on a subject, you cannot write about it clearly.* **2** overcast, clouded, gloomy: *It was a cloudy morning when we set sail for the island.* ANT. (**1**) clearheaded, lucid, clarified. (**2**) sunny, clear, brilliant, cloudless.

club *n.* **1** association, society, organization, circle, set: *There was a long waiting list for membership in the club.* **2** cudgel, bat, stick: *The thieves were carrying clubs with which they threatened their victims.*

clue *n.* hint, suggestion, trace, sign, indication.

clumsy *adj.* awkward, ungraceful, unskilful, bungling, ungainly, inept. ANT. graceful, adroit, skilful, polished, dexterous.

cluster *n.* group, batch, bunch: *A cluster of flowers grew near the rock.* *vb.* group, gather, assemble, pack, crowd: *The students clustered around the notice board where the examination results had been put up.*

clutch *vb.* seize, grip, grasp, hold, grab.

coach *n.* **1** vehicle, bus; carriage: *The coach for Brighton leaves at three o'clock.* **2** instructor, trainer, teacher; manager: *Mr. Smith is the coach for the winning team.* *vb.* instruct, train, drill, exercise: *The trainer has a very difficult job trying to coach the members of the team during the season.*

coarse *adj.* rough, crude, rude. ANT. fine, refined, cultivated, genteel, suave.

coast *n.* beach, seashore, shore, shoreline, seaboard: *We like to spend our holidays on the South coast.* *vb.* glide, ride; drift: *Pete came coasting down the hill on his sledge. Some* *people just coast through life letting nothing disturb them.*

coat *n.* jacket, raincoat, overcoat.

coax *vb.* persuade, wheedle, cajole, urge. ANT. bully, force, coerce.

coil *vb.* wind, ring, twist, loop, roll: *Please coil the string round this stick.* *n.* curl, ring, loop: *We need a lot of wire for this job—you'd better go and buy a coil from the shop.*

coincide *vb.* correspond, agree, match, harmonize.

coincidence *n.* chance, accident. ANT. plan, scheme, plot, prearrangement.

cold *adj.* **1** cool, chilly, chill; frigid, freezing: *Winter in Scotland can be very cold.* **2** unemotional, unfriendly, unfeeling, indifferent, heartless: *Susan's attitude toward her classmates was so cold that she had no friends at all.* ANT. (**1**) hot, warm, temperate. (**2**) friendly, warm, compassionate, outgoing.

cold-blooded *adj.* cruel, unfeeling, pitiless, callous. ANT. *feeling, sensitive.*

collaborate *vb.* work together, cooperate.

collapse *vb.* fall; fail, drop: *The walls of the building collapsed during the fire.* *n.* failure, downfall, destruction: *The kingdom was doomed to collapse when the dictator overthrew the government.*

colleague *n.* associate, co-worker; collaborator.

collect *vb.* **1** gather, assemble, accumulate: *I used to collect seashells as a hobby, but now I collect stamps.* **2** obtain, procure, secure, get, raise: *The charity collected hundreds of pounds to help the handicapped.* ANT. (**1**) disperse, dispel, scatter.

collection *n.* accumulation, hoard, store, pile.

college *n.* polytechnic, university; institution, institute; school.

collide *vb.* crash, smash, strike, hit.

collision *n.* crash, smash, smash-up.

colloquial *adj.* popular, everyday, familiar, conversational, informal.

colossal *adj.* enormous, huge, immense, gigantic. ANT. tiny, miniature, minuscule, microscopic.

colour *n.* hue, shade, tone, tinge, tint: *I can't tell the colour of your eyes through those dark glasses.* *vb.* tint, paint, tinge; decorate: *The walls should be coloured to match the carpet.*

column *n.* **1** pillar, post, support, prop: *The columns at the front of that building look most impressive.* **2** article, feature; comment; review: *Lionel writes the fishing column for the local paper each week.*

combat *vb.* fight, battle, oppose, contest, struggle: *The economists seem to be unable to combat inflation effectively.* *n.* fight, battle, contest, conflict, war, struggle: *The two knights were locked in mortal combat.* ANT. *vb.* surrender, yield, succumb.

combination *n.* 1 blending, mixing, compounding: *The combination of flour and water makes a light paste.* 2 blend, mixture, compound, composite: *Gunpowder is a combination of three simple ingredients.* ANT. (1) separation, division.

combine *vb.* blend, mix; unite, join, connect. ANT. separate, divide.

come *vb.* 1 approach, advance, near: *I want you to come here when I call you.* 2 arrive, reach: *Dick came home late last night.* *vb. phr.* **come about** happen, occur, take place: *The accident came about because you were driving recklessly.* **come across** find, stumble upon, discover; meet: *Who should I come across in town today but Old Smithy!* **come into** inherit, receive, acquire, obtain: *He came into a thousand pounds when his aunt died.* **come to** *or* **round** revive, recover, recuperate: *After the blow on his head knocked him out, it took ten minutes for George to come round.* **come upon** discover, find: *Betty came upon an old photograph album in the attic.* ANT. go, leave, depart.

comeback *n.* *Informal:* recovery, revival, return.

comedown *n.* *Informal:* disappointment, blow; defeat, failure; reversal.

comedy *n.* farce, satire, revue, slapstick.

comfort *vb.* soothe, relieve, console, ease, calm, cheer: *Whenever Victoria was upset, her mother was always there to comfort her.* *n.* 1 solace, consolation: *The comfort of knowing that you will stand by is all I need.* 2 relaxation, rest, satisfaction, luxury, ease: *Because she had saved carefully, the old lady was able to live in comfort.* ANT. *vb.* upset, agitate, disturb, discompose. *n.* (1) uncertainty. (2) discomfort.

comfortable *adj.* 1 relaxed, easy, rested, contented, cheerful: *The teacher's friendly manner made us all feel comfortable.* 2 restful, cosy, snug: *This is a very comfortable armchair.* ANT. (1) uncomfortable, strained, tense, edgy.

comical *adj.* funny, ridiculous, humorous; absurd, ludicrous. ANT. serious, earnest.

command *vb.* order, direct, demand, decree, rule: *The major commanded his men to appear in his office.* *n.* order, demand, direction, rule, decree, charge, authority: *By whose* *command was this ship sent into battle?* ANT. *vb.* obey.

commemorate *vb.* celebrate, remember, observe, honour.

commence *vb.* begin, start, open. ANT. end, stop, terminate, finish.

commend *vb.* praise, recommend, applaud, laud. ANT. blame, censure, criticize.

commendable *adj.* praiseworthy, deserving. ANT. deplorable, bad, lamentable.

commendation *n.* praise, approval, recommendation; applause; medal, honour. ANT. condemnation, criticism, censure.

comment *n.* remark, observation; explanation, commentary, review, report, criticism, judgment: *Your comments on how the programme succeeded will be helpful in planning one for next year.* *vb.* remark, explain, observe: *He commented that the carpet might be a little bright for this room.*

commerce *n.* business, trade, marketing.

commercial *adj.* financial, economic, business, trading.

commiserate *vb.* sympathize, console, comfort, feel for.

commission *n.* **1** committee, board: *The price commission refused to allow any increases during the coming year.* **2** order, command, permission, permit: *His commission as a second lieutenant came through today.* **3** fee, share, royalty; (*informal*) rake-off: *The salesman was paid a very good commission on every car he sold.* *vb.* appoint, delegate, authorize, commit, entrust, deputize: *I have been commissioned to bring you home.*

commit *vb.* **1** entrust, delegate, empower, authorize, commission: *The association is committed to raising funds to help the blind.* **2** do, perform, carry out: *The murder was committed by a person or persons unknown.*

commitment *n.* pledge, promise, duty, responsibility.

committee *n.* board, commission, council.

commodity *n.* goods, merchandise, article, wares.

common *adj.* **1** joint, communal, mutual, shared: *My neighbour and I have a common area of ground between our houses. Our common friend, Danny, invited us together.* **2** customary, usual, regular: *This is a common variety of flower and not rare at all.* **3** ordinary, natural, conventional, plain, commonplace, stale, trite: *The film had rather a common plot.* **4** coarse, vulgar, low: *He was nothing but a common criminal.* ANT. (1) separate, different. (2) unusual, rare. (3) distinctive, outstanding, extraordinary. (4) refined, cultivated, genteel.

commonplace *adj.* ordinary, common, everyday, usual, undistinguished, frequent, run-of-the-mill. ANT. unusual, distinctive, original.

commotion *n.* disorder, disturbance, upheaval; fuss; noise, din.

communal *adj.* common, shared, joint.

communicate *vb.* impart, convey, transmit, reveal, disclose, divulge; advertise, publicize, publish. ANT. conceal, withhold, dissemble.

communication *n.* 1 transmission, announcement, disclosure, notification, declaration, publication: *The minister used his press secretary for the communication of his ideas to the media.* 2 message, information, news, report, account, announcement, advice: *The secret communications between the governments were sent in code.*

communist *n.* Marxist; socialist; radical.

community *n.* 1 town, village, city, township: *We moved to a small community in the country.* 2 public, people; society, nation: *The community felt that Mr. Timpson was doing a good job as mayor.*

commuter *n.* driver, motorist; passenger, traveller.

compact[1] *adj.* compressed, packed, tight, thick: *The snow was so compact that I was hardly able to force a shovel into it.* *n.* makeup case, vanity case: *I lost my silver compact at the restaurant when I went to powder my nose.* ANT. *adj.* loose, unconfined, sprawling, unfettered.

compact[2] *n.* agreement, treaty, contract, pact, covenant: *A trade compact was reached by the two countries.*

companion *n.* associate, comrade, mate, partner, colleague, friend.

company *n.* 1 business, firm, partnership, concern: *After all those years of hard work, Len was made chairman of a big paper company.* 2 group, band, party, assembly, throng: *I told the company that had gathered at the steps why I thought they should obey the rules.* 3 companionship, fellowship: *I enjoy the company of my friends.* 4 guest(s), visitor(s): *Are you expecting company for dinner tonight?*

comparable *adj.* relative, alike, like. ANT. different, unalike.

compare *vb.* 1 match, liken; contrast: *The teacher asked us to compare the invention of the telephone with any invention from before 1800.* 2 compete, rival, vie: *Your beauty and hers cannot compare.*

comparison *n.* likening, judgment, contrasting.

compartment *n.* section, division, part.

compel *vb.* force, coerce, drive, impel. ANT. coax, wheedle, cajole.

compensate *vb.* **1** repay, remunerate, recompense, reimburse: *The insurance company compensated my father for the loss of the money.* **2** balance, counterbalance, offset: *No amount of saying you are sorry could compensate for the broken vase.*

compensation *n.* indemnity, reparation, damages; defrayal.

compete *vb.* contest, vie, rival, oppose.

competence *n.* ability, skill, capability. ANT. incompetence, ineptitude.

competent *adj.* capable, skilful, qualified, able, proficient. ANT. incompetent, inept, awkward.

competition *n.* rivalry, contest, tournament, match.

competitor *n.* contestant, rival, opponent. ANT. friend, ally, colleague.

compile *vb.* put together, compose, collect, gather, arrange.

complacent *adj.* self-satisfied, smug, pleased.

complain *vb.* protest, grumble, moan, groan, fret.

complement *vb.* complete, add to, supplement. ANT. conflict, clash.

complementary *adj.* completing, integral; corresponding, reciprocal.

complete *adj.* **1** whole, full, entire: *The complete chemistry set costs a great deal.* **2** ended, over, finished, done, concluded: *The manuscript would be complete if the author could write the last chapter.* *vb.* finish, end, conclude, terminate; close: *I've completed all my homework for tomorrow.* ANT. *adj.* unfinished, incomplete, partial. *vb.* begin, start, commence.

complexion *n.* appearance, skin; colour, texture.

complicated *adj.* complex, involved, intricate. ANT. simple, uncomplicated, rudimentary.

compliment *n.* praise, honour, admiration, approval, commendation, appreciation: *She took it as a compliment when I told her she was too young to go to college.* *vb.* praise, honour, approve, commend, flatter: *I'd like to compliment you on your new dress, Diane.* ANT. *n.* insult, aspersion, affront. *vb.* insult, affront, disparage.

comply (with) *vb.* obey, agree to, conform to, fulfil.

component *n.* part, element, constituent, ingredient.

compose *vb.* **1** create, write, make up: *My sister composes popular songs in her spare time.* **2** constitute, make up, comprise: *There are thousands of minerals that compose the crust of the earth.*

composed *adj.* relaxed, calm, cool, untroubled, peaceful, serene, tranquil, quiet. ANT. agitated, overwrought.

composer *see* **author.**

compound *n.* mixture, combination, aggregate: *Water is a chemical compound made up of the elements hydrogen and oxygen.* *adj.* complicated, complex; combined, mixed: *Bobby suffered a compound fracture of his arm when he fell off the horse.* ANT. *adj.* simple, uncomplicated.

comprehend *vb.* understand, grasp, perceive.

comprehension *n.* understanding, perception, awareness, knowledge.

comprehensive *adj.* inclusive, broad, wide, complete, full. ANT. partial, fragmentary, incomplete, limited.

compress *vb.* squeeze, compact, press, crowd, pack. ANT. stretch, spread, expand.

comprise *vb.* constitute, consist of; contain, include.

compromise *n.* settlement; concessions; (*informal*) give and take, bargaining.

compulsive *adj.* driving, obsessive, crazy, neurotic.

compulsory *adj.* necessary, required, unavoidable, obligatory. ANT. optional, voluntary; unrestricted, free.

compute *vb.* calculate, reckon, work out, figure.

computer *n.* microprocessor; calculator; electronic brain, automaton, robot.

comrade *n.* companion, friend, associate.

conceal *vb.* hide, cover, obscure, secrete. ANT. reveal, show, display, expose.

concede *vb.* admit, allow, acknowledge, yield. ANT. deny, contradict, dispute, negate.

conceit *n.* vanity, egotism, self-esteem. ANT. modesty, humility, humbleness, self-effacement.

conceited *adj.* vain, arrogant, proud, smug, self-important, egotistical. ANT. modest, humble, self-effacing.

conceive *vb.* **1** create, think (up), invent, imagine: *The prisoners conceived a clever plan to escape.* **2** understand, perceive, grasp: *It is difficult to conceive why they chose purple wallpaper with pink polka dots.*

concentrate *vb.* **1** focus, localize, condense: *The rays of light should be concentrated on one point by this lens.* **2** ponder, meditate, think: *Please don't interrupt while I'm concentrating* *on my homework.* ANT. (1) diffuse, scatter, disperse, dissipate.

concentration *n.* application, study, attention. ANT. distraction, confusion.

concept *n.* idea, notion, thought, theory.

concern *vb.* 1 interest, relate to, affect, touch, involve: *I don't see why what I had for breakfast should concern the Prime Minister of Uganda.* 2 worry, trouble, disturb: *I'm concerned about my teenager's staying out after midnight.* *n.* 1 interest, consequence: *International politics are of concern to everyone.* 2 anxiety, worry, care: *My concern about the safety of children is not limited to that of my own.* 3 business, firm, company, partnership: *Larry resigned from one company and started a concern of his own.* ANT. *vb.* (1) bore, tire. (2) soothe, calm. *n.* (1) indifference.

concerning *prep.* about, regarding, respecting.

concert *n.* recital, performance, entertainment.

concerted *adj.* joint, united, combined. ANT. unorganized, individual, separate.

concession *n.* yielding, admission, granting. ANT. demand, insistence.

concise *adj.* brief, succinct, condensed. ANT. long-winded, prosaic, rambling.

conclude *vb.* 1 finish, end, terminate, complete: *We concluded our dinner with a toast to the guest of honour.* 2 arrange, settle, determine, decide: *The treaty was concluded when Japan agreed to stop whaling.* 3 presume, assume, gather, understand, deduce: *I conclude from your comments that you are a socialist.* ANT. (1) begin, start, commence.

conclusion *n.* 1 end, finish, termination, close: *The chairman's remarks came at the conclusion of the conference.* 2 decision, resolution, determination: *Don't jump to conclusions about Eddie just because he wears his shoulder-length hair in curls.* ANT. (1) beginning, start, opening, commencement.

conclusive *adj.* final, definitive, decisive.

concrete *n.* cement: *The airport runway is made of concrete.* *adj.* firm, definite, solid, specific, precise: *I couldn't tell her any concrete reason for not wanting to go without insulting her, so I went.* ANT. (2) vague, undetermined, general.

condemn *vb.* 1 denounce, rebuke, blame: *You mustn't condemn a person just because he cannot do what you can do.* 2 judge, doom, punish, convict, sentence: *The court con-*

demned the man to ten years in jail. ANT. (1) praise, laud, extol, applaud. (2) pardon, absolve, excuse.

condense *vb.* reduce, abbreviate, shorten, abridge, concentrate, compress, digest, diminish. ANT. expand, enlarge, increase.

condescend *vb.* humble oneself, lower oneself, deign, stoop.

condition *n.* **1** state, position, situation: *The doctor told me that I was in excellent physical condition.* **2** requirement, necessity, provision, stipulation: *One of the conditions of employment in that restaurant is that you agree to give all tips to the management.* *vb.* train; accustom to: *He was conditioned to perspire whenever they rang a bell.*

conditional *adj.* provisional, dependent (on), subject (to). ANT. absolute, certain.

conduct *n.* behaviour, manners, deportment, actions: *Your conduct is not proper for an officer of the Navy!* *vb.* **1** behave, act: *I thought that Philip conducted himself very well, considering his lack of experience.* **2** lead, guide, escort: *Kathy got a job conducting tours of York Minster this summer.*

confer *vb.* **1** give, award, bestow, grant: *In his sixtieth year, the university conferred on him their highest honour.* **2** discuss, consult, deliberate: *Don't you think we ought to confer before announcing a hasty opinion by one person?* ANT. (1) withdraw, retrieve.

conference *n.* meeting, discussion, council; consultation.

confess *vb.* admit, acknowledge, grant, concede.

confide *vb.* disclose, reveal, tell, divulge.

confidence *n.* **1** trust, faith, reliance: *My confidence in your abilities has always been justified by your accomplishments.* **2** self-assurance, self-reliance, self-confidence, courage: *Many people would be more successful if they just had more confidence in themselves.* ANT. (1) distrust, mistrust, doubt. (2) shyness, modesty, diffidence.

confident *adj.* sure, certain, self-assured, self-reliant, self-confident, dauntless. ANT. timid, uncertain, shy, self-effacing.

confidential *adj.* secret, private; off the record. ANT. open, disclosed.

confine *vb.* limit, restrict, bound, hinder. ANT. release, free.

confirm *vb.* **1** assure, verify, corroborate, substantiate; strengthen: *I confirmed everything that she had told me.* **2** validate, approve, ratify: *The higher court confirmed the* *lower court's findings.* ANT. (1) deny, disclaim, disavow.

confirmed *adj.* habitual, inveterate, established; chronic, regular. ANT. infrequent, occasional.

confiscate *vb.* take, seize, appropriate.

conflict *vb.* oppose, clash, contend: *It seems obvious that your ideas about bringing up children conflict with mine.* *n.* **1** fight, battle, struggle, encounter, engagement: *We must recognize the eternal conflict between right and wrong.* **2** controversy, disagreement, contest: *I don't want to be caught in the middle of a conflict between political enemies.* ANT. *vb.* agree, harmonize, concur, coincide. *n.* agreement, harmony, concurrence.

conform *vb.* **1** comply, submit, yield, obey: *If you wish to remain a member of this club, you must conform to the rules.* **2** agree, correspond: *The work you are now doing does not conform to our plan.* ANT. (1) rebel; disobey. (2) disagree, vary.

confront *vb.* face, oppose, defy; challenge, meet, brave.

confuse *vb.* **1** puzzle, perplex, bewilder, mystify, baffle, mislead: *The directions for putting the bicycle together confused my father.* **2** mistake, mix up, jumble: *My aunt is often confused with my mother, whom she resembles closely.* ANT. (1) enlighten, edify, illuminate, clarify. (2) differentiate, distinguish.

confusion *n.* **1** perplexity, bewilderment, uncertainty: *At first, there was some confusion among the actors as to where they should stand on stage.* **2** disorder, mess, turmoil, upset: *Your belongings are in such a state of confusion that I don't see how you can find anything.* ANT. (1) enlightenment, understanding, comprehension. (2) organization, tidiness.

congenial *adj.* agreeable, pleasant; friendly. ANT. unfriendly, disagreeable.

congested *adj.* crowded, full, blocked; dense, thick. ANT. empty.

congratulate *vb.* compliment, honour, acclaim, praise.

congregate *vb.* meet, convene, gather. ANT. disperse, scatter, dissipate, dispel.

congress *n.* conference, meeting; legislature, parliament, assembly.

conjunction *n.* junction, link, combination, connection. ANT. disconnection, diversion, separation.

conjurer *n.* magician, wizard, sorcerer.

connect *vb.* **1** unite, join, link, combine: *The front of our train was connected to the rear carriages of the train in the* *station.* **2** associate, relate: *Somehow, I failed to connect her leaving so suddenly with the disappearance of the vase.* ANT. **(1)** separate, disconnect, disjoin. **(2)** dissociate.

connection *n.* **1** junction, union, link; bond, tie: *There was a loose connection that prevented the radio from working.* **2** association, relationship, bond, tie: *I no longer have any connection with that company.* ANT. **(2)** dissociation.

conquer *vb.* **1** succeed, win, gain, achieve: *The army conquered the fort in two days.* **2** defeat, overcome, overpower, subdue: *It may be years before medicine will be able to conquer cancer. The small force conquered the enemy in hard fighting.* ANT. **(2)** give in, surrender, yield.

conquest *n.* triumph, victory. ANT. failure, surrender.

conscientious *adj.* diligent, painstaking, scrupulous, exact. ANT. irresponsible, careless, slovenly.

conscious *adj.* **1** aware: *I suddenly became conscious of a slow scratching sound at the window.* **2** awake, alert: *When Marilyn became conscious again after the blow on her head, she recognized her mother beside her.* **3** deliberate, intentional, purposeful: *I don't like him, so I make a conscious effort to avoid him.* ANT. **(1)** unaware, insensitive. **(2)** asleep, comatose.

consecrate *vb.* hallow, sanctify; dedicate.

consecutive *adj.* successive, continuous, serial, in order. ANT. discontinuous.

consent *vb.* agree, permit, allow, let, assent: *I consented to Laura's going to the theatre with a friend.* *n.* permission, agreement, assent: *You have my consent to leave school early today.* ANT. *vb.* refuse, dissent. *n.* refusal, dissent.

consequence *n.* **1** result, outcome, effect, issue: *Eugene was rude in class, and as a consequence, was reprimanded by the teacher.* **2** importance, significance, value: *Jenny's father is a man of some consequence in this town.* ANT. **(1)** cause, impetus.

conservative *adj.* **1** reactionary, right-wing, conventional: *The conservative sections of society resist change.* **2** moderate, cautious, careful: *After the accident, Ted became a much more conservative driver.* ANT. **(1)** liberal, radical. **(2)** reckless, rash, adventurous, foolhardy.

conserve *vb.* preserve, keep, retain. ANT. squander, waste, use.

consider *vb.* **1** study, think about, deliberate, reflect on, contemplate: *The committee agreed to consider Janet's request for an increase in salary.* **2** think of, regard, look upon, judge, estimate: *Shirley had never considered Tom to be particularly good-looking.* ANT. (1) ignore, disregard, disdain.

considerable *adj.* 1 quite a lot, much, a great deal: *There was a considerable amount of snow last winter. The complaints from the public were considerable.* 2 worthwhile, noteworthy, important, significant: *Albert Einstein was a man of considerable accomplishments.*

considerate *adj.* kind, thoughtful, polite. ANT. inconsiderate, thoughtless, selfish.

consideration *n.* 1 thoughtfulness, kindness, kindliness, concern, courtesy, politeness, sympathy, empathy: *It was Mark's consideration for other people that made him an outstanding social worker.* 2 attention, thought, reflection, study: *I'll give that matter immediate consideration.* 3 payment, fee, pay, recompense, compensation: *For a small consideration, the steward will serve your meals in your cabin.*

consign *vb.* entrust, hand over; deliver, convey.

consist *vb.* comprise, be composed of; include, embrace, contain.

consistent *adj.* 1 agreeing, compatible, harmonious: *Consistent with your wishes, I have asked that the meeting take place tomorrow.* 2 regular, faithful: *He might have been irresponsible about repaying debts to the bank, but he was always consistent about returning money to his friends.* ANT. (1) contrary, opposed, antagonistic. (2) inconsistent, erratic, eccentric.

consolation *n.* solace, comfort, sympathy. ANT. discouragement, discomfort, burden.

console *vb.* solace, comfort, sympathize with. ANT. disturb, upset.

consolidate *vb.* unite, combine; incorporate, solidify.

conspicuous *adj.* noticeable, visible, clear, prominent, obvious, outstanding. ANT. inconspicuous, neutral.

conspiracy *n.* plot, scheme, intrigue.

conspire *vb.* plot, plan, scheme, intrigue.

constant *adj.* 1 unchanging, fixed, stable, invariable, unchangeable: *The constant sunshine in the desert made me long for clouds and rain.* 2 loyal, faithful, steadfast, true, staunch, devoted, steady, firm: *My constant companion during those years was Arthur.* ANT. (1) irregular, off-and-on, periodic. (2) occasional, infrequent.

constitute *vb.* 1 make up, compose, form: *People once thought that all matter was constituted of four elements—earth, air,* *fire, and water.* **2** found, establish, create, organize: *The courts are a duly constituted authority for dispensing justice.* **3** delegate, appoint, commission, authorize: *My father was constituted ambassador to Ethiopia.*

constitution *n.* **1** code, law: *The nation's Constitution has been put to some severe tests during the last decade.* **2** health, physique, vitality: *With your constitution, you should be able to eat anything.*

constrain *vb.* force, compel; restrain; urge.

construct *vb.* build, erect, raise. ANT. destroy, demolish, raze.

construction *n.* building, erection, fabrication.

constructive *adj.* helpful, useful, valuable. ANT. destructive, ruinous.

consult *vb.* discuss, confer, deliberate.

consume *vb.* **1** use, use up, exhaust, expend; eat, devour: *The people in this country consume more sugar than those of any other country.* **2** destroy, devastate: *The barn was quickly consumed by the flames.*

consumer *n.* buyer, user, purchaser.

contact *n.* touching, meeting.

contagious *adj.* infectious; catching, spreading.

contain *vb.* hold, be composed of, include.

container *n.* receptacle, holder; box, case, bin, tin, jar.

contaminate *vb.* pollute, soil, dirty, corrupt, infect, poison.

contemplate *vb.* **1** think about, consider, study, deliberate on, reflect upon: *Desmond was contemplating the outcome of the trial.* **2** intend, plan: *Do you contemplate correcting your behaviour?* **3** view, look at, regard, observe: *Irene was contemplating her reflection in the mirror.*

contemplative *adj.* thoughtful, meditative, studious, pensive. ANT. indifferent, inattentive, thoughtless.

contemporary *adj.* **1** contemporaneous, simultaneous, coexisting, coexistent: *It is useful to compare the diary of Samuel Pepys with other contemporary writings.* **2** modern, up-to-date, fashionable: *The room was decorated in contemporary style.* ANT. (**1**) antecedent; succeeding.

contempt *n.* scorn, disdain, malice. ANT. admiration, approbation.

contemptible *adj.* low, base, mean, detestable, miserable. ANT. admirable, honourable.

contemptuous *adj.* scornful, disdainful, insolent, sneering. ANT. respectful, polite; flattering; humble, modest, self-effacing.

contend vb. 1 combat, dispute, struggle, contest: *We need to contend for higher moral standards these days.* 2 claim, assert, maintain, argue: *The lawyer contended that his client was innocent.*

content adj. happy, satisfied, pleased, contented. ANT. dissatisfied, restless, discontented.

contentious adj. controversial; quarrelsome, argumentative, hostile.

contest n. competition, match, tournament: *Class 3b won the contest for the best road safety poster.* vb. dispute, oppose: *The miner contested the right of anyone to trespass on his property.*

contestant n. competitor, opponent, rival; player.

continual adj. regular, consecutive, connected. ANT. irregular, intermittent, occasional.

continue vb. 1 persist, carry on: *If you continue in your present manner, you will be punished for it.* 2 proceed, resume, recommence, renew: *The trial continued after an hour out for lunch.* 3 endure, last, remain, stay: *After he was discovered to be dishonest, the manager realized he couldn't continue in his job.* ANT. discontinue, stop, cease, interrupt.

continuous adj. uninterrupted, continuing, ceaseless, incessant, unceasing, constant, unending. ANT. irregular, intermittent, sporadic.

contract n. agreement, bargain, pact; treaty: *The contract between the company and the union was signed yesterday.* vb. 1 agree: *The firm contracted to supply paper to the printers.* 2 diminish, reduce, condense, shrink: *The armadillo contracts into a little ball when it is threatened.* 3 get, acquire, go down with: *I contracted a bad cold while out fishing.* ANT. vb. (2) expand, swell, enlarge.

contradict vb. deny; oppose, object to; defy, challenge. ANT. agree.

contrary adj. 1 opposed, opposite, disagreeing, conflicting, opposing: *If you say he should be released and I say he should be jailed, we obviously hold contrary opinions.* 2 disagreeable, hostile, perverse, stubborn, obstinate, headstrong: *If you agree with me, then why are you being so contrary?* ANT. (1) similar, like, complementary. (2) obliging, agreeable, tractable.

contrast n. difference, distinction, disagreement: *There is a marked contrast between what you are saying today and what you said yesterday.* vb. distinguish, differentiate; contradict, differ: *One of our exam questions was to contrast the American Revolution with the Russian Revolution.* ANT. *n.* similarity, agreement, likeness.

contribute *vb.* donate, give, bestow, grant, provide, offer. ANT. withhold, deny.

contribution *n.* donation, gift, grant, offering.

contrite *adj.* remorseful, sorry, repentant, regretful; penitent.

contrive *vb.* 1 invent, make, form, hatch: *We must contrive a plan to get even with those children who stole our bicycles.* 2 manage, arrange; engineer: *Despite visiting hours being over, I contrived to see my sister in hospital.*

control *vb.* 1 manage, direct, rule, dominate, command: *My uncle controls four companies.* 2 check, restrain, curb, manage: *That woman couldn't control her children and they annoyed everyone in the waiting room.* *n.* 1 management, direction, rule, mastery, command: *After buying large amounts of its shares in the stock market, Cawdry gained control of the company.* 2 check, restraint: *You will have to keep yourself under control if you want to sit in this theatre.*

controversial *adj.* contentious; debatable, arguable.

controversy *n.* dispute, argument, quarrel, debate, disagreement. ANT. agreement, harmony, accord.

convalesce *vb.* get well, recover, improve, recuperate.

convenience *n.* 1 availability, accessibility: *We all know the convenience of having a post office nearby.* 2 advantage, assistance, help, aid, service, benefit: *When you live in the country, a car is a great convenience.* ANT. (2) inconvenience.

convenient *adj.* suitable, ready; accessible, handy, nearby, available. ANT. inconvenient, awkward.

convent *n.* nunnery, community, sanctuary; school.

convention *n.* 1 conference, meeting, assembly: *The American political convention nominated Mr. Harris as state senator.* 2 custom, practice; rule, law: *The karate contestants followed the convention of bowing to each other politely before and after the match.*

conventional *adj.* everyday, common, usual, regular, habitual, accustomed, routine. ANT. unusual, extraordinary, exotic, bizarre.

converge *vb.* meet, unite, join, concentrate. ANT. diverge, separate.

conversation *n.* talk, discussion, chat, dialogue.

converse *vb.* talk, chat, discuss, speak.

convert *vb.* 1 change, alter, transform, turn: *The alchemists tried to convert lead into gold.* 2 win over: *I was converted from atheism to Christianity.*

convey *vb.* bear, carry, communicate.

conveyance *n.* vehicle, car, lorry, van; train; plane.

convict *vb.* pronounce guilty, sentence: *Keith was convicted of robbery.* *n.* criminal, prisoner: *The convict had his personal belongings taken from him when he went into prison.*

convince *vb.* persuade, win over; prove, demonstrate.

cook *vb.* prepare, heat; fry, grill, roast, boil.

cool *adj.* 1 chilly; cold, frosty, wintry, icy, frigid: *The summer evenings are always cool in the mountains.* 2 calm, composed, quiet, collected: *When everyone about her would get excited about something, she always remained cool.* 3 unfriendly, distant, chilly: *After we broke her window with the ball, Mrs. Thompson gave us a cool reception.* *vb.* 1 chill: *You should cool the wine before serving it.* 2 calm, quiet, moderate: *My enthusiasm for the job cooled when I found out how little it paid.* ANT. *adj.* (1) warm, hot, heated. (2) excited, overwrought, hysterical. (3) friendly, warm, outgoing. *vb.* (1) warm, heat. (2) excite, agitate.

cooperate *vb.* 1 join forces, work together, unite, combine: *If everyone cooperates, we can get the work done more quickly.* 2 contribute, help, support: *We tried to get the mule into the barn, but it refused to cooperate.*

cope (with) *vb.* manage, deal with, face, endure.

copious *adj.* plentiful, abundant, ample. ANT. scarce, meagre, scanty, paltry.

copy *n.* reproduction, imitation, facsimile, duplicate, likeness; carbon, print: *Please send me a copy of your article.* *vb.* reproduce, duplicate, imitate: *If you copy these letters for yourself, your handwriting will get better.* ANT. *n.* original.

cordial *adj.* friendly, polite, genial, affable, warmhearted. ANT. hostile, unfriendly, ill-tempered.

core *n.* centre, kernel, heart. ANT. outside, surface, exterior.

corner *n.* niche, recess; angle, bend, turn.

corporation *n.* association, organization, partnership.

corpse *n.* body, remains, carcass, cadaver.

correct *adj.* true, accurate, right, proper, precise, exact: *The only version that is correct is the one prepared by our own students.* *vb.* 1 set right, rectify, emend; better: *The teacher corrected our papers before handing them back to us.* 2 warn, caution, rebuke, admonish, punish: *Each time she said something they didn't like, her parents corrected her.* ANT.

adj. incorrect, wrong, inexact, erroneous.

correspond *vb.* **1** match, compare, agree, coincide, fit, suit: *The two parts of this machine don't correspond.* **2** communicate, write: *While I was away at school, I corresponded regularly with my brothers and sisters.* ANT. (**1**) diverge, differ, vary.

corridor *n.* hall, hallway, passage, passageway; foyer, lobby.

corroborate *vb.* support, confirm, uphold.

corrode *vb.* eat away, erode, wear away.

corrupt *adj.* **1** dishonest, untrustworthy, crooked, treacherous, unscrupulous: *Before my uncle became mayor and improved matters, this town had the most corrupt officials you could find.* **2** wicked, debased, low, evil, perverted: *The minister preached against all of the corrupt practices among some of the people.* *vb.* bribe, pervert, deprave, debase: *The gangsters used money, then threats, to try to corrupt the detectives.* ANT. *adj.* (**1**) honest, upright, scrupulous. (**2**) pure, sanctified. *vb.* purify, edify, sanctify.

cost *n.* **1** price, value, charge: *What is the cost of that puppy in the window?* **2** sacrifice, loss, penalty, damage: *Risking the cost of our friendship, I must tell you that you are very mean to your mother.*

costly *adj.* expensive, dear. ANT. inexpensive, low-cost, cheap.

costume *n.* clothing, dress, attire, clothes, garb, apparel.

cosy *adj.* warm, snug, comfortable; friendly. ANT. unpleasant, uncomfortable; cold.

couch *n.* sofa, settee.

council *n.* committee, board, cabinet.

counsel *n.* **1** advice, opinion, guidance: *Your counsel in matters relating to marriage is meaningless, since you never got married.* **2** barrister, lawyer: *If learned counsel will permit, I should like to cross-examine this witness.* *vb.* advise, guide: *He counselled me to remain quiet in court.*

counsellor *n.* adviser, guide, helper; friend.

count *vb.* **1** enumerate, number, reckon, total, compute, tally: *I counted 13 buns in the bag from the bakery—a baker's dozen.* **2** amount to something, add up, figure: *Your score on the last test won't count because you copied the answers from a neighbour.* *n.* sum, total, number: *Take a count of the books on that shelf.*

countenance *n.* **1** face, visage, aspect, appearance: *I like to see the smiling countenances of my students each morning.* **2** approval, support, encouragement, assistance: *I cannot give* *countenance to such activity.* vb. approve, support, favour, encourage, assist: *I refuse to countenance absence from school to watch a football game.* ANT. vb. prohibit, forbid.

counter n. 1 table, board, bench, ledge: *In this cafeteria we have to queue at the counter to get served.* 2 disc, token; coin: *You can buy counters for the slot machines over there.*

counteract vb. offset, thwart, counterbalance, neutralize, defeat.

counterfeit adj. 1 fake, fraudulent, spurious, false: *I thought we had become millionaires when the money was found, but it turned out to be counterfeit.* 2 pretended, pretend, simulated, sham: *Your counterfeit expression of love doesn't fool me.* n. forgery, imitation, fake: *This document is a counterfeit.* vb. 1 forge, fake, falsify, imitate, copy: *The police found the men counterfeiting bank notes in the basement.* 2 pretend, sham: *At the funeral, those who were glad that George was gone counterfeited great sorrow.* ANT. adj. genuine, real, authentic.

country n. 1 nation, state: *How many foreign countries have you travelled to?* 2 rural area, farmland, forest: *We gave up our flat in the city and bought a house in the country.*

couple n. pair; team, brace.

coupon n. ticket, card, slip, certificate.

courage n. bravery, spirit, daring, fearlessness, valour, mettle, pluck. ANT. cowardice, fear, fearfulness, weakness.

courageous adj. brave, fearless, dauntless, intrepid, plucky, daring, heroic, valorous. ANT. cowardly, fearful, afraid, timid.

course n. 1 advance, progress, passage: *In the course of life it often becomes necessary to suffer hardship for the sake of others.* 2 direction, way, bearing: *When I saw St. Paul's Cathedral I knew we were on the wrong course for Scotland.*

court n. 1 square, yard, courtyard, enclosure, quadrangle: *The presence of trees in courts provides a good shade from the sun in summer.* 2 tribunal, assize, sessions: *The witnesses went to court and gave evidence.* vb. woo, attract, pursue; make overtures; (*informal*) go out with: *We courted for two years before we got married.*

courteous adj. polite, well-mannered, gracious, respectful. ANT. rude, impolite, discourteous.

courtesy n. politeness, graciousness, respect. ANT. rudeness, discourtesy.

covenant n. agreement, promise, pledge, contract; testament.

cover vb. 1 coat, spread; protect: *Please cover the furniture to* *keep the dust off.* **2** conceal, hide; mask: *Miriam covered the scratch on the table with a lamp.* **3** include, embrace: *This book covers every subject thoroughly.* *n.* **1** lid, top, stopper, covering: *Evelyn couldn't get the cover off the box.* **2** shelter, protection, refuge: *During the thunderstorm, we sought cover under an overhanging rock.* ANT. *vb.* uncover, expose, reveal.

coward *n.* shirker, weakling, (*slang*) chicken. ANT. hero.

coy *adj.* bashful, shy, timid, modest: *If you want another helping of food, don't be coy—just ask for it.* ANT. bold, brash, forward.

crack *vb.* **1** break, snap, split: *Just as Walter was looking at himself in the mirror, it cracked.* **2** solve, decode, decipher, unravel: *Have you cracked the code yet?* *n.* **1** snap: *There was the crack of the rifle and the rabbit lay dead.* **2** break, flaw, split, fissure: *Be careful not to drink from the side of the glass with the crack in it.*

cracker *n.* biscuit, wafer.

craft *n.* **1** skill, ability, talent, expertness: *Have you ever seen an expert cabinetmaker at his craft?* **2** handicraft, trade, occupation, profession: *The harpooner has not plied his craft for many years.* **3** cunning, deceit, trickery, guile: *Charles used every bit of his craft to get Jennie to marry him.*

craftsman *n.* artisan; carpenter, potter; specialist.

crafty *adj.* cunning, clever, shrewd, sly. ANT. guileless, gullible, open, naive.

cramp *n.* pain, spasm, paralysis: *He had cramp in his legs and found he couldn't get out of bed.* *vb.* restrict, confine; restrain, hamper, hinder: *I feel cramped with six other people working in the same office.*

crank *n.* **1** starting handle; device, brace: *The car won't start; I'll try using the crank.* **2** *Informal:* eccentric, (*slang*) weirdo, (*slang*) nutcase; fanatic: *I think he's a crank collecting bits and pieces off old cars.*

cranky *adj.* *Informal:* eccentric, odd, strange, peculiar.

crash *vb.* shatter, smash, dash: *It was a miracle that you weren't even scratched when the car crashed into the wall.* *n.* smash, smash-up: *Twenty people were hurt in the crash.*

crass *adj.* stupid, gross; thick.

crate *n.* container, case, pack, box.

crave *vb.* desire, yearn for, want, long for, hunger for. ANT. renounce, relinquish.

crawl *vb.* creep, worm along.

crazy *adj.* mad, insane, lunatic. ANT. sane, rational, lucid.

creak *vb.* squeak; grate.

crease *n.* fold, wrinkle, furrow; pleat.

create *vb.* **1** originate, invent, beget: *The composer created a new piece to honour his parents on their anniversary.* **2** make, form, construct, design: *The early settlers in America created farms and homes out of the wilderness.* ANT. destroy, abolish.

creation *n.* **1** beginning; invention; construction: *The creation of the aeroplane was a marvellous feat.* **2** earth, universe, nature: *As you look at creation, don't you sometimes think it wonderful?*

credible *adj.* believable, conceivable; trustworthy. ANT. incredible, unbelievable, inconceivable.

credit *n.* **1** honour, merit, recognition: *Philip and Peter deserve a lot of credit for taking care of their aged mother.* **2** belief, trust, faith: *How can anyone place any credit on what you say when they know how you lied in the past?* **3** repute, reputation, name, standing, rank: *My credit is good enough to get a loan for a new car.* *vb.* **1** believe, accept, trust: *Even though I credit your explanation of the flat tyre, you shouldn't have been out so late.* **2** attribute: *The museum experts credited the painting to my grandfather.* ANT. *n.,vb.* discredit.

creditable *adj.* praiseworthy, worthy. ANT. discreditable, dishonourable, shameful.

creed *n.* belief, credo, doctrine, faith.

creek *n.* inlet, bay, cove, arm.

creep *vb.* crawl, worm along; slither.

crew *n.* group, team, squad, company; sailors.

crime *n.* wrongdoing, misconduct, wrong, offence; violation, misdemeanour, felony.

criminal *adj.* illegal, unlawful, felonious: *Maltreating a child is a criminal offence.* *n.* crook, lawbreaker, felon, convict, culprit, offender, delinquent: *The escaped criminals were being sought by the police.*

cripple *vb.* maim, disable, injure, hurt, damage: *The fall from the second-storey window crippled him for life.* *n.* invalid, handicapped person, disabled person: *Confined to a wheelchair after his accident, Jim remained a cripple for the rest of his life.*

crisis *n.* emergency, dilemma, trauma, climax.

criterion *n.* standard, basis, principle, norm.

critic *n.* **1** judge, reviewer, commentator: *Who is the drama critic of that newspaper?* **2** faultfinder, censor, slanderer: *I*

*may make a mistake once in a while, but who appointed you as
my critic?*

critical *adj.* 1 faultfinding, carping, condemning, reproachful,
disapproving: *Please stop nagging me: you have no reason to
be so critical of everything I do or say.* 2 dangerous, risky,
hazardous, perilous: *His health was in a critical condition and
the doctor ordered him to rest.* 3 crucial, important, decisive: *The timing in putting a new product on the market can be
critical.* ANT. (1) praising, flattering. (2) safe, sound. (3)
unimportant, trivial.

criticism *n.* 1 censure, faultfinding, objection: *Your harsh
criticism of my work is meaningless as you've never even seen
it.* 2 review, commentary; evaluation, analysis: *His criticism
of Shakespeare's plays is masterly.*

criticize *vb.* judge, censure; scold, rebuke, chastise.

crooked *adj.* 1 bent, twisted, curved, hooked, zigzag: *A
crooked path wove among the boulders to the pond.* 2
Informal: dishonest, criminal, corrupt: *The directors were
embarrassed when they discovered that the treasurer was
crooked and had stolen money.* ANT. (1) straight. (2)
honest, upright.

crop *n.* harvest, produce, yield: *Because of lack of rainfall the
crop will be poor this year.* *vb.* cut, lop, mow, clip: *I think
you look better with your hair cropped short.*

cross *vb.* 1 go across, traverse; intersect: *Don't cross the street
without looking first!* 2 mingle, mix, interbreed: *If you cross
a scottie with a poodle you get a "scoodle."* 3 thwart,
frustrate, oppose: *Once Reginald has his mind made up, it's
not a good idea to cross him.* *adj.* irritable, annoyed, testy,
ill-natured, bad-tempered, snappish; mean, angry: *Our
teacher was very cross with those children who hadn't done
their homework.* ANT. *adj.* good-natured, cheerful.

crouch *vb.* stoop, duck. ANT. stand.

crowd *n.* throng, swarm, host, flock, mob, pack: *There was a
crowd of people waiting in front of 10 Downing Street to see
the prime minister.* *vb.* 1 throng, swarm, mob: *We crowded
onto the football field after the game.* 2 squeeze, cramp,
pack; shove, push: *We were crowded into the tiny cabin.*

crown *n.* 1 circlet, coronet, tiara: *The princess wore a gold
crown studded with precious stones.* 2 head, skull: *Jack fell
down and broke his crown.* *vb.* install, invest, endow: *She
was crowned queen in a ceremony that lasted for seven hours.*

crucial *adj.* decisive, critical, significant, important.

crude *adj.* 1 rude, vulgar, coarse; unrefined, unpolished, graceless: *Roy's manners are very crude.*   **2** unfinished, raw, coarse: *On the workbench stood a crude sculpture of a figure that I couldn't recognize until I was told it was of my sister.* ANT. (1) polite, cultured; refined.   (2) finished, polished.

cruel *adj.*   heartless, mean, merciless, pitiless, ruthless, brutal, inhuman.   ANT. kindhearted, compassionate, merciful.

cruelty *n.*   harshness, brutality, savagery.   ANT. kindness, compassion.

cruise *vb.*   travel, drift, coast; tour: *The car cruised along at a steady speed.*   *n.* tour, voyage, journey: *My grandfather went on a world cruise when he retired.*

crumb *n.*   bit, fragment, particle, scrap.

crumble *vb.*   break up, disintegrate, fall apart.

crumple *vb.*   collapse, crush; fold, crease; shrivel.

crunch *vb.*   bite, chew, munch; masticate.

crush *vb.*   break, smash, crash: *The machine quickly crushed all of the stones into smaller sizes suitable for driveways and other uses.*

cry *vb.*   **1** shout, yell, scream, roar, bellow: *When I saw the rock falling I cried out as loudly as I could.*   **2** weep, wail, sob, bawl: *When the baby cries, either feed her, change her, or make sure nothing is hurting her.*   ANT. (2) laugh.

cuddle *vb.*   embrace, hug, kiss, caress.

cue *n.*   sign; hint, suggestion; reminder.

culminate *vb.*   finish, end, conclude, reach a climax.

culprit *n.*   offender; criminal.

cult *n.*   **1** sect, group, faction, clique: *My daughter's got caught up in a way-out cult and won't talk to me any more.*   **2** fad, craze, fashion: *Milly is into the latest cult and goes around with a ring through her nose.*

cultivate *vb.*   **1** farm, till, plant, seed, harvest: *Although he owns a huge area of farmland, Mr. Snyder cultivates only half of it.*   **2** educate, refine, teach, nurture: *Our parents cultivated the habit of reading in all their children.*

cultural *adj.*   educational, civilizing, instructive, elevating.

culture *n.*   **1** civilization, society: *Western and eastern cultures differ widely.*   **2** refinement, breeding, cultivation, upbringing: *From her bad manners and rude behaviour you could tell at once that she was totally lacking in culture.*

cumulative *adj.*   increasing, intensifying, advancing, snowballing.

cunning *adj.*   **1** clever, tricky, wily, foxy, crafty: *Even at the age of three, Betsy was cunning enough to get what she wanted from anyone.*   **2** skilful, clever, ingenious: *That box was* *carved by a cunning hand from a solid piece of wood.*   n. **1** wiliness, foxiness, shrewdness, cleverness, slyness, deceit: *Another example of his cunning was the way he was able to persuade people to give him their money for his fake schemes.* **2** skill, ability: *Her cunning was matched only by her beauty.*   ANT. *adj.* (**1**) simple, naive, gullible.   n. (**1**) simplicity, openness.

cup *n.*   mug; container; vessel.

cupboard *n.*   cabinet, sideboard, locker.

curb *n.*   check, restraint, control: *The new tax law was an effective curb on expense accounts for executives.*   *vb.* check, restrain, control: *It required stern measures to curb wastage in the use of the country's resources.*   ANT. *vb.* encourage, foster.

cure *n.*   remedy, treatment, medicine: *People used to think that sulphur and molasses were a cure for almost anything.*   *vb.* heal, remedy: *The salesman told us that snake oil would cure my broken leg.*

curious *adj.*   **1** inquisitive, inquiring, interested; nosy, prying: *If you weren't so curious about things that don't concern you, you wouldn't get into so much trouble.* **2** peculiar, odd, strange, unusual, queer: *There was a curious animal with a red plume and a white tail and blue fur sitting on the fence.*   ANT. (**1**) indifferent, uninterested.

curl *vb.*   coil, twist, bend, loop, wind: *Please curl the string around this stick.*   *n.* curve, coil, spiral, lock, tress: *My girlfriend has some lovely curls in her hair.*

current *adj.*   present, up-to-date, modern: *The current craze for horror films is bad for children.*   *n.* stream, tide: *The current carried the boat down the river and out into the sea.*   ANT. *adj.* out-of-date, outmoded, old-fashioned.

curse *n.*   **1** oath, ban: *The witch's curse caused the children to shout and dance wildly.* **2** trouble, misfortune, evil: *The rain, originally a blessing, turned into a curse after two weeks without stopping.*   *vb.* swear, denounce, condemn: *When the police finally caught the thief, he cursed them for finding him.*   ANT. *n.* (**1**) benediction, blessing. (**2**) boon, advantage.

curtail *vb.*   cut short, shorten, abridge.

curtain *n.*   screen, shade, blind.

curve *vb.,n.*   bend, twist, arch: *The road curves round to the left. The curves on that figure are most attractive.*

cushion *n.*   bag; pillow, bolster, rest, support: *There was a comfortable red cushion at each end of the couch.*   *vb.*

protect; lessen, suppress, absorb: *This foam rubber is packed into the box to cushion the shock during shipping.*

custom *n.* habit, practice, convention, rule.

customary *adj.* usual, common, habitual, regular. ANT. unusual, rare.

customer *n.* client, patron, buyer, consumer.

cut *vb.* **1** gash, slash, prick, nick: *I cut my finger on the point of the blade.* **2** sever, slice, carve, cleave, slit: *That knife isn't sharp enough to cut the bread.* **3** mow, lop, chop, crop: *The grass was cut once this week already.* **4** decrease, lower, lessen: *The government may cut spending in order to reduce inflation.* *vb. phr.* **cut back** reduce, decrease: *The budget for school supplies was cut back by 20 per cent.* **cut in** interrupt, interfere, butt in: *When the teacher was talking, Phil cut in to ask if he could leave the room.* **cut off** stop, cease, end, terminate: *The chairman cut off the debate after 20 minutes.* **cut short** finish, stop, end: *The performance was cut short by the power failure.* *n.* incision, slash, gash, slit: *The nurse bandaged the cut on Janet's finger.*

cute *adj.* sweet, delightful, charming, appealing, attractive.

cycle *n.* **1** circle, series, revolution, period: *Many poems have been written about the cycle of the four seasons.* **2** bicycle, bike; tandem; motor cycle: *He rode his cycle to work.* *vb.* ride, travel: *Don't cycle two abreast on busy roads.*

cylinder *n.* vessel; drum; barrel, column, trunk.

cynical *adj.* sarcastic, mocking, sneering, scornful, contemptuous.

d

dabble *vb.*   play, trifle, fool.

daft *adj.*   *Informal:* silly, foolish; simple, stupid.   ANT. clever, bright, intelligent.

dagger *n.*   sword, blade, knife.

dainty *adj.*   delicate, petite, pretty, beautiful, graceful, fine, elegant.   ANT. clumsy, oafish, lumpish.

dally (with) *vb.*   play, toy, flirt.

dam *n.*   barrier, dike, bank, wall: *The beavers built a dam across our stream and flooded part of our land.*   *vb.* obstruct, block, stop; restrict, check, slow: *A huge tree fell down in the storm and dammed up the drain.*

damage *n.*   impairment, injury, harm; destruction: *The hurricane caused millions of pounds worth of damage on the island.* *vb.* impair, injure, harm, mar: *The telephone lines were damaged in the storm. Gossiping about a person can damage his reputation.*   ANT. *vb.* repair, rebuild, improve, fix.

damn *vb.*   condemn; curse.   ANT. bless.

damp *adj.*   moist, soggy, dank; humid: *When the weather is damp, I can't open this cupboard door because it sticks.*   *n.* moisture, dampness, humidity, wetness: *The damp in the walls causes a growth on them.*   ANT. *adj.* dry, arid.

dampen *vb.*   **1** moisten, wet: *It is better to dampen clothes before ironing them.*   **2** stifle, deaden, moderate: *The noise of the traffic outside was dampened by the thick stone walls.*

dance *vb.,n.*   step; polka, tango, waltz; (*slang*) boogie: *Would you like to dance with me? The dance begins at eight tonight.*

danger *n.*   peril, risk, hazard, uncertainty, threat.   ANT. safety, security.

dangerous *adj.*   perilous, hazardous, risky, uncertain, unsafe.   ANT. safe, secure.

dangle *vb.*   hang; sway, droop.

dare *vb.*   **1** brave, risk: *The acrobat dared to walk the tightrope over the river, a long way below.*   **2** challenge: *Rosemarie dared George to swim across the lake.*

daring *adj.*   brave, fearless, intrepid, courageous, bold, valiant: *Entering the lion's cage carrying only a chair and whip is very daring.*   *n.* bravery, courage, valour: *Vincent's reputation for daring began when he saved three children from a* *burning house.* ANT. *adj.* afraid, fearful.   *n.* cowardice, timidity.

dark *adj.* **1** shadowy, unlit, murky, dim, dusky, shaded, sunless, black: *The half of the earth facing away from the sun is always dark.* **2** dismal, sad, gloomy, unhappy: *The period before the war was a dark time for many people.* ANT. **(1)** light, illuminated, bright. **(2)** cheerful, happy.

darken *vb.* shade, blacken; cloud over. ANT. brighten.

darkness *n.* dark, dusk, gloom; night. ANT. lightness, brightness; day.

darling *n.* beloved, dear, sweetheart, favourite: *Anthony was the darling of all the teachers.* *adj.* dear, beloved: *Robert's mother called him "Darling baby" until he was 25 years old.*

darn *vb.* mend, repair; embroider.

dart *n.* arrow, barb, missile: *The dart hit the target but missed the bull's-eye.* *vb.* run, scurry, scamper, hasten, dash: *From the top of the tall building, the people on the street below looked like ants darting to and fro.*

dash *vb.* **1** strike, smash, beat, break: *In the darkness, we could hear the surf dashing on the rocks in front of the ship.* **2** run, scurry, scamper, rush, dart: *In the rush hour, thousands of people dashed down the stairs into the underground station.* *n.* bit, sprinkling, scattering, pinch, hint: *Add just a dash of pepper before serving.*

data *n.* information, facts, evidence; statistics.

date *n.* time, day, moment; year.

daunt *vb.* frighten, discourage, intimidate. ANT. encourage, enspirit.

dauntless *adj.* brave, fearless, undaunted, bold, intrepid, courageous, valiant. ANT. cowardly, timid, fearful.

dawdle *vb.* linger, idle, lag behind, dally. ANT. hurry.

dawn *n.* **1** sunrise, daybreak: *The duel was arranged: it would be pistols at dawn in the park.* **2** beginning, origin, start: *At the dawn of civilization, man already used a highly developed language.* ANT. **(1)** sunset, dusk, nightfall. **(2)** end, finish, conclusion.

daydream *vb.* muse, fantasize.

daze *vb.* stun, confuse, perplex, puzzle: *The author was dazed by the publicity and fame his first novel had brought him. Roger was dazed by the blow he received on the head.* *n.* stupor, confusion, bewilderment: *I just walked around in a daze after learning about winning the scholarship.*

dazzle *vb.* astonish, bewilder, surprise, stupefy, stun, impress.

dead *adj.* **1** deceased, lifeless, defunct; gone, departed: *Donald's great grandfather has been dead for 20 years. Janet forgot to water her violets for a week, and when she looked at them, they were dead.* **2** inert, motionless, still, inoperative, inactive: *The engine went dead right in the middle of a traffic jam.* ANT. (1) alive, animate. (2) active, functioning.

deaden *vb.* numb, paralyse, anaesthetize.

deadlock *n.* stalemate, standstill, impasse.

deadly *adj.* **1** fatal, lethal, mortal: *He was going to take his own life by drinking the deadly poison but he came to his senses in time.* **2** deathly, ghastly, ghostly: *Margaret's face turned deadly pale when she learned of the accident.*

deaf *adj.* **1** unhearing, stone-deaf: *After the explosion, Tim was deaf in one ear for almost a week.* **2** unaware, stubborn, inattentive, oblivious: *My father was deaf to my requests for more money.* ANT. (2) conscious, aware.

deal *vb.* **1** treat, cope, act, attend: *Our former headmaster had methods for dealing with mischievous boys.* **2** trade, barter, do business, bargain: *My company refuses to deal with anyone who isn't completely honest.* **3** give, distribute, apportion, deliver: *I was dealt three aces and two kings.*

dear *adj.* **1** loved, beloved, darling: *His dear wife met his train every evening.* **2** expensive, costly, high-priced: *That new hat was much too dear for someone on my salary.* ANT. (1) hateful. (2) cheap, inexpensive, reasonable.

dearth *see* **lack.**

death *n.* demise, decease, passing, extinction. ANT. life; birth.

debased *see* **corrupt.**

debate *vb.* argue, dispute, contend, discuss: *We debated the merits of different types of wine until midnight.* *n.* discussion, dispute, argument, controversy: *The debate in the House of Commons on the new education bill went on for a week.* ANT. *n.* agreement.

debt *n.* obligation, liability.

debut *n.* (first) appearance, introduction; presentation.

decadent *adj.* corrupt, immoral, degenerate.

decay *vb.* **1** rot, spoil, decompose: *If you don't keep fresh food under refrigeration, it will decay rapidly.* **2** deteriorate, decline, wither, perish, die: *In the Dark Ages, western culture decayed so badly that there was little literature for several hundred years.* *n.* **1** decline, downfall, collapse: *The decay of the Roman Empire was caused by internal corruption.* **2**

rot, decomposition; mould, rottenness: *The decay in her teeth was very bad because she ate so many sweets.* ANT. *vb.* grow, progress, flourish.

deceased *adj.* dead; former, late, previous.

deceit *n.* deceitfulness, deception, fraud, dishonesty, guile. ANT. honesty, uprightness; forthrightness, openness.

deceitful *adj.* insincere, false, dishonest, fraudulent, deceptive. ANT. honest, sincere.

deceive *vb.* mislead, cheat, swindle, defraud, hoax, hoodwink, fool.

decent *adj.* proper, becoming, respectable; fitting, appropriate. ANT. indecent, improper, indecorous, unsuitable.

deception *n.* trickery, treachery, craftiness, deceit. ANT. honesty, openness, frankness, probity.

deceptive *adj.* false, misleading, unreliable. ANT. real, true, authentic.

decide *vb.* determine, settle, choose, resolve. ANT. hesitate, waver.

decision *n.* conclusion, judgment, resolution, settlement.

deck *n.* platform, level, floor, storey.

declaration *n.* announcement, pronouncement, statement, assertion, affirmation, notice.

declare *vb.* say, state, proclaim, announce, pronounce, affirm, assert. ANT. deny, suppress.

decline *vb.* 1 refuse, deny, reject: *He declined the nomination for the post of treasurer.* 2 lessen, deteriorate, weaken, fail, diminish: *Profits continued to decline after the company stopped advertising.* *n.* 1 lessening, weakening, deterioration: *After the accident, my brother's health went into a decline, but then he recovered completely.* 2 descent, slope, incline, hill: *Sledges may be ridden down declines.* ANT. *vb.* (1) agree, accept. (2) improve, increase, grow. *n.* (1) improvement.

decompose *vb.* rot, decay, moulder; break up, disintegrate.

decorate *vb.* ornament, paint, colour, enhance, adorn. ANT. spoil, deface.

decoration *n.* 1 ornamentation, adornment, furnishing: *The decorations for our Christmas tree are stored in the attic.* 2 medal, badge, citation, award: *My father won seven decorations for bravery during the war.*

decrease *vb.* lessen, diminish, decline, dwindle: *The number of complaints about the new cars decreased after the manufacturer recalled them for repairs.* *n.* lessening, reduction, decline: *It will be a long time before we see any decrease in the cost of living.* ANT. *vb.* increase, expand. *n.* increase, expansion.

decree *n.* edict, order, declaration, proclamation: *The new government issued a decree that petrol would be rationed.* *vb.* order, declare, announce, pronounce: *The king decreed that all prisoners would have their sentences reduced.*

decry *vb.* disapprove, criticize, disparage.

dedicate *vb.* **1** consecrate, sanctify, hallow: *The grounds were dedicated as a cemetery for those who had died in the war.* **2** set apart *or* aside, apply, devote, assign: *He dedicated all of his free time to helping the elderly.*

deduce *vb.* conclude, reason, infer.

deduct *vb.* subtract, take away. ANT. add, increase.

deed *n.* **1** act, action, achievement, feat: *For his deed of heroism in rescuing the little girl, the boy received a medal.* **2** title, document, certificate: *After we met the lawyers at the bank, we were given the deed to the house.*

deem *vb.* judge, determine, regard, consider, hold.

deep *adj.* **1** low; bottomless, profound: *They say that this pool is so deep that it has no bottom.* **2** serious, bad: *That boy will find himself in deep trouble one of these days.* **3** learned, intellectual: *I can see from your expression that you are thinking deep thoughts.* **4** absorbed, involved, engrossed: *The two men were deep in conversation, and I didn't want to interrupt.* ANT. *adj.* (**1**) shallow. (**3**) light.

deface *vb.* spoil, mar, scratch, disfigure. ANT. beautify, decorate.

defeat *vb.* **1** overcome, conquer, vanquish, overthrow, suppress: *The small scouting patrol was completely defeated by the enemy's superior forces.* **2** thwart, foil, spoil, frustrate: *The shower defeated our plans for a picnic.* *n.* conquest, overthrow: *Loss of the fighter plane spelled defeat for us.* ANT. *vb.* (**1**) surrender, submit, yield.

defect *n.* flaw, weakness, imperfection, blemish: *There was a defect in the new toaster, so we returned it and got our money back.* *vb.* desert, abandon, leave, forsake: *The men who defected from the army were all rounded up and punished.* ANT. *n.* perfection, flawlessness. *vb.* join, support.

defective *adj.* flawed, faulty, inoperable, inoperative, imperfect. ANT. perfect, flawless, faultless.

defence *n.* **1** protection, resistance: *Until recently, man was unable to provide a natural defence against certain diseases.*

2 trench, bulwark, fortification, fort, barricade, rampart, fortress: *The orange crates were no defence against the oncoming tanks.*

defend *vb*. **1** protect, guard, safeguard, shield: *The main army went out into the battle and left only 50 men to defend the women and children in the fort.* **2** support, uphold, maintain: *She tried to defend her son's behaviour, but everyone knew he had been wrong.* ANT. attack.

defer *vb*. delay, put off, postpone. ANT. hurry, speed, hasten, rush.

defiant *adj*. antagonistic, obstinate, rebellious, resistant, disobedient. ANT. submissive, yielding.

deficiency *n*. lack, scarcity, need, insufficiency. ANT. abundance, profusion.

deficit *n*. lack, shortage, deficiency; loss. ANT. excess; profit.

defile *vb*. corrupt, pollute, debase, adulterate. ANT. purify, cleanse.

define *vb*. **1** explain, describe, interpret; name, designate: *This dictionary defines words very thoroughly.* **2** set off, distinguish, mark off: *I could see his outline defined against the curtain.*

definite *adj*. **1** certain, fixed, settled, determined: *Our plans for Christmas are definite—we're having dinner at your house.* **2** clear, sharp, distinct, obvious, plain: *There, in the stone, was the definite outline of a dinosaur's foot.* ANT. indefinite, undetermined.

definition *n*. meaning, sense, explanation, interpretation, description.

deformed *adj*. misshapen, disfigured; twisted, warped, ugly.

defraud *vb*. cheat, swindle, trick.

defy *vb*. challenge, oppose, dare, flout. ANT. yield, submit, surrender.

degree *n*. **1** measure, extent, standard, order: *He reached a high degree of competence by sheer hard work.* **2** award, qualification: *After three years at college she was awarded a B.A. degree.*

dejected *adj*. depressed, unhappy, disheartened, discouraged, downhearted, sad. ANT. happy, cheerful, optimistic.

delay *vb*. **1** postpone, put off, hold up: *The post was delayed for three days over the Christmas holidays.* **2** wait, hesitate, pause, hold back: *When you hear the fire alarm, line up in the corridors and don't delay.* *n*. hold-up, pause, postponement: *During the strike, there was a three-week delay in the delivery of fresh produce.* ANT. *vb*. advance, forward.

delegate *n.* representative; ambassador, emissary; envoy, deputy: *Three universities sent delegates to the convention.* *vb.* appoint, nominate, deputize, commission, authorize: *I was delegated to ask the teacher whether the class could have a party.*

delete *vb.* cancel, erase, remove, cross out. ANT. add, include.

deliberate *adj.* 1 intentional, considered, planned, calculated, premeditated: *I believe that there was a deliberate effort to set fire to the house.* 2 careful, cautious, slow: *The old man's deliberate walk was recognized by all who knew him.* *vb.* consider, reflect, ponder, weigh, judge: *We deliberated for a long time before deciding what we would give to our teacher for a wedding present.* ANT. *adj.* (1) accidental, unintentional, unplanned.

delicate *adj.* 1 dainty, fine, fragile, frail: *The delicate cobwebs sparkled in the morning dew.* 2 frail, weak, precarious: *For a month after his operation, my uncle was in delicate health, but he's fine now.* 3 sensitive, critical, precarious, perilous: *The situation between Greece and Turkey has always been delicate.* ANT. (2) strong, healthy, robust.

delicious *adj.* tasty, appetizing, delectable, delightful. ANT. unpleasant, horrible, unpalatable.

delight *n.* pleasure, joy, enjoyment: *He is a loving father and takes great delight in his children.* *vb.* please, entertain, satisfy: *Nothing delights me more than a good Christmas party.* ANT. *n.* revulsion, disgust, displeasure. *vb.* displease, revolt, disgust.

delightful *adj.* charming, pleasing, refreshing, pleasant, pleasurable. ANT. disagreeable, unpleasant, nasty.

delinquent *n.* (young) offender, wrongdoer, criminal.

deliver *vb.* 1 distribute, give out; convey, hand over: *The Post Office delivers millions of letters each day.* 2 address, present: *Yesterday my father was to have delivered a speech to 400 people.* 3 liberate, set free, release, save, rescue: *May God deliver us from evil.* ANT. (3) confine, imprison, enslave.

delivery *n.* 1 conveyance, handing over, transfer, distribution: *The delivery of the goods took place at the station.* 2 manner, style, diction, articulation: *It was clear that the minister was the right man to speak at the dinner: his delivery was faultless.*

deluge *n.* 1 downpour, cloudburst: *It's rained nonstop all day—there's a deluge outside!* 2 flood, rush, overflow: *There was a deluge of fan mail for the new rock star.* *vb.* flood;

inundate, overwhelm: *Last month the whole area was deluged by continuous rain storms.*

delusion *n.* fantasy, illusion, vision.

demand *vb.* **1** ask for, claim, request: *I demanded my rights.* **2** command, direct: *The teacher demanded that the noisy children leave the room.* **3** require, need: *This night job demands more than I expected.* *n.* **1** request, claim: *Wage demands are increasing. Women's demands for voting rights equal to men's were a long time being met.* **2** obligation: *This job puts too many demands on my free time.* **3** call, market: *There is a great demand for felt-tip pens these days.* ANT. *vb.* **(1)** relinquish, waive, give up.

demarcation *n.* limit, boundary, separation.

demolish *vb.* destroy, ruin, raze, devastate. ANT. build, construct, erect.

demolition *n.* destruction, wrecking. ANT. construction, erection.

demon *n.* devil, evil spirit, imp. ANT. angel.

demonstrate *vb.* **1** prove, verify, establish: *The prosecutor demonstrated the suspect's guilt beyond all shadow of doubt.* **2** explain, describe, illustrate: *The simple screw demonstrates an application of the principle of the inclined plane.* **3** protest, march: *The angry workers went to London to demonstrate about their low pay.*

demonstration *n.* **1** show, exhibition, exhibit, presentation, display: *There was a demonstration at the planetarium that showed how the planets revolve around the sun.* **2** protest, march, rally: *The trades union leaders called on their members to join the demonstration in the city centre.*

demoralize *vb.* dishearten, discourage, unnerve. ANT. encourage, inspire.

denote *vb.* designate, indicate; stand for, mean.

denounce *vb.* condemn, deplore; blame, accuse.

dense *adj.* **1** thick, solid, impenetrable: *A dense fog covered the moors.* **2** packed, crowded: *On New Year's Eve a dense mass of people gathered in Trafalgar Square to see the new year in.* ANT. **(2)** sparse, scanty.

dent *n.* indentation, depression, dip; hole.

deny *vb.* **1** contradict, disagree, dispute, repudiate: *The suspect denied that he had taken the necklace from the case.* **2** refuse, reject, disallow: *You can't deny me the right to answer your charge.* ANT. **(1)** admit, concede, confess. **(2)** allow, permit.

depart *vb.* leave, go, set out. ANT. arrive, come.

department *n.* section, branch, subdivision.

departure *n.* going, leaving, setting out.

depend (on) *vb.* 1 rely, confide, trust: *We are all depending on Samantha to win the swimming race.* 2 be dependent, hinge, rest: *Whether we win or not will depend on the total score.*

dependable *adj.* reliable, trustworthy, steady, faithful.

depict *see* **describe.**

depleted *adj.* used up, consumed, exhausted, drained, empty.

deplorable *adj.* regrettable, grievous, lamentable.

deposit *vb.* 1 put, place, put down, set down: *The lorry deposited the goods at the quayside.* 2 save, bank; store: *No matter how little money you have, you should get into the habit of depositing some in the bank regularly.* *n.* 1 sediment, lees, dregs: *Port leaves a deposit at the bottom of the bottle.* 2 addition, entry: *Please make this bank deposit for me when you go to town.* ANT. *vb.* (2) withdraw. *n.* (2) withdrawal.

depot *n.* store, warehouse, depository, wharf.

deprave *see* **corrupt.**

depreciate *vb.* reduce, decline, decrease; decay, deteriorate.

depress *vb.* 1 dispirit, dishearten, discourage; dampen: *Paul was depressed for three days after losing the championship match.* 2 devalue, devaluate, cheapen: *The pound was depressed yesterday on the international money market.* ANT. (1) cheer, exhilarate, exalt.

depression *n.* 1 cavity, dip, hole, dent: *All that remained of the flying saucer was a smoking depression in the ground where it had stood.* 2 despair, gloom, melancholy, sorrow, sadness, hopelessness: *My mother went into a period of depression after my brother broke his arm.* 3 decline, recession, hard times: *Some people thought that the business depression of the 1970s would be worse than that of the twenties.* ANT. (1) bank, elevation. (2) elation, happiness. (3) boom.

deprive *vb.* deny, strip; rob. ANT. supply, provide.

depth *n.* deepness, profundity. ANT. height, tallness, loftiness.

deputy *n.* assistant, lieutenant, aide, delegate.

derelict *adj.* dilapidated, decrepit, neglected; deserted, abandoned, forsaken.

derive *vb.* receive, obtain, get, acquire.

derogatory *adj.* offensive, pejorative, disparaging, insulting. ANT. flattering, complimentary, appreciative.

descend *vb.* move lower, climb down. ANT. ascend, climb.

descent *n.* fall, drop, decline. ANT. ascent, rise.

describe *vb.* portray, characterize, picture, narrate, relate, recount, represent.

description *n.* account, narration, report, record.

desert[1] *n.* waste, wasteland, wilderness: *It may sometime be necessary to irrigate the deserts to provide more farmland.* *adj.* wild, barren, uninhabited: *Robinson Crusoe was cast ashore on a desert island.*

desert[2] *vb.* abandon, leave, forsake: *When the cat deserted her kittens, our dog adopted them and took care of them.* ANT. join, accompany.

deserter *n.* fugitive, runaway, defector, renegade; traitor. ANT. loyalist.

deserve *vb.* earn, merit, be worthy of, warrant.

design *vb.* **1** plan, intend, scheme, plot: *The trapdoor was designed to open if anyone tried to open the jewel case.* **2** create, originate: *My sister designs clothes for a large manufacturer in Paris.* *n.* **1** pattern, plan, blueprint, sketch: *These designs for the new monument were copied from old books.* **2** meaning, intention, purpose, end, aim: *Veronica's design for the future did not include Harry as her husband.*

desirable *adj.* wanted, sought-after, wished-for; good, excellent. ANT. unwanted, hated; unattractive, repellent.

desire *vb.* **1** crave, long for, want, covet: *What I desire most of all right now is a delicious nutty bar of chocolate.* **2** ask, request: *If you call the servants, they will see that you have what you desire.* *n.* need, longing, want, craving, wish: *The magician said he could satisfy every one of Harvey's desires.* ANT. *vb.* (1) loathe, abhor, detest.

desk *n.* bureau, table; counter.

desolate *adj.* **1** deserted, empty, lonely: *During the winter, the beach was desolate.* **2** miserable, sad, unhappy, wretched: *When you're away from me I am just desolate.* ANT. (1) crowded, populous, teeming. (2) cheerful, happy.

despair *n.* hopelessness, desperation, discouragement: *When the hundredth experiment resulted in failure, the research staff were in deep despair.* *vb.* lose heart, lose hope: *When I lost my watch while rowing on the lake, I despaired of ever seeing it again.* ANT. *n.* joy, hope, optimism.

desperate *adj.* despairing, hopeless, reckless. ANT. calm, collected.

despicable *adj.* mean, base, low, contemptible, worthless. ANT. admirable, honourable, worthy.

despise *vb.* scorn, dislike, disdain, condemn. ANT. admire, like, honour.

despite *prep.* notwithstanding, regardless of, in spite of, even with.

despondent *adj.* dejected, discouraged, downcast, disheartened, sad. ANT. happy, joyful.

despot *n.* dictator, tyrant, autocrat, oppressor.

dessert *n.* sweet, pudding, (*informal*) afters.

destiny *n.* fate, fortune, lot.

destroy *vb.* **1** ruin, demolish; deface, spoil: *These trees were destroyed by disease.* **2** kill, slay, end, extinguish: *When I saw the train pulling out of the station, my holiday plans were destroyed.* ANT. (**1**) create, start, undertake.

destruction *n.* devastation, demolition, ruin, extinction. ANT. creation, beginning.

detach *vb.* separate, disengage, divide. ANT. attach, connect.

detail *n.* feature, aspect; item, circumstance.

detain *vb.* delay, restrain, hold back, stop. ANT. forward, hurry, rush.

detect *vb.* determine, discover, ascertain, learn, find out.

detective *n.* policeman, officer.

deter *vb.* prevent, discourage, dissuade. ANT. encourage.

deteriorate *vb.* decay, degenerate, decline; impair; disintegrate. ANT. improve.

determine *vb.* **1** decide, settle, resolve: *It was only a few minutes to determine who had eaten the sweets—he had chocolate all over his chin.* **2** fix, establish, define: *I wasn't able to determine exactly where my property ended and my neighbour's began.*

detest *vb.* despise, hate, loathe. ANT. like, love, appreciate.

devastate *vb.* **1** lay waste, ravage; sack: *The nuclear bomb devastated a large area of land.* **2** *Informal:* overwhelm, confound: *The news of the death of her friend devastated her.*

develop *vb.* **1** grow, expand, enlarge, advance, mature: *Anne has developed from a child into a beautiful, charming young lady.* **2** reveal, disclose, become known, unfold: *The plot of the play developed only slowly.* ANT. (**1**) deteriorate, degenerate.

deviate *vb.* diverge, wander, turn aside.

device *n.* machine, tool, utensil, instrument.

devious *adj.* **1** underhand, insincere, dishonest; sly: *The managing director was very devious in his approach to other firms.* **2** roundabout, indirect: *Why did we have to drive the long way home along that devious route of yours?* ANT. (1) open, fair; honest. (2) direct.

devise *vb.* invent, create, originate, concoct.

devote *vb.* apply, dedicate, give, commit. ANT. relinquish, withdraw, withhold, ignore.

devour *vb.* gorge, gulp.

devout *adj.* **1** religious, pious, devoted: *He is a devout Christian and goes to church twice on Sunday.* **2** genuine, earnest, sincere, heartfelt: *I am a devout believer in treating others the way I'd want them to treat me.* ANT. (1) irreligious. (2) indifferent, scornful.

diagram *n.* plan, outline, sketch; chart.

dictate *vb.* **1** speak, deliver, record: *If he dictates too fast, I cannot take it down in shorthand.* **2** order, command, direct: *The general dictated the conditions under which he would accept a surrender.*

dictator *n.* tyrant, despot.

die *vb.* **1** decease, perish, expire, go, pass away: *Because of the advances in medicine, people aren't dying until they are much older.* **2** decrease, diminish, fade, sink, decline, wither, wane, fail: *The candle, like the roses in the vase, is dying.* ANT. (2) flourish, grow.

difference *n.* disagreement, inequality, contrast. ANT. similarity, likeness, kinship, compatibility.

different *adj.* **1** unalike, unlike, differing, changed: *You and your sister are as different as chalk and cheese.* **2** various, miscellaneous: *There are five different flavours of ice cream to choose from.* ANT. (1) similar, alike, identical.

differentiate *vb.* distinguish, separate.

difficult *adj.* **1** hard, laborious, strenuous: *Handling a horse-drawn plough is difficult.* **2** intricate, complicated, obscure: *That college textbook is much too difficult for a child to understand.* ANT. (1) easy. (2) simple, uncomplicated.

difficulty *n.* **1** worry, hardship, trouble: *Getting a good job after school can be a difficulty these days.* **2** predicament, fix, trouble: *Barbie got herself into some difficulty at school last week.*

dig *vb.* excavate, burrow, scoop out.

digest *vb.* **1** eat, consume: *After a huge meal, some snakes spend days digesting their food.* **2** study, consider, reflect on: *Give me a few minutes to digest the teacher's remarks* *before replying.* **3** summarize, shorten, abridge: *How can you digest the encyclopedia into such a small book?* *n.* summary, abridgment, abstract, synopsis, precis: *Why should anyone want to read digests of great authors' books when the real pleasure comes from reading the originals?*

dignified *adj.* noble, serious, stately, solemn, elegant.

dignify *vb.* exalt, ennoble, elevate, honour. ANT. humiliate, degrade, shame.

dignity *n.* distinction, stateliness, bearing.

dilapidated *adj.* old, shabby; decaying, tumbledown.

dilemma *n.* predicament, quandary.

diligent *adj.* hardworking, persevering; careful, attentive. ANT. lazy.

dilute *vb.* water down, thin, weaken, mix.

dim *adj.* unclear, faint, shadowy, vague: *I could hardly make out the dim outline of the house in the fog.* *vb.* obscure, dull, darken: *The houselights were dimmed as the curtain went up for the last act of the play.* ANT. *adj.* bright, brilliant. *vb.* brighten, illuminate.

dimension *n.* (usually **dimensions**) measure, size, extent; importance.

diminish *vb.* lessen, shrink, reduce, decline. ANT. enlarge, increase.

diminutive *adj.* little, small, tiny, minute. ANT. big, large, great, huge, gigantic.

din *see* **noise.**

dine *vb.* eat, feast, lunch, soup.

dinghy *see* **boat.**

dip *vb.* plunge, immerse, submerge, wet: *Dip the burning stick into the water to make sure it's out.* *n.* plunge, swim: *I like to take a dip in the pool before breakfast.*

diploma *n.* award, certificate.

diplomat *see* **ambassador.**

diplomatic *adj.* polite, tactful, gracious, discreet. ANT. impolite, rude, thoughtless, ungracious, tactless.

direct *vb.* **1** command, manage, control, regulate: *The new director directed the company through one of its most profitable periods.* **2** aim, sight, point, level: *Completely frustrated, Betty directed her gaze skyward as if in appeal to a higher power.* **3** indicate, guide, conduct, show: *Please direct me to the nearest police station.* *adj.* **1** straight, unswerving: *When my son comes home after school, he makes a beeline for the kitchen to eat some biscuits.* **2** plain, straightforward, frank, sincere, earnest: *Please stop wavering* *and give me a direct, honest answer to my question.* ANT. *adj.* (1) crooked, indirect, swerving. (2) dishonest, untruthful.

direction *n.* 1 way, route: *After all I had told her, she drove off in the wrong direction.* 2 management, guidance, supervision: *Under her direction, the school became one of the best in the country.*

directly *adv.* straight, immediately, at once.

director *n.* manager, leader, executive; supervisor.

directory *n.* list, classification, record.

dirt *n.* soil, filth, pollution, filthiness. ANT. cleanness, cleanliness.

dirty *adj.* soiled, unclean, filthy, polluted: *I wouldn't drink that dirty water if I were you.* *vb.* soil, foul, befoul, spot, pollute: *The town's water was dirtied by the drains from the chemical-company plant.* ANT. *adj.* clean, pure, spotless. *vb.* clean, cleanse, purify.

disability *n.* incapacity, unfitness, injury.

disable *vb.* cripple, incapacitate, weaken.

disadvantage *n.* 1 inconvenience, drawback: *The only disadvantage of my new job is that I have to get up at 5 o'clock.* 2 handicap, hindrance, obstacle: *Her disadvantage is that she cannot type.* ANT. benefit, advantage, convenience.

disagree *vb.* argue, object, oppose. ANT. agree.

disagreeable *adj.* quarrelsome, offensive, rude. ANT. friendly, agreeable, pleasant.

disagreement *n.* conflict, controversy, quarrel, clash, opposition.

disappear *vb.* vanish, fade; cease, end. ANT. appear, emerge.

disappoint *vb.* fail, dissatisfy; disconcert. ANT. satisfy, please, gratify.

disappointment *n.* defeat, dissatisfaction, failure, discouragement. ANT. satisfaction, pleasure, gratification.

disapproval *n.* condemnation, censure; discontent, dissatisfaction. ANT. approval, praise.

disaster *n.* calamity, misfortune, accident, catastrophe.

disastrous *adj.* unfortunate, catastrophic, calamitous.

disc *n.* 1 record: *Have you bought the number one disc yet?* 2 counter, token: *We have to buy discs for the buses in this town.*

discard *vb.* throw away, get rid of, reject.

discern *vb.* see, distinguish, recognize, differentiate, perceive.

discharge *vb.* 1 let go, dismiss: *When business got bad, three of us were discharged from our jobs.* 2 relieve, unload, unburden: *Marie's responsibilities were not discharged until she finished washing the dishes.* **3** fire, shoot: *The rabbit ran off into the woods when the gun discharged.* *n.* **1** explosion, firing, detonation: *The sudden discharge of the gun made me jump.* **2** release, liberation; dismissal: *My father's discharge from the navy became final this week.* ANT. *vb.* (1) employ. *n.* (2) employment.

disciple *n.* follower, supporter; student, pupil.

discipline *n.* **1** training, practice, exercise, drill: *If you want to do well in sports, you must follow a strict discipline. Discipline in the armed services is not as severe as it once was.* **2** order, system, control: *A neatly written paper shows good discipline.* *vb.* **1** train, control, drill, teach: *Your puppy will make a better pet if you discipline him properly.* **2** punish, correct, chastise: *In the old days, parents disciplined their children much more strictly than they do now.* ANT. *n.* (2) carelessness, negligence, sloppiness, messiness.

disclose *vb.* reveal, show, expose, uncover. ANT. hide, disguise, mask, conceal.

disconnect *vb.* separate, divide, unhook, detach, disengage. ANT. connect, engage, attach, bind.

discontinue *vb.* cease, end, stop; interrupt. ANT. begin, start, launch, initiate.

discord *n.* conflict, disagreement. ANT. agreement, accord, concord.

discount *n.* rebate, deduction, allowance, concession, premium.

discourage *vb.* dishearten, depress, deject. ANT. encourage, inspire.

discourtesy *n.* disrespect, impoliteness, rudeness. ANT. courtesy, politeness.

discover *vb.* find; learn, find out, ascertain, determine. ANT. conceal, hide.

discreet *adj.* tactful, judicious, prudent, wise; cautious, careful. ANT. careless, incautious, tactless, indiscreet, imprudent.

discretion *n.* tact, prudence, wisdom, carefulness, thoughtfulness.

discriminate *vb.* distinguish, differentiate, tell apart.

discuss *vb.* talk about, deliberate, consider.

discussion *n.* talk, conversation; dialogue; conference.

disdain *vb.* scorn, reject: *She disdains the way her sister dresses.* *n.* scorn, contempt, haughtiness: *He treats everyone who has less money than he with disdain.* ANT. *vb.*

admire, respect, esteem, prize. *n.* admiration, respect, honour.

disdainful *adj.* scornful, contemptuous, haughty, arrogant. ANT. admiring; humble.

disease *n.* illness, sickness, affliction, ailment, complaint, disorder, malady, infirmity.

disgrace *n.* shame, dishonour, embarrassment: *Tim had to live with the disgrace of having been caught cheating.* *vb.* shame, dishonour, embarrass, humiliate: *The army deserter was told that he had disgraced his country.* ANT. *n.* honour, esteem. *vb.* honour, respect.

disguise *vb.* mask, hide, screen, conceal, camouflage: *The detective disguised himself as a woman and waited in the street for the robber to attack.* *n.* mask, camouflage, cover: *In her disguise as a flower girl, no one could recognize the society lady at the party.* ANT. *vb.* reveal, display, show.

disgust *vb.* nauseate, sicken; offend, revolt, repulse: *The sight of an operation disgusts me.* *n.* distaste, nausea; aversion, revulsion: *Looking at the dead horse filled him with disgust.* ANT. *n.* liking, admiration.

disgusting *adj.* revolting, repulsive, nauseating, repugnant. ANT. attractive, appealing.

dish *n.* **1** plate; bowl, container: *Who's going to wash the dishes after dinner?* **2** food, meal; course: *That dish certainly looks tasty!*

dishonest *adj.* corrupt, fraudulent, crooked. ANT. honest, straightforward, upright.

disintegrate *vb.* break down, shatter; divide, separate; decay.

dislike *vb.* disapprove of; hate, detest, loathe.

dismal *adj.* gloomy, sorrowful, depressing, melancholy, dreary, sombre. ANT. cheerful, happy, charming, light-hearted.

dismay *vb.* scare, frighten, alarm; discourage, dishearten: *We were dismayed to learn that the only roads to town were blocked by snow.* *n.* fear, terror, horror, dread: *You can imagine the neighbours' dismay when the poisonous snake escaped.* ANT. *vb.* hearten, encourage.

dismiss *vb.* discharge, release, let go, liberate. ANT. engage, employ, hire.

disobey *vb.* break, violate, transgress; neglect, ignore, disregard. ANT. keep, obey.

disorder *n.* confusion, turmoil, tumult, chaos. ANT. order, neatness, organization.

dispatch *vb.* **1** send off *or* away: *I dispatched the letter the very* *same day the request came.* 2 conclude, achieve, finish: *I had only one more thing to do and dispatched that as quickly as I could.* *n.* 1 message, report, communication, communiqué: *The dispatch from the front lines said that our troops were advancing.* 2 speed, promptness, quickness, swiftness: *My next visitor is a bore, and I shall get rid of him with dispatch.* ANT. *n.* (2) slowness, reluctance, hesitancy.

dispense *vb.* distribute, apportion, give out.

disperse *vb.* scatter, spread (out), separate. ANT. gather, collect, assemble.

display *vb.* 1 exhibit, show, demonstrate: *There are strict rules about how flags should be displayed.* 2 reveal, uncover, show: *Many people display their lack of knowledge as soon as they start talking.* *n.* showing, exhibit, exhibition, demonstration: *I have never seen such a display of community spirit as during the parade.* ANT. *vb.* (2) disguise, hide, conceal, cover.

dispose *vb.* deal with, arrange, settle; adjust.

disposition *n.* nature, character, temperament, personality.

dispute *vb.* 1 argue, debate, quarrel, contest: *How can you dispute my statement that my birthday is March 21st?* 2 oppose, deny, contradict: *The committee disputed the wisdom of the report's recommendations and rejected them all.* *n.* argument, quarrel, debate, controversy: *There was a dispute at the door about whether the tickets were valid or not.* ANT. *vb.* agree, concur. *n.* agreement, unanimity.

disqualify *vb.* debar, incapacitate, disable.

disregard *vb.* ignore, overlook, neglect: *In taking on people, employers must learn to disregard race, colour, creed, and sex and to consider only character and qualifications.* *n.* inattention, neglect, oversight: *The policeman jumped into the icy waters with total disregard for his own safety.*

disrespectful *adj.* rude, impudent, impolite, impertinent; cheeky. ANT. respectful, polite, courteous.

disrupt *vb.* interrupt, break; upset; intrude.

dissatisfaction *n.* disappointment, discouragement, discontent. ANT. satisfaction, enjoyment.

dissolve *vb.* 1 liquefy, melt, run: *Salt dissolves in water.* 2 discontinue, terminate: *Parliament was dissolved before the general election.* ANT. (1) harden, solidify.

distance *n.* length, space, extent, reach.

distant *adj.* remote, far, afar, away, separated. ANT. near, close.

distinct *adj.* 1 individual, separate, different: *In nature each* *species is distinct from every other, even though some may seem alike.* **2** clear, definite, obvious, plain: *I have a distinct recollection that you promised to take me to the ice rink.* ANT. (2) indistinct, vague, uncertain, obscure.

distinction *n.* **1** honour, renown, fame, repute, prominence, importance: *It is a great distinction to be selected a winner of the Nobel prize.* **2** difference; characteristic: *Until a child is taught what they mean, he is unable to make a distinction between right and wrong.*

distinguish *vb.* **1** separate, divide, differentiate, classify: *It is hard for anyone but the specialist to distinguish one seashell from another.* **2** perceive, discern, recognize: *Even at that great distance I was able to distinguish George in the crowd.* ANT. (1) blend, join, confuse.

distinguished *adj.* renowned, famous, honoured, eminent, illustrious, noted, important, celebrated. ANT. obscure, unknown, undistinguished.

distort *vb.* **1** deform, contort, twist, warp: *His face had been distorted by old age.* **2** misrepresent, alter, misinterpret, pervert: *Do news bulletins sometimes distort the truth?*

distract *vb.* **1** divert, occupy: *I always found the radio too distracting when I was trying to do my homework.* **2** confuse, bewilder: *Penny seemed distracted and unable to concentrate on what I was saying.* ANT. concentrate, focus.

distraction *n.* **1** amusement, entertainment, diversion: *After studying for days for examinations, Jonathan felt he needed some distraction and went to the disco.* **2** confusion, turmoil, conflict: *She felt a great distraction within herself at the enormity of the decision she had to take.*

distress *n.* **1** anguish, trouble, anxiety, worry, wretchedness; pain: *Maggie caused her mother great distress whenever she stayed out late at night.* **2** danger, peril; disaster: *The small boat was in distress because of the storm.* *vb.* worry, trouble, grieve, make wretched: *Bill was distressed to learn that the headmaster had written to his father.* ANT. *n.* (1) happiness, tranquillity, peacefulness. *vb.* please, charm, satisfy.

distribute *vb.* share, deal, dispense, issue, mete out, allocate, apportion. ANT. collect, gather, assemble.

district *n.* region, area, neighbourhood, section.

distrust *vb.* suspect, doubt, mistrust: *The bank manager distrusted the new cashier.* *n.* suspicion, doubt, mistrust: *A good relationship between people must be founded on confi-*

dence, without distrust. ANT. *vb.* trust. *n.* trust, confidence.

disturb *vb.* **1** annoy, bother, vex: *Please don't disturb me when I am practising on the piano.* **2** worry, trouble: *Even though the doctor said you were fine, the condition of your cold disturbs me.* ANT. calm, pacify.

disturbance *n.* **1** commotion, disorder, confusion: *The marchers in the street caused quite a disturbance to the traffic.* **2** riot, brawl, fight: *The police were called to control a disturbance between the political groups.* ANT. calm, serenity, tranquillity.

disuse *n.* neglect, decay, abandonment. ANT. use, employment.

ditch *n.* channel, furrow, trench.

dive *vb.* plunge, jump, dip, plummet, submerge.

diverge *vb.* branch off, separate, fork. ANT. join, converge, merge.

diverse *adj.* assorted, various, different. ANT. same, similar.

diversion *n.* **1** detour, redirection: *There is a long diversion on the Oxford road because of road works.* **2** entertainment, amusement, sport, recreation: *What do you do as a diversion if you live in such a small town?*

divert *vb.* turn aside *or* away, deflect.

divide *vb.* **1** separate, split, part, detach, sever: *Divide that apple into six pieces so we can share it.* **2** apportion, share, allot, allocate, distribute, deal *or* dole out: *After the apple is cut up, we can divide it among the six of us.* **3** disunite, split up, estrange: *Disagreements about women's rights divided the political party from the start.* ANT. (1) join, merge, combine. (2) gather, collect. (3) unite, unify.

divine *adj.* godly, heavenly, almighty, holy, transcendent. ANT. earthly, worldly.

division *n.* **1** separation, partition, sharing: *In olden times, conquering soldiers were entitled to a division of the valuables in the cities and towns they captured.* **2** section, part, segment, portion: *My father fought in the 3rd Division during the war.* ANT. (1) agreement, union.

divorce *n.* dissolution, annulment; separation. ANT. marriage, wedding.

divulge *vb.* reveal, release, disclose, expose; admit. ANT. conceal, hide.

dizzy *adj.* giddy, unsteady, lightheaded. ANT. clearheaded, rational, unconfused.

do *vb.* **1** perform, execute, enact, carry out, accomplish, effect: *Success depends on everyone doing his job the best he can.* **2** finish, conclude, complete, achieve, attain: *Don't just talk about it, do it!* *vb. phr.* **do away with** kill, murder, execute: *The pirates did away with all those who refused to join them.* **do down** belittle, humiliate: *Some elder brothers always do their younger brothers down.* **do in** *Slang:* kill, murder: *The thugs did the old lady in savagely.* **do up 1** wrap, enclose, tie: *This is a beautiful gift—all done up with a red ribbon!* **2** redecorate, remodel: *The Robinsons have done up their entire house.*

docile *adj.* submissive; meek, mild, humble, tame. ·

dock *n.* wharf, pier, landing place.

doctor *n.* physician, general practitioner, surgeon; specialist.

doctrine *n.* teaching, teachings; dogma, belief, principle.

document *n.* form, certificate, record.

dodge *vb.* evade, elude, avoid; equivocate.

dog *n.* bitch, hound; puppy.

dole *n.* unemployment benefit: *Don's father has been on the dole ever since he lost his job at the factory.* *vb.* deal, distribute, mete: *The Red Cross doled out the food to the flood victims.*

doll *n.* figure, model, dummy, toy.

domestic *adj.* **1** home-loving, homely: *I am really very domestic and like nothing better than a good book and comfortable chair by my own fireside.* **2** native, home-grown, homemade: *If you buy domestic products, you stimulate the economy of your own country.* ANT. (2) foreign, alien, outside.

domesticate *vb.* tame, train, teach; housetrain.

dominant *adj.* ruling, commanding, governing; prevailing, predominant.

dominate *vb.* control, rule, govern, influence, manage, subjugate, tyrannize.

donation *n.* gift, contribution, present, offering.

doom *n.* **1** fate, destiny, fortune: *The criminal had to wait till the judge passed sentence before learning his doom.* **2** death, ruin, destruction: *The entire regiment rode to its doom as the flood waters closed in on them.* *vb.* destine, predestine, ordain, foreordain; decree; condemn: *The entire project is doomed to failure if you take that attitude.*

door *n.* entrance, opening, gateway; gate, portal.

dot *n.* mark, spot, point, speck, particle.

double *adj.* twofold; dual, repeated, coupled: *Give me a* *double portion of chips, please.* vb. multiply, duplicate: *The inflation rate doubled last year.*

doubt vb. distrust, mistrust, question, suspect: *The detective doubted that Professor Twinkle had been home all evening after he noticed the mud on his shoes.* n. **1** uncertainty, misgiving, scepticism, disbelief: *I have my doubts about the truth of your story of being brought up by wolves.* **2** indecision, hesitancy: *When we saw the fox running away with the chicken between its jaws, we no longer had a doubt about the identity of the culprit.* ANT. vb. trust, believe. n. belief, trust, confidence, reliance.

doubtful adj. dubious, uncertain, questionable, unsettled, undetermined, unsure. ANT. certain, definite, sure, settled.

downcast adj. dejected, sad, depressed, downhearted, discouraged, unhappy, dispirited, despondent, crestfallen. ANT. cheerful, happy, lighthearted, encouraged.

downfall n. ruin, fall, destruction.

downgrade vb. lower, reduce, decrease, diminish; depreciate. ANT. upgrade, improve, appreciate.

downhearted adj. sad, gloomy, depressed, downcast. ANT. cheerful, happy, enthusiastic.

doze vb. nap, sleep, slumber.

drab adj. dingy, dull, shabby; dreary.

draft n. sketch, plan, drawing, outline.

drag vb. pull, draw, tow.

drain vb. **1** draw off, empty, tap: *The man drained his glass in one gulp. The conservationists fight the draining of swamps where birds, fishes, and other wildlife breed.* **2** exhaust, sap, waste; milk: *Your annoying manner drains me of all patience.* n. tap, duct, channel, pipe: *I pulled the stopper out of the sink and watched the water go down the drain.* ANT. vb. (1) fill.

drama n. play, piece, show, production.

dramatist n. playwright, author, writer.

drastic adj. severe, extreme; excessive, flagrant. ANT. moderate, cautious.

draw vb. **1** sketch, trace, depict, picture: *The artist drew an excellent likeness of Anne in only a few minutes.* **2** drag, haul, tow, pull, tug: *The oxen drew the heavy wagon up the muddy hill.* **3** attract: *The parade drew a large crowd to the arena where the circus was to take place.* vb. phr. **draw back** withdraw, recoil, retreat: *She drew back when she saw the box was full of snakes.* **draw on** employ, use, exploit: *When you want to get something done properly, you must draw on all your resources.* **draw up** draft, prepare: *Our lawyer drew up* *the documents for us to sign.* ANT. *vb.* (2) push, propel.

drawback *n.* disadvantage, hindrance, defect, shortcoming. ANT. advantage.

drawing *n.* sketch, picture, plan.

dread *vb.* fear: *I used to dread being in that teacher's class.* *n.* fear, terror, horror: *Moriarty never overcame his dread of high places.* ANT. *n.* confidence, security.

dream *n.* 1 reverie, daydream: *I had a dream about you yesterday.* 2 fantasy, hope, wish, fancy: *His dreams of glory included landing on Mars and becoming a millionaire.* *vb.* imagine, fantasize, invent, fancy: *She dreams of becoming a model.*

dreary *adj.* dismal, gloomy, cheerless, chilling, depressing. ANT. cheerful, hopeful, bright, encouraging.

dress *n.* 1 frock, skirt: *I like that low-cut dress on you.* 2 costume, attire, garb, wardrobe, clothing, garments, clothes, apparel; habit; livery: *Will Nancy's party require everyone to wear evening dress?* *vb.* 1 clothe, garb, don, wear, attire; robe: *How are you going to dress for the masked ball?* 2 prepare, treat, attend: *The doctor dressed my cuts and bruises and I was almost as good as new.* ANT. *vb.* (1) undress, disrobe, strip.

drift *vb.* · float, sail, wander: *The empty boat drifted about in the current until it finally came to rest on the beach.* *n.* tendency, intention, direction: *In women's fashions there seems to be a drift toward repeating the styles of the 1930s and 1940s.*

drill *n.* borer, gimlet, awl.

drink *vb.* swallow, sip, gulp: *You shouldn't drink a lot of cold water when overheated from exercise.* *n.* sip, gulp; beverage, potion, refreshment: *There's nothing like a drink of tea when you're thirsty.*

drip *vb.* drop, dribble, trickle.

drive *vb.* 1 control, direct, run, handle: *Do you know how to drive a car?* 2 impel, propel, push, urge: *I tried to reach the canoe but was driven back by the wind and the waves.* *n.* 1 ride, journey, trip, outing, tour, run: *On Saturdays we go for a drive in the country.* 2 pressure, energy, urge, vigour, effort, force: *Some people just have more drive than others.*

drivel *vb.* dribble; drip, slobber, drool: *The dog drivelled at the mouth.* *n.* nonsense, twaddle, balderdash: *What drivel some people speak!*

drizzle *vb.* spit, rain, spray.

droop *vb.* sag, sink, settle. ANT. straighten, rise.

drop *vb*. **1** drip, dribble, trickle: *The rain ran down the roof and dropped into the barrel.* **2** fall, tumble: *At the sound of the first shot, the soldiers dropped to the ground.* *n.* **1** droplet, gob, drip; trickle: *There's a drop of rain right at the end of your nose.* **2** decrease, reduction, fall, slump, slip, decline: *I haven't noticed a drop in the price of gum.*

drove *n*. herd, flock.

drown *vb*. **1** die; kill: *The boys fell into the canal and drowned.* **2** drench, flood, inundate: *The waters drowned the crops.*

drowsy *adj*. sleepy, tired.

drug *n*. medicine, remedy: *There's a drug for almost everything today; whether it cures or not is another matter.* *vb.* anaesthetize, stupefy, numb, benumb: *The doctor drugged me so I wouldn't feel the pain when he set my broken arm.*

drum (up) *vb*. attract, summon, call; obtain, evoke.

drunk, drunkard *n*. drinker, alcoholic; dipsomaniac.

dry *adj*. **1** arid, dehydrated, waterless, parched: *If you don't believe that the desert is dry, you've never been there.* **2** dull, boring, tedious, tiresome: *I found that course on lampshade making too dry to hold my interest.* *vb.* dehydrate, desiccate: *Partly dried plums are called prunes.* ANT. *adj.* (1) wet, soaked, moist. (2) interesting, attractive, fascinating.

dubious *adj*. doubtful, questionable, suspect.

due *adj*. **1** owing, payable, owed, unpaid: *My rent is due at the end of the month.* **2** expected, imminent: *The ship was due yesterday.*

dull *adj*. **1** boring, tiring, tiresome, uninteresting: *Instead of seeing a film on the history of piracy, we saw a dull one on how to grow turnips.* **2** blunt, dulled: *That knife is so dull it couldn't cut a banana.* **3** slow, dumb, stupid, unimaginative: *That fellow is the dullest one in our class.* **4** unfeeling, insensible, lifeless, dead: *She's so dull that nothing interests her except eating and sleeping.* ANT. (1) fascinating, interesting, engaging. (2) sharp, keen. (3) bright, intelligent, quick. (4) alert, animated, spirited.

dumb *adj*. **1** dull, stupid, ignorant: *Sadie is so dumb she failed every subject in school.* **2** speechless, mute: *Some people who seem to be dumb are really only deaf.* ANT. (1) intelligent, bright, lucid, quick.

dump *n*. heap, pile: *We put the old fridge on the dump.* *vb.* throw down, empty, unload: *He dumped the heavy bags on the floor.*

dungeon *n*. prison, cell, jail, keep.

durable *adj.* lasting, firm, enduring. ANT. perishable, short-lived.

duration *n.* length, span, term, period.

duress *n.* compulsion, coercion, constraint; force.

dusk *n.* gloom, twilight.

dust *n.* powder, dirt, sand; granules, particles.

dutiful *adj.* faithful, obedient, docile. ANT. disobedient, headstrong, unruly.

duty *n.* **1** obligation, responsibility, conscience, faithfulness: *It is every citizen's duty to report a crime when he sees one.* **2** function, responsibility, part, assignment: *Every person in this naval unit is expected to perform his duty no matter what the cost may be.*

dwarf *n.* runt, midget: *Only a dwarf could have crawled through that opening.* *vb.* stunt, reduce, minimize: *I'm quite tall, but that football player dwarfed me easily.* *adj.* small, tiny, minuscule: *A dwarf apple tree gives large apples.* ANT. *n.* giant.

dwell *vb.* reside, live, abide.

dwindle *vb.* diminish, wane, lessen, decrease. ANT. increase, wax, gain, grow.

e

eager *adj.* enthusiastic, keen, fervent.   ANT. indifferent, uninterested, uninvolved.

early *adj.* premature; advanced; recent, new.   ANT. late.

earn *vb.* deserve, merit, win; realize, collect; clear, net.

earnest *adj.* sincere, serious, determined, eager.   ANT. insincere, frivolous, indifferent.

earth *n.* **1** world, globe: *The earth is about 93 million miles from the sun.* **2** sod, turf, dirt, soil, ground: *When planting tomatoes, make sure the earth is pressed firmly around the roots.*

earthly *adj.* worldly, everyday, mundane.   ANT. heavenly.

earthquake *n.* tremors, movement, vibrations.

earthy *adj.* **1** earthen, earthlike: *The earthy pots lay about the Indian campfire.* **2** coarse, unrefined, crude, vulgar: *The audience was shocked by the comedian's earthy humour.* ANT. (2) refined, elegant, tasteful.

ease *n.* **1** naturalness, facility, skilfulness, cleverness: *It is such a pleasure to watch the ease with which a master craftsman works.* **2** comfort, rest, relaxation, repose, contentment, contentedness: *My father takes his ease on Sundays by watching football on TV.*   *vb.* comfort, relieve, alleviate, soothe; lighten, lessen, reduce: *That liniment certainly helped ease the pains in my legs. If you'll ease up on the brake, we can let the car roll ahead a little.*   ANT. *n.* (1) difficulty, trouble, effort.   *vb.* aggravate, worsen, heighten, intensify.

easy *adj.* **1** simple, effortless: *Preparing a dictionary is not as easy as it may seem.* **2** comfortable, unhurried, leisurely: *After a heavy Christmas dinner we used to take an easy walk on the common for half an hour.*   ANT. difficult, awkward, strenuous.

easygoing *adj.* relaxed, carefree, calm, light.

eat *vb.* **1** consume, chew, devour, swallow: *Eat your spinach and you'll be as strong as Popeye.* **2** dine, lunch, breakfast; feast: *We eat at about seven o'clock in the evening, after my father returns from work.*

eavesdrop *vb.* listen in, overhear, tap, (*slang*) bug.

eccentric *adj.* odd, peculiar, strange.

echo *n.* reverberation, repetition, imitation.

economical *adj.* thrifty, sparing, careful, frugal. ANT. wasteful, lavish, unsparing.

ecstasy *n.* rapture, delight, pleasure. ANT. misery, unhappiness, agony.

edge *n.* border, rim, brink, threshold, boundary, margin: *The northern edge of the lake is where we swim. Don't cut yourself on the sharp edge of that piece of paper.* *vb.* **1** border, trim: *She edged the neck and sleeves of the dress with lace.* **2** inch, move little by little, sidle: *Roger edged over to Michele and grasped her hand.* ANT. *n.* middle, centre.

edgy *adj.* nervous, tense, irritable, touchy. ANT. tranquil, undisturbed, peaceful, bland.

edit *vb.* **1** revise, alter; compile, arrange: *It requires several people to edit manuscripts before books or newspapers can be published.* **2** be in charge of, direct, publish: *I know the man who edits the local newspaper.*

educate *vb.* teach, train, instruct.

education *n.* **1** instruction, training, schooling: *There are many excellent schools and colleges where you can get a good education.* **2** culture, learning, knowledge: *It is almost impossible to do the things you want to do without the proper education.*

eerie *adj.* weird, strange, fearful, spooky.

effect *n.* **1** result, outcome, consequence, end: *There was a time when the effect of being naughty was a sound spanking.* **2** significance, importance, meaning: *Some kinds of punishment have almost no effect at all.* *vb.* accomplish, achieve; cause, make; bring about: *Conservation of our natural resources has effected many changes in the development of large cities.* ANT. *n.* (1) cause.

effective *adj.* productive, efficient, practical. ANT. ineffective, wasteful, useless.

efficient *adj.* **1** effective, useful, serviceable: *The lever is a very efficient machine.* **2** competent, apt, adept, able, capable, talented, skilled, clever: *Phil has proved himself to be one of the most efficient workmen in the plant.* ANT. (1) useless, unworkable. (2) inefficient, ineffective, clumsy, awkward.

effort *n.* endeavour, attempt, try; struggle.

eject *vb.* force out, expel, emit; dismiss.

elaborate *adj.* ornate, ornamented, decorated, decorative; complicated, complex: *The Victorian style of architecture is one of the most elaborate that was ever developed.* *vb.* decorate, embellish; develop, detail: *The director of the department elaborated on his plan for reorganizing the* *division.* ANT. *adj.* simple, unadorned, stark.

elapse *vb.* pass (by), transpire.

elastic *adj.* flexible; resilient, pliable. ANT. rigid, inflexible, stiff.

elect *vb.* choose, select, vote for.

elegant *adj.* fine, refined, cultivated; tasteful, choice. ANT. crude, unpolished, coarse, tasteless.

elementary *adj.* **1** basic, primary, fundamental: *An elementary rule of competition is good sportsmanship.* **2** simple, uncomplicated: *The explanation of how the prisoner escaped from the locked cell is elementary.* ANT. (2) complex, complicated, involved, sophisticated.

elevate *vb.* raise, lift. ANT. lower, drop.

eligible *adj.* qualified, fit, worthy, suitable. ANT. ineligible, unqualified.

eliminate *vb.* remove, get rid of, leave out, omit.

elope *vb.* run away, abscond.

elude *vb.* evade, avoid, dodge.

embarrass *vb.* shame, abash, confuse.

emblem *n.* sign, token, symbol, badge, mark.

embrace *vb.* **1** hug, clasp: *When I found her in the crowd, I embraced my mother.* **2** include, contain, cover: *The categories of animal, vegetable, and mineral embrace most things on earth.* ANT. (2) exclude, bar.

emerge *vb.* come forth, appear; surface. ANT. recede, retreat, disappear.

emergency *n.* crisis, predicament.

eminent *adj.* distinguished, famous, celebrated, renowned, important, prominent. ANT. unknown, undistinguished, ordinary, commonplace.

emit *vb.* discharge, expel, eject.

emotion *n.* feeling, sentiment.

emotional *adj.* **1** passionate, ardent, stirring: *That display was one of the most emotional scenes I've ever seen.* **2** hysterical, overwrought, zealous, enthusiastic, impetuous: *I can't understand why my mother gets so emotional just because I keep breaking my arm playing football.* ANT. calm, tranquil, placid.

emphasis *n.* stress, accent.

emphasize *vb.* stress, affirm; highlight, underline.

emphatic *adj.* definite, positive, energetic, forceful, strong. ANT. quiet, lax, unforceful.

employ *vb.* **1** take on, engage, hire: *The company employs people according to their skill.* **2** use, apply, utilize: *He* *employed underhand tactics to achieve his own purposes.*

employee *n.* worker, labourer, wage-earner, servant. ANT. employer, boss.

employer *n.* boss, proprietor, owner, management, manager, supervisor, superintendent. ANT. worker, employee.

employment *n.* work; job, position.

empty *adj.* bare, unoccupied, void, blank: *Except for the gold coin, the box was empty. I sat staring at the empty sheet of paper, wondering what to write about.* *vb.* void, clear, unload, evacuate: *Empty that bucket of water outside.* ANT. *adj.* full, filled. *vb.* fill.

enable *vb.* allow, sanction; empower, authorize.

enchant *vb.* charm, fascinate, delight, bewitch. ANT. bore, tire.

enclose *vb.* surround, encircle.

encounter *vb.* meet, come across, face: *We encountered our old neighbours while shopping at the supermarket.* *n.* meeting; appointment, rendezvous: *Let me tell you about an encounter I once had with a king from the east.*

encourage *vb.* cheer up, hearten, help, strengthen, comfort. ANT. discourage, depress.

encouragement *n.* support, reassurance, inspiration, stimulus; approval, help. ANT. discouragement, disapproval.

end *n.* 1 extremity, termination: *After winding it for three hours, I finally came to the end of the string.* 2 limit, bound: *Before Einstein, scientists used to think that space had no end.* 3 finish, conclusion, close: *The symphony came to an end and we all applauded.* 4 aim, purpose, object, intent: *What end have you in reading all those books?* *vb.* stop, finish, terminate, close, halt: *I wish that nations could end all their arguing so we could have peace.* ANT. *n.* beginning, start, opening, launch. *vb.* begin, start, initiate.

endeavour *vb.* try, attempt, strive, struggle: *If you promise to be good, I'll endeavour to forgive you.* *n.* try, attempt, exertion, struggle: *She has made a serious endeavour to memorize her part in the school play.*

endless *adj.* infinite, unlimited, boundless, immeasurable.

endorse *vb.* 1 confirm, approve, sanction, uphold: *The chairman endorsed the comments from the speaker from the floor of the meeting.* 2 sign: *He endorsed the cheque before it could be cashed.*

endow *vb.* give, bestow. ANT. divest.

endure *vb.* 1 last, continue, persist: *The kinds of governments that limit the power of the people cannot endure for long.* 2

suffer, bear, undergo, experience: *I don't think I could endure the pain and discomfort of another broken arm.* ANT. (1) cease, end, perish, die.

enemy *n.* foe, adversary, opponent, antagonist, rival. ANT. friend, colleague, cohort, ally.

energetic *adj.* vigorous, active, forceful, potent. ANT. lazy, indolent, sluggish, lax.

energy *n.* power, force, strength, vigour. ANT. lethargy, feebleness.

enforce *vb.* urge, compel, insist on.

engage *vb.* 1 employ, hire, take on: *He was engaged as a departmental manager but soon rose to be a director.* 2 occupy, involve, absorb, engross: *She was engaged in a new research project.* ANT. (1) dismiss, fire, discharge.

engaged *adj.* 1 betrothed, spoken for: *Vera and Ed were engaged for only a few months before their marriage.* 2 occupied, busy: *I can't connect you now, the line is engaged.*

engaging *adj.* beguiling, enchanting, charming. ANT. boring, ordinary.

engine *n.* motor, machine; locomotive.

engross *vb.* absorb, occupy, involve, consume.

enhance *vb.* heighten, intensify, improve, increase.

enjoy *vb.* have a good time; delight (in), like.

enjoyment *n.* delight, pleasure, satisfaction. ANT. displeasure, dissatisfaction.

enlarge *vb.* increase, amplify, extend, expand, magnify. ANT. decrease, diminish, wane, shrink.

enlighten *vb.* inform, teach; illuminate. ANT. confuse.

enlist *vb.* enrol, enter, sign up, register. ANT. leave, abandon, quit.

enormous *adj.* huge, immense, gigantic, vast, colossal, stupendous. ANT. small, diminutive, tiny, slight, infinitesimal.

enquire *vb.* ask, question; investigate, examine.

enquiry *n.* examination, study, investigation.

enrage *vb.* infuriate, anger, madden. ANT. soothe, appease, calm.

enrol *vb.* enlist, register, sign up. ANT. leave, quit, abandon.

ensue *vb.* follow, succeed; arise, result. ANT. precede.

ensure *vb.* guarantee, secure, assure; necessitate, require.

enter *vb.* come *or* go in, turn into, make one's way into. ANT. leave, depart.

enterprise *n.* 1 project, venture, undertaking: *America is one of the few countries where a new enterprise can succeed.* 2

initiative, courage, boldness, drive, energy: *Bob has the enterprise necessary to do well in anything he gets involved in.*

enterprising *adj.* resourceful, energetic. ANT. indolent, lazy, unresourceful, sluggish.

entertain *vb.* amuse, divert; interest. ANT. bore, tire.

entertainment *n.* amusement, enjoyment, pleasure, fun; sport, games, recreation.

enthusiasm *n.* eagerness, zeal, earnestness. ANT. indifference, unconcern.

enthusiast *n.* fan, fanatic, devotee; supporter.

enthusiastic *adj.* eager, zealous, earnest. ANT. indifferent, aloof, unconcerned.

entice *vb.* attract, draw, lure, tempt.

entire *adj.* whole, complete; intact, undivided. ANT. partial, incomplete, separated, divided.

entitle *vb.* authorize, allow, empower.

entrance *n.* entry, door, access, gate, opening. ANT. exit.

entreat *vb.* beg, plead, implore.

entreaty *n.* appeal, plea, request, supplication.

envelop *vb.* surround, wrap, enclose, contain.

environment *n.* surroundings, habitat, conditions.

envisage *vb.* contemplate, expect, foresee.

envy *n.* jealousy, covetousness: *Millie regarded her sister's new coat with envy.* *vb.* covet; grudge: *You shouldn't envy your friends' property.*

epic *n.* saga, story, legend.

episode *n.* event, occurrence, incident.

equal *adj.* **1** equivalent; same, identical: *All men and women are supposed to be equal in the eyes of the law. Four is equal to two plus two.* **2** even, regular, uniform: *Equal rights are provided for in the constitution.* *vb.* match: *The wealthy man said that he would equal any contribution to the library fund.* *n.* match, counterpart; competitor, rival; double, twin: *Herr Schmidt is my equal in our firm in Germany.* ANT. *adj.* **(1)** unequal, different. **(2)** uneven, irregular.

equip *vb.* furnish, provide, supply, fit out.

equipment *n.* material, materials, utensils, apparatus.

equivalent *adj.* equal, same; comparable; interchangeable: *Turps and turps substitute have many equivalent uses.* *n.* counterpart, equal; match: *The equivalent of a tape recorder for recording pictures is a video recorder.*

equivocate *vb.* prevaricate, hedge; dodge.

era *n.* period, time, age.

eradicate *vb.* destroy, obliterate, stamp out.

erase *vb.* remove, obliterate, expunge; cancel. ANT. include, add.

erect *adj.* upright, vertical, straight: *Sometimes I get a little dizzy when I stand erect after bending over.* *vb.* build, construct, raise; set up: *The men erected the temporary building in less than two days.* ANT. *adj.* horizontal, flat. *vb.* demolish, knock down, flatten.

erode *vb.* wear down, grind down; deteriorate, decay.

errand *n.* job, task; mission.

erroneous *adj.* mistaken, wrong, inaccurate, incorrect, false, untrue. ANT. correct, right, accurate, true.

error *n.* mistake, oversight, inaccuracy, slip, blunder.

erupt *vb.* eject, emit; break out.

escalate *vb.* increase, intensify, make worse.

escape *vb.* **1** run away, steal away, flee: *Three prisoners have escaped from the county jail.* **2** avoid, elude, evade: *Running away through the swamp, the men escaped their pursuers.* *n.* flight, departure; release: *The criminal's escape was reported on the radio.*

escort *n.* guard, protection, convoy; guide: *The murderer was brought to the jail by an armed escort.* *vb.* accompany, attend, usher; guard, protect: *The shipment of gold was escorted by ten men with guns.*

especially *adv.* particularly, unusually, chiefly, specially.

essay *n.* composition, commentary; thesis, dissertation.

essence *n.* root, character, principle, nature, basis.

essential *adj.* important, necessary, vital, critical, indispensable: *In addition to knowing the subject he is teaching, it is essential that a teacher be kind and understanding.* *n.* necessity, requirement: *Oxygen is an essential for all mammals.* ANT. *adj.* unimportant, dispensable, inessential, unnecessary.

establish *vb.* found, form, set up, begin. ANT. discontinue, disperse, scatter.

estate *n.* property, land, grounds, holding.

esteem *vb.* prize, value, regard highly, revere, respect: *The students as well as the teachers esteemed the headmaster of the school as a great educationalist.* *n.* respect, reverence, regard, honour, admiration: *The captain was held in esteem by his crew.* ANT. *vb.* disdain, disregard, scorn. *n.* scorn, contempt.

estimate *vb.* value, gauge, evaluate, judge: *The expert estimated that our paintings were worth almost one million pounds.* *n.* value, evaluation: *The insurance company* *considered the estimate too high for repairing the old car.*

eternal *adj.* everlasting, endless, perpetual. ANT. brief, passing, temporary, transient.

etiquette *n.* decorum, (good) manners, social graces.

evacuate *vb.* withdraw, abandon, leave, desert.

evade *vb.* elude, avoid, escape, dodge. ANT. meet, confront, face.

evaporate *vb.* vaporize; disappear, vanish. ANT. appear; condense.

evasive *adj.* equivocating, deceitful, cagey. ANT. straightforward, open.

even *adj.* **1** level, smooth, flat: *It was easier to walk where the ground was even.* **2** equal, balanced, square: *If I give you the pound I owe you we'll be even.* **3** parallel: *The police car drew up even with us.* *adv.* just, exactly: *Even as I was watching, the sun disappeared and it started to rain.* ANT. (1) bumpy, irregular. (2) unequal, unbalanced. (3) divergent.

evening *n.* dusk, twilight, nightfall, sundown. ANT. dawn, sunrise.

event *n.* occurrence, incident, episode.

eventual *adj.* ultimate, consequent. ANT. current, present.

ever *adv.* **1** always, continuously, constantly: *The sea, like the clouds in the sky, is ever changing.* **2** at all, at any time: *Haven't you ever told a lie?* ANT. never.

evict *vb.* expel, dismiss, remove.

evidence *n.* **1** proof, testimony, grounds: *I know you think he took your umbrella, but have you any real evidence?* **2** indication, sign: *The best evidence I have is that I saw him using it when it was raining.*

evident *adj.* clear, plain, obvious, apparent. ANT. unclear, obscure, doubtful, uncertain.

evil *adj.* **1** sinful, immoral, wicked, bad: *Some people think that any kind of entertainment on Sunday is evil.* **2** harmful, injurious: *Drinking alcoholic beverages is an evil practice.* *n.* harm, woe; badness, wickedness, sin: *Evil to him who does evil.* ANT. *adj.* (1) virtuous, moral, upright, good. (2) beneficial, advantageous, useful. *n.* goodness, virtue, uprightness.

evoke *vb.* call up, summon, arouse.

evolve *vb.* develop, grow, emerge, result.

exact *adj.* correct, accurate, precise; faultless. ANT. inexact, inaccurate, faulty.

exactly *adv.* precisely, accurately; just.

exaggerate *vb.* overstate, magnify. ANT. minimize, understate, diminish.

examination *n.* **1** inspection, scrutiny, investigation: *The jury was cautioned to rely only on a careful examination of the testimony and the evidence.* **2** test: *I haven't yet revised for my geography examination.*

examine *vb.* inspect, investigate, scrutinize.

example *n.* instance; sample, specimen, model; illustration.

exasperate *vb.* annoy, infuriate, bother, disturb.

exceed *vb.* beat, surpass, outdo, excel.

excel *vb.* outdo, surpass, exceed.

excellence *n.* superiority, distinction. ANT. inferiority, poorness, badness.

excellent *adj.* fine, superior, wonderful, marvellous. ANT. poor, bad, terrible, substandard.

except *prep.* save, but, excepting, barring, excluding.

exceptional *adj.* unusual, different, strange, irregular, abnormal. ANT. unexceptional, ordinary, commonplace.

excess *adj.* profuse, abundant, immoderate: *The government checked up on all companies they thought might be making excess profits.* *n.* profusion, lavishness: *An excess of wealth can lead people to forget God.* ANT. *adj.* sparse, inconsequential, meagre.

excessive *adj.* immoderate, inordinate, extreme, extravagant. ANT. moderate, reasonable.

exchange *vb.* swap; transfer, trade, barter: *I exchanged the damaged article for a new one.* *n.* **1** trade, interchange: *In exchange for the three neckties, Suzie took a pair of warm gloves.* **2** market: *Don't invest all your money in the stock exchange.*

excite *vb.* stir up, arouse, stimulate; move. ANT. lull, bore.

excited *adj.* aroused, stimulated, restless, distracted. ANT. calm, composed.

excitement *n.* enthusiasm, stimulation, agitation.

exciting *adj.* moving, interesting, stimulating; impressive. ANT. boring, dull.

exclaim *vb.* shout, cry, speak out; yell.

exclamation *n.* outcry, shout, clamour.

exclude *vb.* keep out, shut out, bar. ANT. include, embrace, involve.

exclusion *n.* bar, exception, rejection. ANT. inclusion.

exclusive *adj.* **1** limited, restricted, restrictive, selective: *Do I have your exclusive permission to represent you?* **2** select, fashionable, choice: *We can't afford to stay at an exclusive* *hotel, so we go to a boarding house.* ANT. **(1)** general, unrestricted. **(2)** ordinary, unfashionable, common.

excuse *vb.* forgive, pardon: *Please excuse Phil for speaking rudely; he didn't mean it.* *n.* explanation, reason, plea, apology: *The teacher accepted Sam's excuse for lateness.* ANT. *vb.* condemn, denounce; deplore.

execute *vb.* **1** carry out, do, complete, achieve: *Every employee is expected to execute the orders given to him by his boss.* **2** kill, put to death, hang: *Three men convicted for murder were executed last week.*

executive *adj.* administrative, managing: *The executive powers of government are in Whitehall.* *n.* manager, administrator, official, supervisor: *The aircraft shuttle service between the cities is intended primarily for business executives.*

exempt (from) *vb.* release, free, excuse: *John was exempted from doing his exam because of his illness.* *adj.* free, excused, not liable, not subject to: *Some people are exempt from paying tax.*

exercise *n.* **1** practice, drill, training; gymnastics: *The old man said he did exercises every morning.* **2** use, application, employment: *The exercise of a citizen's rights is a duty.* *vb.* train, drill, practise: *The soldiers exercised on the parade ground.*

exertion *n.* effort, attempt, endeavour, strain.

exhaust *vb.* **1** wear out, tire, fatigue: *I was exhausted from chopping wood for three hours.* **2** use (up), consume; spend: *If man isn't careful he may exhaust many of the natural resources of the earth.* ANT. **(1)** refresh, renew. **(2)** replenish, replace.

exhibit *vb.* **1** show, display, demonstrate: *At the Trade Fair some manufacturers exhibited their future product designs.* **2** betray, reveal: *With a sneer Sophie exhibited her hatred of modern art.* *n.* show, display, demonstration, exhibition: *We saw an interesting exhibit of weaving at the country fair.* ANT. *vb.* conceal, hide, disguise.

exhibition *n.* display, presentation, show, demonstration, performance.

exhilarating *adj.* invigorating, enlivening, inspiring.

exile *vb.* banish, cast out, expel, deport: *The government once exiled criminals to distant colonies.* *n.* banishment, deportation, expulsion: *The exile of the king was forced by the revolutionaries.*

exist *vb.* be, live; survive, endure.

exit *n.* way out, door, gate. ANT. entrance, way in.

expand *vb.* enlarge, swell, inflate; bloat.   ANT. shrink, shrivel, contract.

expanse *n.* area, stretch, extent, reach, span, sweep.

expect *vb.* anticipate, await, look forward to.

expedition *n.* journey, voyage, trip, excursion.

expel *vb.* drive out *or* away, discharge; banish, deport, exile. ANT. invite; accept.

expend *vb.* use, consume, exhaust.   ANT. conserve, reserve, ration.

expense *n.* cost, price, charge, payment.

expensive *adj.* dear, costly, high-priced.   ANT. cheap, inexpensive, modest, low-priced.

experience *n.* **1** skill, wisdom, judgment; knowledge, contact; observation: *I have had a little experience in dealing with naughty children.* **2** incident, event, adventure: *His trip to the USA was an experience he'd never forget.*   *vb.* feel, live through, undergo: *No one can know what war is like until he has experienced it.*   ANT. *n.* inexperience, naivety.

experienced *adj.* skilled, accomplished, expert, practised, able, qualified.   ANT. inexperienced, untutored, naive, unpractised.

experiment *n.* test, trial; research: *Some people don't approve of doing experiments on animals.*   *vb.* test, prove, try, examine: *The scientists are going to experiment on human beings for the next space launch.*

expert *n.* authority, specialist: *It takes years of training to become an expert in Chinese art.*   *adj.* skilful, experienced, knowledgeable, skilled: *The factory has three job openings for expert tool makers.*   ANT. *adj.* unskilled, untrained, inexperienced.

expire *vb.* **1** terminate, end, cease: *My subscription expires with the next issue of the magazine.* **2** die: *The old man expired on the steps of the church.*

explain *vb.* **1** clarify, define, interpret: *Scientists cannot explain precisely how the earth began.* **2** justify, account for: *How do you explain what you were doing at the cinema when you were supposed to be at school?*

explanation *n.* **1** description, definition, interpretation: *Please give me an explanation of how a dictionary is written.* **2** account, justification; reason; excuse: *The teacher refused to accept Beth's explanation of why she was late.*

explicit *adj.* expressed, stated, plain.   ANT. implicit, implied.

explode *vb.* blow up, burst, detonate, go off.

exploit *n.* feat, accomplishment, achievement.

explore *vb.* investigate, examine.

explosion *n.* blast, burst, detonation, firing.

export *vb.* sell *or* send abroad. ANT. import.

expose *vb.* reveal, bare, uncover, display, disclose. ANT. conceal, hide, cover, mask.

express *vb.* state, declare: *A civilized person learns to express himself clearly.* *adj.* **1** specific, precise, exact, special: *I went to the market for the express purpose of buying celery and then forgot it.* **2** nonstop, quick, direct, rapid, fast: *The express train doesn't stop at those small stations.* ANT. *adj.* (2) local, stopping.

expression *n.* **1** statement, declaration: *The teacher asked for an expression of interest from all those who wanted to go to the museum.* **2** look; air: *Michele had a horrified expression on her face when we showed her the snake.*

exquisite *adj.* **1** delicate, dainty, elegant, beautiful: *Have you ever noticed the exquisite workmanship of the crown jewels?* **2** fine, excellent, superb, matchless, perfect: *The exquisite furnishings of the palace were known throughout the world.*

extend *vb.* **1** stretch, stretch out: *The forest extended as far as the eye could see.* **2** lengthen: *The ladder can be extended by as much again.* **3** give, offer, grant; yield: *We all extend to you our best wishes on your birthday.* ANT. (2) shorten, abbreviate, curtail.

extension *n.* stretching, expansion, enlargement, increase.

extensive *adj.* wide, broad, spacious, vast. ANT. confined, restricted, narrow.

extent *n.* degree, measure, amount, range.

exterior *n.* outside, face, surface, covering: *The exterior of our school is painted white.* *adj.* outside, outer, external: *Exterior paints are made with materials that resist weathering.* ANT. *n.* interior, inside, lining. *adj.* inner, internal, interior.

external *adj.* exterior, outer, outside. ANT. internal, interior, inner, inside.

extinct *adj.* dead, lost, gone, vanished. ANT. alive, present, extant, flourishing.

extinguish *vb.* put out, quench, smother, choke.

extra *adj.* additional, supplementary, another; spare, reserve.

extract *vb.* draw out, withdraw, pull out, remove: *The knight extracted the sword from the stone where it had been embedded.* *n.* essence, distillate: *I bought a jar of yeast extract from the grocer's.* ANT. *vb.* insert, introduce, penetrate.

extraordinary *adj.* unusual, exceptional, rare, uncommon, remarkable. ANT. ordinary, commonplace, usual.

extravagant *adj.* wasteful, lavish, excessive. ANT. frugal, economical, prudent, thrifty, provident.

extreme *adj.* **1** utmost, greatest: *Tim's extreme nervousness made his hands shake.* **2** furthest, outermost, endmost, ultimate: *In the picture at the extreme right you can see a mouse.* **3** excessive, immoderate: *This morning I am suffering from an extreme pain in the neck.* *n.* end, limit, extremity: *I can understand your being angry, but jumping up and down is going to extremes.* ANT. *adj.* (**3**) modest, moderate, reasonable.

f

fable *n.* 1 parable, tale, legend, myth, story: *Aesop's Fables are among the most popular in the world.* 2 falsehood, fib, fiction, tale; lie: *That story about his getting a medal for swimming was a complete fable.*

fabric *n.* cloth, material, textile.

fabricate *vb.* make, manufacture, assemble, construct, form. ANT. destroy, demolish, raze.

fabulous *adj.* fantastic, unbelievable, amazing, astonishing, astounding. ANT. commonplace, ordinary.

face *n.* 1 look, expression; features, visage, countenance: *Roger made a funny face when the teacher wasn't looking. She has a friendly face.* 2 front, façade: *The face of the cliff was too steep for us to climb.* *vb.* meet, encounter, confront: *I'll never be able to face Louis now that I know he tried to kiss my sister.* ANT. *vb.* avoid, evade, shun.

facetious *adj.* jocular, joking, flippant.

facility *n.* 1 ease, skill, skilfulness, ability: *The instructor skis down that steep slope with such great facility.* 2 equipment, material: *This laboratory is equipped with every modern research facility.* ANT. (1) difficulty, effort, labour.

fact *n.* truth, certainty, actuality, reality.

faction *n.* (splinter) group, clique, gang, party.

factor *n.* element; part, constituent; cause.

factory *n.* (assembly) plant, workshop, shop.

factual *adj.* real, actual; accurate. ANT. invented, fabricated, incorrect.

faculty *n.* ability, capacity, talent.

fad *n.* craze, fashion, vogue. ANT. custom, convention.

fade *vb.* 1 pale, bleach, discolour: *These curtains have faded from being in the bright sunlight.* 2 diminish, weaken, fail: *My strength began to fade and I was afraid I couldn't hold on any longer.* ANT. (2) increase, grow.

fail *vb.* 1 fall short, miss, founder: *The explorer failed in his attempt to find the source of the Nile.* 2 disappoint: *Don't fail me now that I've invested so much in your success.* 3 fade, weaken; dwindle: *Her strength failed when she reached the top.* ANT. (1) succeed.

failure *n.* nonperformance, breakdown, collapse, loss, decline. ANT. success, achievement, accomplishment.

faint *adj.* **1** dim, faded, indistinct: *The writing on the wall of the tomb was too faint to read.* **2** feeble, weak, halfhearted: *We heard faint cries coming from inside the chest.* *vb.* collapse, swoon, lose consciousness: *Ted's mother fainted when the hospital phoned about his accident.* ANT. *adj.* (**1**) clear, sharp, distinct. (**2**) strong, forceful, loud.

fainthearted *adj.* timid, shy, bashful; cowardly. ANT. brave, courageous, stouthearted, fearless.

fair[1] *adj.* **1** just, impartial, unbiased, objective, unprejudiced; honest: *The umpire made a fair decision when he said the batsman was out.* **2** ordinary, average, not bad: *My marks for maths were fair.* **3** blonde, light, white: *She had fair hair but a swarthy skin.* **4** beautiful: *Every knight yearned to save a fair damsel in distress.* **5** sunny, pleasant, bright, unclouded: *The weather man predicted it would be fair for our picnic tomorrow.* ANT. (**1**) unfair, unjust, biased. (**3**) dark, black, swarthy. (**4**) stormy, cloudy, threatening.

fair[2] *n.* exhibit, exhibition, festival, bazaar, carnival: *Are you coming to the fair with us?*

fairy *n.* pixie, sprite, elf, brownie.

faith *n.* **1** trust, reliance, belief: *I have faith in everything you say.* **2** belief, religion, creed: *The rights of every human being are equal regardless of their faith.* ANT. (**1**) mistrust, distrust, disbelief.

faithful *adj.* **1** loyal, devoted, trustworthy, trusty, true: *My dog is the only faithful friend I have.* **2** credible, accurate, strict: *The artist had painted a faithful copy of the picture.* ANT. (**1**) disloyal, faithless, treacherous. (**2**) inaccurate, erroneous, wrong.

fake *adj.* false, counterfeit, phoney: *The counterfeiters were printing fake pound notes until they were arrested.* *n.* fraud, cheat; counterfeit, forgery, imitation: *The man who promised to cure your cold is a fake. This diploma is a fake.* ANT. *adj.* genuine, real, authentic.

fall *vb.* **1** drop, descend; plunge, topple: *After lightning had struck it in the storm, the tree began to fall.* **2** die: *Two thousand brave soldiers fell in the last battle of the war.* **3** lower, decrease, diminish: *The price of sugar has fallen during the last month.* *n.* drop, decline, collapse, spill: *Prices haven't taken a fall like that for many years.* ANT. *vb.* (**1**) rise, soar, ascend. (**3**) rise, increase, climb. *n.* rise, ascent, increase.

fallacy *n.* error, inaccuracy, inconsistency.

fallible *adj.* erring, untrustworthy; imperfect. ANT. infallible, inerrant; trustworthy.

fallow *adj.* uncultivated, unplanted; neglected; inactive.

false *adj.* **1** untrue, wrong, fanciful, inaccurate: *I knew that your excuse was false, because I saw you do it.* **2** artificial, fake, unreal: *False eyelashes don't suit you.* ANT. (1) true, accurate. (2) real, authentic, genuine.

falsehood *n.* fib, story, untruth, lie. ANT. truth.

falter *vb.* stumble, hesitate, tremble.

fame *n.* name, reputation, renown, honour, glory. ANT. anonymity.

famed *adj.* renowned, known; famous. ANT. unknown, anonymous, obscure.

familiar *adj.* **1** known, common, frequent, well-known: *That song sounds familiar—I think it's* Greensleeves. **2** close, intimate: *Jennie was a familiar friend at our house.* **3** well-acquainted, well-versed: *I am quite familiar with the rules of the club.* ANT. (1) unfamiliar, unknown, foreign, alien. (2) rare, distant. **3** ignorant, unaware.

familiarity *n.* knowledge, understanding, awareness, comprehension. ANT. ignorance.

family *n.* relatives, tribe, relations.

famine *n.* want, hunger, starvation. ANT. plenty.

famished *adj.* starving, hungry, ravenous.

famous *adj.* well-known, renowned, celebrated, famed, eminent, illustrious. ANT. unknown, obscure, anonymous.

fanatic *n.* enthusiast, zealot, devotee; fiend; addict; (*informal*) crank.

fancy *n.* imagination, fantasy; taste: *My mother said that the pink tiles in the kitchen didn't suit her fancy.* *adj.* **1** ornate, ornamented, elaborate: *The decorations on that dress are too fancy for my taste.* **2** special, deluxe: *We received a basket of fancy fruit for Christmas.* *vb.* like, desire, wish: *I just fancy an ice cream.* ANT. *adj.* plain, unadorned, simple, undecorated.

fantastic *adj.* unbelievable, incredible, unreal, unimaginable.

far *adj.* distant, removed, remote. ANT. close, near.

farce *n.* humour, comedy, burlesque; skit.

fare *n.* charge, tariff, ticket; fee.

fascinate *vb.* attract, charm, bewitch, enchant. ANT. bore.

fashion *n.* **1** manner, way, method: *The teacher spoke to the children in a friendly fashion.* **2** style, mode, custom, vogue: *Alexandra's mother dresses in the fashion of the 1930s.* *vb.*

make, shape, mould, form: *The potter fashioned the vase in a few minutes.*

fashionable *adj.* stylish, chic, modish, smart. ANT. unfashionable, dowdy.

fast *adj.* **1** quick, rapid, swift, speedy: *A fast car could get me to the airport in an hour* **2** secure, solid, staunch, firm: *Before leaving the house, we made sure that the lock was fast on the door.* *adv.* **1** quickly, rapidly, swiftly, speedily: *How did you get back here so fast?* **2** tightly, securely, firmly: *The fishermen held fast to the overturned boat.* ANT. *adj.* **(1)** slow, crawling. **(2)** loose, insecure.

fasten *vb.* attach, fix, join, secure. ANT. loosen, loose, free, release, unclasp.

fat *adj.* **1** fatty, oily, greasy: *The doctor told me not to eat so many fat foods.* **2** obese, plump, stout, chubby: *Betty used to be fat, but since she has started slimming, she has lost a lot of weight.* **3** thick, wide: *The lawyer carried a fat briefcase into court.* ANT. **(2)** thin, lean, emaciated, slim, scrawny.

fatal *adj.* **1** deadly, lethal, mortal: *The wound from the sword proved to be fatal, and the soldier died that night.* **2** disastrous; critical, decisive: *Any mistake in timing during a rocket launching could be fatal for the entire project.*

fate *n.* fortune, luck, chance, destiny.

fatherly *adj.* paternal, paternalistic, protective, kind.

fathom *vb.* penetrate, comprehend, understand.

fatigue *n.* weariness, exhaustion, tiredness.

fatten *vb.* stuff, feed; cram.

fault *n.* **1** defect, imperfection, flaw, blemish, weakness: *The mechanic could find no fault with the engine in my car.* **2** blame, responsibility: *It's your own fault you have a cold if you won't wear your scarf.*

faulty *adj.* defective, imperfect, damaged, broken. ANT. perfect, flawless, whole.

favour *n.* good deed, good turn, service, kindness: *He did Ken a favour by helping him to clean his car.* *vb.* prefer, support, want to: *We favour going to Germany for our holiday.* ANT. *vb.* disapprove of.

favourable *adj.* hopeful, encouraging, promising, beneficial. ANT. unfavourable, discouraging.

favourite *n.* pet, darling: *Jane is the teacher's favourite.* *adj.* favoured, preferred, liked: *My favourite ice cream is chocolate.*

fear *n.* fright, dread, terror, alarm, dismay, anxiety: *As the* *killer approached him with knife drawn, Ron felt his fear overcome him.* *vb.* dread, be afraid of: *This snake is completely harmless, and you have nothing to fear.*

fearful *adj.* afraid, frightened; apprehensive.

fearless *adj.* brave, courageous, bold. ANT. fearful, timid, cowardly.

feasible *adj.* practicable; possible, likely; probable.

feast *n.* banquet; dinner, barbecue: *After the wedding ceremony, we were all treated to a feast at the bride's father's home.* *vb.* dine, banquet: *We feasted on venison and roasted ox.*

feat *n.* achievement, act, deed.

feature *n.* quality, characteristic, trait: *One of the features of life in a democratic country is political independence.* *vb.* star, promote: *Last week the television programme featured my favourite pop star.*

fee *n.* pay, payment, remuneration.

feeble *adj.* weak, frail; ineffective, powerless. ANT. strong, powerful, potent.

feed *vb.* nourish, satisfy: *My father had six mouths to feed and always worked very hard.* *n.* fodder, forage, food: *The farmer stocked up on feed for his cattle for the winter.*

feel *vb.* **1** touch, stroke; grasp, grip: *The blind lady felt the raised dots in her Braille hymnbook.* **2** experience, sense; perceive: *I tried to feel pity for the doomed criminal.*

feeling *n.* **1** emotion, sentiment, sympathy: *Finding her lost kitten gave Susan a feeling of joy.* **2** attitude, belief, thought, opinion: *My mother had a feeling that I would do well in school.*

feign *vb.* pretend, simulate, fabricate.

fellow *n.* man, chap; boy.

female *adj.* feminine, womanly. ANT. male, masculine.

fence *n.* rail, barrier, paling.

ferocious *adj.* fierce, savage, bloodthirsty, wild. ANT. gentle, playful, calm, harmless.

fertile *adj.* productive, rich, fruitful. ANT. barren, sterile, unproductive.

fervent *adj.* passionate, ardent, eager, zealous.

festival *n.* celebration, carnival.

festive *adj.* merry, gay, joyful, joyous. ANT. sad, mournful, morose, gloomy.

fetching *adj.* *Informal:* attractive, charming, pleasing.

feud *n.* quarrel, argument, dispute, strife.

fever *n.* illness, disease, sickness.

fiasco *n.* disaster, calamity, catastrophe.

fickle *adj.* changeable, capricious, inconstant. ANT. steady, constant.

fiction *n.* story, tale, novel.

field *n.* land, ground, plot, patch; meadow, pasture.

fierce *adj.* savage, ferocious, furious, violent, wild. ANT. gentle, peaceful, harmless.

fight *n.* battle, war, conflict, combat: *When the enemy gunboat fired a shot across our bows, we knew we had a fight on our hands.* *vb.* combat, battle, struggle: *Brothers shouldn't fight each other.*

figure *n.* **1** pattern, design: *The wallpaper has some pretty figures on it.* **2** form, outline; shape; mould; frame: *We could see the figure of a man against the sky at the top of the hill.*

file[1] *n.* **1** line, row, rank, column: *The soldiers stood in one long file.* **2** cabinet, index, portfolio, pigeonhole: *He kept all his papers in a file.* *vb.* **1** classify, arrange, index: *The secretary filed her boss's letters.*

file[2] *n.* steel, sharpener: *He used the file to remove the loose ends.* *vb.* smooth, scrape, rub down: *The craftsman filed the wood.*

fill *vb.* stuff, pack, plug; occupy. ANT. empty.

filth *n.* dirt, foulness, pollution, sewage.

filthy *adj.* dirty, foul; polluted, contaminated. ANT. clean, pure, unspoiled.

final *adj.* last, ultimate, terminal, concluding. ANT. first, initial, beginning, starting.

find *vb.* discover, come across; observe.

fine *adj.* **1** excellent, superior, superb, choice, exquisite, perfect: *After living in France, we developed a taste for fine foods and wines.* **2** thin, minute; powdered: *The holes in the strainer are too fine to allow the tea leaves to pass through. The stone was ground down to a fine consistency.* ANT. **(1)** inferior, poor, squalid. **(2)** coarse, broad.

finish *vb.* **1** end, terminate, close, conclude: *Please finish whatever you are doing so that you can help me wash the dishes.* **2** consume, use up, complete: *Finish your first course and then we'll see if you deserve ice cream for dessert.* *n.* **1** conclusion, end, close, termination: *I've written a new finish for my play; do you want to read it?* **2** surface, gloss, polish: *We had to have a new finish put on the table because you spilled paint on it.* ANT. *vb.* **(1)** begin, start, open. *n.* **(1)** opening, start, beginning.

fire *n.* blaze, burning, conflagration, combustion.

firm *adj.* **1** rigid, stiff, solid; unchanging, inflexible, steadfast, unshakable: *Quentin was firm in his conviction that his father was innocent of the theft. The house was on a firm foundation.* **2** compact, dense, hard: *For a really sound sleep, I prefer a firm mattress.* *n.* company, business, concern; partnership: *My uncle works for a firm that manufactures paint.* ANT. *adj.* (1) limp, drooping, soft, weak. (2) soft, squashy.

fit *adj.* **1** suited, suitable, appropriate, proper, fitting: *It wasn't a fit night out for man or beast.* **2** ready, prepared, suited, fitted: *We had all our equipment and were fit to go camping.* **3** healthy, strong; sound, well: *The doctor said I could keep fit if I continued to get exercise.* *vb.* **1** hang, be comfortable for: *That dress doesn't fit you at all.* **2** agree, suit, harmonize: *They made the punishment fit the crime.* **3** equip, provide: *We were fitted out for the safari by the biggest store in London.* *n.* **1** fitting, tailoring; measure: *The shoes were a good fit.* **2** spasm, convulsion, seizure, attack: *Dinah was doubled up in a fit of laughing.*

fitting *adj.* suitable, apt, proper. ANT. unsuitable, inappropriate, improper.

fix *vb.* **1** attach, rivet, fasten, pin, tie, secure, affix: *The teacher fixed the sign to the notice board.* **2** repair, mend: *The man at the shop on the corner is good at fixing record players.* **3** determine, establish, settle, arrange: *We fixed a time for my next appointment.* *n. Informal:* predicament, dilemma: *There he was, alone in the middle of London, with no money: in a real fix.*

flabbergast *vb.* astound, amaze, confound.

flabby *adj.* loose; weak, yielding.

flake *n.* layer, chip; wafer, slice, shaving.

flame *n.* fire, blaze.

flap *vb.* wave, flutter, fly.

flare *n.* flash, blaze, sparkle, glimmer.

flash *n.* **1** flame, flare: *The people's faces were lit up by the flash from the camera.* **2** instant, wink, second, twinkling: *In a flash, Santa Claus was back up the chimney.* *vb.* gleam, sparkle, twinkle, glitter: *Maureen's eyes flashed with anger.*

flat *adj.* **1** level, even, smooth: *The land was as flat as a pancake as far as the eye could see.* **2** dull, uninteresting, boring, lifeless: *We all found the play a little flat.* *adv.* evenly, smoothly: *That rug should lie flat on the floor. The*

poster was pasted down flat against the wall. ANT. *adj.*
(1) uneven, rough, bumpy. (2) interesting, stimulating.

flatter *vb.* praise, adulate; grovel.

flavour *n.* 1 taste, savour, tang: *This pie has the flavour of lemon.* 2 quality, characteristic, essence, character: *That painting really gives you the flavour of the sea.* *vb.* season, spice: *Vickie flavoured the salad with mayonnaise.*

flaw *n.* imperfection, spot, fault, blemish, defect.

flee *vb.* run away, desert, escape.

fleeting *adj.* temporary, brief, passing, swift. ANT. permanent, fixed, stable, lasting.

flesh *n.* fat, meat, tissue.

flexible *adj.* 1 elastic, supple, pliant, pliable: *You'll need a flexible wire to reach into that clogged drain.* 2 yielding, easy, agreeable, adaptable: *My plans for this evening are flexible, so I can meet you at any time.* ANT. inflexible, rigid, firm, unyielding, fixed.

flicker *vb.* twinkle, glimmer, flash.

flight *n.* 1 departure, leaving, take-off: *The plane's flight was delayed by the fog.* 2 fleeing, running away, escape; retreat: *The flight of the Israelites from Egypt is recorded in the Bible.*

flimsy *adj.* weak, wobbly, frail, fragile. ANT. strong, firm, stable.

fling *vb.* toss, throw, pitch: *Walter flung the curtain aside and stepped into the room.* *n.* party, celebration, fun: *Roberta has had her fling and can now get back to more serious things.*

flippant *adj.* frivolous, offhand; impudent, rude, impertinent. ANT. serious, sober, earnest.

flirt *vb.* make advances, toy with, ogle at.

flit *vb.* fly, skim, dart.

float *vb.* drift, flow; swim; sail. ANT. sink, go down.

flock *n.* group, gathering; herd, flight, swarm, school.

flog *vb.* beat, whip, thrash, strike.

flood *n.* deluge, overflow: *After two weeks of rain, we knew that the river would rise over its banks and cause a flood.* *vb.* deluge, overflow, inundate: *When the sink drain clogged up, the water flooded the kitchen floor.*

floor *n.* ground, bottom, surface.

flop *vb.* 1 bend, fall, tumble, slump: *Relaxed, her head flopped backwards.* 2 *Informal:* fail, founder: *The whole scheme flopped when we couldn't raise any interest.* ANT. (2) succeed.

flourish *vb.* 1 grow, succeed, prosper: *Because of his hard* *work, Dick's business flourished, and he was soon employing twenty people.* **2** wave, brandish: *The Samurai flourished his great sword.* ANT. **(1)** decline, die.

flow *vb.* **1** stream, pour, run: *The mill stream flowed right under the middle of the building.* **2** spurt, squirt, gush, spout: *We couldn't stop the oil from flowing out of the broken pipe.* *n.* outpouring, discharge, stream: *The doctor first tried to stop the flow of blood from the wound.*

fluctuate *vb.* waver, vary, falter.

fluent *adj.* eloquent, articulate, glib.

fluid *n.* liquid; gas: *Water is one of the most common fluids on earth.* *adj.* flowing, liquid, liquefied, running: *You have to heat the butter or lard until it is fluid for this recipe.*

flush *adj.* even, level, flat.

fly *vb.* **1** soar, wing, hover, flit: *At the sound of our footsteps, the scarlet bird flew away.* **2** flee, escape; rush, dart: *The minute the door was left open unguarded, the prisoners flew out.*

foam *n.* lather, froth.

focus *n.* centre, middle, nucleus, core.

foe *n.* enemy, adversary, antagonist, opponent. ANT. friend, ally.

fog *n.* **1** mist, cloud, haze: *We couldn't see our way in the dense fog.* **2** confusion, daze, stupor: *Millie is in such a fog that she hardly recognizes her friends.*

foil[1] *n.* **1** metal, sheet, leaf: *The mirror had tin foil on the back of it.* **2** contrast, setting, background: *The brooch acted as a superb foil against the girl's jacket.*

foil[2] *vb.* frustrate, thwart, baffle, hamper: *The police foiled the robbers' plans by turning up just as they were about to break into the bank.*

fold *vb.* bend, double, crease: *After folding your paper in half, write your name at the top on the left.* *n.* lap, pleat, tuck, overlap: *Put two folds into the napkin when you set the table.*

folder *n.* binder, pocket, envelope.

follow *vb.* **1** succeed, ensue: *The mother duck swims along first, and the baby ducklings follow.* **2** obey, heed, observe: *If you want to play any game at all, you must follow the rules.* **3** chase, pursue, track; trace: *Bloodhounds can follow even the faintest scent.* ANT. **(1)** lead, precede.

follower *n.* pupil, disciple, adherent. ANT. leader, director.

following *n.* supporters, disciples, public.

folly *n.* silliness, stupidity, absurdity. ANT. wisdom; sensibleness.

fond adj. **1** attached, partial: *I am very fond of chocolate ice cream.* **2** affectionate, loving, tender: *Julie was aware of the fond looks being given her by Patrick.*

fondness n. liking, affection, partiality. ANT. unfriendliness, hostility.

food n. sustenance, refreshment, nourishment, provisions.

fool n. **1** clown, jester: *The king always insisted on having the fool at his side.* **2** idiot, dunce, simpleton, blockhead, ninny, nincompoop, (*informal*) nitwit, oaf: *If you think you can commit a crime without getting caught you are a fool.* vb. **1** jest, joke, play: *I didn't mean anything cruel—I was just fooling.* **2** deceive, trick, hoax, hoodwink: *The magician had us all fooled—we were sure the hat was empty, but he pulled two rabbits from it!*

foolish adj. silly, senseless, stupid, simple. ANT. sensible, sound, reasonable, rational.

forbid vb. ban, prohibit. ANT. allow, permit, let.

force n. strength, power, energy, might: *The force of the wind is strong enough to knock down that building.* vb. **1** compel, oblige, coerce, make: *I was forced to accept a purple car because it was the only one available.* **2** drive, impel, push: *We forced our way through the crowd.*

forecast vb. predict, foresee; prophesy: *He forecast that he would win the race—and he did.* n. prediction, prognosis: *Let's hear the weather forecast to find out what the weather will be like tomorrow.*

forefather n. ancestor, forebear; predecessor.

foreign adj. strange, unfamiliar, alien, different, exotic. ANT. familiar, ordinary, commonplace.

foreigner n. alien, stranger, outsider, newcomer. ANT. native, resident.

foreman n. supervisor, superintendent, overseer, boss.

foresight n. prudence, forethought, provision.

forest n. wood, woods, woodland, grove, copse.

forever adv. always, evermore, everlastingly. ANT. temporarily, fleetingly.

forfeit vb. lose, give up, abandon, relinquish.

forget vb. **1** think no more of, not remember: *We should both forgive and forget other people's wrongs.* **2** disregard, neglect, overlook, ignore: *You can forget Old Scottie when you're picking the football team; he's not played for years now.* ANT. (1) remember, recall.

forgive vb. pardon, excuse. ANT. censure, blame.

forgo vb. release, relinquish, renounce.

forlorn *adj.* miserable, desolate, wretched.

form *n.* **1** shape, figure, outline: *The prince disappeared, then reappeared in the form of a frog.* **2** kind, sort, type, style: *Vinyl is one of the many forms of plastic.* **3** blank, paper, document: *Please fill in this form on both sides.* **4** mould, frame, pattern: *My father made this form so that I could cast my own lead soldiers.* *vb.* **1** mould, fashion, make, model, construct: *As we watched, the glassblower formed a goblet from a blob of molten glass.* **2** instruct, teach, develop, educate: *Many people believe that parents have more influence in forming a child's mind than do teachers.* **3** take shape, grow, develop, appear: *I have watched clouds form in the sky directly over that mountain.*

formal *adj.* **1** conventional, established: *The formal way to do it is to send in an application.* **2** ceremonial, dignified, solemn, stately: *There will be a formal marriage ceremony at the church, and you are expected to wear formal clothes.* ANT. informal, unceremonious.

former *adj.* previous, earlier, erstwhile, one-time. ANT. present, current; future.

formidable *adj.* imposing, alarming, terrifying, frightful, terrible, horrifying.

formula *n.* **1** form, method, order, procedure: *Is there a formula for a happy life? Yes, there is!* **2** equation, rule: *The chemical formula for water is H_2O.*

forsake *vb.* desert, give up, abandon, forgo.

fort *n.* fortress, castle, citadel.

forth *adv.* forward, onward, out.

forthcoming *adj.* future, approaching, prospective, expected.

forthright *adj.* direct, honest, candid, frank, outspoken. ANT. devious, tricky, roundabout.

forthwith *adv.* immediately, at once, without delay.

fortify *vb.* strengthen, bolster, buttress.

fortunate *adj.* lucky, blessed, charmed. ANT. unfortunate, unlucky, cursed.

fortune *n.* **1** luck, chance, lot, fate: *By good fortune, the gypsies were very kind to the lost boy.* **2** wealth, riches: *Nellie will inherit a fortune when her grandfather dies.*

forward *adv.* onward, ahead: *We marched forward till given the order to halt.* *adj.* **1** front, first, leading, foremost: *The forward carriages sank into the marsh before they could stop.* **2** rude, bold, arrogant, fresh, impertinent, impudent: *Manuel's forward attitude made him few friends.* ANT. *adv.*

backward, rearward. *adj.* (1) rear, last. (2) reserved, shy, demure, retiring.

foster *vb.* promote, support, encourage, nourish, cherish.

foul *adj.* 1 dirty, filthy, unclean, impure, polluted: *The people who live in that factory town are always breathing foul air.* 2 evil, wicked, vile, sinful: *What a foul deed! stabbing someone in the back!* 3 stormy, bad, rainy: *We sailed through some foul weather as we rounded Cape Horn.* ANT. (1) clean, pure, immaculate. (2) saintly, good. (3) clear, sunny, calm.

found *vb.* establish, organize.

foundation *n.* basis, establishment, ground.

fountain *n.* spray, jet, spring, stream.

fracas *n.* dispute, brawl, (*informal*) scrap.

fracture *n.* break, crack; rupture: *There was a slight fracture in the dam, but it increased to a dangerous size overnight.* *vb.* break, crack; rupture: *When I fell, my arm was fractured in two places.*

fragile *adj.* delicate, breakable, frail, weak. ANT. sturdy, hardy, stout, strong.

fragment *n.* bit, part, piece, scrap, remnant. ANT. whole.

fragrance *n.* smell, odour, aroma, perfume, scent.

fragrant *adj.* sweet-smelling, aromatic, perfumed, scented. ANT. noxious, smelly.

frail *adj.* weak, fragile, breakable, feeble, delicate. ANT. strong, sturdy, hardy, powerful.

frame *n.* 1 skeleton, framework, support: *The frame of this house is too weak to support a slate roof.* 2 border, case: *The paintings in the museum have gold frames around them.* *vb.* 1 mount, enclose, border: *I have sent the painting of my father out to be framed.* 2 plan, construct, compose, outline: *Let us try to frame our activities for the next few months.*

framework *n.* structure, skeleton, frame; organization.

frank *adj.* candid, open, forthright, honest, unreserved, sincere, direct. ANT. devious, dishonest, tricky.

frantic *adj.* wild, frenzied, delirious, excited; hysterical, mad, crazy. ANT. calm, tranquil, composed.

fraud *n.* deceit, trickery, treachery.

fraudulent *adj.* fake, deceitful, tricky, dishonest.

freak *n.* abnormality, oddity, curiosity.

free *adj.* 1 independent, unrestrained, unrestricted, liberated: *Britain is a free country, but that doesn't mean it costs nothing to live there.* 2 gratuitous, without charge: *The shop was*

*giving away one free bar of chocolate for every five you
bought.* **3** loose, unfastened, unattached: *We tied one end of
the string to a tree and fixed the balloon to the free end.* *vb.*
release, liberate, set free, emancipate: *The hunter freed the
animals caught in the traps. William Wilberforce wanted to
free the slaves.* ANT. *vb.* enslave, entrap, snare.

freedom *n.* liberty, independence, release. ANT. slavery,
servitude, bondage.

freeze *vb.* **1** harden, solidify, ice up *or* over: *The lake near us
froze during the winter.* **2** cool, refrigerate, chill: *My mother
froze the meat by putting it in the freezer.*

freight *n.* cargo, load, shipping, shipment.

frenzy *n.* excitement, agitation; craze.

frequent *adj.* common, customary, habitual: *The wren was a
frequent visitor to the birdtable in our garden.* *vb.* go to,
visit often, attend: *The teacher noticed that you have not been
frequenting the library lately.* ANT. *adj.* infrequent, uncommon.

fresh *adj.* **1** new, crisp, raw; recent, current; late: *These eggs
are very fresh. The farmer had already planted a fresh crop of
wheat.* **2** pure, sweet, drinkable, safe: *The fresh water from
the stream tasted delicious to the mountaineers.* **3** rested,
healthy, energetic, vigorous: *The cowboy exchanged his tired
horse for a fresh one.* **4** different, original: *We need some
fresh ideas for the project.* **5** inexperienced, unskilled,
untrained: *Let's give that young fellow a chance even though
he's fresh from college.* ANT. **(1)** stale, deteriorated; musty;
old, out-of-date. **(2)** impure, polluted, foul. **(3)**
exhausted, tired. **(4)** stale, unoriginal. **(5)** mature, experienced.

fret *vb.* worry, anguish, grieve; distress, torment.

friction *n.* **1** rubbing, abrasion, wearing away: *The friction of
my bicycle wheel against the mudguard slowed my bike
down.* **2** disagreement, tension, conflict, discord: *I came
down for breakfast and could tell there was some friction
between my parents.*

friend *n.* companion, acquaintance, chum, mate. ANT.
enemy, opponent, foe.

friendly *adj.* kind, helpful, sympathetic, kindly. ANT.
unfriendly, antagonistic.

fright *n.* fear, terror, alarm, panic.

frighten *vb.* scare, terrify, panic.

frightful *adj.* awful, horrible, alarming, distressing.

fringe *n.* border, edge; hem, edging, trimming.

fritter (away) *vb.* waste, squander, misspend.

frivolous *adj.* silly, trivial, light, foolish. ANT. serious, sensible.

front *n.* **1** face, façade: *The front of the house is painted green.* **2** beginning, start, head: *Paul always tries to sneak in at the front of the line for ice cream.* *vb.* face, border, look out on: *Our house fronts on the main street.* ANT. *n.* (**1, 2**) back, rear.

frontier *n.* boundary, border.

froth *n.* foam, lather, spray; scum.

frown *vb.,n.* scowl, grimace, glare: *The teacher frowned sternly at the children's misbehaviour, but did not say anything. Paul gave a frown as he didn't want to do what his mother asked.*

fruitful *adj.* fertile, productive, rich, abundant. ANT. barren, lean, unproductive, fruitless.

fruitless *adj.* sterile, unproductive, barren; vain, futile. ANT. fruitful, productive, fertile.

frustrate *vb.* defeat, discourage, prevent. ANT. satisfy.

frustration *n.* disappointment, prevention, thwarting.

fuel *n.* energy source, substance, material.

fugitive *n.* runaway, deserter, refugee.

fulfil *vb.* complete, do, accomplish, realize, effect, carry out.

full *adj.* **1** filled, complete; replete: *Don't talk with your mouth full. Since the heavy rains, the reservoir has been full.* **2** taken, occupied, in use: *Get to the cinema early because later on, every seat will be full.* ANT. empty, vacant.

fumble *vb.* **1** grope, feel for: *He fumbled for his keys in his pocket.* **2** bungle, botch, mishandle: *He fumbled the speech because he was so nervous.*

fume *n.* smoke, vapour, steam, gas: *The fumes from the back of the car were very strong.* *vb.* **1** smoke: *The smoke-stack fumed with a yellow fog.* **2** rage, rave, storm: *The customer was fuming because the waiter spilled the soup over his suit.*

fun *n.* pleasure, amusement, entertainment, merriment, enjoyment, sport, gaiety.

function *n.* **1** use; purpose; activity, operation: *The function of a teacher is to teach; that of a student, to learn. The function of a watch is to keep accurate time.* **2** ceremony, affair, celebration, party, gathering: *The ambassador attended the function at the embassy.* *vb.* operate, work, run: *My new radio doesn't function properly.*

fund *n.* reserve, money, capital; supply.

fundamental *adj.* basic, elementary, essential, principal, underlying, primary: *The conservation of matter is a fundamental law of physics.* *n.* basics, elements, essentials, principle: *Before learning the details, you must learn the fundamentals.*

funeral *n.* burial, cremation, requiem, mourning.

funny *adj.* humorous, amusing, comic, comical, laughable. ANT. serious, sad.

fur *n.* coat, skin, belt, hide, hair.

furious *adj.* enraged, angry, raging. ANT. calm, serene.

furnace *n.* boiler, heater, kiln.

furnish *vb.* **1** supply, provide: *My uncle Harry is in business to furnish companies with the very best staff.* **2** decorate, appoint, outfit: *We furnished our living room with a new corner suite.*

further *adj.* more, additional.

furthermore *adv.* further, also, moreover.

fury *n.* **1** rage, anger, wrath, frenzy: *Imagine my father's fury when he found the scratch on his new car!* **2** violence, ferocity, ferociousness, fierceness: *After a short period of calm, the hurricane struck again in its full fury.* ANT. serenity, calmness.

fuse *vb.* join, combine, integrate, merge.

fuss *n.* bother, to-do, commotion: *Why make so much fuss about some water on the kitchen floor?* *vb.* bother, annoy, pester, irritate: *I'll get the work done faster if you stop fussing about it all the time.*

fussy *adj.* fastidious, over-particular, choosy, finicky, pedantic. ANT. careless, casual.

futile *adj.* **1** useless, pointless, vain, idle, worthless: *Trying to persuade Thomas to do his homework is futile during the cricket season.* **2** unimportant, minor, trivial: *Don't waste your time on futile activities.* ANT. (1) worthwhile, valuable. (2) important, serious, weighty.

future *adj.* coming, to come, approaching, impending, imminent, destined. ANT. past, bygone, former.

g

gadget *n.* device, contraption, appliance.

gag[1] *vb.* stifle, choke, muffle, stop up: *The prisoner was gagged to keep him quiet.*

gag[2] *n.* *Slang:* joke, story; hoax: *John likes to crack lots of gags to make his friends laugh.*

gain *vb.* 1 obtain, get, acquire, win, earn: *The home team gained a victory in the last few minutes of the game.* 2 improve, better, advance: *The profits from the investments gained value over the years.* 3 increase in: *The train gained speed as it travelled downhill.* *n.* 1 addition, increase: *The gains by the winning party in the election totalled 30 seats.* 2 improvement: *We have been making gains in our fight against poverty.* ANT. *vb.* lose. *n.* loss.

gallant *adj.* 1 brave, valiant, bold, courageous: *Many gallant soldiers died in that battle.* 2 polite, chivalrous, courteous, noble: *Our grandfather had a reputation among the ladies for being gallant.*

gallop *vb.,n.* leap, jump, spring: *The horses galloped along the track. The sudden gallop of the pony frightened the little girl.*

gamble *vb.* 1 bet, wager, game: *The countess gambled until she lost all of her money at the casino.* 2 trust, hope, expect: *Don't gamble on it being fine tomorrow.* *n.* chance, risk: *It's a gamble whether my talk with Lester will do any good.* ANT. *n.* certainty.

game *n.* 1 amusement, entertainment, play, sport, pastime: *The games will start as soon as all of the children arrive.* 2 contest, competition: *The game between the two teams was cancelled because of rain.*

gang *n.* band, troop, group, company, crew; horde.

gangster *n.* crook, criminal, gunman, hit man.

gap *n.* space, interval; break.

gape *vb.* stare, gaze; wonder, be amazed.

garish *adj.* gaudy, showy; ostentatious; colourful. ANT. unobtrusive, unassuming, modest; dull, drab, dowdy.

gasp *vb.* puff, pant, wheeze: *Harold finally reached the surface of the pond, gasping for breath.* *n.* breath; puff, pant: *She gave a gasp as she saw the door handle turn.*

gate *n.* barrier, bar, entrance, door.

gather *vb.* 1 assemble, collect, accumulate, come *or* bring together: *At Christmas, we gather our friends around us for a party. The relatives of the dead man gathered at the grave.* **2** understand, learn, assume: *I gathered from what the teacher said that the exam would be next week.* ANT. (**1**) disperse, scatter, dispel.

gathering *n.* crowd, meeting, assembly, company, throng.

gauge *vb.* estimate, judge; measure, check: *The chairman gauged the atmosphere of the meeting and called on the members to vote.* *n.* **1** instrument, device: *We measured the tyre pressures with a pressure gauge.* **2** standard, criterion, mark: *Exams are a gauge of one's abilities.*

gay *adj.* **1** joyful, joyous, jovial, gleeful, merry, cheerful, happy: *What a gay time we had at Cecile's house last night!* **2** bright, colourful, brilliant: *The ballroom was decorated in gay colours for the dance.* ANT. sad, mournful, sombre, sorrowful.

gaze *vb.* stare, gape, goggle at, look.

gear *n.* **1** wheel, cog, lever: *The driving mechanism on a car has a number of gears.* **2** equipment, material, supplies: *The angler took his fishing gear with him.* **3** *Slang:* clothes, accessories: *Young people's gear is by no means cheap.*

gem *n.* jewel, stone, ornament.

general *adj.* **1** indefinite, miscellaneous, inexact, vague: *Our general plans mean that we will be leaving tomorrow, but we haven't worked out the details yet.* **2** common, usual, regular, customary: *The general way to do it isn't good enough.* ANT. (**1**) definite, specific, exact, precise.

generate *vb.* create, produce, make.

generous *adj.* **1** charitable, liberal, unselfish: *Mr. Storm made a generous contribution to the museum.* **2** noble, (*informal*) big, honourable: *The committee has been very generous with its efforts to help the elderly.* ANT. (**1**) stingy, mean, selfish, tightfisted.

genial *adj.* easygoing, cheerful, warmhearted, cordial. ANT. unfriendly, cold.

genius *n.* **1** ability, talent, intellect, gift, aptitude: *My brother has a genius for mathematics.* **2** prodigy, brain: *My brother is a genius at mathematics.*

gentle *adj.* **1** mild, kindly, kind: *Ken is so gentle he'd never say anything to hurt anyone's feelings.* **2** tame, cultivated, civilized: *That tiger cub is as gentle as a lamb.* ANT. (**1**) rough. (**2**) uncivilized.

genuine *adj.* **1** real, actual, true: *If that were a genuine diamond, you'd be able to scratch glass with it.* **2** sincere, unaffected, definite: *When I told you that I loved you, my feelings were completely genuine.* ANT. (1) fake, bogus, counterfeit, false. (2) insincere, pretended, sham.

germ *n.* seed; microbe, bacteria; (*informal*) bug.

get *vb.* **1** acquire, obtain, secure, procure, gain: *Where did you get that funny hat?* **2** become, grow, develop: *We all get old.* **3** fetch: *Go and get your coat: we're leaving.* **4** carry, take: *Get that bicycle out of the street!* **5** prepare, ready, make ready: *You'll have to get your own breakfast.* **6** persuade, induce, urge: *Sam can get anyone to do anything.* **7** come, approach, near: *Get over here to my house as soon as you can.* **8** arrive at, reach, come to: *When does the train get to London?* *vb. phr.* **get along** succeed, prosper: *Will he be able to get along without his mother?* **get by** manage, survive: *I'll get by all right on a few pounds a week.* **get in** enter; arrive: *Get in the car at once! My train gets in at noon.* **get off** disembark, alight: *The train stopped with a jerk and he got off.* **get over** **1** overcome, recover, survive: *My father had malaria during the war and he's never got over it.* **2** appreciate, understand, believe: *I can't get over seeing you again after all these years.* **get up** arise, rise: *I get up at eight o'clock to go to school.*

ghastly *adj.* **1** *Informal:* horrifying, horrible, frightful, frightening, dreadful: *Being in a war is a ghastly experience.* **2** pale, wan, white, deathly: *When Clare put down the phone she looked ghastly.*

ghost *n.* **1** spectre, phantom, spirit, (*informal*) spook: *Have you ever seen a ghost?* **2** trace, glimmer, vestige, hint, suggestion: *Without a lot of practice, our team hasn't the ghost of a chance of winning the game.*

giant *n.* ogre, colossus, monster: *The giant broke the telephone pole as if it were a matchstick.* *adj.* gigantic, huge, colossal, monstrous, enormous: *I had a giant ice-cream cornet and now I can't eat my dinner.* ANT. *n.* dwarf, midget. *adj.* small, tiny, minuscule, infinitesimal.

gibberish *n.* nonsense, rubbish, claptrap, balderdash.

giddy *adj.* dizzy, unsteady, lightheaded.

gift *n.* **1** present, offering, donation: *Although I like to receive gifts, I get much pleasure from giving them, too.* **2** talent, genius, ability, aptitude: *Martin's gift for playing the oboe won him a scholarship.*

gigantic *adj.* huge, enormous, giant, large. ANT. small, little, tiny, infinitesimal.

gingerly *adj.* cautious, timid, gentle: *We made gingerly pro-*

gress along the slope of the cliff. adv. carefully, cautiously, gently: *The bomb squad handled the mysterious package very gingerly.* ANT. *adv.* roughly.

girl *n.*   lass; miss.   ANT. woman; boy.

gist *n.*   substance, essence, point.

give *vb.*   **1** provide, donate, supply, contribute, grant, present: *I never realized how much your father has given to the town, both in time and money.* **2** yield, give in, give way: *I felt the floor begin to give a little where we were standing.* **3** produce, develop, yield: *This orchard won't give fruit for seven years.* **4** sacrifice, give up, donate: *I have but one life to give for my country.*   *vb. phr.* **give away** betray, reveal, divulge: *Whenever Peter tells a lie, he gives himself away by stuttering.*   **give in** yield, submit, surrender; admit: *The weather was so beautiful that the teacher finally gave in and let the children go home early.*   **give off** emit, discharge: *The chemicals give off a smell like burning rubber.*   **give out** **1** distribute, deal, dole: *The man at the corner is giving out free sweets.* **2** weaken, tire: *My arm gave out and I couldn't play tennis any more.* **3** publish, make known *or* public, publicize, advertise: *The office refused to give out any information until the dead man's relatives had been informed of his death.*   **give up** **1** stop, cease, discontinue, end: *I've tried to give up smoking, but I can't.* **2** surrender, yield, submit, cede: *The robbers gave up when surrounded by the police.* ANT. *vb.* (1) take.

glad *adj.*   **1** pleased, happy, satisfied, delighted: *I'm so glad that you're coming to my party!* **2** good, encouraging, pleasing: *I heard the glad tidings: Marie is going to get married!* ANT. (1) unhappy, sad, morose. (2) gloomy, sombre, dismal.

glamour *n.*   allure, charm, attraction.

glance *vb.,n.*   peek, glimpse, look: *She glanced in my direction but I still tried to avoid her. I caught a glance of the car as it sped around the corner.*

glare *n.*   dazzle, flash, brilliance: *I couldn't make out who it was in the glare of the spotlight.*   *vb.* scowl, stare, glower: *The speaker would glare in the direction of anyone who caused a disturbance.*

glass *n.*   beaker, tumbler, cup; goblet.

glasses *n.pl.*   spectacles, eyeglasses; contact lenses.

glaze *vb.*   coat, cover, gloss, shine, burnish.

gleam *vb.,n.*   beam, glow, glimmer; shine, sparkle: *The mooon gleaming on the water looked like a silver path to the horizon.*

The gleam of candlelight on silver and crystal will always remind me of my father's home.

glee *n.* merriment, joy, cheer, mirth.

glib *adj.* easy, slick, smooth.

glide *vb.* slide, slip, flow.

glimpse *n.* sight, glance, impression.

glisten *vb.* shine, glitter, shimmer, glimmer, sparkle.

glitter *vb.* sparkle, glisten, shimmer, glimmer, shine: *The calm sea glittered in the sunlight.* *n.* light, sparkle, splendour, brilliance: *The pop star stood on stage amidst the glitter of all the lights.*

global *adj.* worldwide, international, universal; round-the-world.

globe *n.* sphere, orb, ball.

gloom *n.* **1** darkness, shade, shadows, dimness: *I heard footsteps but could see nothing in the gloom.* **2** sadness, melancholy: *A feeling of gloom came over us when we thought about the hungry people.* ANT. (1) brightness. (2) cheerfulness, happiness.

gloomy *adj.* **1** sad, downcast, downhearted, glum, unhappy: *The staff were gloomy because the prospect of redundancy hung over them.* **2** dark, dim, shadowy, dismal: *The gloomy old house had not been lived in for years.* ANT. (1) happy, cheerful, merry, highspirited. (2) sunny, bright.

glorify *vb.* **1** praise, worship, exalt: *The congregation glorified God as the missionaries told them that many people had been converted.* **2** honour, acclaim, commend, extol, eulogize: *The headmaster glorified the achievements of his senior pupils.*

glorious *adj.* **1** famous, renowned, noted, famed, distinguished, splendid, celebrated: *It is our glorious tradition that attracts members to the club.* **2** *Informal:* delightful, admirable, wonderful: *I've had a glorious day here in York.*

glory *n.* **1** honour, eminence, renown: *His bravery in battle has won him much glory.* **2** splendour, magnificence, grandeur: *Can we ever forget the glory that was Greece?*

glossary *n.* lexicon, dictionary.

glow *n.* **1** gleam, light: *I saw the glow of the city against the sky as we approached.* **2** warmth, heat: *The fire cast a warm glow on the children's faces.* *vb.* **1** gleam, glimmer, shine: *The hot embers glowed in the fireplace after the flames died down.* **2** radiate, shine: *The children's faces glowed with the expectation that Santa Claus would soon be there.*

glue *n.* adhesive, paste, gum.

glut *n.* surplus, excess, saturation. ANT. insufficiency, deficiency, deficit.

gnash *vb.* grind, snap, bite.

gnaw *vb.* eat, chew, erode.

go *vb.* **1** leave, depart, withdraw: *All evening long, people kept coming and going in the large hall.* **2** proceed, move, travel, visit: *Let's go to the cinema. My parents went to the United States for a holiday.* **3** become: *Stop teasing me or I'll go crazy.* **4** operate, function, work, run: *The car won't go unless you turn the key.* **5** pass, elapse: *When you're busy, the day goes very quickly.* *vb. phr.* **go about** be busy, work, engage in: *Mrs. Smith went about her daily business quietly and efficiently.* **go by** pass, proceed: *I go by your house every day.* **go off** explode, blow up: *Don't let that firework go off in your hand!* **go on** **1** continue, persevere, persist: *I just can't go on without you.* **2** happen, take place, occur: *At our house there's a lot going on all of the time.* **go over** examine, scan, study: *The actor went over his lines again before the rehearsal.* **go through** experience, undergo, endure: *Please don't ask me any more questions: I've gone through enough for one day.* **go with** harmonize, match, suit, agree, complement: *This grey hat will go with almost anything in my wardrobe.* **go without** fall short, want, need, require, sacrifice: *When times are hard, we sometimes have to go without.* ANT. *vb.* (1) come.

goal *n.* aim, object, target, end, purpose.

go-between *n.* mediator, intermediary, middleman, agent.

God *n.* supreme being, deity; spirit.

good *adj.* **1** well-behaved, obedient; upright, moral, righteous: *If you are a truly good person, other people won't always like you.* **2** qualified, suited, suitable, apt, proper, capable, fit: *We have had a great many good applicants for the job.* **3** generous, kindly, kind, friendly, gracious, obliging: *There's nothing more important than having good neighbours.* **4** pleasant, agreeable, pleasurable, satisfactory, fine: *Did you have a good time at the party?* **5** healthy, sound, normal: *You have good hearing to be able to hear a footstep at that distance!* **6** favourable, excellent, profitable: *Business prospects are good for the future.* *n.* **1** benefit, welfare, advantage, profit: *You'll do it now, if you understand it's for your own good.* **2** virtue, righteousness: *Embrace the good and shun evil.* **3** kindness, beneficence: *The good that men do is often buried with them when they die.* ANT. *adj.* (1) disobedient, naughty; bad, evil, corrupt. (2) unsuitable. (3)

unkind, unfriendly. **(4)** unpleasant, (*informal*) lousy. **(5)** unhealthy, ill, sick. **(6)** unfavourable, hopeless, desperate. *n.* **(1)** disadvantage. **(2, 3)** evil, wickedness.

good-bye *interj.* cheerio, so long, see you soon, au revoir, adieu, farewell. ANT. hello.

good-looking *adj.* attractive, beautiful, pretty; handsome. ANT. ugly; plain.

good-natured *adj.* kind, friendly, gracious.

goodness *n.* honesty, virtue, good, integrity. ANT. dishonesty, badness, evil, corruption, sin.

goods *n.pl.* **1** commodities, wares, merchandise; freight: *The goods were brought out of the factory and put onto the lorry.* **2** property, possessions: *I've got so many goods; what am I going to do when I move?*

gorge *n.* pass, defile, ravine: *The outlaws lay in wait for the stagecoach at the edge of the gorge.* *vb.* stuff, cram, fill: *Of course you can't eat your dinner after gorging yourself on sweets.*

gorgeous *adj.* splendid, magnificent, grand, dazzling. ANT. ugly, squalid.

gossip *n.* **1** prattle, hearsay, rumour: *Don't believe what you hear about Henry—it's just gossip.* **2** scandalmonger, blabbermouth, meddler: *That nosy Mrs. Parker is just a loudmouthed gossip.* *vb.* prattle, tattle, chatter, blab: *I knew they must have been gossiping about me because they stopped talking the minute they saw me.*

govern *vb.* rule, control, guide, run; command.

government *n.* **1** rule, control, command, direction, authority, jurisdiction: *The United Kingdom has a democratic form of government.* **2** Parliament, council: *Both central and local government can levy taxes.*

gown *n.* dress, frock; robe.

grab *vb.* seize, clutch, grasp.

grace *n.* **1** gracefulness, ease, elegance: *I admire the grace with which you got rid of that awful person.* **2** charm, attractiveness, beauty: *The princess is noted for her grace.*

graceful *adj.* elegant, artistic, becoming. ANT. awkward, clumsy, ungainly.

gracious *adj.* **1** kind, friendly; courteous, polite: *It was very gracious of you to allow me to invite my friend for dinner.* **2** tender, merciful, compassionate: *How gracious your wife is to take care of me when I'm ill.* ANT. **(1)** rude, impolite, discourteous, thoughtless.

grade *n.* **1** position, degree, class, category: *There are several* *grades of blue.* **2** mark, evaluation, award: *She got a poor grade in her maths test.* *vb.* arrange, class, categorize: *She graded the eggs according to size.*

gradual *adj.* little by little, slow, moderate. ANT. sudden.

graft *vb.* join, unite, splice.

grand *adj.* **1** elaborate, great, royal, stately: *Kings and queens have always lived in a grand style.* **2** splendid, magnificent, sumptuous: *A grand feast was arranged for the visitors.* ANT. poor, mediocre; plain.

grandiose *adj.* flamboyant, elaborate, rich.

grant *vb.* **1** give, bestow, confer, award: *Charles was granted a leave of absence from the university.* **2** agree, allow, concede, accept: *The detective reluctantly granted that I couldn't have been at the scene of the crime.* *n.* award, bequest, gift: *My sister received a £1,000 grant for study abroad.* ANT. *vb.* (1) deny, withhold.

graphic *adj.* vivid, distinct, expressive; strong.

grapple *vb.* grip, seize, clutch.

grasp *vb.* **1** seize, hold, grab, clasp, grip, clutch: *Howard grasped the gun by the barrel and wrenched it from the robber's hand.* **2** perceive, understand, comprehend: *I don't quite grasp what you're trying to tell me.* *n.* **1** grip, clutches, clasp, hold: *The coin fell from my grasp and slipped down between the bars of the grating.* **2** reach, understanding, capacity: *That book is beyond the grasp of a seven-year-old.*

grateful *adj.* appreciative, thankful. ANT. ungrateful, thankless, grudging.

gratify *vb.* satisfy, please. ANT. frustrate.

gratitude *n.* thankfulness, appreciation, indebtedness. ANT. ingratitude, ungratefulness.

grave¹ *n.* tomb, vault, crypt: *The mourners stood round the grave as the coffin was laid in.*

grave² *adj.* **1** sober, thoughtful, solemn, serious: *When I saw the doctor's grave expression I knew something was wrong.* **2** important, serious, weighty: *Solving the problems of inflation and unemployment are very grave matters.* ANT. (1) happy, merry, frivolous, jolly. (2) trivial, unimportant.

gravity *n.* **1** gravitation, pressure, force: *Objects fall to the ground because of gravity.* **2** seriousness, importance; concern: *It wasn't until fourteen people had to go to hospital that we realized the gravity of the disease.* ANT. (2) triviality.

graze¹ *vb.* scrape, brush: *The child grazed its knee on the side of the fence.*

graze² *vb.* feed, pasture, forage: *The sheep were grazing on the grass.*

grease *n.* oil, fat, lubricant.

great *adj.* **1** large, big, huge, enormous, immense, gigantic: *A great mountain loomed before us.* **2** noteworthy, significant, important, worthy, distinguished, remarkable: *Shakespeare is undoubtedly a very great writer.* **3** chief, leading, main, principal: *Sheldon has always been a great friend of mine.* ANT. (1) small, diminutive. (2) insignificant, trivial. (3) minor.

greed *n.* avarice, greediness, covetousness. ANT. generosity, selflessness, unselfishness.

greedy *adj.* selfish, covetous, grasping, avaricious. ANT. generous, giving, unselfish.

greet *vb.* meet, welcome, salute, address.

grey *adj.* dull, drab, sombre.

grid *n.* framework, network, system.

grief *n.* sorrow, sadness, distress, suffering, anguish, woe, misery. ANT. joy.

grieve *vb.* **1** lament, mourn, weep: *Peggy grieved over the loss of her puppy for weeks.* **2** distress, sorrow, sadden, hurt: *It grieves me to realize that all people are not honest.* ANT. rejoice, celebrate.

grievous *adj.* dreadful, awful, gross, shameful, outrageous, regrettable, lamentable.

grim *adj.* **1** stern, severe, harsh: *The headmaster gave the students a grim warning about mugging old ladies.* **2** ghastly, sinister, frightful, horrible, grisly: *The skull nailed to the tree was a grim reminder that we were far from being safe.*

grime *n.* dirt, filth; soil; soot.

grin *vb.,n.* smile, beam; smirk: *The little girl grinned with delight as she was given the huge teddy bear for her birthday. His broad grin showed that he knew the answer to the riddle.*

grind *vb.* **1** powder, pulverize, mill, crush: *The corn was ground between the two stones.* **2** sharpen; smooth, even: *Try to grind down the rough spots.*

grip *n.* hold, grasp, clutch, clasp: *My grip on the branch was weakening and I was about to plummet to the rocks below.* *vb.* seize, grasp, hold, clutch: *Grip the handle tightly and don't let go until I tell you to.*

groan *vb.* moan; sob: *Did you have a bad dream? I heard you groaning in your sleep last night.* *n.* moan, sob, cry: *The old man's groans could be heard throughout the whole hospital ward.*

groove *n.* slot, channel, scratch, furrow.

grope *vb.* feel for, touch; fumble.

gross *adj.* **1** improper, rude, coarse, indecent, crude, vulgar: *Her gross behaviour shocked her parents.* **2** flagrant, outrageous, extreme; grievous, shameful: *The innocent man's conviction was a gross miscarriage of justice.* ANT. (**1**) refined, cultivated, polite.

ground *n.* **1** land, earth, soil: *My great-grandfather built his house on a small plot of ground.* **2 grounds** basis, reasons, foundation, base: *You have no grounds for saying such things about me.* *vb.* train, educate, instruct: *I was well grounded in history.*

groundless *adj.* unfounded, baseless.

group *n.* gathering, collection, set, assembly, assemblage: *A group of us went out for pizza. There is an interesting group of exhibits at this end of the hall.* *vb.* gather, collect; sort, classify: *Group all of the red flowers together.*

grovel *vb.* crawl, fawn, sneak.

grow *vb.* **1** enlarge, increase, swell, expand: *Watch that house grow.* **2** develop, flower: *The rosebushes grow very well in this soil.* **3** cultivate, raise, produce, nurture: *My father grows tomatoes every year.* ANT. (**1**) shrink, decrease.

growl *vb.,n.* rumble, snarl, gnarl: *The surly old man growled an excuse angrily. The dog gave out a steady growl as we came nearer.*

growth *n.* increase, development.

grudge *n.* resentment, ill will, spite, bitterness.

gruff *adj.* surly, rough, abrupt, blunt.

grumble *vb.* complain, protest, fuss.

grunt *vb.* grate, snort, croak.

guarantee *n.* warranty, commitment, promise, pledge: *The manufacturer's guarantee says that they will replace any defective parts for nothing.* *vb.* warrant, promise, pledge, ensure: *I can safely guarantee you'll be home before midnight.*

guard *vb.* protect, preserve, shield, defend: *Two armed men were guarding the security van.* *n.* sentry, patrol, watchman, sentinel: *There is a guard at every door during the king's visit.* ANT. *vb.* neglect, ignore, disregard.

guess *vb.* estimate, surmise, reckon: *Guess what's for tea!* *n.* notion, opinion, hypothesis, theory: *I'll give you three guesses how I got here last night.*

guest *n.* visitor, caller, company. ANT. host.

guide *vb.* **1** lead, direct, conduct, steer, pilot: *I wish I had someone who could guide me through the forest.* **2** influence, affect: *Let good judgment guide you throughout your life.* n. director, pilot, helmsman, leader: *We were able to hire a Sherpa guide for the climb.* ANT. vb. (1) follow. n. follower.

guilt n. blame, fault; responsibility; remorse, self-reproach.

guilty adj. responsible, culpable, blameworthy. ANT. innocent, blameless, guiltless.

gulf n. 1 chasm, abyss, ravine, canyon: *The gulf that separated us from the lion was fortunately too wide for him to leap over.* 2 inlet, sound, bay: *Have you ever been to the Gulf of Mexico?*

gulp (down) vb. swallow, bolt down; eat, drink.

gum n. adhesive, glue, resin.

gun n. rifle, shotgun; pistol, revolver; machine gun.

gurgle vb. chortle, chuckle; murmur, ripple.

gush vb. spout, spurt, flow, pour, stream.

gutter n. drain, ditch, sewer.

h

habit *n.* **1** addiction, compulsion, disposition: *Reginald has a nasty habit of biting his nails.* **2** custom, practice: *You ought to get into the habit of brushing your teeth after every meal.*

haggard *adj.* gaunt, drawn, worn. ANT. fresh, animated, bright, clear-eyed.

hail¹ *n.* ice, sleet; rain: *The hail beat on the windows during the storm.*

hail² *vb.* greet, welcome, address: *The tax refund was hailed by many as the solution to the crisis.*

hair *n.* growth, locks; beard, moustache.

hale *adj.* hearty, healthy, robust, vigorous. ANT. feeble, weak.

halfhearted *adj.* indifferent, uncaring, cool, unenthusiastic. ANT. enthusiastic, eager, earnest.

halfwit *n.* dunce, idiot, dope, fool, simpleton.

hall *n.* passage, corridor, hallway; vestibule, lobby, foyer.

hallow *vb.* set apart, consecrate, sanctify.

halt *vb.* stop, cease, hold: *The train halted in the station to let passengers get on and off.* *n.* stop, end: *The government has called a halt to wasteful spending.* ANT. *vb.* start, begin. *n.* start, beginning.

hamper¹ *vb.* hinder, prevent, obstruct, thwart: *I was hampered from swimming by my clothes and heavy shoes.*

hamper² *n.* basket; pannier, creel: *We carried our sandwiches in a wicker hamper.*

hand *n.* **1** fingers, palm, fist: *Stretch out your hand, please.* **2** helper, farmhand, assistant, labourer: *We have three hired hands at the farm.* **3** aid, help, support: *Can someone please give me a hand with this piano?* *n. phr.* **at hand** near, nearby, close: *The boy's tenth birthday was at hand.* **by hand** manually: *This desk was made entirely by hand.* **on hand** available, ready, convenient, in stock: *We always keep spare parts for the engine on hand.* *vb.* give, pass, deliver: *Please hand me that wrench.* *vb. phr.* **hand down** pass on, bequeath, give: *That hunting rifle has been handed down from generation to generation in our family.* **hand in** deliver, submit, give in: *We handed in our essays yesterday.* **hand out** distribute, pass out: *A man in the street was handing out these leaflets.*

handicap *n.* disadvantage, hindrance: *A person's lack of education is a handicap in getting some jobs.* *vb.* hinder, thwart, hamper: *The brace on the girl's teeth handicapped her speech.*

handicapped *adj.* disabled; crippled.

handle *n.* knob, crank, grasp: *Take hold of the door handle and turn it.* *vb.* feel, touch: *It is dangerous to handle some chemicals.*

handsome *adj.* **1** good-looking, fine, comely: *Don is as handsome as a film star.* **2** generous, large, big, liberal, ample: *My employer gave me a handsome bonus at Christmas.* ANT. (1) ugly, unattractive. (2) mean, petty, stingy, niggardly.

handy *adj.* **1** ready, at hand, near, nearby, close: *I always keep a notepad handy by the telephone.* **2** helpful, clever, useful: *A can opener is a very handy gadget.* ANT. (2) inconvenient.

hang *vb.* **1** suspend, dangle, drape: *The flag was hung from the railing of the balcony.* **2** execute, kill, lynch: *The murderer was hanged the next morning.*

hanker *vb.* yearn, desire, crave.

haphazard *adj.* random, chance, accidental. ANT. intended, designed, deliberate.

happen *vb.* occur, take place, come to pass.

happiness *n.* joy, delight, joyfulness, elation, ecstasy. ANT. sadness, gloom, melancholy.

happy *adj.* **1** pleased, contented; satisfied: *I'm so happy to see you I could hug you! Jimmy was happy to be home again.* **2** lucky, fortunate: *By a happy coincidence, the policeman came along just then and the thief ran off.* ANT. (1) sad, gloomy, sorrowful. (2) unlucky, inconvenient, unfortunate.

harass *vb.* **1** torment, bother, trouble.

harbour *n.* port, haven, anchorage: *Rotterdam is one of the busiest harbours in the world.* *vb.* shelter, protect: *The farmer and his wife harboured the runaway criminal for two weeks and then the police found him.*

hard *adj.* **1** firm, solid, rigid, unyielding, compact, dense: *I could not dig the shovel into the hard ground. This stale bun is as hard as a rock.* **2** difficult, laborious, exhausting: *Hard work never hurt anybody.* **3** difficult, complicated, puzzling, tough, intricate: *We won't get any of the really hard problems to solve till we get to college.* **4** severe, stern, harsh, strict, demanding: *Things will be hard for anyone who disobeys.* **5** shrewd, hardheaded, unsympathetic, cool, cold: *Shirley really drives a hard bargain.* *adj. phr.* **hard up** *Informal:*

poor, up against it, poverty-stricken; broke: *When Jack became unemployed, his family were really hard up.* *adv.* energetically, vigorously, forcefully, earnestly: *My father has worked hard all his life.* ANT. *adj.* (1) soft, pliable, yielding. (2) easy, undemanding, comfortable. (3) simple, uncomplicated, direct. (4) lenient, easygoing.

harden *vb.* solidify, petrify. ANT. soften, loosen.

hardly *adv.* scarcely, barely.

hardship *n.* difficulty, trouble, affliction.

hardy *adj.* vigorous, sturdy, tough, strong. ANT. weak, feeble, frail, fragile, decrepit.

harm *n.* 1 damage, hurt, injury: *Your father wouldn't let any harm come to you.* 2 evil, wickedness, wrong: *Although they don't want to admit it, gossips really want to do harm.* *vb.* hurt, damage, injure: *Alan is so gentle, he wouldn't harm anyone.*

harmful *adj.* mischievous, hurtful, injurious. ANT. beneficial, advantageous.

harmless *adj.* innocent, painless. ANT. harmful, injurious, dangerous.

harmonious *adj.* 1 melodious, tuneful: *Those boys certainly make a harmonious trio.* 2 amicable, congenial: *The two companies reached a harmonious settlement of the legal case before it came to court.* ANT. (1) discordant, dissonant. (2) quarrelsome, discordant, disagreeable.

harmony *n.* agreement, accord, unity. ANT. discordance, disagreement, conflict.

harness *n.* bridle, yoke, straps: *The horse's harness was attached to the cart.* *vb.* yoke, control: *For many years scientists have been developing means for harnessing tides for electric power.*

harrowing *adj.* tormenting, nerve-racking, distressing.

harsh *adj.* 1 rough, severe, tough, unpleasant, unkind, stern, cruel: *The police may have to take harsh measures to control hooliganism.* 2 rough, coarse, jarring: *The harsh cry of the raven was heard in the woods.* ANT. (1) easy, soothing, gentle. (2) melodious, pleasing.

harvest *n.* crop, yield: *The new fertilizers helped give the most successful harvest ever.* *vb.* gather, collect, pick, glean, reap: *What is not sown cannot be harvested.*

haste *n.* 1 rush, hurry, rapidity, speed: *Those who were not fighting the fire left the dangerous area with haste.* 2 scramble, hurry, flurry, rush, heedlessness: *If you marry in haste,* *you may repent at leisure.* ANT. (1) sluggishness, sloth.

hasten *vb.* **1** hurry, rush, run, scurry, scamper, dash, sprint: *Timothy hastened to be first in the line to receive the prize.* **2** quicken, urge, press, speed: *Mother hastened us on to school in the mornings.* ANT. (1) dawdle, linger, tarry.

hasty *adj.* quick, rapid, swift. ANT. slow, dawdling.

hat *n.* cap, hood, bonnet, headgear, headpiece; helmet.

hatch *vb.* brood, breed, bring forth, incubate.

hate *vb.* detest, abhor, loathe, despise; dislike: *I have never understood why Cinderella's stepmother and half-sisters hated her so.* *n.* hatred, loathing, abhorrence; dislike: *Judges have a hate of injustice.* ANT. *vb.* like, love, admire. *n.* liking, love, esteem.

hateful *adj.* detestable, loathsome, offensive. ANT. lovable, likable, admirable.

hatred *n.* hate, loathing, aversion. ANT. liking, appreciation.

haughty *adj.* aloof, proud, prideful, arrogant. ANT. humble, simple, unaffected.

haul *vb.* drag, draw, pull, tow.

have *vb.* **1** hold, possess, own: *Dick has a pony that he got for his birthday.* **2** contain, include: *The van has room for all our furniture.* **3** get, receive, obtain, take, gain, acquire: *Have another biscuit with your tea.* **4** engage in, experience, undergo: *My father had 20 years of army service.* **5** maintain, uphold, hold, believe, say, assert, testify: *As the officer would have it, we drove into the river on purpose.* **6** bear, give birth to, bring forth, beget: *Anne has just had twins.* *vb. phr.* **have to** must, be compelled to; need to: *Do you have to go now?*

hazard *n.* peril, risk, danger: *Driving too fast is a hazard not only to yourself but to other drivers.* *vb.* offer, tender, dare: *I'd hazard a guess that you're fifteen years old.*

hazardous *adj.* perilous, dangerous, risky. ANT. safe, secure.

hazy *adj.* **1** misty, murky, unclear: *The day began hazy, but it later became very hot.* **2** vague, obscure: *I don't understand what you mean: what you said is still rather hazy in my mind.* ANT. (1) clear. (2) definite.

head *n.* **1** skull: *Robert was hit on the head and he fell down, unconscious.* **2** leader, commander, director, supervisor, chief: *We went to talk to the head of the English department about our exams.* **3** source, start, beginning, origin: *It took explorers many years to find the head of the Nile.* *vb.* lead, direct, command: *Isaac will head this project and tell the* *workers what they must do.* *adj.* chief, leading, principal, main: *The head buyer for the firm has been with them for forty years.*

headquarters *n.pl.* head office, base, centre.

headstrong *adj.* stubborn, obstinate, wilful. ANT. amenable, easygoing.

headway *n.* progress, movement, advance.

heal *vb.* cure, restore.

health *n.* wholeness, fitness, strength.

healthy *adj.* strong, robust, vigorous, sound: *Two weeks after his operation, Adam was healthy enough to go camping.* ANT. unhealthy, ill, sick, unwholesome.

heap *n.* pile, stack, mound, collection, accumulation: *There was a heap of rubbish at the side of the road.* *vb.* pile, stack, collect, accumulate: *We kept heaping the sand in one place till there was a very high mound.*

hear *vb.* listen; detect, perceive.

heart *n.* 1 centre, core: *The heart of the problem was that we didn't believe anything Jack said.* 2 sympathy, feeling, sentiment; tenderness; pity: *Dave has so much heart he'd do anything for you.*

hearty *adj.* warm, cheery; lively.

heat *n.* 1 warmth, hotness, temperature: *The heat from the fire singed the blanket.* 2 passion, excitement; ardour, zeal: *They said that he struck her in the heat of the moment.* *vb.* warm, inflame, cook: *It takes a long time to heat water on a wood stove.* ANT. *n.* (1) coolness, cold, coldness, iciness, chilliness. *vb.* cool, freeze, chill.

heathen *adj.* pagan, ungodly, unchristian, barbaric. ANT. godly.

heave *vb.* 1 hoist, boost, raise: *With one final push they heaved up the box.* 2 haul, pull, tug: *Three men heaving on the rope couldn't lift the safe.*

heaven *n.* paradise; firmament; empyrean. ANT. hell.

heavenly *adj.* 1 blissful, divine, saintly, angelic, holy, blessed: *The minister had a heavenly expression on his face.* 2 celestial: *Astronomers observe the motions of the heavenly bodies.* 3 *Informal:* wonderful, super: *That gateau we had for tea was absolutely heavenly.*

heavy *adj.* 1 weighty, ponderous: *That trunk is too heavy for you to lift by yourself.* 2 intense, concentrated, severe: *There was a very heavy snowfall last week.* 3 burdensome, oppressive, harsh, depressing: *The atmosphere was heavy when I walked into the courtroom.* 4 sad, oppressed, serious, grave, gloomy, mournful, melancholy, dismal: *He told us the bad news with a heavy heart.* 5 boring, dull, tiresome: *I found the play quite heavy going.* ANT. (1) light, buoyant, airy. (2) light, insignificant, minimal. (4) cheerful, happy.

hectic *adj.* active, rushed; excited.

heed *vb.* obey, regard, observe: *You'd better heed the advice your parents give you.* *n.* attention, mind: *Don't pay heed to what Jean says, as she's only teasing you.* ANT. *vb.* ignore, disregard, overlook, disdain.

height *n.* 1 altitude, elevation, tallness: *What is the height of that block of flats?* 2 mountain, peak, prominence: *We looked down on the valley from the height.* 3 extreme, climax, maximum: *Crossing the street with your eyes closed is the height of stupidity.* ANT. depth.

heir *n.* inheritor, successor, descendant.

hell *n.* perdition, inferno, underworld. ANT. heaven.

hello *interj.* hi!, good morning, good afternoon, good evening. ANT. good-bye, farewell, cheerio.

help *vb.* 1 aid, assist, support; back, encourage: *Can someone please help me lift this piano? In these times we help all the needy people we can.* 2 avoid, prevent: *I can't help hiccuping.* 3 serve: *Please, help yourself to some more corned beef.* *n.* aid, assistance, support, relief: *We need all the help we can get.*

helper *n.* assistant, aide; supporter.

helpful *adj.* advantageous, profitable, valuable. ANT. useless, futile, worthless.

helpless *adj.* 1 dependent, feeble, weak, disabled: *My brother has been helpless in a wheelchair since his operation.* 2 unresourceful, incompetent, inept, incapable: *Sarah is completely helpless when faced with a machine that won't work.* ANT. (1) strong, independent. (2) competent, resourceful, enterprising.

hem *n.* edge, border, edging.

herald *n.* messenger, bearer; forerunner, harbinger.

herb *n.* plant, spice, flavouring.

herd *n.* flock, crowd, group, drove, pack: *A herd of elephants stampeded towards us, and we had no place to hide.* *vb.* group, gather, crowd: *The guide herded all of the tourists into the coach for the ride home.*

heresy *n.* unorthodoxy, heterodoxy; nonconformity.

heritage *n.* inheritance, legacy, patrimony.

hermit *n.* recluse, anchorite, eremite.

hero *n.* champion, idol, star, paladin.

heroic *adj.* valiant, brave, dauntless, gallant, courageous, bold, fearless. ANT. cowardly, fainthearted, timid.

heroism *n.* bravery, valour, gallantry, courage, boldness. ANT. cowardice, timidity.

hesitate *vb.* **1** pause, wait, delay: *He who hesitates is lost except when crossing the street.* **2** stutter, stammer: *The actor hesitated for a moment or two at the beginning of his speech.* ANT. (1) proceed.

hidden *adj.* concealed, latent; obscure; invisible, unapparent, withheld. ANT. showing; revealed.

hide *vb.* conceal, cover, mask, screen, camouflage, cloak, shroud, veil: *You can't hide your true feelings from me.* *n.* skin, pelt, leather, fur: *The hides of buffaloes were once worth a lot of money.* ANT. *vb.* show, display, reveal.

hideous *adj.* ugly, frightful, frightening, shocking, horrible, horrifying, terrible, terrifying, monstrous, gross, grisly. ANT. beautiful, lovely.

hierarchy *n.* system, authority; bureaucracy, government.

high *adj.* **1** tall, lofty, towering: *That's a very high building.* **2** raised, shrill, high-pitched, strident, sharp: *She speaks in a very high voice that gets on my nerves.* **3** important, prominent, powerful: *A high official in the government gave me the news.* **4** dear, expensive: *The jeweller asks high prices for gold these days.* ANT. (1) low, short. (2) deep. (3) lowly, unimportant, insignificant. (4) reasonable, inexpensive.

highlight *n.* outstanding feature, best part: *The highlight of our holiday was a day at the zoo.* *vb.* emphasize, stress, feature: *The politician highlighted low investment in industry in his speech.*

highly *adv.* very, extremely.

hike *n.* walk, trek, ramble.

hill *n.* mound; headland, incline.

hinder *vb.* interrupt, hamper, slow, delay, obstruct, interfere with, block, thwart, prevent, stop. ANT. advance, further, promote.

hindrance *n.* delay, interruption, obstruction, interference, barrier, obstacle.

hinge *n.* pivot, link, joint, flap: *The door has two hinges to the door frame.* *vb.* depend, rely, pivot: *Success of the project hinges on getting enough people to support it.*

hint *n.* suggestion, tip, clue; whisper, taste, suspicion: *If you don't get the answer in ten seconds, I'll give you a hint. There* *was just a hint of curry in the soup.* vb. suggest, mention: *Are you hinting that Felix has been going out with my girlfriend?*

hire vb. 1 employ, engage, retain, enlist: *The factory hired 200 people today.* 2 rent, lease, charter: *We hired a car at the airport and drove it about on holiday.* n. rent, rental, lease, let, charter: *The marina advertised boats for hire.* ANT. (1) dismiss, fire.

hiss vb. 1 boo, disapprove, shout down: *The hecklers hissed loudly while the prime minister spoke to the crowd.* 2 spit, buzz, fizz, seethe: *The snake's hiss frightened the little boy.*

historic adj. significant, important, famous.

history n. chronicle, record, account, narrative, tale, memoir, story.

hit vb. 1 strike, smite: *The ball hit the wall and bounced off. Stop hitting children smaller than yourself.* 2 find, come upon, discover: *The young couple hit upon a plan to elope, avoiding their parents' protection.* n. blow, stroke: *She gave him a hit right in the face.*

hitch vb. tie, fasten, tether, harness: *The cowboy hitched the horses to the wagon.* n. hindrance, interruption, interference: *There's been a hitch in our plans and we can't go on the picnic.*

hoard vb. amass, save, store: *During the shortage, some people hoarded sugar and coffee.* n. store, stock, cache: *The police found a hoard of gold coins in a box in the chimney.* ANT. vb. spend, use, squander.

hoarse adj. rough, raucous, deep, husky, grating, harsh. ANT. clear.

hoax n. (practical) joke, trick; deception.

hobble vb. limp, stumble, dodder, totter.

hobby n. pastime, diversion, leisure activity.

hoist vb. lift, raise, heave, elevate: *It will take four men to hoist that ladder up to the roof.* n. crane, derrick; lift: *The hoist was too weak to lift the piano.*

hold vb. 1 grasp, clasp, grip, clutch: *The woman disappeared into the crowd, leaving me there holding the baby.* 2 have, keep, retain: *I am holding onto the book and don't intend to lend it to anyone.* 3 contain: *This bottle holds exactly one litre.* 4 possess, have: *My uncle holds a history degree from Oxford.* 5 conduct, observe, engage in: *The society is holding a meeting next month.* 6 think, believe, maintain, consider, judge: *We hold these truths to be important: life, liberty, and the pursuit of happiness.* 7 remain, stick, adhere, cohere, cling: *Will that tiny drop of glue hold the entire model together?* **8** exist, be valid, be true: *Laws still hold even when people break them.* *n.* **1** grasp, grip: *Get a good hold on the fishing rod.* **2** sway, influence, control: *Geoff's new girlfriend has quite a hold on him.*

hole *n.* **1** opening, tear, rip, aperture: *I'm so embarrassed! I had a hole in my sock when I took off my shoe.* **2** burrow, pit, cave, den, lair: *The bear crawled into his hole to hibernate for the winter.*

holiday *n.* time off, leave, vacation, rest.

hollow *adj.* **1** empty, unfilled: *The wall made a hollow sound where it was tapped, so we knew it wasn't solid.* **2** empty, false, flimsy, meaningless: *We lost so many men in the battle that ours was a hollow victory.* *n.* cavity, hole, depression, pit: *The dog crawled into the hollow in the rock and went to sleep.* *vb.* excavate, dig, shovel: *The pirates hollowed out a place in the hillside where they hid the treasure.* ANT. *adj.* **(1)** full, filled, solid.

holy *adj.* **1** blessed, sacred, hallowed, consecrated: *We visited many holy places in our tour of Jerusalem.* **2** saintly, pious: *Holy people take time to worship God every day.* ANT. **(1)** profane, unconsecrated, unsanctified.

homage *n.* respect, reverence, honour.

home *n.* **1** family: *Wherever my wife and children are is home to me.* **2** house, residence, abode, dwelling: *Several thousand homes have been built in the area already.*

homeless *adj.* destitute, desolate; wandering, vagrant.

homesick *adj.* nostalgic; lonely.

homework *n.* (*informal*) prep, study, assignment, work.

honest *adj.* **1** truthful, trustworthy, moral, upright, honourable: *The bank tries to employ honest people.* **2** open, candid, forthright, frank, straightforward: *If you want my honest opinion, I think you treated her very badly.* ANT. **(1)** dishonest, fraudulent.

honesty *n.* **1** integrity, uprightness, trustworthiness, fairness, honour: *Honesty is a virtue that we seek in all people.* **2** frankness, candour, sincerity: *In all honesty, you did steal the money, didn't you?* ANT. **(1)** dishonesty, fraud.

honorary *adj.* complimentary, gratuitous.

honour *n.* **1** respect, esteem, distinction: *It was an honour to be selected to head the social committee.* **2** principle, character, honesty, uprightness: *Although Jane didn't have to return the money, she did so as a matter of honour.* *vb.* **1** respect, esteem: *We honoured the memory of the past president with a* *special dinner.* **2** admire, revere: *The returning football team were honoured by thousands of supporters.* **3** accept, acknowledge, clear: *The bank refused to honour my cheque.* ANT. *n.* **(1)** dishonour, disgrace, shame. *vb.* **(1)** dishonour, disgrace, shame.

honourable *adj.* **1** honest, noble, just, fair: *The hero fought well and went to an honourable death.* **2** illustrious, famed, distinguished: *The honourable chairman of the council received a special award.* ANT. **(1)** dishonourable, shameful, humiliating.

hood *n.* covering, bonnet, veil.

hook *n.* clasp, catch, fastener.

hoop *n.* ring, band, circle.

hoot *vb.,n.* howl, bellow, yelp; screech, shriek: *The workers hooted with laughter at jokes all afternoon and forgot their work. The owl's hoot could be heard a long way away in the stillness of the night.*

hop *vb.,n.* leap, jump: *Why do you keep hopping about on one leg? Because with each hop I am giving the other leg a rest.*

hope *n.* **1** expectation, anticipation; desire: *My parents have high hopes for me, which is why I am going to university.* **2** trust, faith, confidence: *There may not be food on the table, but there's hope in our hearts.* *vb.* desire, aspire, expect: *I hope Hugh will invite me to the dance.* ANT. *n.* **(2)** hopelessness, despair.

hopeful *adj.* confident, optimistic. ANT. hopeless, despairing.

hopeless *adj.* **1** despairing, desperate, forlorn: *With the score 5 to nothing, the situation looks hopeless.* **2** incurable, fatal, disastrous: *His condition is hopeless: I don't think your horse will live.* ANT. hopeful, promising.

horizontal *adj.* level, even, plane, flat, straight. ANT. vertical, upright.

horrible *adj.* horrifying, awful, terrible, horrid, dreadful, ghastly. ANT. wonderful, splendid.

horrid *adj.* shocking, horrifying, horrible, revolting, repulsive.

horror *n.* **1** terror, dread, alarm: *The horror of the murders shocked the nation.* **2** loathing, hatred, aversion: *Phil had a great horror of seeing the animal in such pain.*

hospital *n.* clinic, infirmary, medical centre, nursing home.

hospitality *n.* generosity, liberality, graciousness, warmth, welcome.

host *n.* entertainer, master of ceremonies, compere.

hostage *n.* security, captive, prisoner.

hostel *n.* guest house, inn, boarding house.

hostile *adj.* unfriendly, antagonistic, warlike. ANT. friendly, hospitable.

hot *adj.* **1** burning, fiery, blazing; sizzling, roasting, frying, broiling, boiling, scorching, searing: *It can get very hot in the middle of the desert at noon.* **2** spicy, sharp, biting: *If you didn't put so much pepper on that curry, it wouldn't be so hot.* **3** violent, passionate, intense, ardent: *The question of how to save fuel and energy is a hot issue today.* ANT. **(1)** cold, cool, chilly, freezing. **(2)** bland, tasteless.

hotel *n.* guest house, inn, motel, hostel.

hotheaded *adj.* reckless, rash, unruly; touchy, testy, short-tempered, irritable. ANT. calm.

hound *n.* dog, beagle, greyhound: *The local gentry took part in the fox hunt with hounds.* *vb.* pursue, harass, harry, pester: *Pete was constantly hounded by the people to whom he owed money.*

house *n.* building, dwelling, residence: *I have to be back at my house by noon.* *vb.* accommodate, shelter, lodge: *The new hall of residence will house more than 500 students.*

hover *vb.* float, glide, fly.

howl *vb.,n.* wail, yowl, cry; yell: *Crowded in the lonely hut, we heard the wolf howling in the distance. With a howl, the dog leaped at the robber.*

hubbub *n.* noise, commotion, fuss, uproar, turmoil.

huddle *vb.* crowd, throng, bunch, nestle.

hue *n.* colour, shade, tone, tint.

hug *vb.,n.* embrace, clasp, press, grasp: *Monica hugged the frightened puppy close to her. Laura's father came home and gave her a big hug and a kiss.*

huge *adj.* enormous, gigantic, immense, colossal, tremendous; large, big. ANT. small, tiny, miniature.

hum *vb.,n.* buzz, drone, whirr, murmur: *The sound of bees humming in the garden is a real delight. The constant hum of traffic in the town is something you can get used to.*

human *adj.* individual, personal; social.

humane *adj.* kind, thoughtful, kindly, merciful, kindhearted, tender, gentle, softhearted. ANT. cruel, mean, heartless.

humble *adj.* **1** lowly, unassuming, modest, unpretending, unpretentious: *My father came from humble origins but is now the general director of a bank.* **2** polite, courteous, respectful: *You should be more humble when talking to your elders.* *vb.* lower, reduce, degrade, downgrade, shame: *Meeting the Prince of Wales face to face humbled me greatly.* ANT. *adj.* **(1)** vain, proud, haughty.

humid *adj.* moist, damp, close, muggy, sticky.

humiliate *vb.* degrade, disgrace, shame, humble.

humorous *adj.* funny, comical, comic, amusing. ANT. serious, unfunny, sober, sombre.

humour *n.* 1 amusement, joking, clowning, fun: *I really like the style of humour of the Marx Brothers.* 2 mood, temper, disposition: *If you want to ask Dorothy for a favour, you'd better wait till she's in a good humour.*

hump *n.* bump, mound, protuberance, elevation.

hunch *n.* guess, feeling, intuition, notion.

hungry *adj.* famished, starved. ANT. full, sated, glutted.

hunt *vb.* 1 chase, track, pursue, stalk: *Do you want to come to our country house and hunt game at the weekend?* 2 seek, probe; scour: *She's been hunting for that book everywhere.* *n.* chase, pursuit; search: *I went along on a fox hunt just for the ride.*

hurdle *n.* 1 fence, barricade, barrier: *The athletes ran the race, leaping over the hurdles.* 2 difficulty, impediment, obstacle: *There are many hurdles in life to overcome.*

hurl *vb.* fling, throw, pitch, cast.

hurry *vb.* 1 rush, run, speed, race, hasten: *Dinner is probably ready, so I'd better hurry home.* 2 rush, hasten, urge, accelerate: *The police hurried the people along the street away from the fight.* *n.* rush, haste, bustle: *Stop pushing! What's the hurry?* ANT. *vb.* (1) linger, tarry, dawdle.

hurt *vb.* 1 damage, harm, injure: *Did you hurt yourself when you fell down the stairs?* 2 wound, distress, afflict, pain: *If you tell Liz that she can't go because she's too young, you'll hurt her feelings.* *n.* injury, harm, pain: *I feel the hurt of knowing I'll never see him again.*

hush *vb.,n.* silence, quiet, still: *Hush the children will you; I'm trying to read! It is so peaceful in the hush of the evening.*

hustle *vb.* hurry, hasten, race, run, speed.

hut *n.* cottage, shed, lodge, shelter.

hypnotize *vb.* mesmerize, entrance, charm, fascinate.

hypocrisy *n.* sham, hollowness, affectation.

hypocrite *n.* actor, pretender, deceiver, fraud.

hysterical *adj.* raving, frenzied, uncontrolled, delirious.

i

icy *adj.* freezing, frozen, cold; slippery.

idea *n.* **1** thought, conception, concept: *I've just had a great idea: let's go to the zoo this afternoon!* **2** notion, understanding: *I haven't the slightest idea what you're talking about.* **3** opinion, plan, belief, view: *The head of the company asked me what my ideas were for expansion.*

ideal *n.* **1** model, example, paragon, standard: *My ideal kitchen appliance is one that does the dishes by itself.* **2** aim, objective, target, goal: *The ideals of the United Nations are peace and friendship throughout the world.* *adj.* perfect, complete, fitting, supreme: *This is an ideal spot for a picnic.*

identical *adj.* alike, indistinguishable, like; same. ANT. unalike, different.

identify *vb.* name, describe, classify; recognize.

identity *n.* individuality, character, uniqueness, personality.

idiosyncrasy *n.* peculiarity, quirk, mannerism, eccentricity.

idiot *n.* fool, nincompoop, dunce, moron.

idiotic *adj.* stupid, senseless, foolish, inane, moronic, half-witted, simpleminded, dim-witted. ANT. intelligent, bright, brilliant, smart.

idle *adj.* **1** unemployed, inactive, unoccupied, unused: *Five hundred men were made idle by the redundancies at the factory.* **2** lazy, sluggish: *An idle mind finds nothing interesting in the world.* ANT. **(1)** active, busy, occupied, engaged.

idol *n.* **1** image, symbol, graven image, god, statue: *The natives fell to their knees before an idol of their water god.* **2** favourite, pet, darling: *The Monster was the name of the new rock group that was the idol of the teenagers.*

ignition *n.* firing, combustion, timing.

ignorant *adj.* **1** untrained, uneducated, illiterate, untaught: *Some of the applicants were too ignorant to qualify for the job.* **2** unaware, unmindful, uninformed: *Ignorant of the fact that she had just written him a letter, Bill tried to ring her up.* ANT. **(1)** educated, cultivated, cultured, schooled, learned. **(2)** aware, informed.

ignore *vb.* disregard, overlook, omit, neglect. ANT. notice.

ill *adj.* sick, unwell, unhealthy, diseased, ailing. ANT. well, healthy, fit.

illegal *adj.* unlawful, forbidden, illicit. ANT. legal, lawful, legitimate.

illegible *adj.* unintelligible, unreadable, indecipherable. ANT. legible.

ill-mannered *adj.* rude, impolite, uncouth. ANT. polite, courteous.

illness *n.* sickness, infirmity, disease, ailment.

illuminate *vb.* 1 light, light up, brighten, lighten: *A strange green glow illuminated the sky.* 2 enlighten, explain, clarify, interpret: *The difficult lecture was illuminated by many illustrations and examples.* ANT. (1) darken, shadow, becloud, obscure.

illusion *n.* mirage, delusion, hallucination, vision, fantasy. ANT. reality, actuality.

illustrate *vb.* 1 illuminate, decorate, adorn, embellish: *The book was illustrated with colour photographs.* 2 demonstrate, show: *The salesman illustrated the use of the gadget by peeling potatoes with it.*

illustration *n.* 1 picture, photograph: *This book contains hundreds of illustrations.* 2 example, explanation: *Dictionaries often give illustrations of how words are used.*

illustrator *n.* artist, painter.

image *n.* 1 likeness, representation, reflection: *Betsy stared at her own image in the mirror.* 2 idea, picture, notion, conception: *In my mind there is an image of what I would want to become when I grow up.*

imaginary *adj.* unreal, fanciful, whimsical. ANT. real, actual.

imagination *n.* imaginativeness, originality, inventiveness, ingenuity.

imagine *vb.* 1 conceive, picture, envisage, envision: *Imagine yourself sitting in a restaurant eating your favourite food.* 2 suppose, believe, think: *I couldn't imagine what had happened to you.*

imbecile *n.* *Informal:* fool, idiot, bungler.

imitate *vb.* follow, copy, mimic, duplicate, reproduce.

immature *adj.* youthful, young; simple, naive. ANT. mature, wise, experienced.

immediate *adj.* 1 instant, instantaneous, present: *My immediate reaction to your request for a loan is "no."* 2 near, next, close; prompt: *Let's take care of the immediate problems now and leave the others till later.* 3 direct: *The immediate result of the plan was to give housing to the elderly.* ANT. (1) long-range, distant. (2) future.

immediately *adv.* at once, instantly, forthwith, directly, promptly.

immense *adj.* huge, enormous, vast, gigantic, great, large, big. ANT. small, tiny.

immerse *vb.* dip, plunge, submerge.

imminent *adj.* approaching, forthcoming, impending.

immobile *adj.* fixed, motionless, stationary. ANT. mobile, moving.

immoderate *adj.* excessive, extravagant, extreme. ANT. moderate, reasonable.

immoral *adj.* corrupt, wicked, dissolute. ANT. good, upright.

immortal *adj.* everlasting, eternal, timeless, undying, endless. ANT. mortal, perishable.

immune *adj.* insusceptible, protected; exempt.

impact *n.* 1 contact, striking, collision: *The bullet struck the wall with such impact that it went right through.* 2 impression, effect, result, consequence: *The impact of the Reformation on Church history was very great.*

impair *vb.* mar, damage, spoil, destroy.

impartial *adj.* unbiased, unprejudiced, fair. ANT. biased, prejudiced, unfair,

impatient *adj.* restless, anxious; irritable. ANT. patient, self-controlled; unexcited.

impediment *n.* hindrance, obstruction, obstacle.

impend *vb.* loom, menace, threaten.

impersonate *see* mimic.

impertinent *adj.* impudent, insolent, rude, disrespectful. ANT. polite, courteous, respectful.

impetuous *adj.* rash, hasty, impulsive. ANT. careful, cautious, thoughtful, prudent.

implant *see* instil.

implement *n.* tool, utensil, instrument, device: *The die-cutter uses precision implements in his trade.* *vb.* complete, fulfil, achieve, realize: *The government implemented their election promises and lowered income tax.*

implicit *adj.* 1 implied, indirect: *The meaning of what he was trying to say was implicit rather than immediately obvious.* 2 unquestioning, absolute, certain: *Young children have an implicit trust in their parents.* ANT. explicit, plain.

implore *vb.* beg, beseech, entreat.

imply *vb.* hint, suggest, indicate, mention. ANT. state, declare.

impolite *adj.* rude, unpleasant, discourteous, insolent, impertinent, uncivil.   ANT. polite, courteous, respectful.

import *vb.*   bring *or* come in, ship in; buy abroad.   ANT. export.

important *adj.*   **1** significant; essential, primary, principal: *Filling in a form is an important part of applying for a job.*   **2** famous, distinguished, notable: *We have had some very important people visiting us.*   ANT. (**1**) unimportant, trivial, trifling, secondary.   (**2**) inconsequential, anonymous.

impose *vb.*   require, levy, demand.

impossible *adj.*   inconceivable, unimaginable, unworkable, preposterous.   ANT. possible; probable, likely.

impostor *n.*   pretender, charlatan, cheat, dissembler.

impotent *adj.*   weak, powerless, inept.   ANT. powerful, strong.

impoverish *vb.*   make poor, ruin, bankrupt.

impractical *adj.*   unworkable, unrealistic, unreal.   ANT. practical, workable, plausible, viable, feasible.

impregnate *vb.*   soak, saturate, fill up, permeate, pervade, infuse.

impress *vb.*   **1** influence, affect; awe: *All of the parents were impressed by their children's achievements in the art class.*   **2** imprint, emboss, indent, mark, print: *The Roman general impressed his seal on the document.*

impression *n.*   **1** effect, mark, influence: *The prime minister's speech made a deep impression on me.*   **2** mark, dent, indentation, depression: *The thief's shoe made an impression in the flower bed outside the window.*   **3** opinion, belief, guess, theory: *I have the impression that you'd rather not go.*

impressive *adj.*   striking, awe-inspiring, stirring, moving; grand, magnificent.   ANT boring, tedious.

improbable *adj.*   doubtful, unlikely.   ANT. likely, probable.

improper *adj.*   **1** unsuitable, unfit, inappropriate: *The manager told us that blue jeans and sweatshirts were improper attire for the restaurant.*   **2** indecent, naughty, unbecoming: *My father used to punish any of us whom he heard using improper language.*   ANT. proper, fitting, appropriate.

improve *vb.*   better, amend, repair, ameliorate.   ANT. worsen, impair.

improvement *n.*   change, development, growth; addition; modernization; amelioration.   ANT. deterioration, worsening.

improvise *vb.*   ad-lib, extemporize; invent, devise.

impudent *adj.*   impertinent, fresh, insolent, insulting, rude.   ANT. courteous, polite, respectful.

impulse *n.*   **1** whim, hunch, fancy, caprice, urge: *Fanny got an* *impulse to place a bet on a horse called "Bottoms Up."* **2** force, surge, pulse: *The impulse of the waves keeps the pump going automatically.*

impulsive *adj.* hasty, rash; spontaneous, automatic. ANT. careful, cautious, prudent.

impure *adj.* adulterated, contaminated, mixed, tainted; unclean. ANT. pure, spotless, clean.

impute *vb.* attribute, ascribe, reckon.

inaccessible *adj.* far, remote, (*informal*) ungetatable. ANT. near, close.

inaccurate *adj.* incorrect, wrong, mistaken, faulty. ANT. accurate, correct, right.

inactive *adj.* motionless, still, inert, idle.

inadequate *adj.* insufficient; weak, feeble; unsatisfactory. ANT. adequate, sufficient, satisfactory.

inanimate *adj.* lifeless, mineral, inorganic. ANT. animate, lively.

inappropriate *adj.* unsuitable, improper, unfit; untimely. ANT. appropriate, suitable.

incapable *see* **incompetent.**

incense[1] *n.* fragrance, odour, scent, aroma: *There was a strong smell of incense in the church.*

incense[2] *vb.* enrage, infuriate, anger: *Terry's father was incensed to learn that he had taken the car without his permission.*

incentive *n.* inducement, stimulus, impulse, encouragement, influence. ANT. discouragement, disincentive.

incessant *adj.* unending, eternal, continuous, perpetual, constant, relentless. ANT. intermittent, irregular, spasmodic.

incident *n.* event, occurrence, happening.

incidental *adj.* secondary, unimportant, trivial. ANT. fundamental, basic.

incite *vb.* provoke, stir up, arouse.

inclination *n.* **1** tendency, predisposition, preference, prejudice: *My inclination is to do nothing for a week and see what happens.* **2** slope, slant, incline, lean: *The inclination of the Leaning Tower of Pisa continues to increase every year.* ANT. (1) disinclination, reluctance. (2) uprightness, straightness.

incline *vb.* **1** lean, slope, tilt, slant: *The hill inclines steeply near the top.* **2** tend, be disposed: *I incline to think you're right.*

include *vb.* embrace, encompass, contain, involve. ANT. exclude, omit.

incoherent *adj.* disordered, unclear, inarticulate.

income *n.* salary, earnings, wages, pay; revenue, receipts, return. ANT. expenditure.

incompatible *adj.* conflicting, inconsistent, contrary, contradictory.

incompetent *adj.* unfit, incapable, unqualified; clumsy, awkward. ANT. competent, able, skilled.

incomplete *adj.* unfinished, imperfect. ANT. complete, finished.

inconvenient *adj.* inappropriate, awkward, troublesome, untimely. ANT. convenient, handy.

incorrect *adj.* wrong, inaccurate, mistaken, erroneous. ANT. correct, accurate, proper, suitable.

increase *vb.* swell, enlarge, extend, grow, prolong, lengthen, broaden: *My boss increased my salary this year.* *n.* enlargement, growth, expansion: *There has been a huge increase in the price of cheese during the past year.* ANT. *vb.* decrease, shrink, lessen, diminish. *n.* decrease, lessening, shrinkage.

incredible *adj.* unbelievable, improbable. ANT. credible, plausible, believable.

incriminate *vb.* involve, accuse, blame, implicate.

indebted *adj.* appreciative, grateful, thankful.

indecent *adj.* immoral, offensive, shocking, shameful. ANT. decent, upright.

indecision *n.* hesitancy, irresolution, uncertainty.

indeed *adv.* really, in fact, truthfully, surely, honestly.

indefinite *adj.* uncertain, unsure, vague, unsettled, confused; confusing. ANT. definite, decided, unequivocal.

indemnity *n.* compensation, reimbursement, restitution.

independence *n.* liberty, freedom; sovereignty, autonomy. ANT. dependence, reliance.

independent *adj.* **1** free, autonomous, self-ruling, self-determining: *Many African countries, once under British rule, have become independent.* **2** unconventional, uninhibited, self-confident: *Karen is an independent girl for her age.* ANT. **(1)** dependent, subject.

index *n.* list, classification, catalogue, file; appendix.

indicate *vb.* **1** signify, symbolize, mean: *Yellow lines near the kerb indicate that you cannot park there.* **2** point out, show, designate: *The policeman indicated that the best route to the park would be straight ahead.*

indifferent *adj.* unconcerned, uncaring, cool, insensitive, nonchalant. ANT. concerned, caring, earnest.

indignant *adj.* angry, irritated, aroused, exasperated, irate. ANT. serene, calm, content.

indiscreet *adj.* tactless, rash, imprudent. ANT. cautious, tactful.

indispensable *adj.* necessary, essential, required. ANT. dispensable, unnecessary.

indisposed *adj.* ill, sick, unwell. ANT. well, healthy.

individual *adj.* single, separate, apart, different, distinct; special: *Each member of the team has his own individual number.* *n.* person, human, human being: *Each individual will be given his own reading list for the summer.*

indoctrinate *vb.* teach, influence, inculcate, force into, brainwash.

indolent *adj.* lazy, idle, slow, sluggish, inactive. ANT. vigorous, active, dynamic.

induce *vb.* persuade, influence, convince. ANT. dissuade, discourage.

inducement *n.* lure, enticement, incentive, stimulus. ANT. discouragement.

indulge *vb.* yield to, gratify, satisfy.

industrious *adj.* hard-working, busy, diligent, persistent. ANT. lazy, indolent.

inefficient *adj.* wasteful, extravagant; incompetent, incapable. ANT. efficient; effective.

inevitable *adj.* unavoidable, inescapable, sure, certain.

inexpensive *adj.* low-priced, modest, economical; cheap. ANT. expensive, costly, dear.

inexperienced *adj.* untrained, green; uninformed, naive. ANT. skilled, experienced, seasoned, trained.

infamous *adj.* **1** scandalous, shocking, shameful, disgraceful: *Her infamous conduct was known to many in the town.* **2** notorious, wicked, evil, bad: *Everyone knows about the infamous Spanish Inquisition.*

infantile *adj.* childish, immature, babyish, naive. ANT. grown-up, mature, adult.

infatuated *adj.* fascinated, inflamed, charmed.

infect *vb.* contaminate, taint, pollute.

infectious *adj.* catching, communicable, contagious, transferable.

inferior *adj.* lower, second-rate; mediocre. ANT. superior, higher.

infinite *adj.* vast, boundless, innumerable, endless, unlimited, limitless. ANT. finite, limited.

inflame vb. excite, arouse, incite, fire. ANT. calm, soothe.

inflammation n. irritation, soreness; infection.

inflate vb. swell, expand, blow up, distend. ANT. deflate, collapse.

inflexible adj. rigid, unbending, firm, unyielding, immovable, steadfast. ANT. flexible, pliant, yielding, giving, elastic.

inflict vb. **1** give, deliver, deal: *The gang that attacked us inflicted serious injuries to those who resisted.* **2** impose, levy, apply: *The government inflicts heavy taxes on rich people.*

influence n. effect, sway, weight, control: *The politician had great influence throughout the city.* vb. affect, control, sway, impress: *The scientist insists on keeping an open mind and will be influenced only by actual facts.*

inform vb. notify, advise, tell, relate.

informal adj. relaxed, friendly, easygoing. ANT. official, formal, conventional.

information n. facts, data, knowledge; intelligence.

informative adj. enlightening, instructive, educational.

informer n. betrayer, traitor, tattler, (*slang*) rat.

infrequent adj. occasional, scarce, sparse. ANT. frequent, regular.

infuriate vb. anger, annoy, enrage.

ingenious adj. clever, skilful, imaginative, inventive.

ingredient n. element, component, constituent.

inhabit vb. occupy; live, dwell, *or* reside in.

inhabitant n. resident, citizen; native.

inheritance n. heritage, legacy, patrimony.

initial adj. first, basic, primary, elementary. ANT. last, final, terminal.

initiate vb. start, begin, commence, open. ANT. stop, finish, terminate.

initiative n. enterprise; enthusiasm; energy, vigour.

inject vb. inoculate, vaccinate.

injure vb. harm, hurt, wound, damage.

injury n. harm, damage, hurt, impairment.

inmate n. prisoner, convict, internee; patient.

inn n. public house, tavern; hotel.

innocent adj. **1** not guilty, blameless, faultless, virtuous: *The defendant was found to be innocent and was set free.* **2** unknowing, naive, unsophisticated: *Innocent young people are not allowed to see that kind of film.* ANT. (**1**) guilty, blameworthy. (**2**) sophisticated, wise, worldly.

innumerable adj. numberless, countless, immeasurable.

inquisitive *adj.* prying, curious, intrusive, (*slang*) nosy. ANT. uninterested, incurious.

insane *adj.* **1** mad, crazy, deranged, lunatic, demented, mentally unsound: *The murderer was declared legally insane.* **2** foolish, stupid, idiotic: *You're insane to dive off that tower into a small tank of water.* ANT. (**1**) sane, coherent, rational.

insert *vb.* introduce, put in; infuse.

inside *n.* interior, lining; heart, centre.

insignificant *adj.* unimportant, irrelevant, trifling. ANT. important, significant.

insipid *adj.* boring, uninteresting, tasteless. ANT. lively.

insist *vb.* demand, require, command.

insolent *adj.* impertinent, rude, disrespectful, insulting. ANT. polite, courteous, respectful.

inspect *vb.* examine, investigate, study.

inspection *n.* examination, investigation, enquiry.

inspiration *n.* impulse, stimulus, spur, motivation, incentive; thought, idea.

inspire *vb.* stimulate, encourage, invigorate; quicken, animate.

instability *n.* unsteadiness, imbalance, disequilibrium. ANT. stability, balance.

install *vb.* establish, set up, put in, place.

instance *n.* case, example, occasion, illustration.

instant *n.* moment, flash, twinkling.

instantly *adv.* at once, immediately, right away, directly, instantaneously.

instil *vb.* implant, infuse, imbue; introduce.

instinct *n.* feeling, intuition.

institute *vb.* establish, organize, found, launch, begin, initiate.

institution *n.* organization, establishment, association; college, hospital.

instruct *vb.* **1** teach, educate, train, tutor, school, drill: *The gym teacher instructed us in the art of self-defence.* **2** order, command, direct: *We were instructed to be very quiet during the ceremony.*

instruction *n.* **1** teaching, training, education, guidance: *Miles plays the violin beautifully, but he's never had any instruction.* **2** direction, order, command: *The instruction was to proceed to the end of the street and turn right.*

instrument *n.* tool, implement, device; means.

insufficient *adj.* inadequate, unsatisfactory; poor, meagre.

insulate *vb.* protect, treat; wrap, cushion, line.

insult vb. offend, outrage, humiliate: *I won't insult you by telling you what I think of that cake you baked.* n. offence, affront, outrage, scorn: *Even though you love your dog, telling me that I look like him is an insult.* ANT. vb. flatter, praise. n. flattery, praise.

integrity n. honesty, uprightness, honour, principle, virtue.

intellect n. 1 judgment, understanding: *The men who planned the raid were of low intellect.* 2 intelligence, mind, mentality, brains: *There can be no doubt that Albert Einstein was a man with enormous intellect.*

intellectual adj. intelligent, learned: *I don't think you will find this comic too intellectual.* n. academic, scholar: *The intellectuals are all in favour of higher government grants to the arts.*

intelligence n. ability, skill, aptitude; understanding.

intelligent adj. bright, clever, quick, astute, alert. ANT. stupid, slow, unintelligent, dumb.

intelligible adj. comprehensible; clear, plain, obvious.

intend vb. mean; expect; plan, propose.

intense adj. 1 deep, profound, concentrated, serious, earnest: *Felicity was wrapped up in her own intense thoughts.* 2 concentrated, great, heightened, intensified, exceptional: *The intense heat from the burning building scorched the trees nearby.*

intensify vb. raise, magnify, reinforce, sharpen.

intent n. aim, purpose, intention: *The man had been arrested for attacking the pedestrian with intent to kill him.* adj. concentrated, set; steadfast: *Philip was intent on becoming a doctor, and after years of study, his ambitions were fulfilled.*

intention n. plan, intent, purpose, expectation, design, aim.

intentional adj. purposeful, deliberate, planned, intended. ANT. accidental, chance.

intentionally adv. purposefully, on purpose, deliberately; maliciously. ANT. accidentally.

intercept vb. stop, seize, ambush; deflect, (*informal*) head off.

interest n. 1 concern, care, attention: *The scientist examined the fossil with interest.* 2 profit, advantage, benefit, gain: *It's in your own interest to do well at school.* 3 right, share, ownership, claim: *Yes, I do have a small interest in that publishing company.* 4 addition, increase: *Nowadays the interest you have to pay if you borrow money is about ten per cent.* vb. attract, engage, absorb: *What you say about your uncle's jewel collection interests me.* ANT. n. (1) disinterest, apathy. vb. bore, weary.

interested *adj.* **1** absorbed, engrossed; stimulated, excited, inspired: *Are you interested in model railways?* **2** concerned, involved, affected: *You cannot be impartial: since you own a share in the property, you are an interested party.* ANT. **(1)** bored. **(2)** disinterested, indifferent.

interesting *adj.* attractive, fascinating, absorbing, engrossing. ANT. uninteresting, boring, tedious, wearisome.

interfere *vb.* meddle, butt in, intervene.

interference *n.* **1** meddling, prying, intrusion: *Your interference in matters that don't concern you has gone far enough.* **2** obstruction, obstacle, barrier: *Every time I have tried to settle the question the others have created some interference.*

interior *n.* inside, centre: *The interior of the house was painted yellow.* *adj.* inside, central, inner, internal: *The interior sections of the island were mostly swamplands.* ANT. *n.* exterior, outside. *adj.* external, outer, ouside.

intermediate *adj.* middle, mean, half-way.

interminable *adj.* endless, never-ending, long; boring, dull.

intermittent *adj.* occasional, periodic, spasmodic, discontinuous.

internal *adj.* **1** inner, interior, inside; private, intimate: *They received internal injuries in the car crash.* **2** domestic, native: *Diplomatic relations are an international, not an internal matter.* ANT. external, outer, surface.

international *adj.* foreign, worldwide, multinational. ANT. national, domestic, internal.

interpret *vb.* **1** explain, define; make sense of; understand: *The way Lorenzo interpreted your remark, he thinks you don't like him.* **2** translate, paraphrase: *Because the ambassador understood not one word of Russian, he hired Ivan to interpret what was being said.*

interpretation *n.* explanation; account, rendition, reading.

interpreter *n.* translator, linguist.

interrogate *vb.* cross-examine, question, ask.

interrupt *vb.* **1** intrude, break in, interfere, cut in (on): *Please don't interrupt me when I'm talking. If you always interrupt, how can you know what others think?* **2** discontinue, stop, hinder, obstruct: *The trees on this side of the house interrupt the view of the seashore.*

interval *n.* gap, pause, intermission.

intervene *vb.* come between, interfere, interrupt, intrude.

intimate *adj.* **1** close, familiar, personal: *Shellie is one of my most intimate friends.* **2** private, personal, confidential, secret: *We have always shared the most intimate details of our lives with each other.* **3** thorough, complete, detailed: *I have an intimate understanding of the way in which a car engine works.* *vb.* hint, suggest, imply: *Charlie intimated that if I were to offer to lend him my car, he would accept.*

intimidate *vb.* scare, frighten; threaten.

intolerable *adj.* unbearable, insufferable; painful. ANT. tolerable, bearable.

intolerant *adj.* prejudiced, biased, bigoted. ANT. tolerant, broadminded, fair.

intrepid *adj.* bold, fearless, daring, courageous. ANT. cowardly.

intricate *adj.* complex, involved; puzzling, tricky; obscure. ANT. clear, easy.

intrigue *vb.* attract, charm, interest, captivate: *The dark-haired girl at the table in the corner intrigues me.* *n.* plot, scheme, conspiracy: *The cafés of Casablanca were famous as the scenes of many international intrigues.*

introduce *vb.* **1** present; acquaint: *We were introduced to each other at Flora's house in Putney.* **2** submit, propose, present, offer: *The government has introduced a bill to change the education system in this country.*

introduction *n.* **1** presentation, acquaintance, contact: *The meeting began with the introduction of three new members.* **2** preface, foreword, preliminaries; prelude: *The introduction in this book is very short: just two pages.*

intrude *vb.* interfere, infringe, interrupt.

intruder *n.* prowler, thief, trespasser, robber.

invade *vb.* attack, penetrate, occupy, overrun; encroach upon.

invalid[1] *n.* patient, sufferer, convalescent: *We visited the invalids in hospital.*

invalid[2] *adj.* inoperative, null and void; abolished: *The return half of a day-return ticket is invalid on the day after you bought it.* ANT. valid, operative; permitted.

invasion *n.* intrusion, attack, encroachment.

invent *vb.* **1** originate, create, devise: *Thomas Edison invented the electric light bulb.* **2** make up, concoct, contrive: *I think Andrew invented the story about being in the army, as he's only nine years old!*

invest *vb.* lay out, put money in; loan, lend.

investigate *vb.* examine, inspect, explore, study.

investigation *n.* examination, exploration, enquiry, study, research, search.

invisible *adj.* imperceptible; hidden, concealed, inconspicuous. ANT. obvious, visible, clear.

invite *vb.* **1** ask, request the company of: *After we got to know them a little, we invited our neighbours for dinner.* **2** request, encourage, urge: *Applications are invited for the teaching post at the school.*

inviting *adj.* alluring, luring, appealing, tempting, attractive, encouraging. ANT. uninviting, unattractive.

involuntary *adj.* automatic, reflex, uncontrolled; unintentional. ANT. voluntary, willed, wilful.

involve *vb.* **1** include, contain, embrace: *If your plans for having dinner involve me, please remember I don't like cauliflower.* **2** complicate, confuse, entangle: *"This is one of the most involved cases I have ever tried," said the judge.*

inward *adj.* internal, inner, inside. ANT. outward.

irony *n.* satire, absurdity; ridicule, mockery.

irrational *adj.* **1** illogical, absurd, unreasonable: *The girl's irrational behaviour baffled the doctor for months.* **2** senseless, stupid, incoherent: *Man sometimes behaves as an irrational being.*

irregular *adj.* **1** uneven, unequal, crooked: *The irregular surface of this wall must accumulate a lot of dust.* **2** disorderly, random, unsettled, disorganized: *The hours kept by the staff are irregular, and you can never be sure when someone is in the office.* ANT. (1) regular, even.

irrelevant *adj.* unimportant, unrelated, unconnected, extraneous.

irresistible *adj.* compelling, alluring, overwhelming.

irreverent *adj.* disrespectful, impolite; sacrilegious, profane, blasphemous.

irritable *adj.* sensitive, touchy, testy, peevish, short-tempered. ANT. cheerful, happy.

irritate *vb.* **1** annoy, vex, pester, bother: *I find your constant whining about going swimming very irritating.* **2** redden, chafe, inflame: *Stop scratching your eye or you'll irritate it.* ANT. (1) soothe, pacify, calm.

isolate *vb.* separate, disconnect, segregate, detach.

isolation *n.* separation, detachment; loneliness, solitude, seclusion, confinement.

issue *n.* **1** number, copy, edition: *Have you seen Wednesday's issue of the newspaper?* **2** problem, question, concern;

matter, subject: *The television programme dealt with current events and with issues of importance to all of us.* *vb.* **1** appear, emerge, come out, come forth: *The smoke issued from the chimney in great black clouds.* **2** publish, distribute, put out, send out, circulate, release: *A quarterly magazine is issued four times a year.*

j

jail *n.* prison: *After spending 20 years in jail, the man was afraid to face the responsibilities of freedom.* *vb.* imprison, confine, detain, lock up: *She was jailed for shoplifting.*

jailer *n.* keeper, guard, warden.

jam *vb.* pack, crowd, force, ram, push, squeeze, wedge: *I don't see how they can jam eight tomatoes into that tiny can.* *n.* preserve, conserve: *Do you like jam in sandwiches?*

jar[1] *n.* pot, jug, bottle, pitcher; container: *I bought a jar of honey from the supermarket.*

jar[2] *n.* jolt, shock: *The fall gave her system quite a jar.* *vb.* clash, disagree, grate: *The colours in your living room jar.*

jealous *adj.* envious; covetous.

jealousy *n.* envy; covetousness; greed.

jeer *vb.,n.* laugh, scoff, taunt: *The boys jeered as the headmaster went by. A huge jeer rose from the crowd as the prisoners came out of the courtroom.*

jerk *vb.* twitch, quiver, shake: *When you jerked the tablecloth, you spilled the milk.* *n.* twitch, spasm, shake, quiver: *With a quick jerk, the horse threw the boy to the ground.*

jet *n.* **1** spurt, squirt: *When I turned on the tap, a jet of water hit me in the face.* **2** aeroplane, jumbo jet: *The jet took off from Heathrow bound for the United States.*

jewel *n.* gem; emerald, ruby, diamond, pearl.

job *n.* **1** work, employment, trade, profession, position, calling, career, business: *With so many people unemployed, my father was lucky to have a job.* **2** task, chore, duty: *Mother told me she had some jobs she wanted done around the house after school.*

jog *vb.* **1** push, shake, jar: *Sandra jogged her boyfriend as he had fallen asleep.* **2** run, trot: *Many people now go jogging to keep fit.*

join *vb.* unite, connect, couple, assemble, link, fit, attach. ANT. split, separate, divide, sunder.

joint *n.* connection, link, coupling, union, junction: *I could see where the glue was oozing out of the joint between the parts.* *adj.* common, mutual, combined, connected: *If we make a joint effort, we can do it more quickly.* ANT. *adj.* separate, divided.

joke *n.* jest, prank, game, caper, antic; anecdote: *Tying a tin to a dog's tail isn't a funny joke.* *vb.* jest, banter, laugh: *You go to your office by helicopter every day? You must be joking!*

jolly *adj.* joyful, spirited, happy, cheerful, glad. ANT. sad, sombre, gloomy, melancholy.

jolt *vb.,n.* jar, bump, bounce, shake, shock: *The electric wire touched my finger and jolted me. Everett got quite a jolt when he sat on that drawing pin.*

journal *n.* **1** diary, account, record: *Some people keep a journal every day of everything that happens to them.* **2** periodical, magazine, newspaper: *The reading room contains many journals.*

journalist *n.* writer, reporter, correspondent, editor.

journey *n.* trip, voyage, excursion, tour: *Our journey to Istanbul took three days on the train.* *vb.* travel: *The student journeyed for two weeks to visit his old professor.*

jovial *adj.* jolly, convivial, hearty.

joy *n.* delight, pleasure, happiness, gladness, satisfaction. ANT. unhappiness, misery, sadness, gloom.

judge *n.* **1** justice, magistrate: *The judge pronounced judgment on the men and sentenced them to 18 months imprisonment.* **2** arbiter, referee, umpire, arbitrator: *How can you be a judge of the matter when you don't know all of the facts?* *vb.* **1** sentence, condemn, convict: *Mr. Justice Smith judged the prisoners in the dock.* **2** decide, determine, consider, reckon: *He judged the festivities worthy of his support.*

judgment *n.* **1** decision, verdict, estimation, opinion: *In our judgment, the horse should not have been disqualified.* **2** understanding, wisdom, discretion, sense, common sense, intelligence: *I think you showed good judgment when you reported that suspicious man to the police.*

jug *n.* jar, bottle, flagon, flask, pitcher.

jump *vb.,n.* leap, spring, bound, vault, skip, hop: *Don't try jumping over that puddle or you'll fall into it. He's going to attempt a jump over the river next year while riding a horse.*

jumpy *adj.* nervous, apprehensive, touchy, sensitive, excitable. ANT. calm, tranquil, unruffled.

junction *n.* **1** intersection, crossroads: *The accident happened at the junction, as the two cars collided.* **2** connection, joint, weld, seam: *The rust started at the junction where the two sides of the box come together.*

jungle *n.* bush, forest, thicket, undergrowth.

junk *n.* rubbish, waste, salvage, scraps.

just *adj.* **1** fair, impartial: *I think that the umpire's decision was* *just—the man was out.* **2** rightful, lawful, legal; proper; deserved: *Since we had paid for the land, we had just title to it.* ANT. **(1)** biased, unfair, partial.

justice *n.* fairness, equity, impartiality, fair-mindedness.

justify *vb.* **1** vindicate, clear, acquit, excuse: *I don't see how you can justify murder except in self-defence.* **2** defend, explain, excuse: *Tom tried to justify his actions by claiming that he had been very tired.*

k

keen *adj.* **1** enthusiastic, eager, interested: *I don't know if Ward is so keen to publish the book any more.* **2** sharp, acute: *This hunting knife has such a keen edge I can split a hair with it.* **3** quick, shrewd, bright, clever, intelligent: *John has a keen wit.* ANT. (1) apathetic, reluctant. (2) blunted. (3) dull, stupid, slow, obtuse.

keep *vb.* **1** retain, hold, withhold, preserve, maintain: *When you borrow books from the library, you're supposed to return them, not keep them.* **2** continue, persist in: *I wish you wouldn't keep saying the same thing over and over again.* **3** save, store, hold: *You can't keep eggs for a month outside the refrigerator without their becoming rotten.* *vb. phr.* **keep back** delay, hinder, hold, check: *I couldn't keep back a sneeze.* **keep on** continue, persist in: *If you keep on shouting you'll get hoarse.* **keep up** maintain, sustain, support: *The firm kept up its rate of progress for 3 years and then went bankrupt.* *n.* **1** living; room and board, maintenance, subsistence: *The farmhand worked just for his keep during hard times.* **2** tower, dungeon: *The knight rescued the damsel from the keep of the king's castle.*

keeper *n.* jailer, warden, custodian, guard.

key *n.* **1** latchkey; master key; skeleton key: *He opened the front door with his key.* **2** clue; answer: *The key to the puzzle is to spell the words backwards.*

kick *vb.* boot, strike, hit, tap.

kidnap *vb.* abduct, capture, seize, carry away, make off with, hold for ransom.

kill *vb.* **1** slay, execute, assassinate, murder: *The tiger killed two people and then ran into the jungle.* **2** destroy, cancel, abolish: *Your attitude could kill any feeling of love I might have towards you.*

kind[1] *n.* sort, class, type, variety: *What kind of bird is that?*

kind[2] *adj.* friendly, gentle, kindly, mild, kindhearted, goodhearted, warm, tender, affectionate: *He was very kind to his elderly neighbours.* ANT. cruel, brutal, mean, hardhearted.

kindle *vb.* **1** ignite, fire, light: *You'll need some paper to kindle a fire.* **2** excite, arouse, inflame, provoke: *The new girl in* *the class knew how to kindle a spark of dislike into a flame of hatred.*

kingdom *n.*   monarchy, realm, domain, empire.

kiosk *n.*   booth, stall, stand.

kiss *vb.*   **1** embrace: *The friends kissed as they met again.*   **2** touch, brush, graze: *The billiard balls kissed lightly.*

kit *n.*   set, collection; outfit, equipment.

knife *n.*   blade, cutter, spear; penknife.

knob *n.*   **1** handle, doorknob: *You have to turn the knob if you want to open the door.*   **2** bump, projection, protuberance: *There's a knob on my head where the ball hit me.*

knock *vb.,n.*   rap, thump, whack, thwack, tap: *Please knock on my door at seven tomorrow morning. I have a headache from that knock I got yesterday.*

knot *n.*   tie, splice, hitch; twist, tangle.

know *vb.*   **1** recognize: *I don't think I know you—have we met?*   **2** understand, comprehend, see: *Do you know what I'm talking about?*   **3** distinguish, discriminate: *I wouldn't know him from Adam.*

knowledge *n.*   **1** facts, information, learning, data: *Sidney's knowledge of physics is rather limited.*   **2** understanding, wisdom, judgment: *Man's knowledge of himself has increased enormously in the past century.*

l

label *n.* marker, mark, sticker, tag, stamp: *The label on this vase says it was made in Denmark.* *vb.* mark, stamp: *All medicines should be labelled to show their ingredients.*

laborious *adj.* difficult, tiring, burdensome, hard. ANT. easy, simple, restful, relaxing.

labour *n.* 1 work, toil, drudgery: *Clearing out your attic would provide labour for five men for a week.* 2 workingmen, workers, working class: *Management and labour reached an agreement last night, and the bus drivers returned to work today.* *vb.* work, toil, strive: *My father laboured for many years for others before he could buy his own farm.*

lack *n.* shortage, need, dearth, want, scarcity: *Driving over the speed limit shows a lack of good judgment. The lack of vitamins and protein in their diet made many of the people very weak and ill.* *vb.* want, need, require: *We are lacking three people to make up the football team.* ANT. *n.* abundance, quantity, plenty, profusion.

lad *n.* boy, youth, fellow, chap, stripling.

lag *vb.* fall behind, dawdle, linger, loiter, tarry, straggle: *Deliveries are lagging two weeks behind orders.* *n.* slack, slowdown, tardiness: *The lag in sales is due to economic difficulties.*

lame *adj.* crippled, disabled, limping; deformed.

lament *vb.* mourn, weep, bemoan, grieve; regret: *The widows of the men killed in the explosion lamented their loss.* *n.* mourning, lamentation, moan, wail, moaning, wailing, weeping: *The widow's lament was great for many days after the accident.*

lamentable *adj.* deplorable, unfortunate, shocking.

lamp *n.* light, light bulb, candle.

land *n.* ground, earth: *The hovercraft moved off the land into the sea.* *vb.* come down, touch down, arrive: *The aeroplane landed at Gatwick airport.*

lane *n.* passage, alley, way, alleyway.

language *n.* 1 tongue, speech: *My uncle speaks three foreign languages.* 2 dialect; jargon; patois: *The technical language of mathematics is hard to understand.*

lapse *vb.* stop, end, cease; decline, deteriorate, weaken.

large *adj.* big, great, massive, huge, vast, enormous, immense. ANT. small, little, tiny, diminutive.

largely *adv.* mainly, chiefly, mostly, principally.

lash *n.* whip, thong, cane, rod, knout: *The thief received five lashes in the public square.* *vb.* whip, strike, scourge, beat: *The prisoner was lashed as a punishment.*

lass *n.* girl, maiden, damsel.

last *adj.* final, latest, ultimate, extreme, concluding: *The last time I saw her, she was wearing a green hat and coat.* *vb.* continue, remain, endure: *This pair of blue jeans has lasted for three years.* ANT. *adj.* first, initial, starting, beginning.

late *adj.* overdue, behind time; slow. ANT. early.

latitude *n.* freedom, scope, range, extent.

laugh *vb.,n.* chuckle, giggle, snicker, guffaw: *I wasn't laughing at you because you're not funny. Margaret gave a little embarrassed laugh when asked why she was late.*

laughable *adj.* amusing, funny, humorous, comical, ridiculous.

launch *vb.* 1 fire, drive, propel: *The rocket was launched to the moon at dawn.* 2 initiate, originate, start, begin: *The firm launched its sales offensive in October.* ANT.(2) stop, finish, terminate.

lavish *adj.* generous, profuse, abundant, liberal. ANT. meagre, scanty; sparing; mean.

law *n.* rule, statute, order, decree, ruling.

lawful *adj.* legal, legitimate. ANT. illegal.

lawless *adj.* uncontrolled, uncivilized, wild, untamed, savage, violent. ANT. law-abiding, obedient, tame.

lawyer *n.* barrister, counsel, advocate.

lax *adj.* lenient, slack, remiss. ANT. strict.

lay[1] *vb.* 1 put, place, set, deposit: *Please lay the book on the table.* 2 attribute, reckon: *The blame was laid fair and square on Peter.* 3 wager, bet, risk, hazard, stake: *I'll lay you five to one that my horse wins.*

lay[2] *adj.* 1 unordained, laic, laical: *John's uncle is a lay member of the church, not a minister.* 2 amateur, nonprofessional: *Since I wasn't a scientist, I could give only a lay opinion about the effects of the atomic power plant.*

layer *n.* coat, coating, stratum, bed.

lazy *adj.* idle, indolent, inactive, sluggish. ANT. ambitious, active, forceful.

lead *vb.* 1 guide, conduct, direct, steer: *The blind man's dog led him carefully across the street.* 2 command, direct: *We need a strong man to lead us through the coming difficulties.* ANT. follow.

leader *n.* director, chief, commander, head, manager, ruler. ANT. follower, disciple.

league *n.* alliance, union, combination.

leak *vb.* drip, flow.

lean[1] *vb.* **1** slant, tilt, slope: *The Tower of Pisa leans over a little more each year.* **2** rely, depend, trust: *When you go in to take the examination, you won't be able to lean on your teacher's help.*

lean[2] *adj.* slender, slim, thin, lanky, skinny: *The tall lean cowboy · sauntered into the saloon.* ANT. *adj.* fat, heavy, obese.

leap *vb.,n.* jump, vault, spring, bound: *Jennie leapt up to kiss me when I entered the room. With a leap, the tiger was attacking the elephant.*

learn *vb.* master, acquire, gain, determine, find out, discover; memorize.

learned *adj.* scholarly, wise, educated, knowledgeable, well-informed. ANT. ignorant, uneducated, unlettered, illiterate.

learning *n.* knowledge, scholarship, education.

lease *vb.* let, hire, rent, charter.

least *adj.* **1** smallest, tiniest, minutest: *Mother gave me the least amount of rice she could: one grain!* **2** slightest; trivial: *Don gets annoyed at the least little thing.* ANT. (**1**) most.

leave *vb.* **1** depart, go, quit; desert, abandon: *Evelyn left two days ago. The man in the witness box admitted to leaving his wife and two children.* **2** bequeath, will: *Oscar's grandmother left him some money when she died.* *n.* **1** permission, allowance, liberty, freedom, consent: *Do I have your leave to speak to the minister?* **2** vacation, holiday: *Andy will be on leave from the navy all next month.* ANT. *vb.* (**1**) arrive, come.

lecture *n.* speech, talk, address, lesson: *Last night we attended an illustrated lecture on bird watching.* *vb.* speak *or* talk (to), address, teach, instruct: *The professor lectured the students about the plays of Shakespeare.*

ledge *n.* shelf, strip, ridge, step.

legal *adj.* lawful, legitimate; honest. ANT. illegal.

legend *n.* story, tale, myth, folk tale, fable.

legendary *adj.* **1** mythical, fictitious, fanciful, imaginary: *Nobody is exactly sure whether King Arthur was real or legendary.* **2** famous, celebrated, notorious: *The wealth of the Rhodes family is legendary in these parts.*

legible *adj.* decipherable, readable, plain. ANT. illegible, unclear.

legitimate *adj.* legal, lawful, right, proper, correct, valid. ANT. illegitimate.

leisure *n.* relaxation, ease, recreation, rest.

leisurely *adj.* unhurried, casual, relaxed, comfortable. ANT. hectic, hurried, pressed, forced, rushed.

lend *vb.* loan, entrust, advance. ANT. borrow.

length *n.* extent, measure, reach, stretch; longness.

lengthen *vb.* extend, stretch, reach, prolong, grow, increase. ANT. shorten, contract, shrink.

lenient *adj.* tolerant, indulgent, pardoning; soft, gentle. ANT. severe, strict, austere.

lessen *vb.* reduce, diminish, decrease, shrink, dwindle, decline. ANT. increase, swell, expand, multiply.

lesson *n.* 1 exercise, drill, assignment, homework: *I hope that all the students have completed the lesson for today.* 2 instruction; example, model: *Your catching a cold ought to be a lesson to you to wear your coat.*

let *vb.* 1 permit, allow, grant: *Please let me go to the disco.* 2 lease, rent: *There's a flat to let in our block.*

lethal *see* **fatal.**

letter *n.* note, message, communication, epistle.

level *adj.* 1 even, smooth, flat, uniform: *The new board you put into the floor isn't level with the others.* 2 horizontal, plane, flat: *On a level road, this car runs very smoothly.* 3 equivalent, equal: *My boat drew up level with the leader's and then we started to pull ahead.* *vb.* 1 even, equalize; smooth: *I have to level the ground before planting the seeds.* 2 demolish, destroy, raze, flatten: *The entire centre of the city was levelled by the bomb.*

lever *n.* bar, lifter, prize, crowbar.

levy *n.* tax, charge, tool, fee, duty.

lewd *adj.* obscene, immoral, indecent.

liable *adj.* subject, accountable, answerable, responsible.

liar *n.* deceiver, fibber, cheat.

liberal *adj.* 1 generous, openhanded, unselfish, kind: *Arnold has always been a very liberal tipper in this restaurant.* 2 tolerant, unprejudiced, unbigoted, openminded: *I have always taken a liberal attitude towards women's rights.* ANT. (1) stingy, mean, niggardly, tightfisted, selfish.

liberate *vb.* free, release, loose, deliver. ANT. imprison, confine, jail.

liberty *n.* freedom, independence. ANT. bondage, servitude, slavery.

licence *n.* permit, authorization.

license *vb.* permit, allow, sanction, authorize.

lick *vb.* stroke, touch, rub, tongue.

lid *n.* cover, top, cap.

lie[1] *n.* falsehood, prevarication, fib, untruth, fiction, perjury: *It's a lie to say that I stole that cherry pie—my twin brother did it.* *vb.* fib, prevaricate, misinform: *Don't lie to me! I know you have no twin brother.*

lie[2] *vb.* 1 recline, repose: *I lay in bed till noon today.* 2 be situated *or* located: *The valley lies between the two mountains.* *n.* position, situation, location, site: *I've just started this job, so give me a chance to see the lie of the land.*

life *n.* 1 being, animation, existence, vitality: *There's still a breath of life in the injured man.* 2 biography: *I've just finished reading a life of Churchill.* 3 vigour, vitality, energy, spirit, sparkle: *Irene is always the life of the party.*

lifeless *adj.* dead; inanimate; heavy, dull, slow.

lift *vb.* raise, elevate.

light[1] *n.* 1 illumination, radiance, brilliance, brightness: *There's not enough light here to read by.* 2 lamp, fixture, chandelier, candle, bulb: *Please turn off the lights when leaving the room.* *vb.* 1 illuminate, brighten: *That one candle isn't enough to light this room.* 2 ignite, fire, burn, kindle: *I lit a fire in the sitting room.* *adj.* 1 bright, clear, luminous, lit, illuminated: *This is a pleasant light room to be in.* 2 pale, whitish, bleached: *Your light yellow dress looks very good on you.* ANT. *n.* (1) dark. *vb.* (1) darken. (2) extinguish. *adj.* dark.

light[2] *adj.* 1 unsubstantial, airy, buoyant, dainty: *If all the books are removed this bookcase is very light.* 2 giddy, frivolous: *Sometimes I think you're a bit light in the head.* 3 trivial, shallow, slight: *I enjoy a little light reading before going to sleep.* ANT. (3) serious, heavy, weighty.

lightheaded *adj.* 1 silly, frivolous: *Why do you always get so lightheaded when you're playing games at a party?* 2 giddy, dizzy: *The effects of the anaesthetic made me feel lightheaded.* ANT. (1) sober, rational. (2) clearheaded.

lighthearted *adj.* gay, carefree, cheerful, merry, happy, glad. ANT. sad, melancholy, sombre, serious.

like *vb.* admire, esteem, fancy, care for, cherish, adore, love: *Do you like me as much as I like you? I like scones for tea.* *adj.* alike, similar; resembling: *The two brothers were very like each other.* ANT. *vb.* dislike, hate. *adj.* dissimilar, different.

likely *adj.* probable, liable, possible, reasonable.

likeness *n.* **1** resemblance, similarity: *Yes, there is a likeness between you and Napoleon.* **2** image, representation, picture, portrait: *The king's likeness appears on all postage stamps, coins, and bank notes.*

likewise *adv.* similarly; besides, also.

liking *n.* affection, partiality, fondness. ANT. dislike, antipathy.

limit *n.* **1** boundary, bound, extent, frontier, end: *The limits of our property are marked by those huge trees.* **2** restraint, check, restriction: *There is no limit to your rudeness!* *vb.* check, hinder, restrain, restrict, confine: *You ought to limit the amount of sugar you eat.*

limp[1] *adj.* flabby, soft, supple, flexible: *After being left out in the rain, the pages of the book were all soggy and limp.* ANT. stiff, rigid, hard.

limp[2] *vb.* hobble, falter, stagger: *The pirate came limping into the cabin on his pegleg.* *n.* hobble, lameness: *This limp comes from my sprained ankle.*

line *n.* **1** row, array, file, sequence, series: *There was a line of medicine bottles on the shelf.* **2** mark, stroke; outline: *After drawing a line at the top of your paper, write your name on it.* **3** seam, crease, wrinkle: *The palmist told my fortune from the lines on my hand.* **4** division, limit, boundary: *I draw the line when it comes to five packets of crisps in one day.* **5** wire, cable; pipe; track: *When digging along the railway line, the men had to be careful to avoid cutting the telephone, power, and gas lines.* *vb. phr.* **line up** align, file, array: *I want all the children who are going to the zoo to line up outside at once.*

linger *vb.* loiter, stay, remain, tarry, dawdle.

link *n.* tie, bond, connection, connector, loop, coupling: *I cannot see any link between your wanting to see a film and Bob's washing his car.* *vb.* connect, tie, couple: *The chains were linked to each other.*

lip *n.* brim, edge, rim.

liquid *see* **fluid.**

list *n.* series, roll, record, register: *Is Bob's name on the list of candidates?* *vb.* record, register, post, file: *At the bottom of the application form, please list all personal references.*

listen *vb.* hear, attend.

literal *adj.* word for word, verbatim, exact, faithful, precise.

literate *adj.* educated, informed; intelligent. ANT. illiterate, unread, unlettered, ignorant.

literature *n.* writings, poetry, plays, novels, essays.

litter *n.* rubbish, waste, refuse: *Please don't throw litter on the streets.* *vb.* strew, scatter, disorder: *The park was littered with sweet wrappers after the children had left.*

little *adj.* 1 small, tiny, wee, minute: *This little book has more information in it than many large ones.* 2 brief, short: *There's only a little time left before my plane leaves.* *adv.* slightly: *Aren't you even a little hungry?* ANT. *adj.* (1) large, big, huge. (2) long, extended.

live[1] *vb.* 1 abide, reside, dwell: *I am going to live in India when I grow up.* 2 exist, be; survive: *No animal, including man, can live without any water at all.*

live[2] *adj.* 1 alive; surviving: *My grandmother used to go visiting carrying a live white mouse on a gold chain.* 2 unrecorded: *Shall we go to town to see a live show tonight?* 3 controversial; important: *The television programme dealt with live issues.* ANT. (1) dead. (2) recorded.

lively *adj.* 1 active, live, vigorous; spry, nimble, quick: *Jack's grandmother is pretty lively for a woman of 92.* 2 animated, spirited: *That certainly was a lively party last night.* ANT. slow, dull, sluggish.

livid *adj.* *Informal:* angry, furious, enraged.

living *n.* livelihood; support.

load *n.* burden, weight; cargo, shipment, delivery: *That's quite a load you're carrying. I've ordered another load of coal for the winter.* *vb.* weight, burden; lade: *We loaded the luggage into the boot of the car.*

loaf *vb.* loiter, lounge, idle.

loan *n.* advance; credit: *I asked the bank to approve a loan of £1000 for my new car.* *vb.* lend, entrust, advance: *The library loans books freely.*

loathe *see* hate.

lobby *n.* vestibule, foyer, entrance hall, anteroom: *Please meet me in the lobby in ten minutes.* *vb.* influence, induce, persuade: *The pressure group tried to lobby the MPs.*

local *adj.* home; civic, suburban; provincial.

locate *vb.* 1 find, discover, unearth: *I haven't been able to locate a copy of the book you asked for.* 2 situate, site, place: *I've been planning to locate the new factory near the motorway junction.*

location *n.* site, situation, spot, place.

lock[1] *n.* tress, braid, plait: *Betty's golden locks flowed down to her shoulders.*

lock[2] *n.* latch, hasp, bolt, padlock: *I have nothing that anyone would want, so I don't have a lock on the door.* *vb.* latch, padlock, bolt, fasten: *Lock the door carefully after I leave and don't let anyone in.*

lodge *n.* cottage, cabin, hut; chalet: *The prince had a hunting lodge in the mountains.* *vb.* **1** stay, reside, abide, board, room, dwell: *I've been lodging with my aunt while looking for a job.* **2** settle, fix, put: *Trying to get the pencil out of the rifle barrel, my finger became lodged in the hole.*

lofty *adj.* **1** tall, high, towering: *A lofty tower block can be seen as you approach the city.* **2** exalted, elevated: *His lofty ideas of himself annoyed everyone.* **3** proud, scornful, haughty: *She's much too lofty to have anything to do with us.* ANT. (1) low. (3) humble.

logical *adj.* reasonable, rational, sensible. ANT. irrational, crazy.

loiter *see* **linger.**

lone *adj.* sole, alone, solitary; apart.

lonely *adj.* solitary, friendless; rejected.

long[1] *adj.* extensive, lengthy, extended: *You have kept me waiting for a long time.* ANT. short, brief, limited.

long[2] (for) *vb.* crave, desire, wish: *I long for a tall glass of iced tea.*

long-suffering *adj.* tolerant, patient, forbearing.

long-winded *adj.* wordy, verbose; dull, boring. ANT. terse, curt.

look *vb.* **1** gaze, glance, survey, watch, regard, see, study: *Look at the girl in the window.* **2** appear, seem: *It looks as if we won't be able to go on our picnic now that it's raining.* **3** seek, search for: *Please look for your keys yourself.* *n.* **1** glance, peek, peep, glimpse: *I've only had one look at the page, but I've memorized it.* **2** gaze, stare; contemplation, study, examination: *The fixed look she gave me made me nervous.* **3** appearance, expression: *You should have seen the look on her face when I told her!*

loom *vb.* threaten, menace, impend; dominate.

loop *n.* circle, coil, ring.

loose *adj.* **1** unfastened, untied, free, undone: *There's a lion loose from the circus!* **2** wobbly, insecure, unscrewed, movable: *The arm of the chair is loose.* **3** baggy, draped, slack: *Now that I've lost all that weight, my trousers are too loose on me.* *vb.* loosen; release, set free: *Whenever anyone came too close to the property, they would loose the guard dogs.* ANT. *adj.* (1) fastened, tied, secure. (2) firm, immobile, secure, steady.   (3) close-fitting, tight, confining.

loosen *vb.*   loose, untie, undo, unchain, unfasten.   ANT. tighten, tie, secure.

loot *n.*   plunder, booty: *The bank robbers escaped with the loot.* *vb.* rob, steal, plunder, rifle, sack: *It was the manager of the bank who had looted the customers' accounts.*

lord *n.*   nobleman, peer; master, ruler, governor.

lose *vb.*   mislay, misplace.   ANT. find, discover, locate.

loss *n.*   **1** damage, injury, hurt: *The insurance was barely enough to cover our losses in the fire.*   **2** want, bereavement, need; misfortune, trouble; death: *The loss of Ben's mother was a loss to us all.*

lost *adj.*   **1** missing, mislaid, misplaced, gone, absent: *The ring, which I thought was lost, turned up in John's pocket.*   **2** wasted, spent, misspent, squandered: *The money lost in gambling every year amounts to millions of pounds.*   ANT. **(1)** found.

lot *n.*   plenty, abundance, group.

lotion *n.*   balm, salve, cream, liniment.

loud *adj.*   noisy, ear-splitting, thunderous, blaring.   ANT. soft, quiet, murmuring.

lounge *vb.*   loaf, idle, laze: *Stop lounging about the house and go out and get yourself a job!*   *n.* living room, sitting room: *Let's go into the lounge and wait for Hattie there, where it's more comfortable.*

love *n.*   adoration, warmth, devotion, tenderness, liking, friendliness, affection: *How can you compare a person's love for his family with his love of ice cream?*   *vb.* worship, adore, treasure, cherish, like: *Darling, when I say I love you, I mean I want to be with you forever.*   ANT. *n.* hate, loathing. *vb.* hate, detest, loathe.

lovely *adj.*   attractive, fair, charming, comely, pretty, beautiful, handsome.   ANT. ugly, hideous.

low *adj.*   **1** low-lying, stooped, crouched: *Sarah jumped over the low wall.*   **2** cheap, inexpensive: *The greengrocer was asking low prices for the vegetables at the end of the day.*

lower *vb.*   **1** reduce, decrease, lessen, diminish: *If you don't eat a balanced diet you lower your resistance to disease.*   **2** soften, quiet, turn down: *Please lower the volume of your stereo.*   **3** degrade, disgrace, humble: *I wouldn't lower myself to talk to someone who's such a bigot.*   **4** sink; drop; *Martin lowered himself carefully into the hot bath. Lower the leaf of* *the table gently.* ANT. **(1, 2, 4)** increase, raise.

loyal *adj.* faithful, true, devoted, dependable; patriotic. ANT. disloyal, treacherous, traitorous.

loyalty *n.* faithfulness, devotion, fidelity; allegiance, patriotism. ANT. disloyalty, treachery, treason.

luck *n.* fortune, chance, success, fluke. ANT. misfortune.

lucky *adj.* fortunate, favourable, blessed. ANT. unlucky, unfortunate.

ludicrous *adj.* absurd, ridiculous, preposterous.

luggage *n.* baggage, suitcases, bags, trunks.

lull *vb.* calm, soothe, quiet: *We were lulled to sleep by the sound of the waves beating on the shore.* *n.* calm, hush, quiet, stillness, silence; pause: *I took advantage of a lull in the activities to steal away unnoticed.*

luminous *adj.* light, glowing, bright, luminescent, fluorescent.

lump *n.* **1** bump, protuberance: *I still have the lump on my head where she hit me.* **2** cube; piece, block: *I have two lumps of sugar in my tea.*

lunatic *n.* madman, maniac; neurotic.

lure *n.* attraction, temptation, bait: *The salesman used the promise of a free information service as a lure to sell the encyclopedia.* *vb.* entice, attract, tempt, draw: *The spider attempted to lure the fly to land on its web.*

lurid *adj.* shocking, sensational; violent, vivid, daring.

luscious *adj.* juicy, delicious, delectable.

lust *n.* desire, drive, passion, craving, appetite: *The dance that Salome did for King Herod was to arouse his lust.* *vb.* desire, long for, crave for: *As he was lusting after money, the poor man found himself committing murder.*

lustre *n.* **1** sheen, gloss, glitter; brightness, brilliance, radiance: *The lustre of the pearls showed up best in candlelight.* **2** fame, glory, repute, honour, distinction: *Although the lustre of his accomplishments had won him praise, he was then awarded the Nobel prize.*

luxurious *adj.* lavish, rich, splendid, deluxe. ANT. sparse, Spartan, simple, crude.

lyric *n.* words, text, libretto.

m

macabre *adj.*   gruesome, horrible, horrifying, ghastly, grim.

machine *n.*   device, contrivance, engine, motor, mechanism.

mad *adj.*   **1** insane, crazy, mentally ill, deranged: *The composer finally went mad and had to be confined in a hospital.*   **2** angry, furious, enraged, irate, raging: *I'm very mad at Nora for not telling me about Ted's surprise party.*   ANT. (**1**) sane, rational, lucid.   (**2**) happy, cheerful, content.

madden *vb.*   enrage, infuriate, anger, vex, annoy.   ANT. mollify, calm, please.

magazine *n.*   periodical, journal, review, publication.

magic *n.*   sorcery, wizardry, sleight-of-hand, witchcraft: *The way that rabbit appeared in the silk top hat was magic.*   *adj.* magical: *This is a magic wand that turns into a snake unless I'm holding it.*

magical *adj.*   magic, marvellous, miraculous; mystical.

magician *n.*   conjuror, sorcerer, wizard, witch, warlock, enchanter.

magnanimous *adj.*   generous, unselfish, kind, benevolent.

magnificence *n.*   splendour, grandeur, luxury.

magnificent *adj.*   **1** splendid, luxurious, rich, lavish, grand: *The throne room of the palace is the most magnificent I've ever seen.*   **2** marvellous, wonderful, extraordinary, impressive: *From our bathroom windows we have a magnificent view of the mountains.*   ANT. plain, simple.

magnify *vb.*   enlarge, increase.   ANT. diminish, reduce.

magnitude *n.*   **1** extent, dimension, size, measure: *Nobody had any idea of the magnitude of the disaster because all telephones and other communications had been cut off.*   **2** importance, consequence, significance: *The results of the research were of some magnitude for all mankind.*

maid *n.*   **1** maidservant, housemaid, chambermaid, servant: *We left the hotel room early so the maid could clean up and make the beds.*   **2** maiden, girl, young woman, lass: *The shepherd was singing a song to a pretty maid who had brought his lunch.*

maim *vb.*   disable, cripple, injure, mutilate, disfigure.

main *adj.*   chief, principal, foremost.   ANT. secondary, accessory.

maintain *vb.*   **1** keep, continue, keep up, preserve, support:

Despite opposition, Johnson maintained his leadership of the political party. **2** preserve, keep, keep up, renew: *If the town maintained the park in good condition, the people would be able to use it.* **3** assert, state, hold, declare; claim, contend: *The man whom the police are questioning maintains that he was nowhere near the scene of the crime.* ANT. (1) discontinue.

maintenance *n.* **1** upkeep, preservation: *This is a delicate machine, and maintenance and repairs are costly.* **2** support, living, subsistence, bread, livelihood: *On the salary you are paying me I don't even have money for maintenance.*

majestic *adj.* **1** royal, kingly, princely, regal, noble, grand, stately: *The star of the play made a majestic entrance and everyone applauded.* **2** splendid, magnificent: *The decorations in the grand ballroom of the hotel are truly majestic.* ANT. (1) lowly, base. (2) squalid.

majesty *n.* dignity, nobility, grandeur.

major *adj.* greater, larger; important, chief. ANT. minor, inconsequential.

majority *n.* greater part, preponderance, mass, bulk. ANT. minority.

make *vb.* **1** fabricate, manufacture, produce, form, build, construct, create: *By using assembly lines, it became possible to make a car in an hour.* **2** become, develop into: *I think that Barbie would make an excellent prefect.* **3** cause, render; occasion: *Eating chocolate all afternoon made him feel sick.* **4** do, effect, execute, perform, accomplish: *Alan made a bow and the curtain came down at the end of the play.* **5** compel, cause, force: *Patrick's mother makes him wear the velvet suit with the lace collar whenever they go visiting.* **6** earn, gain, obtain, acquire, get: *My guess is that as a director of the company, Abernathy makes about £25,000 a year.* **7** reach, arrive at: *I don't see how we can make Edinburgh if you drive so slowly all the time.* **8** appoint, elect, select, assign: *Ernie's father was made head of the town committee on preservation of trees.* **9** amount to, add up to, equal, total: *6 and 3 makes 9.* *vb. phr.* **make believe** pretend, fantasize, imagine: *Let's all make believe that we're sailing across the ocean in a big ship.* **make do** get by, manage, survive: *"I expect we'll make do somehow," mother used to say, and we always did.* **make for** head towards, aim for: *We're making for the Lake District on our holiday.* **make good** repay, compensate, reimburse: *The company had to make good the loss of my wallet.* **make it** succeed, triumph: *After working hard for 20 years, Prof. Kelly has finally made it to the top of his profession.* **make out** discern, perceive, understand, recognize: *Hubert mumbles so, I can hardly make out what he's saying.* **make up** 1 create, invent, fabricate: *The students made up a story about life as a lorry driver and then put it on as a play.* 2 compose, form, join, constitute: *Do we have enough people to make up a football team?*

male *adj.* masculine, manly, virile. ANT. female, feminine, womanly.

malice *n.* spite, resentment, viciousness, grudge, bitterness. ANT. love, kindness.

maltreat *vb.* hurt, abuse, injure.

mammoth *adj.* huge, colossal, enormous, immense, gigantic. ANT. small, tiny, minuscule.

man *n.* 1 mankind, humanity; human beings: *Man has lived on earth for thousands of years.* 2 gentleman, chap, fellow: *The men came in the room and the ladies left.* 3 manliness, courage, bravery: *The man in him was quickened as he contemplated the task before him.*

manage *vb.* 1 direct, guide, lead, supervise, superintend, control, conduct, administer, rule: *My uncle manages an aircraft factory.* 2 succeed, contrive; arrange, bring about: *I managed to cling to a small tree that saved me from falling off the cliff.* ANT. (1) mismanage, bungle.

manageable *adj.* controllable; docile, tractable, willing; obedient. ANT. unmanageable; wild, recalcitrant.

management *n.* 1 control, supervision, direction, regulation, administration, care: *The management of the company was in the hands of the owner's son.* 2 directors, authorities: *The management consulted with the union officials before declaring the redundancies.*

manager *n.* supervisor, superintendent, overseer, executive, director, boss.

mandate *n.* commission, authority, support; command.

mangle *vb.* mutilate, destroy, disfigure, tear.

mania *n.* craze, obsession, passion.

maniac *see* **lunatic**.

manipulate *vb.* handle; manage, use.

manner *n.* way, method, style, fashion, custom.

manoeuvre *n.* plan, action, strategy, tactics: *In war, political and military manoeuvres are both important.* *vb.* plot, scheme, contrive: *Three men manoeuvred for the leadership, when they heard that the present director was retiring.*

manual *n.* handbook, guidebook, instruction book: *I looked in my car manual to see how to change the oil.* *adj.* **1** physical: *Ian sometimes did a manual job in his holidays.* **2** human: *Manual cataloguing of books takes a long time; doing it by computer would be much quicker.* ANT. *adj.* (1) mental. (2) automatic, computer-operated.

manufacture *vb.* make, assemble, fabricate, construct: *The company manufactures toys in the factory down the road.* *n.* making, assembly, fabrication, construction, production: *The Black Country is an important centre for the manufacture of locks and drains.*

many *adj.* numerous, abundant, plentiful. ANT. few.

map *n.,vb.* chart, graph, plan: *This map of England doesn't show the county boundaries. The survey team was mapping the area using photographs taken from an aeroplane.*

mar *vb.* spoil, impair, harm.

march *n.* walk, parade, advance; procession: *The march, which covered a distance of 25 miles, tired the soldiers out.* *vb.* move, proceed, walk, parade: *The protesters marched to Trafalgar Square and held a rally.*

margin *n.* edge, rim, border.

marine *adj.* maritime, oceanic, nautical.

mark *n.* **1** impression, effect, trace, imprint, stamp, brand: *The teachers at the school have left their mark on their students.* **2** sign, symbol, emblem, badge: *The king made his mark on the treaty by using his signet ring.* **3** target, goal: *The first three arrows were wide of the mark, but the last hit the bull's-eye.* *vb.* **1** stamp, brand, imprint, identify: *The bookplate marks this book as one of mine.* **2** distinguish, characterize: *Her face was marked by anger.* **3** note, heed, notice, pay attention to, attend, register: *Mark what I say about these chemicals or you may get hurt.* *vb. phr.* **mark down** reduce, cut: *The prices of cars have been marked down 10 per cent.* **mark off** separate, segregate, designate: *These spaces in the car park have been marked off for executives' cars.* **mark up** increase, raise: *These cameras were marked up for only a small profit over cost.*

market *n.* marketplace, stall, bazaar; supermarket, shop, store: *We have to go to the market to do our week's shopping tomorrow.* *vb.* sell, merchandise: *This company has been marketing cosmetics for almost 50 years.*

marriage *n.* **1** wedding, nuptials: *There aren't many people old enough to remember the marriage of the king.* **2** matrimony, wedlock; union: *Marriage is a solemn condition, but it can be* *rewarding for the right couple.* **3** alliance, association, confederation: *The marriage of the company making toothpaste with the one making toothbrushes worked out very successfully.* ANT. divorce, separation.

marry *vb.* wed; betroth; join, unite.

marsh *n.* swamp, bog, fen, morass, quagmire.

marshal *vb.* arrange, order, organize, rank.

martyr *n.* sufferer, victim, sacrifice.

marvel *n.* wonder, miracle, phenomenon: *The electric light was one of the marvels of the late 19th century.* *vb.* wonder, stare, gape: *The children marvelled at how an elephant could dance so gracefully.*

marvellous *adj.* wonderful, miraculous, wondrous, extraordinary, amazing, astonishing, astounding. ANT. commonplace, ordinary, usual.

masculine *adj.* male; manly. ANT. feminine, female, unmasculine.

mask *n.* protection, protector; disguise, camouflage: *You must wear a mask when operating this machinery. The beautiful ladies all wore masks to the ball.* *vb.* conceal, hide, disguise, veil, screen: *I find it difficult to mask my contempt for someone who would strike a person when he's down.*

mass *n.* **1** pile, heap, quantity, aggregation: *A huge mass of building materials was being accumulated near the foundation.* **2** size, bulk, magnitude, extent: *The mass of the sun is many times greater than that of the earth.* *vb.* gather, amass, accumulate, collect, marshal, assemble: *The armies were massed on the battlefield.*

massacre *n.* slaughter, genocide, killing, butchery, extermination: *The massacre of the missionaries horrified the rest of the population.* *vb.* slay, murder, kill, butcher, exterminate: *The Nazis were guilty of massacring millions of innocent people.*

massage *vb.* rub, knead, caress; stimulate.

massive *adj.* **1** huge, immense, gigantic, tremendous: *Behind the town was a massive pile of rocks from the last avalanche.* **2** large, bulky, weighty, ponderous: *A massive rock was balanced on the edge of the cliff, about to topple into the valley below.* ANT. (1) small, little, tiny. (2) light, weightless.

mast *n.* spar, pole; post.

master *n.* **1** expert, maestro, genius: *From what the museum curator could see, this artist was a master with a brush.* **2** ruler, leader, chief, commander, captain, boss, director, supervisor, superintendent: *In ancient Greece and Rome,* *slaves assumed the names of their masters.* *vb.* **1** learn, understand, grasp: *Jane eventually mastered the German language.* **2** conquer, overcome, subdue, overpower: *The inexperienced chessplayer was easily mastered by the professional.* *adj.* **1** major, chief, principal: *The man was a master bridge player.* **2** expert, skilful, skilled: *My cousin Peter has a licence as a master mariner.*

masterly *adj.* skilful, expert, superb, adroit. ANT. clumsy, maladroit, awkward.

mastermind *n.* genius, expert: *Robin is a mathematical mastermind who can solve these problems in seconds.* *vb.* manage, direct, supervise; organize: *The woman who masterminded the bank robbery escaped and now lives in Brazil.*

masterpiece *n.* masterwork, perfection, model, classics.

mat *n.* cover, covering; rug.

match *n.* **1** equal, equivalent, peer: *Stan is very good at tennis, but he's finally met his match in Paul.* **2** competition, contest, sport: *The wrestling match has been postponed.* *vb.* **1** even, equal, balance, equate: *I'm afraid that with your experience of the game you won't match the champion.* **2** agree, resemble, harmonize: *I'm sorry to tell you that your green polka-dot tie doesn't match that pink and purple shirt.*

matchless *adj.* unequalled, unrivalled, peerless, incomparable. ANT. unimpressive, ordinary.

mate *n. Informal:* associate, companion, comrade: *The man said he'd get two of his mates to help him move the piano.* *vb.* breed: *What would happen if you mated a goat with a bluebottle? You'd get a butterfly!*

material *n.* **1** substance, matter, stuff; fabric: *We were unable to identify the material of which the flying saucer was made.* **2** cloth, fabric, textile: *The shop sells material by the metre.* *adj.* physical, real, touchable, palpable, tangible: *You cannot discuss the spiritual world in terms of material objects.* ANT. *adj.* immaterial, intangible, spiritual.

maternal *adj.* motherly; loving, caring, sympathetic; protective.

matter *n.* **1** substance, material: *The matter of which the universe is composed is almost infinite in its variety.* **2** subject, affair, business, interest: *We have a matter to discuss before you can go.* **3** trouble, difficulty: *What's the matter? You look pale.* *vb.* count, signify, mean: *Does it matter whether you paint the table before or after the bookcase?*

mature *adj.* **1** ripe, aged, ready, seasoned: *When these tomatoes are mature, each will weigh a lot.* **2** adult, full-grown, matured, grown: *The play my parents saw last night is suitable only for mature audiences.* *vb.* age, ripen, develop: *This tree hasn't matured enough to be transplanted.* ANT. *adj.* (1) young, youthful. (2) immature, innocent, naive.

maximize *vb.* increase, develop, enlarge, extend. ANT. minimize, reduce.

maximum *n.* height, climax, greatest number. ANT. minimum.

maybe *adv.* perhaps, possibly. ANT. definitely, certainly.

maze *n.* network, labyrinth, tangle.

meadow *n.* pasture, field, plain.

meagre *adj.* scanty, sparse, frugal, mean. ANT. plentiful, bountiful, ample, abundant.

meal *n.* snack, refreshment; breakfast, dinner, lunch.

mean[1] *vb.* **1** intend, plan, expect, propose: *What do you mean to do when you arrive in Manchester?* **2** indicate, denote, signify, say, express, suggest: *You ought to know that I say what I mean, and I mean what I say.*

mean[2] *adj.* **1** unkind, cruel, nasty, rude: *I think it was very mean of you to tell Sarah that her dress is ugly.* **2** stingy, miserly, tight, selfish: *Scrooge was so mean that he didn't even give his employees a day off at Christmas.* ANT. (1) gentle, thoughtful, kind. (2) generous, openhanded.

mean[3] *n.* average, centre, middle: *Each family has a mean number of 2.4 children.*

meaning *n.* sense, signification, denotation; significance, import, gist.

means *n.pl.* **1** wealth, riches, money: *The bank manager is a man of means and should contribute more than just a pound to charity.* **2** support, agency, resources: *What means can we use to persuade him to give more?*

measure *n.* **1** extent, size, weight, volume, bulk, dimension; depth, breadth, height, length: *It is difficult to comprehend the measure of the universe because the earth is so small by comparison.* **2** rule, test, standard, trial: *By that measure, all the students in the class have done rather well.* *vb.* rule, weigh, count, estimate, gauge: *How do astronomers measure the distance from the earth to the nearest star? Not in the same way you measure flour for baking a cake or cloth for making a coat.*

measureless *adj.* limitless, immeasurable, boundless, immense, vast, infinite. ANT. measurable, ascertainable.

meat *n.* flesh; food.

mechanic *n.* machinist, workman, operator.

mechanism *n.*   machine, machinery, device, tool, contrivance.

mechanize *vb.*   equip, industrialize, automate.

medal *n.*   award, decoration, medallion, badge, reward.

meddle *vb.*   interfere, pry, intrude, snoop.

meddlesome *adj.*   meddling, troublesome, interfering, obstructive.

mediate *vb.*   intervene, intercede, reconcile.

medical *adj.*   pathological, healing, remedial, pharmaceutical.

medicine *n.*   drug, remedy, potion, prescription, cure.

mediocre *adj.*   average, ordinary, fair, dull.   ANT. excellent.

meditate *vb.*   think, ponder, reflect, contemplate.

medium *n.*   **1** average; mean: *There must be some medium between your being either very good or very naughty.*   **2** means, mechanism, factor; agency, instrument: *The telephone is the medium by which we can communicate with people across a distance.*   *adj.* average; middling: *The medium-priced suits are on this rack.*

medley *n.*   mixture, variety, conglomeration.

meek *adj.*   humble, patient, submissive.

meet *vb.*   **1** encounter, come across: *I don't think that we have met before.*   **2** converge, connect, join, unite: *This road meets the motorway at the new intersection.*   **3** settle, satisfy, fulfil, answer, discharge: *I don't know if Hugo has the money to meet his obligations.*   **4** convene, gather, assemble, congregate: *The committee is supposed to meet next week.*   *n.* contest, meeting, competition, match: *The athletes' meet took place on the cinder track.*   ANT. *vb.* **(1)** miss.   **(2)** diverge, split.   **(4)** scatter.

melancholy *n.*   sadness, gloom, depression: *Since she moved from the country to the city, Janet seems so full of melancholy.*   *adj.* sad, gloomy, depressed, downcast, downhearted, unhappy: *The cry of the owl sounds so melancholy—like the howl of the wolf.*   ANT. *adj.* happy, joyful, jubilant.

mellow *adj.*   **1** ripe, mature, full-flavoured: *This pear is so mellow I can eat it with a spoon.*   **2** smooth, sweet, melodious: *The mellow sounds of the orchestra filled the room where we were dining.*   *vb.* ripen, mature, develop, soften: *This whisky has mellowed with age.*   ANT. *adj.* **(1)** immature, unripened.

melodious *adj.*   tuneful, harmonious, sweet, dulcet; pleasant.   ANT. jarring, grating, discordant, tuneless, unmelodious.

melody *n.*   tune, air, music, song.

melt *vb.*   **1** liquefy, dissolve: *The ice in my ginger ale has melted.*   **2** fade out, blend, dwindle, vanish, disappear: *As* *we approached their village, the natives seemed to melt away into the jungle.* **3** soften, relax: *The giant's heart melted when he saw the children, and he let them play in his garden.* ANT. (1) harden, freeze, solidify.

member *n.* partner, sharer, participator.

memorable *adj.* historic, unforgettable, important, significant. ANT. forgettable, passing, transitory.

memorial *n.* commemoration, remembrance; pillar, column; inscription.

memorize *vb.* learn, remember, record. ANT. forget.

memory *n.* **1** recollection, recall, remembrance, retrospection: *As she got older, her memory grew worse.* **2** mental image, thought, representation: *After more than ten years, my memory of the conversation is not very accurate.*

menace *n.* threat, warning, intimidation: *That driver is a menace to everyone else on the road.* *vb.* threaten, intimidate, warn: *As I stepped nearer to the gate, a huge dog leapt out and menaced me.*

mend *vb.* **1** repair, patch, restore, fix: *There's a man down the street who mends broken china.* **2** improve, recover, recuperate, heal: *Greg's broken arm mended very quickly.* ANT. (1) ruin, destroy, spoil. (2) worsen, deteriorate.

menial *adj.* lowly, common, servile.

mental *adj.* intellectual, reasoning, thinking. ANT. physical.

mention *vb.* refer to, introduce, touch on: *Please don't mention the subject of your leaving to mother.* *n.* reference, remark: *I do seem to remember that the speaker made some brief mention of the other candidates.*

merchandise *n.* wares, stock, goods, commodities: *The shopkeeper said that he doesn't keep that kind of merchandise and would have to order it.* *vb.* sell, promote: *The sales manager suggested merchandising the posters through bookshops.*

merchant *n.* storekeeper, shopkeeper, retailer, trader, dealer; businessman.

merciful *adj.* kind, compassionate, lenient, forgiving, tenderhearted, kindhearted, sympathetic. ANT. unjust, unforgiving, harsh, mean.

merciless *adj.* cruel, ruthless, pitiless, savage, hard, hardhearted, unfeeling. ANT. merciful, benevolent, openhearted.

mercy *n.* **1** compassion, sympathy, pity, consideration, leniency, kindness, tenderness: *The prisoners begged for mercy, and the chief allowed them to be released.* **2** disposal, discretion, disposition: *The poor fly was caught in the web* *and was now at the mercy of the spider.* ANT. **(1)** cruelty, ruthlessness, pitilessness.

mere *adj.* bare, scant. ANT. considerable, substantial.

merely *adv.* barely, hardly, only, simply.

merge *vb.* join, unite; blend, fuse.

merger *n.* amalgamation, combination, incorporation.

merit *n.* worth, value, quality, worthiness: *I think that there is a great deal of merit in wanting to conserve energy.* *vb.* deserve, earn, qualify for, be worthy of: *Joe merited that commendation for bravery for saving the girl from drowning.*

merry *adj.* cheerful, cheery, joyful, happy, jolly, jovial. ANT. sad, doleful, gloomy.

mesh *n.* network, net, web.

mess *n.* **1** untidiness, confusion, disorder, muddle, jumble: *I've never seen a mess like the one in Sophie's room—everything's strewn about.* **2** difficulty, trouble, predicament: *Pete has got himself into a mess with the history teacher again: something about late homework.* *vb.* confuse, muddle, dirty: *It takes an hour to straighten up and clean a room that you mess up in a minute.*

message *n.* **1** communication, note, letter; memorandum, memo: *The courier carried the message for three weeks through the jungle.* **2** information, news, word, advice: *I have a message for you from your mother: Don't forget to brush your teeth.*

messenger *n.* courier, bearer, runner, agent.

messy *adj.* dirty, disorderly, disordered, confused, confusing; untidy, sloppy, slovenly. ANT. neat, orderly, tidy.

metal *n.* mineral, iron, copper; alloy, brass, steel.

mete (out) *vb.* administer, distribute, allot.

meter *n.* device, recorder, gauge; measure, scale.

method *n.* way, technique, manner, approach, means.

methodical *adj.* systematic, orderly, businesslike. ANT. irregular, disconnected, confused.

meticulous *adj.* precise, accurate, exact, painstaking, scrupulous.

middle *n.* centre, midpoint, median: *You are not allowed to walk down the middle of a motorway.* *adj.* centre, central, halfway, intermediate: *Bill lives in the house at this end, John in the one at the other end, and Betty lives in the middle one.* ANT. beginning, end.

midst *n.* middle, centre, thick, heart.

might *n.* power, strength, force, vigour. ANT. weakness, frailty, vulnerability.

mighty *adj.* strong, powerful, muscular. ANT. weak, frail.

migrate *vb.* move, resettle; immigrate, emigrate. ANT. remain, stay, settle.

mild *adj.* 1 calm, gentle, temperate, pleasant: *After a bitter cold winter, we experienced a mild spring.* 2 amiable, kind, compassionate, peaceful, calm: *Tom is known to have a mild disposition.* 3 bland, soothing: *This is a sharp, not a mild, cheese.* ANT. (1) stormy, turbulent. (2) violent, excitable, hot-tempered.

militant *adj.* aggressive, belligerent, offensive, pugnacious.

military *adj.* armed, martial; operational, strategical.

mimic *vb.* impersonate, copy, imitate, ape: *Have you seen Stuart mimicking the headmaster?* *n.* impersonator, comedian, mime: *I love seeing mimics imitating famous people!*

mind *n.* 1 intellect, brain, intelligence, reason, understanding, sense: *Albert Einstein had the mind of a genius.* 2 inclination, intention: *I have a mind to dismiss the entire class early for being so good.* *vb.* 1 object (to), care (about), dislike: *Do you mind moving your car a little, so I can drive mine out?* 2 care for, look after, watch, tend: *Stefanie minds three children after school.* 3 pay attention, obey, heed, attend: *Mind what your father says to you now!*

mine *n.* 1 pit, shaft, excavation; lode, vein: *The mine was rich in coal and could be worked for 25 years.* 2 source: *Jim was a mine of information about football.* *vb.* dig, excavate, drill, quarry: *My grandfather mined in South Africa.*

mineral *n.* rock, deposit, metal, ore.

mingle *vb.* combine, mix, blend. ANT. separate, sort.

miniature *adj.* tiny, small, midget, little, minute. ANT. large, giant.

minimize *vb.* diminish, decrease, lessen, reduce. ANT. maximize, enlarge.

minimum *n.* smallest number, least, lowest (point), nadir. ANT. maximum.

minister *n.* clergyman, pastor, parson, preacher, vicar, curate, chaplain, deacon, cleric, reverend.

minor *adj.* smaller, lesser, secondary, petty, unimportant: *The department stores no longer consider shoplifting a minor offence.* *n.* boy, girl, child, youth, adolescent: *No minors were allowed to attend the film.* ANT. *adj.* major. *n.* adult, grown-up.

mint *vb.* coin, punch, stamp, strike.

minute[1] *n.* jiffy, moment, instant, second: *When my wife says "Wait a minute," I sometimes have to wait an hour.*

minute² *adj.* tiny, wee, microscopic, minuscule: *I've never understood how the fly's minute wings could carry it so quickly.* ANT. large, huge, immense.

miracle *n.* marvel, wonder, phenomenon.

miraculous *adj.* marvellous, wonderful, incredible, phenomenal, extraordinary. ANT. ordinary, commonplace, everyday.

mirror *n.* looking-glass, glass; reflector: *I don't always like what I see when I look in the mirror.* *vb.* reflect: *The image of the building is mirrored in the pond.*

mirth *n.* glee, joy, gaiety, joyousness, jollity, joyfulness, merriment, laughter. ANT. gloom, sadness, seriousness.

miscarry *vb.* fail, go wrong. ANT. succeed.

miscellaneous *adj.* diverse, different, mixed, varied.

mischief *n.* 1 playfulness, roguishness, rascality: *That red-headed boy is full of mischief—putting a drawing pin on teacher's chair.* 2 trouble, harm, damage, injury: *The vandals who broke into the school last night did a lot of mischief.*

mischievous *adj.* roguish, playful, naughty. ANT. good, well-behaved.

miser *n.* niggard, skinflint, tightwad, Scrooge; hoarder. ANT. philanthropist, benefactor.

miserable *adj.* 1 unhappy, uncomfortable, wretched, heartbroken: *Ted was miserable when he wasn't chosen for the team.* 2 poor, penniless, needy, poverty-stricken: *The miserable people in other countries have no one to turn to for help but us.* 3 mean, contemptible, hateful, low, wretched, bad: *What rotten miserable person has been teasing these animals?* ANT. (1) happy, joyful, content. (2) wealthy, well-off, prosperous. (3) noble, honourable. (4) lucky, fortunate.

miserly *adj.* stingy, tightfisted, pennypinching, cheap, mean; selfish. ANT. generous, openhanded, extravagant.

misery *n.* 1 unhappiness, suffering, anguish, woe, agony, distress: *During the famine I saw almost more misery than I could stand in one lifetime.* 2 grief, sorrow: *We all tried to console the widow in her misery.* ANT. (1) delight, joy.

misfortune *n.* bad luck; calamity; disappointment, nuisance. ANT. good fortune.

misgiving *n.* doubt, hesitation, suspicion, mistrust, uncertainty.

mishap *n.* accident, misadventure; disaster, catastrophe.

misjudge *vb.* prejudge, misconstrue, misinterpret.

mislay *vb.* lose, misplace. ANT. find, discover.

mislead *vb.* deceive, delude, (*informal*) take in; trick.

misprint *n.* error, mistake; literal.

miss *vb.* 1 need, want, desire, yearn for: *His wife missed him very much when he was away from home.* 2 drop, fumble: *Sonia missed the ball completely, even when we threw it gently.* *n.* slip, failure, error, blunder, fumble: *A miss is as good as a mile.*

missile *n.* projectile, shot, weapon.

mission *n.* task, duty, work, undertaking.

missionary *n.* evangelist, preacher, minister; witness.

mist *n.* fog, cloud, haze, steam.

mistake *n.* error, slip, fault: *Lester, this homework is full of mistakes and you must do it again.* *vb.* misunderstand, misjudge, confuse; misinterpret: *I mistook the reflection of the searchlight on the clouds for a flying saucer.*

mistaken *adj.* wrong, incorrect, confused, misinformed, inaccurate. ANT. correct, right, accurate.

misunderstand *vb.* misinterpret, misjudge, confuse, jumble, mistake. ANT. comprehend, perceive.

mitigate *vb.* moderate, lessen, relieve, alleviate.

mix *vb.* combine, blend, mingle: *When you mix the chemicals together be careful that they do not explode.* *n.* combination, blend, mixture: *The people on that island are an unusual mix of natives and immigrants. Use a cake mix when preparing this cake.* ANT. *vb.* separate, divide.

mixture *n.* 1 mix, confusion, jumble, medley, hotchpotch: *Your jacket and your trousers are a curious mixture of styles.* 2 blend, combination: *I made up this mixture so that we could dip bread in it for French toast.*

moan *vb.,n.* groan, wail, lament, cry: *When I went to see what it was, it turned out to be the wind moaning in the chimney. I thought I heard someone in the next room give a loud moan.*

mob *n.* swarm, crowd, rabble, throng: *There was a mob of people gathered near the ice-cream vendor.* *vb.* swarm, crowd, throng; riot: *The rock star was mobbed when he left the theatre by people wanting his autograph.*

mobile *adj.* movable; free; portable. ANT. immobile, stationary, fixed.

mock *vb.* scorn, deride, ridicule, tease, jeer: *When the singer came out on stage, the audience mocked him, and he wept.* *adj.* imitation, fake; fraudulent, sham: *Mock turtle soup doesn't taste like the real thing.* ANT. *vb.* praise, honour, applaud. *adj.* real, genuine, authentic.

mockery *n.* 1 ridicule, scorn, derision: *Bernard's painting was held up to the mockery of the other students.* 2 travesty, sham, pretext, pretence: *You have made a mockery of a very serious matter by ridiculing it.* ANT. praise, admiration.

mode *n.* manner, method, style, technique, practice, way, fashion.

model *n.* 1 example, pattern, ideal: *I tried to make a vase, using the one over there as a model.* 2 copy, representation, imitation, facsimile: *This aeroplane is an actual working model of the real thing.* 3 version, style, design: *This car is a late model.* 4 mannequin, sitter: *I'd very much like to have you sit as a model for my next painting.* *vb.* 1 form, shape, mould, fashion, pattern, design: *Dick has modelled a figure out of clay. Sandra tries to model herself on her teacher.* 2 sit, pose: *Cordelia models for that high-fashion boutique in town.*

moderate[1] *adj.* 1 reasonable, average, medium, fair: *The doctor said that a moderate amount of coffee would do me no harm.* 2 conservative, middle-of-the-road, cautious: *The minister's plans for economic recovery were moderate, not extreme.* ANT. (1) immoderate, excessive.

moderate[2] *vb.* 1 arbitrate, referee, judge, umpire: *The head of the department moderated the debate between the two teams.* 2 weaken, pacify, lessen, calm, sober, temper: *As the sun sank towards the horizon, the scorching heat of the day was moderated by a cool breeze.* ANT. (2) intensify, increase.

modern *adj.* present-day, up-to-date, recent, novel, new, fresh, modish, stylish. ANT. old-fashioned, antique, out-of-date, outmoded.

modernize *vb.* refurbish, rebuild, improve, renovate, renew.

modest *adj.* 1 humble, unassuming; meek: *Geoffrey was very modest regarding his achievements.* 2 decorous, chaste: *Harriet was wearing a modest black dress buttoned up to the neck.* ANT. (1) vain, proud, arrogant. (2) ostentatious, pretentious, showy, gaudy.

modesty *n.* humility, simplicity, decency, propriety. ANT. vanity, conceit, pride.

modify *vb.* 1 change, alter, vary, adjust: *If you expect to remain as a student in this school, Patrick, you'll have to modify your behaviour.* 2 moderate, temper: *Since she was elected, I think that the record will show that the MP has modified her views on education.*

moist *adj.* damp, humid; muggy, clammy, wet. ANT. dry, arid, parched.

moisten *vb.* dampen; wet; humidify. ANT. dry.

moisture *n.* dampness, wetness; condensation; mist. ANT. dryness, aridity.

molest *vb.* annoy, disturb, pester; attack, assault.

moment *n.* **1** instant, (*informal*) jiffy, flash, twinkling: *The receptionist asked me to sit down and wait a moment.* **2** importance, significance, import, gravity, seriousness, consequence: *It is of no great moment to me whether you go tomorrow or tonight.*

momentary *adj.* brief, temporary, short-lived, fleeting, ephemeral.

momentous *adj.* important, serious, consequential, far-reaching. ANT. unimportant, trivial, trifling.

monarch *n.* king, queen, ruler, emperor, empress, sovereign.

money *n.* **1** coin, cash, currency, notes: *Can you lend me some money to go to the cinema?* **2** funds, capital: *I doubt that the company has the money it needs for expansion.*

monitor *n.* supervisor; director, adviser: *Felicity will be the dining room monitor for today and will try to keep the children under control.* *vb.* watch, observe, control, supervise: *We were able to monitor the actions of the robot from the control booth.*

monopolize *vb.* exclude, corner, (*informal*) hog.

monopoly *n.* **1** control, domination: *Some nationalized industries have a monopoly in the supply of their services.* **2** cartel, ring; protectionism: *The firms were operating a monopoly in the market of selling spare parts for cars.*

monotonous *adj.* boring, dull, tedious, humdrum, tiring, tiresome, wearisome: *Watching a record turning on a record player is terribly monotonous. The politicians gave one monotonous speech after another.* ANT. interesting, fascinating, riveting.

monster *n.* beast, brute, fiend, villain, wretch, demon.

monstrous *adj.* horrible, revolting, shocking, repulsive, hideous, dreadful, terrible; outrageous.

monument *n.* column, pillar, obelisk, stone; statue.

monumental *adj.* **1** huge, enormous, immense, colossal, gigantic: *At the top of the mountain stands a monumental cross.* **2** significant, important: *The invention of the wheel allowed man to make monumental progress.* ANT. (**1**) miniature, tiny. (**2**) insignificant, trivial.

mood *n.* temper, humour, disposition, frame of mind.

moody *adj.* temperamental, changeable; short-tempered, irritable, peevish, fretful, spiteful. ANT. calm, even-tempered, good-natured.

mop (up) *vb.* wipe, wash, clean.

mope *vb.* grieve, lose heart, despair, sulk. ANT. cheer up.

moral *adj.* upright, honest, ethical, just, good, honourable. ANT. immoral, dishonest, sinful, corrupt.

morale *n.* spirit, confidence, assurance.

morbid *adj.* unhealthy, unwholesome; pessimistic; morose.

more *adj.* additional, extra, further. ANT. fewer.

moreover *adv.* also, further, furthermore, in addition, besides.

moron *see* **idiot.**

morose *adj.* gloomy, depressed, sullen.

morsel *n.* bite, titbit, bit, piece.

mortal *adj.* **1** perishable; temporary; human: *Since all men are mortal, we must all die sometime.* **2** lethal, deadly, fatal: *The knight received a mortal wound from the sword and lay dying.* ANT. (1) immortal, imperishable. (2) superficial.

most *adj.* nearly all, a great majority of.

mostly *adv.* generally, chiefly, mainly, for the most part, largely, principally.

motion *n.* movement, change, action: *Because of the breeze, the branches of the trees are constantly in motion.* *vb.* gesture, signal, indicate: *I was about to say something, but Vincent motioned to me to be quiet.* ANT. *n.* stillness, immobility.

motivate *vb.* stimulate, move, cause, prompt.

motive *n.* reason, purpose, idea, cause, ground.

motor *n.* engine, machine, device.

motto *n.* slogan, maxim, byword, catchword; proverb, saying.

mould *n.* **1** cast, cavity, form, pattern: *Joyce makes her jellies in a pretty mould.* **2** decay, mildew: *Mould developed on the damp walls.* *vb.* shape, form, fashion: *Sandra moulds the clay into delicate figures.*

mound *n.* hill, hillock, pile, heap.

mount *vb.* **1** ascend, climb, go up: *The cowboy mounted his horse and rode away. Frank had to mount a ladder to reach the light bulb.* **2** rise, increase, ascend: *As the costs of raw materials mounted, the manufacturers passed them on to the consumer in higher prices.* **3** prepare, make ready, set up: *The enemy was going to mount an attack at dawn.* *n.* **1** horse, steed, charger: *The comical knight rode an old nag as his mount.* **2** mountain; hill: *Mount Everest is the highest peak in the world.* **3** backing, setting; margin: *The drawing* on white card was set off well against the black mount. ANT. vb. (1, 2) descend.

mountain n. peak; height, ridge, range.

mourn vb. lament, grieve, sorrow, bemoan. ANT. rejoice, celebrate.

mournful adj. sad, sorrowful, unhappy. ANT. cheerful, joyful, happy.

mouth n. entrance, opening, aperture.

move vb. 1 advance, proceed, progress, go on; stir, budge, travel, shift; retreat: As soon as anyone moved, the dogs would begin to growl. 2 push, propel, shift: Please move your chair closer to the table. 3 affect, touch, influence: I was deeply moved by the play. n. movement, motion, action: Hilary made a move as if to leave.

movement n. 1 move, motion, action, activity: I noticed a slight movement of the door and knew someone was behind it. 2 effort, action, crusade: There was a movement among the students to help the vagrants of the town.

mud n. dirt, mire; swamp, marsh.

muddle n. confusion, trouble: Dear me! I seem to be in such a muddle today! vb. confuse, mix up, jumble up: I'm sorry, I seem to be muddling you and your sister, as you look so alike.

muddy adj. soggy, miry, marshy.

muffle vb. deaden, soften, quieten, mute, stifle. ANT. amplify, louden.

multiply vb. 1 increase; double, triple, treble: The number of readers of the new magazine multiplied in the beginning. 2 reproduce, propagate: Rabbits multiply very rapidly. ANT. decrease, lessen.

multitude n. throng, crowd, mass, swarm, mob.

mumble see **murmur**.

munch vb. chew, crunch.

murder n. killing, death, slaying, slaughter; manslaughter: The suspect was accused of the murder of three people whose bodies had been found in his cellar. vb. kill, destroy, massacre; slaughter, slay, assassinate: It was found that the killer had murdered the people out of revenge.

murderer n. killer, slayer, assassin; gangster.

murky adj. dim, dark, gloomy; dirty.

murmur n. mutter, mumble, grumble, complaint; whimper: A murmur of protest was heard from the audience when the new rules were announced. vb. mutter, mumble, grumble; whimper: The trees murmured in the icy winds.

museum n. exhibition, archives; art gallery, library.

music *n.*   melody, harmony, tune.

musical *adj.*   tuneful, harmonious, melodious.

musician *n.*   artist, player, performer; composer.

musty *adj.*   old, dusty, fusty, mouldy.

mute *adj.*   dumb, voiceless, silent.

mutilate *vb.*   maim, weaken, damage, injure.

mutinous *adj.*   rebellious, revolutionary, unruly.   ANT. obedient, dutiful, compliant.

mutiny *n.*   rebellion, revolt, uprising: *All of the men who took part in the mutiny were sent home in chains.*   *vb.* rebel, revolt, rise up: *The crew of the* Bounty *mutinied against Captain Bligh and set him and a few men adrift in a boat.*

mutter *see* **murmur.**

mutual *adj.*   **1** reciprocal, alternate: *If you give our employees a discount in your shop, we'll give yours a mutual discount in ours.*   **2** common, shared: *Albert is our mutual friend.*

mysterious *adj.*   secret; puzzling, strange.   ANT. open, direct, obvious.

mystery *n.*   **1** puzzle, riddle, enigma: *The mystery developed as a second man suddenly disappeared.*   **2** strangeness, inscrutability: *There is a strange mystery surrounding the woman who lives in the castle, and we may never know the solution.*

mystify *vb.*   confuse, bewilder, puzzle, perplex.

myth *n.*   **1** legend, tradition, fable: *The ancient Greek and Roman myths still have a profound effect on our literature and language.*   **2** lie, fib, prevarication, fiction: *That whole story she told about being an heiress is just a myth.*

n

nag *vb.* annoy, pester, irritate, torment, vex: *Warren's mother is always nagging him about cleaning up his room.* *n.* faultfinder, carper; pest, nuisance: *Phil's wife is an awful nag.*

nail *n.* spike, brad; screw.

naive *adj.* innocent, credulous, simple, ingenuous. ANT. experienced.

naked *adj.* **1** unclothed, undressed, bare, uncovered, nude: *At night, when it was hot, we used to go swimming naked.* **2** simple, stark, plain, obvious, unadorned, undisguised: *Jack finally told me that he had done the deed, and that's the naked truth.* ANT. (1) covered, clothed, garbed. (2) suppressed, concealed.

name *n.* **1** title, appellation, designation: *My name is George; what's yours?* **2** reputation; character: *Rick has made a name for himself as an author of historical novels.* *vb.* **1** call, title, term, christen, baptize: *We named our first child Nancy.* **2** designate, signify, mention: *By the time he was two, Dan could name all the days of the week and the months.* **3** elect, nominate, appoint: *We named Betty chairwoman of our committee.*

nap *n.* rest, snooze, forty winks, siesta, doze.

narrate *vb.* tell, relate, describe, recount, report.

narrative *n.* story, tale, account, history, description.

narrow *adj.* **1** slender, thin, tapering, tight: *The passageway at the end of the cave was too narrow for me to squeeze through.* **2** close, precarious, perilous, dangerous: *The driver leapt clear of the wreck just as it burst into flames—a narrow escape!* ANT. (1) wide, broad.

narrow-minded *adj.* limited, illiberal. ANT. broad-minded, liberal.

nasty *adj.* **1** disagreeable, unpleasant, foul: *We sometimes get a spell of very nasty weather in February.* **2** dirty, filthy, foul, disgusting, loathsome, polluted, offensive: *There was a very nasty pool of sewage where the factory dumped its wastes.* **3** dirty, filthy, obscene, indecent, improper: *How dare you use such nasty language in the classroom!* **4** ill-natured, mean, spiteful: *Manuel has a very nasty temper.* ANT. (1) pleasant, fair, seasonable. (2) clean, pure. (3) proper, decent. (4) pleasant, even-tempered.

nation *n.* country, state, realm, kingdom, republic.

national *adj.* political, public, civil.

nationality *n.* citizenship; allegiance.

native *adj.* **1** natural, innate, inborn, inbred, hereditary: *English is my native language.* **2** local, original: *Kangaroos are native to Australia.* *n.* national, citizen, inhabitant, resident: *I don't come from around here at all—I'm a native of the Channel Isles.* ANT. *adj.* (2) foreign, alien. *n.* stranger, foreigner, outsider.

natural *adj.* **1** inbred, inborn, innate, inherited, hereditary; original, basic, fundamental: *It's natural for a frightened animal to attack when cornered.* **2** normal, customary, typical, usual; characteristic: *Instead of trying to act in a particular way, just do what is natural for you.* ANT. unnatural, alien, contrary.

naturalize *vb.* adopt, introduce, accustom.

naturally *adv.* **1** normally, usually, typically, ordinarily, customarily: *Naturally I expect everyone to respect his parents.* **2** freely, readily, simply, openly, sincerely: *Please try to behave naturally when you go for the interview: don't put on an act.* ANT. (2) artificially.

nature *n.* **1** world, universe; creation: *It's against the laws of nature to expect things to fall upward.* **2** character, quality, essence: *What is the true nature of water that makes it expand when cooled and contract when warmed?* **3** sort, kind, variety, character: *I don't understand the nature of your question.* **4** manner, disposition, personality, character: *I didn't think it was in Mr. Robinson's nature to get so upset.*

naughty *adj.* **1** disobedient, unruly, unmanageable, insubordinate, mischievous: *Don't be naughty: just do as you are told and behave yourself.* **2** titillating, indecent, improper, rude: *The boys told naughty stories in the locker room after the game.* ANT. (1) good, well-behaved, obedient.

nausea *n.* sickness, vomiting, queasiness.

nauseate *vb.* disgust, repel, sicken.

nautical *adj.* marine, maritime, naval; sea-going.

navigate *vb.* direct, guide, steer, pilot.

near *adj.* close, nearby, neighbouring, adjoining. ANT. far, distant, remote.

nearly *adv.* almost, practically.

neat *adj.* clean, orderly, tidy, trim; smart, elegant. ANT. messy, sloppy, unkempt, disorganized.

necessary *adj.* needed, required, important, essential. ANT. unnecessary, dispensable, unneeded.

necessity *n.* requirement, essential, prerequisite.

need *n.* **1** want, lack, necessity: *I feel the need of a holiday after working so hard for two years.* **2** requirement, necessity: *The need for energy is increasing all of the time in the industrialized nations.* **3** poverty, pennilessness, want: *Every Christmas we make a contribution to families that are in need.* *vb.* want, lack, require, miss: *The poor children needed shoes and clothing and food after the flood had destroyed their home.*

needy *adj.* poor, poverty-stricken, penniless, destitute. ANT. wealthy, well-to-do, affluent, well-off.

neglect *vb.* **1** disregard, overlook, ignore: *The judge ruled that the man had to take better care of the family he had neglected.* **2** omit, skip, miss: *The speaker neglected mentioning all those who had helped elect him.* *n.* disregard, negligence, inattention: *The soldier was reprimanded by his commanding officer for neglect of duty. The house was suffering from neglect and needed painting and some repairs.* ANT. *vb.* (**1**) care, attend. *n.* attention, concern, regard.

negligent *adj.* careless, inattentive, neglectful.

negotiate *vb.* arrange, settle, transact.

neighbourhood *n.* area, vicinity, section, district, locality.

nerve *n.* **1** courage, boldness, bravery, spirit: *It takes some nerve to move to a new district where you don't know anyone.* **2** *Informal:* effrontery, impudence, rudeness, impertinence: *You have a lot of nerve walking into my home without knocking or ringing!* ANT. (**1**) cowardice, weakness, frailty.

nervous *adj.* **1** restless, excited, agitated: *The threatening phone calls made everyone in the town nervous.* **2** timid, shy, fearful: *Mona was very nervous about her interview.* ANT. (**1**) calm, tranquil, placid. (**2**) bold, courageous, confident.

nestle *vb.* settle, shelter, huddle, snuggle, cuddle.

net *n.* web, mesh; fabric.

network *n.* system, organization, complex, structure.

neutral *adj.* **1** uninvolved, inactive, nonpartisan: *I am going to remain neutral in the argument between Cecile and Roger.* **2** dull, drab: *The car was a neutral colour.* ANT. (**1**) prejudiced, biased.

new *adj.* **1** novel, fresh, unique, original, unusual: *Ken announced that he'd discovered a new way to cook chicken.* **2** recent, modern, current, latest: *The new fashions aren't really very becoming to shorter people.* ANT. (**1**) old, ancient, usual. (**2**) outmoded.

newcomer *n.* new boy, beginner, novice; intruder.

news *n.* information, knowledge, data, report.

next *adj.* 1 adjacent, beside, close, touching: *The house was next to the church.* 2 following, succeeding, subsequent: *Who will be the next ruler of the country?* ANT. (1) distant. (2) preceding, previous.

nibble *vb.* peck, nip, bite.

nice *adj.* 1 pleasant, agreeable, pleasing: *Maria certainly has a nice disposition.* 2 kind, thoughtful, friendly, cordial: *Be nice to your sister.* 3 accurate, precise, exact; subtle: *People should learn to make a nice distinction between the meanings of words.* ANT. (1) unpleasant, disagreeable, nasty. (2) thoughtless, unkind. (3) careless, inexact.

niggardly *adj.* stingy, mean, parsimonious. ANT. generous.

night *n.* darkness, blackness; evening. ANT. day; light.

nimble *adj.* agile, spry, lively, quick. ANT. clumsy, awkward.

noble *adj.* 1 honourable, honest, upright, virtuous, dignified: *It is more noble to give than to receive.* 2 aristocratic, titled, high-born, well-born, blue-blooded: *The man who will marry the princess comes from a noble family.* ANT. (1) ignoble, base, dishonest. (2) lowborn.

nod *vb.* approve, agree, consent, bow.

noise *n.* tumult, uproar, clamour, din, racket. outcry. ANT. quiet, silence, peace.

noisy *adj.* loud, tumultuous, booming. ANT. quiet, silent, peaceful.

nominal *adj.* theoretical, titular, ostensible.

nominate *vb.* name, select, choose, propose.

nonchalant *adj.* uninvolved, unconcerned, uncaring, indifferent; easygoing.

nonconformist *n.* rebel, dissenter, radical.

nonsense *n.* trash, rubbish, balderdash, twaddle.

nonsensical *adj.* ridiculous, absurd, silly, stupid, senseless.

norm *n.* standard, model, measure; average.

normal *adj.* regular, usual, customary, typical, common; standard, routine. ANT. odd, irregular, peculiar.

normally *adv.* usually, customarily, regularly, frequently.

notable *adj.* noteworthy, remarkable, noted, unusual, uncommon, conspicuous, distinctive, distinguished: *The union and management negotiators made notable progress in their discussions.* *n.* celebrity, personality, star: *Notables of the stage, film, and television attended the gala dinner.* ANT. *adj.* ordinary, usual, commonplace.

notation *n.* representation, system; signs, symbols.

note *n.* **1** message, memorandum, memo, record: *The secretary took notes of what the members of the council said.* **2** notice, heed: *I have taken note of what you said and will act as you suggest.* **3** eminence, importance, distinction, repute, reputation: *Many people of note came to the farewell party.* *vb.* **1** notice, attend, observe, heed, regard: *The witness testified that he had noted that the back door of the house was open.* **2** write down, record, register: *I noted in my diary all of the interesting things that happened to me and my friends.*

noted *adj.* famous, well-known, celebrated, distinguished, famed, notable. ANT. unknown, anonymous.

notice *n.* **1** sign, poster, announcement, advertisement; note: *In addition to the notices we posted on the board, we also placed one in the newspaper.* **2** observation, attention, heed, note: *Please take notice of the No Smoking signs in the trains.* **3** warning, advice, admonition: *The mechanic gave the garage manager one week's notice of his intention to leave.* *vb.* observe, note, heed, regard, pay attention to: *Notice how carefully the painter works on these miniatures.* ANT. *vb.* ignore, disregard, overlook.

noticeable *adj.* observable, apparent, perceptible; obvious, conspicuous.

notify *vb.* inform, advise, announce, mention, reveal.

notion *n.* idea, fancy, impression, concept, conception.

notorious *adj.* infamous, ill-famed; disreputable.

nought *see* **zero**.

nourish *vb.* sustain, support, feed, supply.

nourishment *n.* sustenance, support, food, nutriment.

novel *n.* book, story, tale; fiction: *Have you read any good novels lately?* *adj.* new, original; unusual, different, odd, strange: *He's so old-fashioned that he thinks the waltz is a novel dance.*

novelty *n.* newness, originality; freshness, recentness.

novice *n.* beginner, learner, tyro; amateur.

nude *see* **naked**.

nuisance *n.* irritation, annoyance, bother, trouble.

null *adj.* invalid, void.

nullify *vb.* annul, cancel, abrogate, abolish.

numb *adj.* dead, deadened, paralysed.

number *n.* **1** total, sum, collection, quantity, amount: *A large number of people visit the museum every year.* **2** numeral, digit, figure: *Pick a number from one to ten but don't tell me what it is.* *vb.* count, total, add, work out, calculate; estimate: *Number the desks in this classroom.*

numerous *adj.* many, copious; numberless. ANT. few, scanty.
nurse *n.* attendant, orderly; sister, matron: *Nurse, will you see to this patient, please?* *vb.* take care of, tend, care for, attend: *When you were sick, wasn't it your mother who nursed you back to health?*
nurture *vb.* nourish, feed; support.
nutrition *n.* food, nutriment, nourishment, sustenance.

O

oath *n.* **1** pledge, promise, vow: *I have sworn an oath never to reveal the secret.* **2** curse, profanity, swearword: *When the hammer struck his finger the carpenter uttered an oath that I shall not repeat.*

obedience *n.* submission, docility. ANT. disobedience, rebelliousness.

obedient *adj.* docile, yielding, respectful, obliging.

obey *vb.* do, carry out, behave, comply with, submit. ANT. disobey; break.

object *vb.* protest, disapprove of, complain: *My mother objected when I said I wanted to climb the mountain alone.* *n.* **1** objective, goal, target, aim: *Our object in staging the rally was to demonstrate against the use of nuclear weapons.* **2** thing, article: *The object on the table was a golden statue.* ANT. *vb.* approve, agree, assent.

objection *n.* protest, disapproval, doubt. ANT. agreement, assent, concurrence.

objective *n.* aim, goal, purpose: *Our objective was to reach the border before dawn.* *adj.* fair, just, impartial, unbiased: *Since you are not involved and won't profit either way, perhaps you can give us an objective opinion.* ANT. *adj.* subjective, biased.

obligation *n.* **1** requirement, responsibility, duty: *Anyone who is elected to an office should be prepared to assume its obligations.* **2** contract, agreement: *The company has taken on the obligation to supply clean towels to the school.*

oblige *vb.* require, force, compel, bind. ANT. free.

obliging *adj.* agreeable, accommodating, kind.

oblique *adj.* slanting, sloping, inclined. ANT. vertical, perpendicular.

obliterate *vb.* destroy; erase, wipe out, delete.

oblivion *n.* forgetfulness, unmindfulness; blankness, emptiness.

oblivious *adj.* forgetful, unaware, unconscious.

obnoxious *adj.* unpleasant, annoying, disagreeable.

obscene *adj.* offensive, outrageous; filthy, foul, unclean.

obscure *adj.* **1** hidden, dim, unclear, indistinct: *The sign was too obscure for me to read what it said.* **2** unknown, inconspicuous: *The best play of the year was written by an obscure playwright.* *vb.* screen, veil, hide, conceal, cover: *The car was completely obscured by the bushes.* ANT. *adj.* (**1**) clear, lucid, illumined. (**2**) famous, distinguished. (**3**) bright.

observance *n.* honouring, keeping; celebration.

observant *adj.* watchful, alert, keen, vigilant, attentive. ANT. unobservant, inattentive.

observation *n.* **1** watching, attention: *Our observation of the cave was rewarded when we saw the men emerge.* **2** comment, remark, opinion: *Wendy made the observation that she considered the book very boring.*

observe *vb.* **1** see, notice, look at, regard, watch: *Observe the way the amoeba surrounds its food, then absorbs it with its body.* **2** honour, keep, celebrate: *I observe the Queen's birthday by putting a flag outside my window.* **3** obey, follow, abide by: *Please observe the speed limit.* ANT. (**1, 2**) ignore, disregard.

obsession *n.* fixation, infatuation, craze, mania, delusion; neurosis.

obsolete *adj.* old-fashioned, outdated, outmoded, antiquated. ANT. new, modern, up-to-date, current, fashionable.

obstacle *n.* block, stop, barrier, interference, obstruction. ANT. aid, support.

obstinate *adj.* stubborn, opinionated, wilful, pigheaded, inflexible. ANT. pliable, pliant, yielding.

obstruct *vb.* block, stop, hinder, interfere. ANT. help, further.

obstruction *n.* obstacle, block, blockage, interference, barrier.

obtain *vb.* **1** get, acquire, gain, procure, secure, attain: *It is sometimes difficult to obtain foodstuffs in country areas.* **2** pertain, be valid, concern: *Which laws obtain in this area?*

obtrusive *adj.* protruding, jutting; noticeable, prominent.

obvious *adj.* clear, unquestionable, transparent, plain, unmistakable. ANT. subtle, hidden, unobtrusive.

obviously *adv.* clearly, plainly, certainly, surely, evidently.

occasion *n.* **1** time, occurrence, happening: *The family gave Dad a gold watch on the occasion of his fiftieth birthday.* **2** opportunity, chance, excuse: *Should the occasion arise, I would love to go the the United States for a holiday.*

occasional *adj.* irregular, random, sporadic. ANT. regular, constant.

occasionally *adv.* now and then, infrequently, seldom, irregularly. ANT. often, regularly.

occult *adj.* magical, mystical, supernatural.

occupant *n.* resident, tenant, inhabitant.

occupation *n.* **1** trade, profession, business, job, employment: *For many years, my uncle's occupation was as an architect.* **2** seizure, capture: *When the soldiers defending the castle surrendered, the enemy's occupation of the mountain was complete.*

occupy *vb.* **1** take up, use, fill, hold: *The parents occupied the back part of the theatre at the school play.* **2** obtain, seize, capture: *The invading army soon occupied the city and its suburbs.* **3** engage, employ, busy, absorb: *Worries about the coming exams occupied Nellie's mind.*

occur *vb.* happen, take place, befall.

occurrence *n.* event, happening; incident.

ocean *n.* sea, deep.

odd *adj.* strange, unusual, peculiar, queer, weird, extraordinary. ANT. ordinary, regular, unexceptional; straightforward.

odious *adj.* repulsive, offensive, disgusting, repugnant.

odour *n.* smell, aroma, scent, fragrance, bouquet, perfume.

offence *n.* **1** sin, wrong, transgression, trespass, crime, wrongdoing, misdemeanour: *The policeman said that the offence I had committed was driving through a red traffic light.* **2** resentment, indignation, anger: *Bill took offence when we suggested he was too cowardly to ask Lucy for a dance.*

offend *vb.* **1** irritate, annoy, vex, anger, provoke, displease: *Marie was offended at Paul's suggestion that she should get rid of her new hat.* **2** outrage, insult: *The sight of the concentration camp offended all of us.* ANT. (1) please, flatter, delight.

offender *n.* culprit, criminal, lawbreaker, transgressor.

offensive *adj.* **1** unpleasant, disagreeable, revolting, nauseous, sickening, nauseating, disgusting: *Certainly, most people find the smell of rotten eggs offensive.* **2** aggressive, attacking: *Our football team then made a number of offensive manoeuvres that gained some ground.* *n.* attack, assault, aggression: *Our team took the offensive and we won.* ANT. *adj.* (1) pleasing, pleasant, agreeable, attractive. (2) defensive, defending.

offer *vb.* **1** present, tender, proffer, submit: *The plan that Bill offered was to be voted on the next day.* **2** volunteer: *Manuel* *offered to help with the collection at the school.* n. suggestion, proposal; presentation: *We have received three offers to buy the car.* ANT. *vb.* refuse, deny. *n.* refusal, denial.

offhand *adj.* casual, informal, impromptu, unprepared. ANT. planned, considered, calculated.

office *n.* **1** suite, offices, office building: *I will be working late at the office tonight.* **2** position, post, situation; occupation: *Which office do you hold in Parliament?*

official *n.* office-holder, functionary, bureaucrat, civil-servant: *When enquiring about my grant, I talked with an official in the education department.* *adj.* **1** formal, conventional: *I think we'd better order the paper through the official channels.* **2** administrative; authorized, authoritative: *The official records of births, deaths, and marriages are kept in that building.*

officious *adj.* interfering, intrusive, impertinent, rude.

offset *vb.* balance, counterbalance, set off, compensate for.

offshoot *n.* branch, by-product, derivative.

offspring *n.* children, descendants, issue, progeny.

off-the-record *adj.* unofficial, restricted, confidential.

often *adv.* frequently, regularly, usually. ANT. rarely, seldom, hardly.

ogre *n.* giant, monster.

oil *n.* lubricant, unction, fat, grease.

O.K. *adj.* *Informal:* correct, fine, all right.

old *adj.* **1** aged, elderly: *My parents aren't very old.* **2** used, worn, dilapidated, faded, broken-down: *There was an old hut in the woods where the boys would meet secretly.* **3** former, ancient, old-fashioned, antique: *My aunt collects old cigar boxes.* ANT. (1) young, youthful. (2) fresh, brand-new.

old-fashioned *adj.* old, antiquated, outmoded, passé. ANT. new, up-to-date, fashionable, current, modern.

omen *n.* portent, sign, indication, warning.

ominous *adj.* threatening, menacing, foreboding, inauspicious.

omit *vb.* **1** leave out, exclude, bar: *It was decided to omit from consideration all those with less than a B average mark.* **2** ignore, neglect, overlook: *By mistake your name was omitted from the list of members.* ANT. include.

onerous *adj.* burdensome, oppressive, troublesome.

one-sided *adj.* partial, biased, prejudiced, unfair. ANT. impartial, just.

only *adj.* single, lone, solitary: *When you have no brothers or sisters you are called an only child.* *adv.* merely, just, but, not more than: *It took me only one hour to walk to work during the railway strike.*

onset *n.* beginning, opening, start, commencement. ANT. end, conclusion, finale.

onwards *adv.* forwards, ahead. ANT. backwards.

ooze *vb.* seep, exude, drip, emit, leak, flow: *The oil oozed from the ground.* *n.* slime, mire, mud: *Many fossils have been found in the ooze at the bottom of the sea.*

opaque *adj.* covered, darkened, murky; dense. ANT. transparent, clear.

open *adj.* **1** unclosed, uncovered, accessible: *The door was open all night—anyone could have walked in. The jar of jam was left open and became mouldy.* **2** free, easy, candid; sincere, honest: *Donald was very open about his plans for the next week.* **3** unoccupied, vacant, unfilled: *The job advertised last week is still open.* *vb.* **1** start, begin, commence: *The chairman opened the meeting with a short speech of welcome.* **2** expand, spread, extend: *When Roger opened his fist, I saw the stain on his fingers, proving that he was the culprit.* ANT. *adj.* (1) closed, shut, sealed. (2) private, secretive. (3) filled, taken. *vb.* (1) finish, end, stop. (2) close, clench.

open-handed *adj.* generous, kind, charitable. ANT. tight-fisted, stingy, mean.

open-hearted *adj.* honest, frank, candid. ANT. devious, insincere.

opening *n.* **1** gap, hole: *The dog escaped from our yard through an opening in the fence.* **2** beginning, start, commencement: *At the opening of the ceremony, a huge limousine arrived.* **3** vacancy, opportunity, chance: *We have an opening for a skilled typist.*

open-minded *adj.* fair, tolerant, liberal, just. ANT. bigoted, intolerant, prejudiced.

operate *vb.* **1** run, work, use, manage: *Do you known how to operate a printing press?* **2** run, work, function, perform: *After it had been repaired, the machine operated normally again.*

operation *n.* **1** performance, function, action: *The operation of this motor is poor and irregular.* **2** administration, direction, supervision, handling: *A new executive was brought in to take charge of the operation of the project.* **3** surgery: *The operation on my toe will be tomorrow.*

operator *n.* operative, machinist, engineer, driver, workman.

opinion *n.* belief, view, sentiment, idea, viewpoint.

opponent *n.* rival, competitor, contestant, antagonist. ANT. ally, colleague, teammate.

opportunity *n.* chance, time, occasion.

oppose *vb.* resist, battle, combat, withstand, thwart. ANT. support, agree to.

opposite *adj.* 1 contrary, reverse, different: *Ken turned the car round and drove off in the opposite direction.* 2 facing: *I walked in and took my place on the opposite side of the room.* ANT. (1) same, like, similar.

opposition *n.* antagonism, resistance, defiance; disapproval. ANT. support, help, cooperation.

oppress *vb.* burden, afflict, torment; depress, worry.

oppression *n.* tyranny, injustice, cruelty, persecution. ANT. freedom, liberty.

oppressive *adj.* burdensome, difficult, hard; stifling.

opt (for) *vb.* choose, prefer, select.

optimism *n.* hopefulness, confidence, cheerfulness. ANT. pessimism, doubtfulness, cynicism.

option *n.* choice, preference, selection.

optional *adj.* voluntary, elective, discretional. ANT. compulsory, obligatory, necessary.

oral *adj.* spoken, uttered, verbal, said, vocal, voiced. ANT. written, printed.

oration *n.* speech, address, sermon, lecture.

orbit *n.* course, path, circuit, lap, revolution: *The planets move in elliptical orbits round the sun.* *vb.* circle, revolve: *The moon orbits round the earth, which orbits round the sun.*

ordeal *n.* trial, calamity, difficulty, misfortune, tribulation.

order *n.* 1 command, direction, instruction, rule: *The sergeant received the order to move the company into the front line area.* 2 requisition, purchase order; contract: *The shop acknowledged receiving our order for two boxes of stationery.* 3 goods, merchandise, shipment: *Two weeks afterwards, our order arrived.* 4 arrangement, classification, system, sequence: *The words in this book are in alphabetical order.* *vb.* 1 command, direct, instruct: *The police were ordered to investigate a report of thefts from the supermarket.* 2 buy, obtain, request: *That is not the stationery we ordered.* 3 arrange, classify, organize: *The teacher thought the material in my essay had been well ordered.*

orderly *adj.* 1 neat, well-organized, regulated: *In contrast to Mary's room, which is a mess, Anita's is very orderly.* 2 disciplined, well-organized, well-behaved: *I want everyone to line up and to go into the corridor in orderly fashion during the fire drill.* ANT. (1) messy, sloppy, undisciplined. (2) disorganized, haphazard.

ordinarily *adv.* usually, commonly, generally.

ordinary *adj.* **1** usual, common, customary, regular, normal: *Just do everything in the ordinary way and try to pretend nobody is watching you.* **2** average, mediocre, everyday, undistinguished: *Although Annette wears fancy clothes for her job in the hotel, she dresses in ordinary clothes during the day.* ANT. (**2**) extraordinary, unusual, special.

organization *n.* **1** formulation, plan, classification: *The experts disagreed on the organization of the information for the files.* **2** group, association, society, institute, league, guild: *The members of the teacher's organization agreed to meet the education officials.*

organize *vb.* **1** arrange, compose, coordinate, shape, regulate, order, classify: *The office manager asked Ronnie to organize the files.* **2** establish, found, form, constitute: *Ten of us decided to organize a swimming and tennis club.*

organized *adj.* orderly, planned, neat, arranged.

orgy *n.* revelry, debauchery, indulgence.

orientate *vb.* adjust, align, position; influence.

origin *n.* beginning, source, root, birthplace, rise, start. ANT. end, termination.

original *adj.* **1** first, primary, beginning: *The original people in this town were Anglo-Saxons.* **2** unique, new, fresh, novel, creative: *The invention of the steam engine, by James Watt, was an original idea.* ANT. (**1**) secondary. (**2**) outmoded, old-fashioned.

originate *vb.* **1** arise, begin, start: *The idea of coining money originated many centuries ago.* **2** invent, create, begin: *I wonder who originated the idea of the Channel Tunnel.*

originator *n.* inventor, creator; discoverer. ANT. imitator, follower.

ornament *n.* decoration, adornment, ornamentation, embellishment.

ornamental *adj.* decorative, ornate, embellishing, adorning.

orthodox *adj.* conforming, conservative, conventional, standard. ANT. unorthodox, unconventional.

oscillate *vb.* waver, sway, swing.

ostensible *adj.* seeming, apparent, superficial.

ostentatious *adj.* showy, pretentious, pompous.

oust *vb.* eject, expel, deprive, dislodge.

outbreak *n.* eruption, bursting, outburst, blast.

outcome *n.* result, end, consequence, upshot.

outdo *vb.* surpass, excel, beat.

outfit *n.* **1** gear, clothing, get-up, garb: *Stephanie arrived at the* *dance wearing a new outfit of gold lamé.* **2** kit, equipment: *My father was given a whole new fishing outfit for his birthday by the family.*

outlaw *n.* criminal, bandit; fugitive.

outlet *n.* opening, break, crack.

outline *n.* **1** edge, border, side: *If you see it against the sky, you will be able to make out the outline of the jagged cliff in the distance. Draw an outline of the map of the British Isles.* **2** plan, sketch, framework: *Nick handed in an outline of the essay he was going to write.* *vb.* draft, sketch, plan, draw: *The playwright outlined the plot of his new musical.*

outlook *n.* **1** view, viewpoint: *Because Tessie comes from a family that has money, her outlook on saving is different from mine.* **2** future, prospect, chance, opportunity: *The outlook for people with qualifications is better than for those without when they leave school.*

output *n.* production; productivity, yield.

outrage *n.* affront, offence, insult: *In wartime, soldiers commit outrages on the people whose land they capture.* *vb.* shock, injure, offend: *I was outraged when I learned that Jim had borrowed the car after I had told him not to.*

outrageous *adj.* shocking, offensive, disgraceful, shameful, gross, contemptible. ANT. reasonable, sensible, prudent.

outset *n.* beginning, start, commencement. ANT. end, climax.

outside *n.* **1** exterior, surface, covering: *The outside of the tin box was brightly coloured.* **2** limit, bounds: *I would guess that, at the outside, 300 students live in that hall of residence.* *adj.* external, exterior, outer: *The outside walls of my house need painting.*

outsider *n.* stranger, alien, foreigner; nonmember.

outspoken *adj.* bold, candid, blunt, frank.

outstanding *adj.* **1** excellent, distinguished; notable, well-known, famous, prominent, conspicuous, leading: *Alan's mother was one of the most outstanding violinists of her time.* **2** unpaid, overdue, due, owing: *I keep all of the paid bills in this drawer and all of the outstanding ones in the other.* ANT. **(1)** ordinary, average.

outward *adj.* external, exterior, outside. ANT. inward.

outwit *vb.* confuse, bewilder, trick, baffle.

overall *adj.* general, complete, comprehensive.

overbearing *adj.* domineering; proud, arrogant.

overcast *adj.* cloudy, clouded, dark. ANT. clear, sunny.

overcome *vb.* **1** conquer, defeat, beat, subdue: *The heavyweight boxer easily overcame any challenger.* **2** overpower, weaken, overwhelm: *The firemen were nearly overcome by the smoke.* ANT. (1) submit, yield.

overcrowded *adj.* congested, full, crowded.

overdue *adj.* late, delayed, due.

overflow *vb.* run over, flood, spill over.

overhear *vb.* eavesdrop, catch, listen in to, hear.

overlook *vb.* ignore, disregard, neglect, miss. ANT. notice.

overpower *vb.* overwhelm, vanquish, overcome, conquer, subdue, defeat, beat. ANT. surrender.

overrule *vb.* disallow, override, nullify, cancel.

oversight *n.* **1** error, overlooking, omission, blunder, neglect, fault: *Through an oversight, the report cards weren't sent out on time.* **2** supervision: *The elders exercise oversight in our church.*

oversleep *vb.* sleep late, sleep in.

overtake *vb.* catch, reach; pass.

overthrow *vb.* overpower, defeat, conquer; upset, overturn: *The army succeeded in overthrowing the government so quickly that no one was hurt.* *n.* defeat, collapse, fall: *The overthrow of the king was being plotted by spies in another country.*

overture *n.* **1** prelude, introduction: *The overture to the opera was played very well.* **2** (often **overtures**) approach, suggestion, advance: *I think we must begin making overtures to take over that company.*

overwhelm *vb.* defeat, overcome, crush, overpower.

own *vb.* possess, have, hold.

p

pace *n.* **1** step: *Take three paces to the right, then one to the left, and dig there for the buried treasure.* **2** speed, rate; velocity: *Anne was typing only three letters an hour and was asked to increase her pace.* *vb.* walk, stride: *John paced the room as he waited for news impatiently.*

pacific *adj.* peaceful, calm, peaceable, tranquil, quiet; gentle. ANT. turbulent, excited, rough.

pacify *vb.* calm, quiet, tranquillize, smooth, lull. ANT. upset, excite, disturb.

pack *vb.* **1** prepare: *Pack your suitcase right away—we're off for a holiday this afternoon.* **2** cram, ram, crowd, stuff, compress: *Those sardines are packed in the can almost as tightly as people on a train during the rush hour.* *n.* **1** bundle, package, parcel, load: *Each hiker carried a pack on his back.* **2** crowd, herd, gang, mob, group: *The pack of wolves had attacked the sheep during the night.*

package *n.* bundle, parcel, pack, packet, load: *The package was weighed at the post office.* *vb.* crate, box, bottle: *The perfume comes packaged in a leakproof container.*

packet *n.* package, bundle; parcel.

pact *n.* agreement, contract, compact, arrangement, deal, settlement, treaty, bargain.

pad *n.* **1** cushion, wadding; stuffing, filling, padding: *If you keep this pad under your sprained knee it will make you more comfortable.* **2** block; bundle: *The detective made notes on a small pad of paper.* *vb.* cushion: *This fragile vase should be carefully padded for shipping.*

paddle *n.* oar, pole, scull, sweep.

pagan *see* **heathen**.

page *n.* **1** leaf, sheet, side: *This book has 60 pages.* **2** servant, boy: *The page came into the room with an important message from the king.*

pageant *n.* spectacle, exhibition, show, display, extravaganza.

pain *n.* **1** distress, suffering, misery, ache, pang, torment, agony: *Harold kept on running in spite of the pain of his sprained ankle.* **2** anguish, misery: *Betty's decision to live away from home caused her parents much pain.* ANT. (1) comfort, ease. (2) delight, joy.

painful *adj.* agonizing, aching, inflamed, sore, throbbing. ANT. soothing.

painstaking *adj.* careful, exacting, scrupulous. ANT. careless, slipshod.

paint *vb.* portray, draw, sketch, depict.

painter *n.* artist, craftsman.

painting *n.* composition, sketch; portrait, water colour, abstract, landscape; art.

pair *n.* couple; brace, team: *A pair of horses drew the carriage.* *vb.* match, mate, couple, join: *The teacher paired us off and we marched out of the room two abreast.*

pale *adj.* 1 white, ashen, colourless, pallid: *Before it becomes warm enough to go sunbathing and get a tan, everyone looks pale.* 2 dim, faint: *The bedroom is being painted pale blue.* ANT. (1) ruddy, flushed. (2) dark, bright.

pamper *vb.* coddle, spoil, cosset, overindulge.

pamphlet *n.* brochure, booklet, leaflet.

pan *n.* vessel, container, bowl.

pander (to) *vb.* please, gratify; provide, minister to.

panel *n.* 1 section, board, inset: *Robert fixed some new panels on the wall.* 2 group, team; committee, commission: *The panel on the television quiz programme consisted of two men and two women.*

pang *n.* pain, hurt, throb.

panic *n.* alarm, fear, dread, fright, terror: *When they saw and smelled the fire, the horses' panic was so great they stampeded.* *vb.* terrify, frighten, alarm: *The civilians were panicked by the scream of the bombs dropping nearby.* ANT. *vb.* calm, soothe, tranquillize.

pant *vb.* puff, gasp, throb; wheeze.

pantry *n.* storeroom, larder, cupboard, scullery.

paper *n.* 1 newspaper, journal: *Have you read the paper today?* 2 document, record, certificate: *When you apply for a job, you should bring all the necessary papers with you.* 3 article, report, essay: *Only invited scholars read their papers at the international meeting.*

parade *n.* march, procession, review; pageant: *Today is the annual Church parade.* *vb.* march, walk, strut: *The pretty girls were parading along the beach.*

paradise *n.* 1 heaven: *Many people believe that if they're good, they'll end up in paradise when they die.* 2 utopia: *We spent our holiday on what was promised in the travel brochure would be a tropical paradise.*

paradox *n.* puzzle, contradiction, mystery, enigma.

parallel *adj.* similar, corresponding, like, resembling: *Our thinking has been parallel on the subject of liberty for many years.* *n.* **1** equal, match, counterpart: *As a scientist, George has no parallel in this country.* **2** similarity, likeness, resemblance, correspondence: *It isn't accurate to draw a parallel between 20th-century rulers and those of the 16th century.* *vb.* resemble, correspond to, match, equal: *My experience parallels yours when it comes to service in the army.* ANT. *adj.* divergent.

paralyse *vb.* deaden, benumb, numb; transfix.

paramount *adj.* pre-eminent, supreme, greatest.

parcel *n.* package, bundle, packet.

parch *vb.* dry up, dehydrate, brown.

parched *adj.* very thirsty; dry; withered.

pardon *n.* excuse, forgiveness; amnesty, acquittal, exoneration: *The general refused to give pardons to the criminals convicted of major crimes.* *vb.* excuse, forgive, acquit, exonerate: *On his birthday the king pardoned all his political opponents still in jail.* ANT. *vb.* condemn, sentence.

pare *vb.* **1** peel, skin: *I know how to pare an apple so that the skin comes off in one long curly piece.* **2** diminish, reduce, cut, trim, crop, shave: *The finance committee is meeting to see if the budget can be pared down a bit.*

park *n.* green, square, land: *I sometimes go for a walk in the park near my home.* *vb.* leave, put, place: *Where can I park my car?*

parody *n.* humour, satire; imitation, mimicry, travesty.

parsimonious *adj.* mean, selfish, stingy. ANT. generous.

part *n.* **1** portion, piece, section, fraction, fragment: *Since I helped to pay for it, part of that apple pie should go to me.* **2** share, allotment, participation, interest: *If everyone does his part, we shall be finished much sooner.* **3** role, character: *Philip played the part of Macbeth.* *vb.* **1** divide, split, break up, disconnect: *The curtains parted to reveal a striking stage set. We had to part at the barrier because only passengers were allowed beyond it.* **2** depart, go, leave, quit: *It is late and we must part now.* ANT. *n.* (1) whole, entirety.

partial *adj.* **1** incomplete, unfinished, undone: *I made a partial payment towards the cost of the car.* **2** prejudiced, biased, one-sided, unfair, unjust: *The umpires and referees in sports should not be partial to one team or the other.* ANT. (1) entire, complete, comprehensive.

participate *vb.* share, partake, join; engage in, be involved.

particle *n.* bit, spot, grain, speck, shred, scrap.

particular *adj.* **1** special, specific, distinct: *This particular house is where I once lived.* **2** careful, finicky, discriminating: *Suzanne is very particular about the people she associates with.* **3** notable, exceptional, remarkable, unusual: *This is a matter of particular importance for the future.* *n.* detail, point, item, feature: *The report on the condition of the playground was correct in every particular.* ANT. *adj.* (2) careless, indiscriminating.

partisan *n.* follower, disciple, supporter, backer: *After the government was overthrown, its partisans continued to fight.* *adj.* partial, biased, prejudiced: *Rupert presented a very partisan view of the conference when he got back.*

partition *n.* **1** division, separation, distribution: *The allies agreed to the partition of Germany after the war.* **2** divider, screen, separator, barrier, wall: *A new partition was installed dividing the office in half.* *vb.* divide, separate, apportion: *We ought to partition a section of the cellar for a workshop.* ANT. *n.* (1) joining, unification.

partner *n.* associate, colleague, participant.

partnership *n.* cooperation, alliance, union.

party *n.* **1** gathering, social; fun: *Are you coming to our party on Saturday?* **2** group; company, crowd: *A party of tourists saw the sights of London.* **3** block, faction, body, organization: *You don't have to join a political party to vote in an election.*

pass *vb.* **1** go, move, proceed, continue: *Have you seen a ginger kitten pass this way?* **2** disregard, bypass, ignore: *The manager passed over George when it was time to consider promotions.* **3** circulate, spend: *The counterfeiter succeeded in passing some false ten-pound notes around.* **4** go by or away, end, terminate, cease, expire: *The day of the horse and cart has passed.* **5** enact, establish, approve: *Parliament has passed the new tax bill.* **6** exceed, surpass: *The club passed its target in raising funds.* **7** spend, while away, fill: *I passed the time waiting for the train in reading a book.* **8** elapse, flow, roll; advance, proceed: *Time passes slowly when you are waiting for someone.* *n.* **1** gorge, ravine, gap: *The army reached the mountain pass before dawn and launched an attack immediately.* **2** permit, admission, permission: *You will need an official pass to visit the arms factory.* **3** toss, throw, hurl: *Namath threw a forward pass that was caught by the fly-half.* ANT. *vb.* (2) consider, notice, note.

passable *adj.* acceptable, satisfactory, adequate, tolerable, fair. ANT. exceptional, extraordinary, superior.

passage *n.* **1** paragraph, section, text: *The speaker read a passage from* Moby Dick *and then discussed its meaning.* **2** passing, transition, movement: *The passage of time seems to slow when you are waiting for someone.* **3** passageway, corridor, hall: *The passage is so narrow that it is difficult for two people to pass.* **4** journey, voyage, trip, crossing, tour: *When he was just a boy, my grandfather worked his passage from England to America as a cabin boy.*

passenger *n.* commuter, traveller; tourist.

passion *n.* **1** emotion, feeling, zeal, rapture, excitement: *The passion Victoria had for the women's lib movement sometimes made her say things she didn't mean.* **2** love, desire, affection, liking, fondness, enthusiasm: *My mother has a strong passion for all of her nine children.* ANT. indifference, apathy, coolness.

passionate *adj.* emotional, excited, impulsive, zealous, enthusiastic, earnest, sincere.

passive *adj.* inactive, inert, lifeless; submissive.

past *adj.* **1** gone, over, finished, done, done with: *The days of regular travel by steam trains are past.* **2** former, preceding, prior: *The past president of the Cricket Club was at the dinner.* **3** recent, preceding: *In the past few days nobody has seen Joan at school.* *n.* **1** antiquity, old times, the (good) old days, days of yore, yesterday: *It always seem as though everything was better in the past.* **2** experiences, former life, secret life: *She may be old now, but that author had quite an exciting past.* ANT. *adj.* (1) ahead. (2) present; future. *n.* (1) present; future.

paste *n.* adhesive, glue: *Let's make some paste to stick the pieces of paper together.* *vb.* stick, glue, fix: *The teacher pasted some paintings on to the boards.*

pastime *n.* amusement, recreation, entertainment; hobby.

pastor *n.* minister, clergyman, priest.

pastry *n.* cake, tart, delicacy; patisserie.

pasture *n.* land, grass, field, meadow.

pat *vb.,n.* tap, stroke; beat; hit: *She patted the cake mixture firmly into the tin. She gave him a friendly light pat on the head.*

patch *vb.,n.* mend, repair: *Do you think that the tailor can patch my torn trousers? My jacket has a patch over each elbow.*

patent *n.* protection, copyright, control, permit: *Dick's got a patent on a new kind of fuel.* *vb.* license, limit, copyright:

Some of the strangest devices you have every seen have been patented.

path *n.* walk, way, trail, track, footpath, lane, pathway.

pathetic *adj.* 1 pitiable, pitiful, moving, touching: *The half-drowned kitten looked so pathetic that we had to take it home and care for it.* 2 *Slang:* worthless, awful, contemptible: *Her first attempts at learning to drive were pretty pathetic.*

patience *n.* 1 calmness, composure, passiveness, serenity, courage: *Our teacher's patience came to an end when Evelyn started to giggle again.* 2 endurance, perseverance, persistence: *It takes a great deal of patience to stand in a queue for four hours to buy a ticket for a concert.* ANT. (1) impatience, restlessness, impetuosity.

patient *adj.* 1 persistent, untiring, persevering: *If you'll be patient, the dentist will be with you in a few more moments.* 2 resigned, submissive: *As Tom grew older, he became more patient with other people's faults.* 3 calm, serene, quiet, unexcited, unexcitable, self-controlled, unruffled, unshaken: *The old pony was very patient when children wanted to ride him. After years of patient research, the scientists finally perfected the medicine.* *n.* invalid; case, inmate: *Danny was a patient in the hospital for a week after he broke his leg.*

patrol *vb.* guard, watch; inspect: *Three security guards are employed to patrol the factory at night.* *n.* guard, protector, watchman: *The patrol walked regularly round the office block, making sure everything was all right.*

patron *n.* 1 customer, client, purchaser, buyer: *The first patrons arrive at the restaurant at six-thirty for breakfast.* 2 supporter, benefactor, backer, philanthropist: *The patrons of the arts centre have contributed thousands of pounds to its funds.*

patronize *vb.* 1 buy at, support: *We always patronize our local shops.* 2 condescend, stoop, talk down to: *The department head didn't like the new clerk because she spoke to him in a patronizing way.*

patter *n.* 1 tapping, patting, rattle: *The patter of rain on the window became louder.* 2 chatter, jabber, prattle: *The saleman's glib patter about the encyclopedias helped him sell several sets.*

pattern *n.* 1 model, guide, example, original: *Penny was building a model car, using a Rolls Royce as a pattern.* 2 design, decoration, figure: *The dress has a beautiful pattern but I don't like the way it fits.* *vb.* model, copy, follow, imitate: *The style of the building was patterned after Georgian designs*.

paunch *n.* belly, abdomen, stomach.

pause *n.* hesitation, rest, wait, interruption, delay, break, intermission, recess: *After a short pause, the speaker went on to discuss the habits of lions in the wild.* *vb.* hesitate, rest, wait, interrupt, break, delay, recess: *You ought to pause to think before replying to that question.* ANT. *n.* continuity, perpetuity. *vb.* continue, perpetuate.

pave *vb.* lay, cover, flag.

paw *n.* foot, claw, talon.

pay *vb.* **1** settle, remit, discharge: *I have very few bills to pay this month.* **2** compensate, recompense, reward, return: *Phil's new job pays him much better than his last one.* *n.* payment, salary, wage, wages, fee, income: *How much is your pay per month?*

payment *n.* sum, recompense, remittance.

peace *n.* **1** quiet, serenity, calm, peacefulness, tranquillity: *Every time I spend a day in a big city, I yearn for the peace of the countryside.* **2** pact, treaty, truce, accord, armistice: *A peace agreement was signed in Geneva this week.* ANT. agitation, upheaval, disturbance.

peaceable *adj.* peaceful, gentle, mild, calm, friendly, amicable, pacific. ANT. hostile, warlike, aggressive.

peaceful *adj.* peaceable, quiet, calm, serene, tranquil. ANT. disrupted, agitated, riotous.

peak *n.* **1** top, summit, point, crest: *We could see the peaks of the Lake District mountains from the railway.* **2** top, maximum, pinnacle: *Prices on the stock market reached their peak of the year today.* ANT. (2) base, bottom.

peal *vb.* sound, ring, chime, resound.

peck *vb.* rip, bite, pick.

peculiar *adj.* **1** unusual, odd, strange, unfamiliar, uncommon, queer, outlandish, curious: *The camel is a very peculiar animal.* **2** characteristic, special, unique, exclusive: *A love of eucalyptus leaves is peculiar to the koala, which looks like a teddy bear.* ANT. (1) ordinary, regular, unspecial.

peculiarity *n.* characteristic, distinctiveness, individuality.

pedantic *adj.* academic, overprecise, fussy.

peddle *vb.* hawk, vend, sell.

pedestrian *n.* walker, stroller: *Pedestrians should watch how they cross the road.* *adj.* ordinary, common, everyday, dull, commonplace: *The comedian told some very pedestrian jokes* *that weren't funny at all.* ANT. *adj.* unusual, fascinating, extraordinary, special.

pedigree *n.* family, descent, ancestry, parentage, line, lineage.

pedlar *n.* salesman, hawker, seller.

peel *n.* skin, rind, peeling: *I slipped on a banana peel and everyone laughed when I fell down.* *vb.* skin, strip, pare: *My uncle can peel an orange so that the skin comes off in one piece.*

peep[1] *vb.,n.* cheep, chirp, squeak: *The baby chicks peeped constantly when they were awake. I don't want to hear a peep out of you after you get into bed.*

peep[2] *vb.,n.* peer, glimpse, look: *Close your eyes and count to 20; and no peeping! We got a peep at what they were doing without their seeing us.*

peer[1] *n.* **1** equal, parallel, match, rival: *As a high-jumper, Kim has no peer.* **2** nobleman, lord: *The peers of the British realm are listed in this book.*

peer[2] *vb.* scrutinize, examine: *The old lady peered at me closely, trying to see if I was someone she knew.*

peg *n.* holder; pin, tack, fastener.

pelt *vb.* **1** throw, hurl: *The natives pelted stones at the visitors.* **2** hurry, speed, dash: *We pelted along the road trying to catch the robbers.* **3** rain, pour: *It was pelting down outside.*

pen *n.* **1** fountain pen, ball-point pen: *Can you lend me a pen so I can write down your name?* **2** enclosure, cage, coop, sty: *Domestic animals like chickens and pigs are often kept in pens.*

penalize *vb.* punish, condemn; sentence.

penalty *n.* punishment; forfeit; fine.

penetrate *vb.* **1** pierce, enter, bore, hole: *The bullet penetrated the wall, just missing my head.* **2** permeate, spread, seep: *The smoke from the fire penetrated all the rooms, and we had to have everything cleaned.*

penetrating *adj.* shrewd, astute; sharp, acute.

peninsula *n.* point, neck, spit, headland.

penitence *n.* repentance, remorse, contrition; regret, sorrow.

penniless *adj.* poor, poverty-stricken, needy, destitute. ANT. rich, wealthy, well-off, prosperous.

people *n.* **1** human beings, humans, persons: *Many people have moved from the country to the cities.* **2** race, nation, tribe, clan, family: *A primitive people was found recently, living in the Philippine Islands.* *vb.* populate: *Australia was origi-*

nally peopled by the Aborigines, long before the white man came.

perceive *vb.* **1** see, discern, notice, observe, distinguish, make out: *It is very difficult to perceive the differences between the monarch and the viceroy butterflies.* **2** understand, comprehend, grasp: *I cannot perceive the purpose in your trying to swim across the river.*

perception *n.* understanding, apprehension, comprehension.

perceptive *adj.* discerning, sharp, acute, observant.

perfect *adj.* **1** faultless, excellent, flawless, pure, ideal: *The acrobat's style was perfect.* **2** complete, finished, whole: *The robbers' plan was perfect: they had thought of everything.* **3** complete, utter, total: *He might have told you he was my brother, but he was a perfect stranger to me.* **4** exact, precise, sharp, correct: *The two pieces of ancient sculpture turned out to be a perfect match.* *vb.* complete, achieve, finish, accomplish: *No one has yet been able to perfect a perpetual-motion machine.* ANT. *adj.* **(1)** imperfect, flawed, second-rate.

perforate *vb.* drill, hole, penetrate.

perforation *n.* hole, slot, notch.

perform *vb.* **1** do, carry out, accomplish, achieve, complete: *With a little coaxing, Harry would perform the trick of walking on his hands.* **2** present, act out, give, produce: *The children performed the play on an outdoor platform in the park.*

performance *n.* presentation, offering, exhibition, appearance.

performer *n.* actor, actress, entertainer.

perfume *n.* **1** scent, essence; toilet water, cologne: *Every Mother's Day I give my mother a bottle of perfume.* **2** odour, scent, fragrance, smell, aroma: *The perfume of the orange blossoms filled the night air.*

perhaps *adv.* maybe, possibly, conceivably. ANT. definitely, absolutely.

peril *n.* danger, hazard, risk. ANT. security, safety.

perilous *adj.* dangerous, risky, hazardous, unsafe. ANT. safe, secure.

perimeter *n.* edge, boundary, border, outline.

period *n.* **1** time, interval, term; era, age, epoch: *My uncle spent a brief period in the navy. The 15th to 17th centuries were a period of exploration and migration.* **2** course, cycle; timing: *The period of the day is marked by the revolution of the earth on its axis.*

periodical *n.* magazine, review, journal.

perish vb. die, expire; pass away, depart.

perk up vb. liven up, revive, cheer up.

permanent adj. 1 enduring, lasting, stable, continuing, long-lived, persisting, persistent; perpetual, everlasting: *Stainless steel is a more permanent material than aluminium for building*. 2 unchanging, unaltered, unchanged, constant, unvarying, invariable: *Because of the accident, Tim has a permanent scar on his arm*. ANT. passing, temporary, fluctuating.

permeate vb. pervade, penetrate, fill, saturate.

permission n. consent, leave; freedom, liberty.

permit vb. allow, let, tolerate, suffer: *No one is permitted to talk during class*. n. permission, authorization: *Only councillors have permits to park in that area*. ANT. vb. forbid, prohibit, disallow.

perpendicular adj. vertical, upright, standing. ANT. horizontal.

perpetual adj. unceasing, continuing, continuous, continual, everlasting, permanent, constant, eternal, ceaseless, undying. ANT. intermittent, inconstant, fluctuating.

perplex vb. confuse, puzzle, mystify, bewilder.

persecute vb. oppress, torment, ill-treat, maltreat, victimize, abuse.

persevere vb. endure, persist, last, continue. ANT. lapse, desist, discontinue, stop.

persist vb. persevere, continue, remain, endure. ANT. stop, desist.

person n. human, human being, individual, someone, somebody.

personal adj. 1 private, secret: *Linda revealed many personal things about herself that I wouldn't repeat to anyone*. 2 individual, special, particular: *My personal opinion is that each one of us ought to do what he does best*. ANT. (1) public, general.

personify vb. represent, symbolize; embody.

personnel n. people, staff, workers.

perspective n. aspect, viewpoint, outlook.

perspire vb. sweat, exude, secrete.

persuade vb. 1 influence, induce, convince: *Peter persuaded me to try to get a job for the summer holidays*. 2 urge, coax, prompt: *You don't have to persuade Anne to eat everything on her plate*. ANT. (1) dissuade, discourage.

persuasive adj. convincing, influential, winning, alluring, compelling. ANT. unconvincing, dubious.

pertinent *adj.* relevant, appropriate, suitable.

pervade *vb.* permeate, spread, fill.

perverse *adj.* deviant, wayward.

pessimism *n.* unhappiness, gloom; doubtfulness, cynicism. ANT. cheerfulness, hopefulness.

pest *n.* 1 nuisance, irritation, irritant, annoyance, (*informal*) tease, bother: *Why must you be such a pest about my keeping my room neat?* 2 disease, germ, virus, bug, insect: *The pests damaged the crops.*

pester *vb.* annoy, irritate, vex, nag, trouble, harass, torment, tease, bother, worry.

pestilence *n.* epidemic, plague, disease.

pet *n.* favourite, darling: *Eunice is the teacher's pet.* *vb.* fondle, caress: *Phoebe had great fun at her aunt's house where she petted the new kittens.*

petition *n.* request, application, appeal, solicitation, entreaty: *Most of the residents signed the petition to save trees along the streets.* *vb.* request, apply, appeal, entreat: *The students got together to petition the teachers to give them less homework.*

petrify *vb.* stun, daze, dull, deaden.

petty *adj.* 1 unimportant, trivial, insignificant, paltry, trifling: *My mother always seems to tell me off about very petty things.* 2 stingy, mean, miserly: *Some people are very generous with themselves but very petty when it comes to others.* ANT. (1) important, vital, significant. (2) generous, bighearted.

phantom *n.* spectre, ghost, apparition: *The old man swore that he had seen a phantom who haunted the ghost town.* *adj.* unreal; imaginary: *He insisted that the ghost was a phantom cowboy who had been killed in a gunfight.*

phase *n.* 1 stage, period, state: *The Neanderthal was thought to be an early phase in the development of modern man.* 2 aspect, side, view, condition: *Each phase of the project should be handled by the person who knows most about it.*

phenomenon *n.* 1 happening, occurrence, fact, incident: *The fish that climbs trees in Borneo is a very strange phenomenon.* 2 marvel, wonder: *Anyone who can balance himself on only on toe is truly a phenomenon.*

phenomenal *adj.* extraordinary, remarkable; stupendous; unusual. ANT. ordinary.

phobia *n.* fear, dread, neurosis.

phone *see* **telephone.**

photograph *n.* photo, picture, snapshot; print; slide.

physical *adj.* 1 bodily, corporeal, corporal: *I have a complete*

physical examination once a year. **2** real, material, natural:
Man cannot fly—it's a physical impossibility. ANT. **(1)**
mental, spiritual.

pick *vb.* **1** choose, select: *I was picked to represent our school
in the debating contest.* **2** gather, harvest, reap, collect,
pluck: *Every autumn our family goes to an orchard where you
can pick all the apples you want.* **3** steal, rob: *My pocket was
picked while I was in the bus.* *n.* choice, selection; best:
*When Josie's dog had puppies, we were allowed the pick of the
litter.*

picture *n.* **1** painting, drawing, photograph, illustration: *I love
the pictures in my family album.* **2** image, likeness, representation: *Jean is the picture of health.* **3** description,
account: *Try to give us a picture of the events of last Saturday.*
vb. **1** describe, represent: *In his story, the writer pictured a
world where there was no evil.* **2** imagine, conceive of: *Can
you picture yourself winning the Miss World contest?*

picturesque *adj.* striking, scenic; attractive, pleasing.

piece *n.* quantity, unit, section, portion, part.

piecemeal *adv.* partially, gradually, bit by bit. ANT. entire,
whole, complete.

pierce *vb.* **1** stab, perforate, puncture: *Once you pierce the skin
of the sausage with a fork, all the juices and fat run out.* **2**
affect, rouse, touch, move, excite, thrill: *Cory's sad story
about the death of her cat pierced our hearts.*

piety *n.* devotion, reverence, holiness.

pigment *n.* paint, dye, colour.

pile *n.* heap, collection, accumulation: *There's a pile of dirty
clothes in the corner of your room and I want it taken away.*
vb. heap (up), accumulate, amass, assemble: *Please ask the
men to pile that firewood near the shed.*

pilfer *vb.* steal, take, (*slang*) nick.

pilgrim *n.* traveller, wanderer.

pilgrimage *n.* tour, journey, trip, expedition.

pill *n.* tablet, medicine, dose, capsule.

pillar *n.* column, shaft, support, prop.

pillow *n.* cushion, pad, bolster.

pilot *n.* aviator; steersman, helmsman: *My uncle was a fighter
pilot in the Air Force. That's nothing: my father is a pilot on a
transatlantic 747.* *vb.* steer, guide: *A man who knows the
harbour waters was brought aboard to pilot the ocean liner up
to the pier.*

pin *n.* **1** fastening, fastener, clip, peg: *A wooden pin was used* *to hold the door shut.* **2** brooch, tiepin: *Sandy's mother wore a diamond pin to the opera last night.* *vb.* fasten, fix: *Hugh pinned the notice onto the board.*

pinch *vb.,n.* nip, squeeze: *Why do grown-ups all like to pinch children's cheeks? The pinch of these tight new shoes is more than I can stand.*

pinnacle *n.* point, peak, tower, summit, climax, crest, zenith.

pioneer *n.* **1** settler, explorer, discoverer: *The spread westward of American civilization was due chiefly to the early adventurous pioneers.* **2** leader, initiator: *Ivor was a pioneer in the field of digital computers.*

pious *adj.* devout, religious, reverent. ANT. impious, irreligious, profane.

pipe *n.* tube; channel, duct, conduit.

piquant *adj.* pungent, penetrating, tart, spicy.

pirate *n.* buccaneer, corsair, privateer, plunderer: *Some books make pirates seem romantic, when in fact they were killers and thieves.* *vb.* steal, rob, plagiarize: *The novel sold very well over here, and soon it was pirated for publication in Taiwan.*

pistol *n.* gun, revolver, weapon.

pit *n.* hole, cavity, hollow, well, excavation.

pitch *vb.* **1** set up, establish: *We pitched camp near the river.* **2** throw, toss, fling, hurl: *It was John's turn to pitch the ball.* **3** plunge, rock: *The huge ship was pitching like a matchbox in the typhoon.* *n.* slant, angle, incline, grade: *In countries where it snows a lot, the roofs of the houses have a very steep pitch.*

pitcher *n.* jug, container, ewer.

pitfall *n.* trap, deadfall, snare.

pithy *adj.* terse, succinct, concise, pregnant.

pitiful *adj.* pitiable, pathetic, distressing, heart-rending.

pitiless *adj.* unpitying, merciless, unmerciful, ruthless, mean, cruel, hard-hearted, stony-hearted. ANT. kind, kindly, gentle.

pity *n.* sympathy, compassion, charity, mercy, tenderheartedness, softheartedness: *I feel so much pity for the animals in zoos that I want to set them free.* *vb.* feel for, sympathize (with), commiserate (with): *Pity the poor children elsewhere in the world, many of whom have nothing to eat.* ANT. *n.* cruelty, pitilessness, vindictivensss.

pivot *n.* lever, fulcrum, hinge, axis.

placard *n.* card, notice, poster.

place *n.* **1** space, plot, region, location, area, spot: *There's a place I know where the sun always shines and the swimming is* *marvellous*. 2 residence, home, house, dwelling: *I love your new place, Anna! Too bad you can't afford to furnish it!* *vb*. 1 put, set, arrange, locate: *Place your hands on top of the table, palms up*. 2 engage, appoint: *We have placed three new people in the accounts department this month*. 3 identify, recognize, connect: *I know that face, but I just can't place it*.

placid *adj*. calm, peaceful, quiet.

plagiarize *vb*. copy, appropriate, forge.

plague *n*. 1 pestilence, Black Death, epidemic: *The plague in Europe in the Middle Ages killed about one quarter of the population*. 2 trouble, vexation, nuisance, irritation: *A plague of locusts destroyed almost the entire crop*. *vb*. trouble, vex, annoy, irritate, pester: *Financial troubles always plagued this family*.

plain *adj*. 1 simple, undecorated, unembellished, ordinary, unadorned: *Sophie was wearing a plain black dress with a shocking pink collar and cuffs*. 2 unattractive: *Peter married a plain girl*. 3 clear, understandable, unmistakable, obvious: *I made it quite plain that Sue would not go out with anyone who drank or smoked*. 4 candid, blunt, outspoken, frank, open, honest, sincere: *If you don't mind some plain speaking, I'd like to know why you arrived home so late*. *n*. plateau, prairie, steppe, savanna, tundra: *The central plains of the United States are extensive farming areas*. ANT. *adj.* (1) fancy, elaborate, ornamented. (2) pretty, beautiful, attractive. (3) disguised, hidden, unclear.

plan *n*. 1 plot, procedure, scheme, design, method: *Donald outlined his plan for selling the textbooks to schools and colleges*. 2 drawing, rendering, map, chart, diagram: *When I checked the plan of the building I found the hidden passageways*. *vb*. plot, scheme, design, arrange, contrive: *The engineers planned to build the plant near the river. If it's sunny on Saturday, we plan to go on a picnic in the park*.

plane *n*. 1 level: *If you are going to be rude, then the plane of this conversation is too low for me*. 2 aeroplane, aircraft: *Tony just got off the plane from London*.

plank *n*. board, timber, wood.

plant *n*. 1 shrub, bush, bulb, flower: *Your garden plants look lovely*. 2 factory, works, installation; machinery: *The printers opened a new plant on the industrial estate*. *vb*. sow, seed: *Sue planted some seeds in her garden*.

plaster *n*. 1 mortar, binding; cement: *We put some plaster on the walls and then wallpapered them*. 2 bandage, dressing,

plate · 230

lint: *I think we'd better put a plaster on that cut.*

plate *n.* dish: *Michael got the plates out of the cupboard for dinner.* *vb.* coat, layer, cover: *The metal was plated with gold.*

platform *n.* 1 stage, pulpit: *The primitive theatre was nothing more than a raised platform on which the actors stood.* 2 policies, principles: *The politicians met to work out the party platform for the coming elections.*

plausible *adj.* reasonable, likely, probably, credible.

play *n.* 1 show, drama, performance: *Each year at Christmas our class put on a play for the rest of the school.* 2 amusement, sport, entertainment, recreation, game, pastime: *There is a time for work and a time for play, and play comes after work.* *vb.* 1 act, perform, present, represent, impersonate: *Richard played the part of the grandfather in our melodrama.* 2 have a good time; sport, frisk, romp, caper, frolic: *After school was over, we all went out to play on the beach.* 3 compete, participate, contend: *My brother taught me how to play chess.* 4 perform on: *Can you play the piano?* *vb. phr.* **play ball** *Informal:* collaborate, cooperate: *If we can get the teacher to play ball, maybe we'll have less homework.* **play down** minimize, belittle, make light of: *If I were you, I would play down my experience as a pickpocket.* **play up** 1 *Informal:* annoy, irritate, antagonize: *Why do you children always play up when we have visitors?* 2 highlight, emphasize, stress: *You ought to play up your good points, like your ability to draw.*

player *n.* sportsman, participant, team member; contestant, competitor.

plaything *n.* toy, game, gadget, trinket.

plea *n.* 1 appeal, request, entreaty: *Ted's plea for fair treatment by his teammates was sincere.* 2 excuse, apology, answer, reply: *My only plea for having given George a box on the ears was that he hit me first.* 3 defence, pleading, case: *The lawyer entered a plea of not guilty for his client.*

plead *vb.* 1 beg, entreat, appeal: *Sonia pleaded with her captors to let her go.* 2 answer, declare, present: *The man pleaded guilty to driving on the wrong side of the road.*

pleasant *adj.* 1 enjoyable, nice, agreeable, pleasurable, satisfying, satisfactory, adequate, acceptable: *We had a pleasant visit at my cousin's, but it could have been much more fun.* 2 affable, agreeable, charming, mild, amiable, friendly, personable, courteous: *Fred's a pleasant enough fellow, but he's not my best friend.* ANT. horrid, disagreeable; sour, nasty.

please *vb.*   **1** gratify, satisfy: *It pleases me to think of my parents getting a good rest from work.*   **2** desire, choose, wish: *You may do as you please about going to the concert.*   ANT. (**1**) displease, annoy, vex.

pleased *adj.*   happy, satisfied; delighted.

pleasing *adj.*   pleasant, agreeable, charming, delightful, engaging.   ANT. irritating, annoying.

pleasure *n.*   **1** delight, satisfaction, enjoyment, gladness, happiness, joy, well-being, gratification: *Stefan gets a great deal of pleasure out of spending a day with his grandchildren.*   **2** luxury, indulgence: *His pleasures are his greatest weakness.*   ANT. (**1**) pain, discomfort, torment.

pledge *n.*   promise, agreement, commitment, oath: *Ronnie gave his pledge to abide by the rules of the club if he became a member.*   *vb.* promise, agree; swear, vow: *Timothy has pledged to help at home after school.*

plentiful *adj.*   abundant, bountiful, fruitful, copious.   ANT. scarce, rare, scanty.

plenty *n.*   abundance, fullness, fruitfulness, bounty, plentifulness.   ANT. need, want, scarcity.

pliable *adj.*   flexible, mouldable, adaptable.

plight *n.*   difficulty, predicament, dilemma, situation, state, condition.

plod *vb.*   walk, trudge; stump.

plot *n.*   **1** plan, scheme, design, intrigue, conspiracy: *Some think that the oil shortage is the result of an international plot.*   **2** story, theme, outline, thread: *The acting in the play was good, but the plot lacked something.*   *vb.* plan, scheme, design, contrive, conspire: *The prisoners spent six months plotting their escape.*

plough *vb.*   furrow, till, cultivate.

pluck *vb.*   snatch, pull, jerk, yank: *You have to pluck the feathers out of a chicken before cooking it, not after.*   *n.* courage, bravery, nerve, boldness, determination, spirit: *It takes pluck to admit when you've done something wrong.*

plucky *adj.*   brave, courageous, undaunted.

plug *n.*   stopper, cork, bung: *She pulled out the plug and let all the water out of the bath.*   *vb.* stop (up), block, obstruct: *The rust inside the pipes plugged up the whole system.*

plump *adj.*   chubby, fat, stout, portly.   ANT. slim, thin, skinny.

plunder *vb.*   rob, pillage, sack, ravage, strip, raid, loot: *The conquering armies plundered the city till nothing of value remained.*   *n.* **1** booty, loot, spoils: *The soldiers needed many wagons to carry off their plunder.*   **2** pillage, robbery, sacking, sack: *The plunder of Troy lasted two months.*

plunge *vb.* **1** submerge, dip, immerse: *I plunged my burnt finger into the cool water.* **2** dive, jump, rush: *Davey plunged into the river to try to save the drowning girl.* *n.* leap, dive, jump: *We all took a plunge into the swimming pool before dinner.*

ply *vb.* travel (between), commute (between), oscillate (between).

pocket *n.* bag, pouch: *Jean's handbag has a number of pockets in it.* *vb.* take, steal; put: *He pocketed Fred's wallet and ran off.*

poem *n.* verse, lyric, sonnet, ballad.

poetry *n.* verse; metre; rhyme.

poignant *adj.* distressing, painful; cutting, piercing.

point *n.* **1** locality, position, location, spot: *Don has reached a point in his life where he doesn't want to waste time any more.* **2** aim, object, intent, purpose, idea: *The point of my story is to show that you cannot afford to be dishonest.* **3** meaning, import, drift: *You don't get the point of the joke, do you?* **4** headland, cape, ness, promontory: *We stood out on the point, near the lighthouse, watching the boats sail past.* *vb.* **1** indicate, show, designate: *The boy pointed to the place in the wall where the man had disappeared.* **2** direct, guide, head, lead, steer; aim: *I pointed the canoe homeward to arrive before sunset. Don't ever point a gun at anyone!*

poise *n.* **1** self-control, control, assurance, composure, dignity; carriage: *Suzanne, although she's only 14, has the poise of a 21-year-old.* **2** balance, steadiness, equilibrium: *That acrobat on the high wire has unbelievable strength and poise.* *vb.* balance; hesitate: *The diver poised on the edge of the high platform before diving into the pool.* ANT. *n.* **(1)** coarseness, ineptitude. **(2)** awkwardness, instability.

poison *n.* venom, virus, toxin, bane: *Children should never be allowed to touch or use poison of any kind. The spitting cobra can project its poison a very long way.* *vb.* infect, contaminate, pollute: *Exhaust fumes from cars poison the atmosphere in large cities.*

poisonous *adj.* toxic, deadly, lethal; dangerous, harmful.

poke *vb.,n.* stab, thrust, jab, punch: *Don't poke that broom handle into the hornets' nest. When I teased Peter he gave me a poke in the ribs.*

pole *n.* post, shaft, stick; pillar, column.

policy *n.* tactic, strategy, procedure, approach, system, rule.

polish *vb.* **1** shine, brighten: *When you've finished making the* *beds, you can polish the silver.* **2** refine, finish: *The president polished his speech while on his way to the meeting.* *n.* **1** gloss, shine, sheen, lustre, brightness: *The furniture has such a high polish that you can see yourself in it.* **2** refinement, finish, elegance: *The lady has excellent taste and polish.* ANT. *vb.* (1) dull, tarnish.

polite *adj.* courteous, thoughtful, considerate, cordial, respectful. ANT. impolite, rude.

poll *n.* vote, voting, election.

pollute *vb.* contaminate, dirty, befoul, taint. ANT. clean, purify.

pomp *n.* magnificence, splendour, brilliance.

pond *n.* pool, fishpond.

ponder *vb.* weigh, consider, study, reflect, deliberate, think, contemplate.

poor *adj.* **1** impoverished, poverty-stricken, needy, destitute, penniless, hard up: *There are many more poor people in India than in all the western countries combined.* **2** bad, substandard, faulty, inferior, worthless: *The machinery made in this factory is of such poor quality that no one wants it.* **3** unfortunate, unlucky, doomed, luckless, unhappy, miserable, pitiful, pitiable: *After the man's wife went away, the poor fellow just didn't know what to do.* ANT. (1) rich, wealthy, prosperous. (2) good, excellent. (3) lucky, fortunate.

popular *adj.* **1** well-liked, well-thought-of, approved, accepted, favourite, celebrated, admired, famous: *Jane was one of the most popular girls in our class at school.* **2** common, general, familiar, ordinary, current, prevailing: *The popular view of the scholar is of someone out of touch with the world, buried in books.* ANT. (1) unpopular, disliked.

populous *adj.* thronged, crowded, teeming, dense.

port *n.* harbour, haven, refuge, dock.

portable *adj.* movable, transportable; handy.

porter *n.* **1** carrier: *The porter took my suitcases off the train.* **2** gatekeeper, doorman; caretaker: *The porter at the door told me where to go.*

portion *n.* **1** share, part, quota, section, segment: *Only a small portion of money from the sale of a book goes to the author.* **2** serving, helping: *Tom ate three portions of apple pie with ice cream after that big dinner.* *vb.* apportion, allot, distribute, deal out: *The profits from the sale were portioned out to us.*

portly *adj.* corpulent, stout, fat, heavy, obese. ANT. slim, thin, slender.

portrait *n.* picture, likeness, representation; painting.

portray *vb.* represent, depict, picture.

pose *vb.* 1 model, sit: *When Janet was a student, she made money posing for fashion commercials.* 2 pretend, feign, act: *Donald posed as an expert on computers, but he'd never even seen one.* 3 assert, state, set forth: *Getting an elephant for a pet poses the problem of how to feed it.* *n.* posture, position, attitude: *If you take a pose so that your face is in the light, I can get a much better photograph.*

position *n.* 1 location, place, locality, site: *The position of that building causes it to block out sunlight during the summer.* 2 condition, situation, state, status: *The position of all the students was the same: all had taken the one-year course and all now had to face the exam.* 3 job, post, employment, situation, office, occupation: *Raquel has just got a very good position in the printing company.* 4 posture, pose, deportment, bearing: *Your telling my wife about that party we attended has put me in an awkward position. For how long can you maintain that position of standing on one leg?* 5 belief, view, attitude, opinion: *My position is that the teachers ought to be paid as much as the government can afford.* *vb.* put, place, situate, locate: *The painting must be carefully positioned in the frame for the best effect.*

positive *adj.* 1 clear, definite, sure, certain, direct, unmistakable: *We gave the tourists positive directions on how to get there, but they still got lost.* 2 sure, certain, definite, obstinate: *Betty was positive that Jim had said to meet him at eight o'clock.* 3 practical, real; beneficial: *I want to see some positive effects before I approve another test of this plane.* ANT. (1, 2) unsure, dubious, mixed-up, confused. (3) negative, adverse.

possess *vb.* 1 have, own, hold: *Everything Tim possesses can fit into his one small knapsack.* 2 occupy, control, dominate, hold: *Whatever possessed you to act in such a way? Dave was possessed by a fit of laughter.*

possession *n.* 1 ownership, occupancy, custody: *When are we taking possession of the house?* 2 property: *That fountain pen is one of my prized possessions.*

possible *adj.* conceivable, imaginable; practical, practicable, feasible. ANT. impossible, unthinkable, inconceivable; impractical.

post *n.* 1 shaft, column, pole, pillar: *We built a bird house and put it on top of a tall post in the garden.* 2 job, position, office: *Donna's father was appointed to an important post in the embassy.* 3 position, station, location: *The sentry left his post to investigate the eerie noises.* 4 fort, camp, base: *The soldiers from the nearby post came into town on Sundays to go to church.* *vb.* 1 send: *The letter I posted in London yesterday was delivered in Leeds today.* 2 assign, station, position: *There were two guards posted at the gate.*

poster *n.* advertisement, bill, placard.

postpone *vb.* delay, defer, put off.

postscript *n.* P.S.; appendix, supplement.

postulate *vb.* assume, suppose, presuppose, posit.

posture *n.* carriage, stance, deportment.

pot *n.* saucepan, pan, vessel.

potent *adj.* powerful, strong, mighty; influential, convincing, effective. ANT. impotent, weak, powerless, feeble.

potential *adj.* 1 possible; likely: *Ken is a potential member of the swimming team.* 2 latent, hidden, dormant: *The potential energy of the hydrogen atom is unbelievably great.* *n.* potentiality, capacity, ability: *Renee has great potential as a soprano.*

pottery *n.* ceramics, china, earthenware.

pouch *n.* sack, bag; container.

pound *vb.* beat, strike, hit.

pour *vb.* flow; discharge, emit.

poverty *n.* 1 need, want, destitution, distress, pennilessness: *Many of Dickens' characters lived in the worst of poverty in 19th-century England.* 2 scarcity, lack, scantiness, scarceness: *Comic books may be fun to read sometimes, but they suffer from a poverty of expression.* ANT. (1) wealth, richness, comfort. (2) abundance, fruitfulness.

powder *n.* particles, pulverulence.

power *n.* 1 ability, capability: *It isn't within my power to grant you permission to stay away from school.* 2 force, energy, strength, might, vigour: *It takes a lot of power to hit a six in cricket.* 3 authority, command, control, rule, sovereignty: *When our party came into power, they passed many laws dealing with union reforms.*

powerful *adj.* 1 strong, mighty, potent: *The blacksmith was a huge powerful man who could lift an anvil with one hand.* 2 influential, effective, convincing: *The police force is a powerful arm of law enforcement in this country.* ANT. (1) weak, powerless. (2) ineffective, inefficient, useless, ineffectual.

practical *adj.* possible, workable, achievable, attainable. ANT. impractical, visionary.

practice *n.* 1 habit, custom, usage, tradition: *Breaking a bottle over the bow of a ship at its launching is a well-established practice.* 2 operation, action, performance: *Your theory sounds fine, but how can it be reduced to actual practice?* 3 exercise, drill, repetition: *Practice makes perfect.*

practise *vb.* 1 exercise, drill, repeat: *If you practise, they may let you play the piano in the school orchestra.* 2 observe, follow, pursue: *You should practise what you preach.* 3 do, exercise, work at; function: *My uncle practises medicine in Bombay.*

practised *adj.* skilled, adept, expert, able. ANT. inept, unskilled.

pragmatic *adj.* practical, realistic, workable, functional.

praise *vb.* commend, laud, applaud, admire, celebrate: *Fran's dog was very pleased when she praised him for doing a trick correctly.* *n.* commendation, compliment, approval: *Praise from one's friends is often more valued than praise from one's parents.* ANT. *vb.* disapprove, condemn, criticize. *n.* criticism, condemnation, disapproval.

prank *n.* trick, joke, caper.

pray *vb.* ask, beseech, beg, entreat, supplicate; worship, adore, thank; confess.

prayer *n.* request, appeal, entreaty, adoration, worship, thanksgiving.

preach *vb.* teach, address, urge, encourage; lecture.

precarious *adj.* perilous, dangerous; uncertain, doubtful. ANT. safe.

precaution *n.* safeguard, measure, step.

precede *vb.* go before, go first. ANT. go after, succeed.

precedence *n.* priority, preference.

precedent *n.* example, criterion, model.

precept *n.* rule, principle, maxim.

precious *adj.* 1 valuable, costly, priceless, expensive, dear: *She kept her most precious jewels in the bank.* 2 beloved, dear, cherished, favourite: *The memory of the ball is so precious to Miranda that she'll never forget it.*

precipice *n.* cliff, crag.

precipitate *adj.* sudden, swift, hasty, speedy. ANT. considered, gradual.

precipitous *adj.* steep, abrupt, sharp.

precis *n.* summary, abstract, abridgment.

precise *adj.* **1** definite, exact, well-defined: *The pirates gave me a precise description of where I could find the buried treasure.* **2** rigid, stiff, inflexible, careful, severe: *Only precise adherence to the rules is tolerated in this school.*

precisely *adv.* exactly, specifically.

precision *n.* exactness, accuracy, correctness.

precocious *adj.* developed, forward, mature.

preconception *n.* assumption, bias, prejudice.

predicament *n.* quandary, dilemma, difficulty.

predict *vb.* foretell, forecast, prognosticate, prophesy.

prediction *n.* forecast, prognostication; prophecy.

predominant *adj.* prevalent, dominant, prevailing. ANT. secondary, accessory.

predominate *vb.* prevail, rule.

pre-eminent *adj.* distinguished, outstanding; incomparable. ANT. inferior, secondary.

preface *n.* introduction, foreword, prelude, preamble, prologue: *To find out what an author has in mind, it's a good idea to read the prefaces of books.* *vb.* precede, introduce, begin: *The speaker prefaced his remarks with some jokes that put everyone at their ease.*

prefer *vb.* favour, select, elect, fancy.

preference *n.* choice, selection, option, decision, pick.

pregnant *adj.* **1** with child: *Mrs. Jones was six months pregnant.* **2** meaningful, significant: *After the preacher had finished his sermon there was a pregnant pause.*

prejudice *n.* favouritism, bias, partiality, unfairness: *He has a strong prejudice against people who make up their minds without weighing both sides of the question.* *vb.* influence, convince, bias, warp: *If everyone claims to be prejudiced in favour of peace, why do we have wars?*

preliminary *adj.* preparatory, introductory: *Before you start recording the talk I'd like to make some preliminary remarks.* *n.* **preliminaries** introduction, preface, prelude: *Now that the preliminaries are over, let's get down to business.*

premature *adj.* untimely, early, unexpected. ANT. prompt.

preoccupied *adj.* distracted, absorbed, engrossed; busy.

preparation *n.* arrangements, plans; measures, provisions.

prepare *vb.* get ready, arrange, plan.

preposterous *adj.* absurd, ridiculous; fantastic, impossible.

prerogative *n.* privilege, right.

prescribe *vb.* direct, designate, order, recommend.

presence *n.* **1** attendance: *Samuel's presence at the meeting will be important to its success.* **2** nearness, vicinity, closeness:

Please don't use such language in my presence. **3** bearing, personality, appearance: *The king of Madagascar was a man of tremendous presence.* ANT. (1) absence.

present[1] *adj.* **1** existing, current; being: *The present membership of the club is 25.* **2** here, attending; near, nearby: *If you hear your name called, please answer "Present."*

present[2] *vb.* **1** give, donate, grant: *The retiring employee was presented with a gold watch.* **2** introduce, acquaint: *May I present my cousin, Andrew?* **3** show, display, exhibit, offer, furnish: *Please present your tickets of the person at the door of the theatre.* *n.* gift, donation, gratuity, tip, largess: *Toby received more presents for his birthday than anyone I know.*

presently *adv.* soon, shortly; right away, directly, immediately.

preserve *vb.* **1** keep, save, maintain: *Preserve your energy for the next race.* **2** can, conserve, cure, salt, pickle: *All of the vegetables we don't eat fresh we preserve and eat during the winter.* ANT. (1) squander, waste, use.

press *vb.* **1** push: *Press the button and the lift will come.* **2** squeeze, compress: *After the grapes have been pressed, the skins and pulp are used to make brandy.* **3** embrace, hug, clasp: *Suzie pressed the shivering kitten to her bosom.* **4** iron, smooth: *Do you think you can press this skirt for me?* **5** urge, insist on: *If I press you, would you be able to buy something for me when you go to town?* **6** push, crush, crowd: *So many people pressed into the underground train that I could hardly breathe.* *n.* journalists, reporters, newspapermen: *The trades union leader gave a full briefing to the press after leaving the meeting.*

pressure *n.* stress, constraint; force.

prestige *n.* reputation, importance, influence, distinction: renown, fame.

presume *vb.* suppose, assume, believe; take for granted.

presumption *n.* **1** supposition, assumption, guess: *Your presumption that I am going out just because you see me wearing a hat happens to be false.* **2** impudence, insolence: *What presumption in speaking to your elders like that!* ANT. (2) humility; shyness; modesty.

presumptuous *adj.* impertinent, bold, impudent, fresh, rude, arrogant, forward.

pretence *n.* **1** deceit, falsification, fabrication: *Tom made a pretence of trying to appear innocent.* **2** lie, falsehood, deception: *Your story about going to the library was nothing but pretence.*

pretend *vb.* **1** imagine, make believe: *Let's pretend that you are a knight and I a damsel in distress.* **2** deceive; falsify, fake, simulate, feign: *Don't try to pretend to us that you didn't know you were absent from school yesterday.*

pretentious *adj.* ostentatious, showy, affected; showing off. ANT. humble, simple.

pretext *n.* appearance, guise; pretence, guise.

pretty *adj.* attractive, fair; lovely, beautiful. ANT. plain; ugly.

prevail *vb.* **1** predominate: *A belief in the supernatural still prevails in many parts of the world.* **2** succeed, win, triumph: *Even though the forces of evil may seem to have the upper hand, in the end good will prevail.* ANT. (2) lose, yield.

prevailing *adj.* current, common, habitual, general, universal.

prevalent *adj.* common, prevailing, widespread, extensive. ANT. rare, infrequent.

prevent *vb.* block, stop, thwart, interrupt, obstruct, retard, hinder, slow, deter, inhibit. ANT. help; allow.

previous *adj.* prior, earlier, former. ANT. later, following, subsequent.

prey *n.* victim: *The rabbit was easy prey for the lion.* *vb.* victimize; seize, raid: *There was a band of thugs in the hills that preyed on the villages for food.*

price *n.* cost, charge, expense, value: *The price of food in Britain has risen a lot in the past months.* *vb.* mark; value, rate; *We shall have to price all these goods before putting them out for sale.*

priceless *adj.* **1** invaluable, inestimable: *The gold jewels were priceless.* **2** *Informal:* very funny, ridiculous: *That joke you told us was priceless—now tell it to the others!*

prick *vb.* stab, pierce: *The needle pricked him slightly as it went through his skin.* *n.* stab, cut, mark: *The prick of the nettles stung her.*

pride *n.* **1** conceit, vanity, arrogance, self-importance, egotism, pretension: *John is so swelled up with pride over his new job that he won't listen to anything I say to him.* **2** self-respect: *Stephanie's pride in her family's position is great but she doesn't boast about it all the time.* **3** enjoyment, fulfilment, satisfaction: *Dick takes so much pride in his vegetable garden each summer.* ANT. (1) humility, humbleness.

primarily *adv.* chiefly, mainly, essentially, firstly, originally. ANT. secondarily.

primary *adj.* **1** chief, main, principal: *My primary purpose in being here is to help you learn.* **2** first, earliest, prime, original: *Our primary consideration should be the safety of the* *participants in the race.* ANT. **(1, 2)** secondary.

prime *adj.* **1** primary; first; chief: *The prime aim in education is to teach understanding rather than just knowledge.* **2** best, top-grade, superior, excellent: *I wish I could eat a prime sirloin steak, medium-rare, right this minute.* *vb.* prepare, make ready: *The speaker was well primed on how he should address his audience.*

primitive *adj.* **1** prehistoric, primeval: *In primitive societies, the men went out to hunt and the women stayed at home.* **2** uncivilized, uncultured, unsophisticated, simple, rough, rude, brutish: *Why is it that so many children today have such primitive table manners?* ANT. **(2)** cultured, sophisticated, cultivated.

principal *adj.* chief, main, leading, prime, first, essential, primary: *The principal problem lies in selecting the right people to do the job.* *n.* chief, head, leader: *The authorities appointed a new principal to the college.* ANT. *adj.* secondary, accessory.

principle *n.* **1** rule, standard: *The cafeteria operates on the principle of first come, first served.* **2** truth, law, postulate, proposition: *Democratic government was founded on the principle that all men have equal rights.* **3** honesty, uprightness, virtue, goodness: *My father was a man of very high principles.*

print *vb.* **1** issue, publish; reissue, reprint: *We printed 2000 copies of the book.* **2** develop; enlarge: *I had the pictures printed on glossy paper.* *n.* **1** mark, fingerprint, sign: *The detectives found three identifiable prints on the door leading to the bedroom.* **2** type, printing: *Make sure you read the small print at the end of the contract before signing it.* **3** copy, lithograph, picture, photograph, etching, engraving: *The public library has a fine collection of prints by famous artists.*

prior *adj.* earlier, sooner, preceding. ANT. subsequent, later.

prise *vb.* lift, raise, lever; open.

prison *n.* jail.

private *adj.* **1** personal, individual; special, particular: *What I have in my bank account is my own private business.* **2** secret, confidential, hidden: *The representative made his views known in a private communication to the reporter.* ANT. **(1)** public, general.

privilege *n.* freedom, liberty; permission, right, advantage.

prize *n.* reward, award, premium, bounty, bonus: *The company gives a yearly prize for the best suggestion made by an employee.* *vb.* value, esteem; estimate, rate: *Don's judg-*

ment is highly prized by the directors of the company. ANT. *vb.* undervalue, disregard.

probable *adj.* likely; feasible; presumable.

probe *vb.* examine, investigate, inquire, scrutinize, explore: *The committee was set up to probe gifts to political parties.* *n.* examination, investigation, inquiry, scrutiny, exploration: *The probe of the MPs' bank accounts revealed nothing of an illegal nature.*

problem *n.* **1** difficulty, predicament, dilemma: *A problem has arisen in connection with my tax refund, causing a month's delay.* **2** question; puzzle, riddle: *I couldn't do the last problem in the maths exam.*

procedure *n.* operation, process, method, system.

proceed *vb.* **1** move ahead *or* on, go on, progress, continue: *Let us now proceed to the next house and interview the people there.* **2** result, issue, spring, emanate: *The next step in the operation will proceed from the last one.* ANT. (1) withdraw, retreat.

proceedings *n.pl.* record, account, annal, document.

proceeds *n.pl.* income, reward, intake, profit, return, yield.

process *n.* course; procedure, method, system, operation: *In the process of saving the puppy, I lost my glasses. The scientist developed a new process for refining iron ore.* *vb.* treat, prepare: *George's grandfather is the man who invented the technique for processing wood into paper.*

procession *n.* parade, train, cavalcade.

proclaim *vb.* announce, advertise, declare.

proclamation *n.* announcement, declaration; promulgation.

prod *vb.* nudge, goad, push, jab.

prodigious *adj.* vast, huge, immense, extensive.

prodigy *n.* marvel, wonder; freak, curiosity.

produce *vb.* **1** bear, bring forth, yield, supply, give: *A ewe rarely produces twin lambs.* **2** create, make, originate, generate, occasion, bring about, give rise to, cause: *Hydroelectricity produces electricity from the power of the flow of water.* **3** show, exhibit, present, display, demonstrate: *The judge said that we had to produce proof of damages in order to have a valid case.* *n.* product, production, fruits, crops, harvest: *We buy all the produce for the restaurant directly from the farmers to ensure freshness.*

product *n.* **1** result, outcome, output, produce: *The product of all that hard work is an essay I'm very pleased with.* **2** goods, stock, commodity, merchandise: *Some shops once refused to sell any products manufactured in your country.*

productive *adj.* fertile, fruitful, rich; creative. ANT. wasteful, useless.

profane *adj.* irreverent, irreligious, disrespectful.

profess *vb.* declare, state, avow.

profession *n.* occupation, calling, vocation, employment, ANT. hobby, pastime.

professional *n.* expert, specialist: *Mark is a real professional at painting model aircraft.* *adj.* 1 trained, expert, qualified: *Patrick is a professional lexicographer.* 2 paid: *Some sports are open to both amateur and professional competitors.* ANT. amateur.

proficient *adj.* skilled, skilful; able, capable. ANT. unskilled, inexperienced.

profit *n.* 1 gain, return, earnings: *If I buy something for £10, sell it for £20 and have expenses of £5, my profit is £5.* 2 advantage, benefit, gain, improvement: *I can't see any profit in continuing this dispute.* *vb.* benefit, improve, better: *It doesn't profit you to say bad things about others.* ANT. *n.* (1) loss, debit. *vb.* lose.

profitable *adj.* beneficial, favourable, productive, useful, lucrative.

profound *adj.* deep, solemn, serious; wise, knowing, knowledgeable, intelligent, learned. ANT. shallow, superficial.

profuse *adj.* abundant, plentiful, bountiful. ANT. meagre, scanty, inconsiderable.

programme *n.* record, plan, calendar, list, agenda; events.

progress *n.* advance, advancement, movement, improvement, development: *The doctor was pleased to see that I was making considerable progress towards recovery.* *vb.* advance, improve, proceed, develop: *If Frank continues to progress in his studies, he may come first in the class.* ANT. *n.* regression.

prohibit *vb.* 1 forbid, disallow, ban: *The fire laws prohibit smoking in some lifts.* 2 prevent, obstruct, stop, hinder: *A sprained ankle prohibited Jane from walking any faster.* ANT. (1) allow, permit. (2) help, encourage.

prohibition *n.* ban, prevention, restriction, embargo. ANT. permission, authorization.

project *n.* 1 plan, proposal, outline, scheme, design: *Your project for the new shopping centre must be approved by the district council.* 2 activity, task: *The children are going to construct a model Indian village as a class project.* *vb.* 1 propose, plan: *How much time do you project will be required to clear the land for the building?* 2 cast, throw: *The image from the film was projected onto the screen.* 3 extend,

protrude, bulge: *The corner of the table projects too far to allow the door to be closed.*

projectile *n.* object, body; missile, weapon.

proliferate *vb.* grow, increase; generate, reproduce.

prolong *vb.* lengthen, extend, increase.

prominent *adj.* **1** well-known, famous, noted, notable, noteworthy, important, eminent, distinguished, leading, celebrated: *A prominent scientist had been invited to give the address on speech day.* **2** noticeable, obvious, conspicuous: *The error in the statistics was too prominent to be ignored.* ANT. insignificant, unimportant.

promiscuous *adj.* immoral, loose, licentious, dissolute.

promise *n.* assurance, pledge, oath, vow, word: *The manager gave his promise that our new dishwasher would be repaired.* *vb.* pledge, vow, assure, swear: *You promised that we could go to the cinema if we finished all our homework.*

promote *vb.* **1** advance, further, support, help, aid, assist: *To promote the sale of the vacuum cleaners, the store offered a week's free trial.* **2** move up, advance: *Vickie was so proud when her father was promoted to foreman of the whole factory.* ANT. (1) hinder, retard. (2) demote.

prompt *adj.* timely, punctual: *The fireman's prompt action saved the lives of three old people. Please try to be more prompt at the dinner table.* *vb.* **1** urge, arouse, incite: *Your reminder prompted me to phone to ask if you could come to dinner.* **2** hint, suggest, propose, mention: *I don't need you to prompt me about buying flowers for my mother's birthday.* ANT. *adj.* late; slow.

pronounce *vb.* **1** utter, proclaim, announce: *The minister said, "I now pronounce you man and wife."* **2** articulate, utter, enunciate: *When he was about nine, Eugene had difficulty pronouncing the letter "L."*

pronounced *adj.* definite, clear, noticeable. ANT. indistinguishable, minor, unnoticeable.

proof *n.* **1** evidence, demonstration, testimony, confirmation: *The man accused of the crime offered proof that he was far away when it was committed.* **2** test, trial: *The proof of the pudding is in the eating.* *adj.* protected, impenetrable, impervious: *This thick plastic is proof against bullets.*

propaganda *n.* information, dogma, doctrines.

propagate *vb.* reproduce, breed; spread.

proper *adj.* **1** suitable, correct, fitting, just: *I think that making children who write on walls clean them is a proper punishment.* **2** polite, well-mannered, decent: *When she's with* *grown-ups, Natalie is always very proper.* ANT. **(2)** rude, impolite, discourteous.

property *n.* **1** belongings, possessions, effects: *Please remove all personal property from your lockers at the end of the school term.* **2** house; land, real estate, tract: *My uncle has just bought a large property in Altrincham.*

prophecy *n.* prediction, augury; forecast.

prophesy *vb.* predict, foretell; divine, augur.

prophet *n.* oracle, fortune teller, forecaster, seer, clairvoyant, soothsayer.

proportion *n.* **1** relation; comparison, balance: *You must be careful to mix the ingredients in the correct proportion or you won't get an edible cake.* **2** part, section, share, piece: *What proportion of the interest in the company do you think the investors have?* *vb.* adjust, balance, arrange: *The club members proportioned the work among themselves.*

proposal *n.* **1** offer, suggestion; scheme, plan: *The company accepted our proposal, and we'll soon have the contract to build the ship.* **2** proposition, engagement: *My proposal of marriage was accepted immediately.*

propose *vb.* **1** present, offer, tender, recommend, suggest: *The union proposed a settlement that would give each employee a 20% rise.* **2** plan, intend, expect, mean: *How do you propose to climb up the face of a sheer cliff?* **3** offer marriage, (*informal*) pop the question; ask for the hand of: *The young man proposed to his girlfriend rather nervously, thinking she might say no.*

prosecute *vb.* accuse, charge with, sue, bring an action against.

prospect *n.* **1** expectation, hope: *Your job prospects won't be very good if you don't complete your education.* **2** view, outlook, panorama: *The prospect from the hotel window was marvellous.* **3** buyer, candidate: *Dan's father will be entertaining two business prospects at dinner tonight.* *vb.* search, explore, dig: *My forefathers went prospecting for gold, but they didn't find any.*

prospective *adj.* proposed, planned, hoped-for.

prosper *vb.* succeed, thrive, rise, flourish. ANT. decline, sink, fail.

prosperous *adj.* wealthy, well-off, rich, thriving, flourishing, well-to-do. ANT. poor, impoverished; failing; unfortunate.

protect *vb.* defend, shield, guard.

protection *n.* **1** guard, security, shield, safety: *The shed provided protection against the rain.* **2** security, assurance :

*Many people have life insurance to provide protection in case
one partner dies.*

protest *n.* objection, complaint; opposition, disagreement:
*Our protest against the way children were treated had no effect
on our parents.* *vb.* object, complain: *If you didn't protest
about the conditions here, no one would do anything to
improve them.* ANT. *n.* approval, agreement. *vb.* approve,
agree.

protocol *n.* etiquette, convention, procedures.

prototype *n.* ideal, original, model.

protrude *vb.* stick out, project, jut out.

proud *adj.* **1** arrogant, haughty, self-important, snooty; conceited, vain: *The people next door are too proud to have
anything to do with us.* **2** self-respecting: *We are justly proud
of our country's fine heritage.* **3** dignified, high-minded,
honourable: *It was a proud moment for my parents when I
was given the prize.* ANT. humble, modest.

prove *vb.* show, demonstrate, confirm, verify, test, examine,
affirm.

proverb *n.* saying, adage, maxim, byword.

proverbial *adj.* well-known, common, general.

provide *vb.* supply, furnish, equip, give, bestow.

province *n.* area, territory, region, district.

provisional *adj.* temporary, transient, passing; conditional.

provisions *n. pl.* store, supplies, stock.

provoke *vb.* **1** bother, vex, irritate, annoy, irk, anger, enrage:
*Don't provoke me any more or I won't let you go to the game
on Saturday.* **2** cause, occasion, bring about: *The articles in
the newspaper provoked many readers to write in.*

prowl *vb.* slink, sneak, lurk.

prudence *n.* **1** carefulness, care, caution, tact; discretion,
circumspection: *Junior employees have to exercise prudence
when they notice the faults of their superiors.* **2** wisdom,
judgment, foresight, common sense: *Don showed prudence
in not asking the teacher a lot of silly questions.* ANT.
rashness, recklessness, foolishness.

prudent *adj.* wise, discreet, careful, sensible. ANT. rash,
reckless, foolish, foolhardy.

pry *vb.* peep, peer, meddle.

pseudonym *n.* assumed name, alias; pen-name, nom de plume.

public *n.* society, community, people: *The public has a right to
know about the workings of government.* *adj.* common;
community, municipal, civil: *This is a public park and I have*

every right to be in it. ANT. *adj.* private.

publish *vb.* 1 issue, distribute, bring out: *During his career, Alfred published many worthwhile works of literature.* 2 announce, declare, proclaim, disclose, reveal, publicize: *The prime minister's honours list was published recently.*

pull *vb.* drag, draw: *Jack pulled the sledge back up the slope.* *vb. phr.* **pull apart** separate, divide: *The referee couldn't pull the wrestlers apart.* **pull away** leave, depart: *Just as I arrived, I saw the train pulling away.* **pull down** wreck, destroy, raze: *The company is going to pull down the old factory.* **pull off** 1 remove: *I pulled off my burning clothes and dived into the water.* 2 achieve, succeed: *The task seemed impossible but she pulled it off very skilfully in the end.* **pull out** leave, depart: *The coach pulls out at midnight.* **pull through** survive, recover: *James has had a serious illness, but the doctor said he'll pull through all right.* **pull up** stop: *I pulled up at the traffic light, waiting for it to change to green.* *n.* 1 wrench, jerk; haul, tow: *I gave a hard pull and the handle came off.* 2 *Informal:* influence, weight: *David's father has a lot of pull in this town.*

pulse *n.* beat, throb, vibration.

pump *vb.* 1 lift, raise, drive: *The natives pumped the water up.* 2 blow: *Your bicycle tyres need pumping up.*

punch *vb., n.* blow, knock, hit: *He punched me on the nose. The punch the boy got dazed him for a few seconds.*

punctual *adj.* prompt, timely, on time. ANT. early; late.

punish *vb.* discipline, chasten, reprove, scold. ANT. reward; praise.

pupil *n.* student, learner.

purchase *vb.* buy, obtain, get, acquire, procure: *We drove into the village once a week to purchase groceries and other supplies.* *n.* acquisition: *Ernest made two purchases in the hardware store.*

pure *adj.* 1 unmixed, genuine, simple, undiluted: *This sweater is made of pure wool.* 2 spotless, untainted, clean, uncontaminated, unpolluted: *The spring gave out abundant pure water.* 3 innocent, good, chaste, virtuous: *The priest led a completely pure existence.* ANT. (1) adulterated, mixed. (2) dirty, foul, tainted. (3) immoral, licentious.

purely *adv.* completely, entirely, totally.

purge *vb.* cleanse, eliminate, eradicate: *The people could not purge themselves from their sins.* *n.* elimination, removal; purification. *Many were forced to resign in the purge on the radicals in the political party.*

purify *vb.* cleanse, refine, purge.

purpose *n.* **1** intention, intent, object, end, aim, objective, goal: *My purpose in life is to help people learn as much as possible about the English language.* **2** use, application: *What is the purpose of this device?* *n. phr.* **on purpose** intentionally, deliberately: *You stepped on my toe on purpose!*

pursue *vb.* follow, chase, hound, track.

pursuit *n.* chase, hunt.

push *vb.* **1** force, shove, thrust: *Kim pushed a pencil through the hole in the wall.* **2** press, shove: *The crowd pushed me right back onto the train I had just left.*

put *vb.* **1** place, set: *Please put the tray on the table.* **2** attach, establish, assign: *Don't put too much emphasis on how much money your friends have.* **3** express, state, say: *It wasn't so much what George said as how he put it that was so clever.* *vb. phr.* **put across** communicate: *The preacher put his message across very well.* **put aside** save, keep: *My mother always put a little money aside for a rainy day.* **put away** **1** save, set aside, store: *I had a little bit put away for your birthday.* **2** lock up: *That crazy old man ought to be put away.* **put down** defeat, repress: *The new commander had the rebellions in the provinces put down.* **put off** **1** delay, postpone: *Don't put off till tomorrow what you can do today.* **2** disconcert: *Stanley was put off by the rude way the hotel manager spoke to him.* **put on** **1** don; wear, dress, attire: *Please don't put on your purple shirt with the green trousers.* **2** pretend, fake, feign: *Don't put on airs with me, young man.* **3** stage, produce, present: *The Royal Shakespeare Company is putting on* Macbeth. **put out** **1** extinguish, douse: *Put out that match!* **2** inconvenience: *I hope it won't put you out if I stay for tea.* **3** extend, offer: *Sam put out his hand and I shook it warmly.* **put through** effect, achieve, do: *The plan was put through with little delay.* **put up** erect, build, construct: *They put up a statue to the statesman in front of the Town Hall.* **put up with** endure, stand, tolerate, suffer: *I can't understand how you can put up with Deirdre's constant complaining.*

puzzle *n.* confusion, question, riddle, problem: *It's a puzzle to me how your cousin, who is so lazy, can keep his job.* *vb.* confuse, perplex, bewilder, mystify: *I was puzzled by your comment, but now I understand what you meant.*

q

quaint *adj.* **1** strange, unusual, odd, curious, uncommon: *Tourists often commented on the quaint customs of village life.* **2** old-fashioned, antiquated: *My aunt still makes quilts using those quaint old stitches.* ANT. (1) common, ordinary.

quake *vb.* tremble, shake, quiver, shudder.

qualifications *n., pl.* accomplishments, attainments; experience, knowledge; abilities, skill.

qualify *vb.* **1** suit, fit: *The interviewer told Rosette that she wasn't qualified for the job.* **2** limit, restrict; restrain, moderate; change: *Instead of making a general statement, you ought to qualify your remarks.*

quality *n.* **1** attribute, property, characteristic, character, trait, feature: *A good doctor has the quality of sympathy in his basic nature.* **2** excellence, worth, value; grade, rank, status, condition: *The quality of some television programmes leaves much to be desired.*

quantity *n.* amount, extent, mass, bulk, measure, number.

quarrel *n.* argument, dispute, disagreement, difference, tiff, fight: *The quarrel between my brother and me arose because he wanted me to stay at home while he went to the bowling alley.* *vb.* argue, dispute, disagree, differ, squabble, bicker, fight: *Our children seldom quarrel about anything.*

quarrelsome *adj.* edgy, irritable, disagreeable; cross. ANT. even-tempered, genial.

quash *vb.* crush, suppress, subdue, put down.

queer *adj.* odd, peculiar, unusual, extraordinary, uncommon. ANT. ordinary, conventional, usual.

quell *vb.* subdue, suppress; allay.

quench *vb.* satisfy, slake.

query *n.* question, enquiry: *If you have a query about your homework, please ask your teacher.* *vb.* question; doubt: *When Andrew failed the exam, he queried the result with his teacher.*

quest *n.* search, journey, hunt.

question *n.* **1** query, enquiry: *Timmy, if you have a question, please raise your hand.* **2** doubt, uncertainty: *There has been some question about whether John could visit us.* *vb.* **1** query, ask; interrogate, interview: *The police questioned the* *man closely.* **2** doubt; suspect: *How dare you question my honesty?* ANT. *n.* (1) answer, solution. *vb.* (1) answer, reply, respond.

questionable *adj.* doubtful, dubious; debatable.

queue *n.* line, file; train, retinue: *British people seem to like standing in queues. vb.* line (up), file: *Please queue at the bus stop.*

quibble *vb.* argue, (*informal*) split hairs, take issue.

quick *adj.* **1** fast, rapid, swift, speedy: *Walter plays a lot of tennis and is very quick on his feet.* **2** impatient, hasty: *He must learn to control his quick temper.* **3** prompt, ready, immediate: *The quick answer to your question is "No," but I should explain that more fully.* ANT. (1) slow, sluggish.

quicken *vb.* hurry, hasten, accelerate.

quiet *adj.* **1** silent, still, soundless, noiseless: *Please be quiet in the library.* **2** tranquil, peaceful, calm, restful: *The patient was finally quiet after a restless night. n.* silence, stillness, peace, peacefulness, calm, calmness: *You could have heard a pin drop in the quiet of the meeting.* ANT. *adj.* (1) noisy, loud, boisterous. (2) perturbed, anxious.

quieten (down) *vb.* **1** still, hush, silence: *You'd better quieten down or the neighbours will complain.* **2** calm, pacify, subdue: *Though Dad was very angry to begin with, we managed to quieten him down when he explained how the accident happened.*

quirk *n.* peculiarity, characteristic; mannerism, idiosyncrasy, foible.

quit *vb.* **1** stop, cease, discontinue: *Quit teasing Anne about having red hair.* **2** resign, leave: *After 25 years without promotion Bill quitted his job.*

quite *adv.* **1** rather, somewhat: *I was quite annoyed when the train was 10 minutes late.* **2** completely, entirely, wholly: *If you have quite finished talking, I should like to say something.*

quiver *vb.* shake, quake, tremble, shudder, shiver, vibrate.

quiz *vb.* question, interrogate, cross-examine.

quotation *n.* extract, citation; passage, sentence; saying.

quote *vb.* cite, recite; mention, refer to.

r

race¹ *n.* **1** contest, competition, match: *When Mel entered the race, he had no idea he would win.* **2** stream, course: *The race under the mill was strong enough to turn the paddle-wheel.* *vb.* **1** run, compete, contend: *Phil wasn't allowed to race on Saturday because of his sore ankle.* **2** hurry, run, speed, dash, hasten: *We raced to finish our homework before the deadline.* ANT. *vb.* (2) dawdle, linger, dwell.

race² *n.* family, kind, strain, breed, people, nation, tribe, stock: *The Mongolian race developed in Asia.*

rack *n.* framework, frame, bracket.

racket *n.* noise, hubbub, disturbance, fuss, uproar, din, tumult.

racy *adj.* lively, spirited, vigorous, fresh; sharp. ANT. dull, deadly.

radiant *adj.* bright, shining, beaming, brilliant. ANT. dim, dark.

radiate *vb.* emit, spread, shed, diffuse.

radical *adj.* **1** basic, fundamental, essential: *We shall have to make radical changes in our plans if we can't use the hall.* **2** extreme, progressive, revolutionary, militant: *The radical element in the organization has been warned about the disturbances.* *n.* progressive, militant, extremist, revolutionary: *The radicals confronted the political leaders with their views.*

rag *n.* cloth; scrap, piece.

rage *n.* **1** anger, fury, wrath: *The director's rage at the news that he had been left out of the screen credits was huge.* **2** fad, fashion, craze, vogue, mania: *Except for a few fanatics, the skateboarding rage has passed.* *vb.* **1** fume, rant, rave, storm: *When he found that the dog had eaten his dinner, Albert raged about the house for an hour.* **2** storm, overflow; burn: *The storm raged all about us. The fire raged out of control for three hours.*

ragged *adj.* torn, tattered, shredded, worn.

raid *n.* **1** attack, assault, invasion: *The commandos planned a raid on the submarine base.* **2** arrest; seizure: *Aunt Martha was caught in the police raid on the gambling casino.* *vb.* attack, assault, invade, maraud: *The ammunition dump was raided last night.*

rail *n.* fence, railing, bar.

rain *n.* drizzle, sprinkle; shower; storm, deluge: *I hope the rain keeps off.* *vb.* pour (down); drizzle: *It's raining again today.*

raise *vb.* **1** lift, elevate, hoist: *Please raise your hand if you wish to speak in class.* **2** rear, bring up; cultivate: *My mother raised 12 children. Mr. Green raises corn on his farm.* **3** rouse, awaken, excite: *Our hopes were raised when we spied a sail.* **4** increase; enlarge: *Your salary will be raised by 10 per cent next week.* ANT. (1) lower. (4) decrease, lessen, reduce.

rally *vb.* **1** reassemble, attack: *The soldiers rallied for the major assault on the town.* **2** summon, call up: *A leader should try to rally other people's support.* *n.* gathering, meeting: *The motoring enthusiasts assembled for their weekly rally.*

ramble *vb.* amble, stroll, saunter, wander, walk: *We rambled through the meadow looking for wild flowers to pick.* *n.* stroll, walk: *Let's take a ramble along the beach.*

rampant *adj.* unrestrained, unchecked; raging, violent.

rancid *adj.* rotten, bad, mouldy, rank.

random *adj.* chance, haphazard, unplanned, unscheduled, irregular, casual. ANT. particular, specific, special.

range *n.* extent, expanse, area, limit: *Sue was interested in a very narrow range of subjects.* *vb.* **1** vary, change: *The weather in our area ranges from bad to awful.* **2** wander, travel, roam, rove, stray: *The prince ranged far and wide, through many lands, seeking adventure.*

rank *n.* grade, level, order, class, standing, degree: *Morris achieved a high rank among the officers in the company.* *vb.* arrange, order, sort, classify: *Eugene ranks at the top of his group.* *adj.* **1** wild, dense, lush, vigorous, luxuriant, abundant: *The vegetation was so rank we could barely make our way through it.* **2** smelly, putrid, offensive, foul, rotten: *A rank odour emanated from the sewer.*

ransack *vb.* **1** examine, search: *We ransacked the attic looking for the lost medals.* **2** plunder, loot, take away: *The enemy soldiers ransacked the town they had captured.*

ransom *n.* deliverance, release; compensation, redemption.

rap *n.* knock, blow, thump: *Every time he played a wrong note, the piano teacher gave him a rap on the knuckles.* *vb.* knock, thump, whack: *When you get there, rap at the door three times and ask for Joe.*

rape *vb.* assault, seduce, ravish.

rapid *adj.* quick, swift, speedy, fast. ANT. slow, sluggish, halting.

rapture *n.* joy, bliss, ecstasy, delight.

rare *adj.* **1** unusual, uncommon, scarce, infrequent: *Good diamonds are expensive because they are rare.* **2** superlative, excellent, fine, choice, matchless: *The museum has a collection of rare paintings by 16th-century artists.* **3** underdone, undercooked, red: *I enjoy eating a rare steak.* ANT. **(1)** common, ordinary, usual, everyday. **(3)** well done.

rascal *n.* **1** villain, scoundrel, rogue, trickster, swindler, scamp: *The rascal told me one story and you another about how much money he needed.* **2** imp, mischief-maker: *That little rascal ate all the biscuits.*

rash[1] *adj.* thoughtless, hasty, impetuous, foolhardy, reckless: *If you think before you act, you can avoid doing many rash things.* ANT. considered, thoughtful, prudent.

rash[2] *n.* eruption, eczema, dermatitis: *You know you have measles when you see a red rash on your chest.*

rate *n.* **1** pace, speed, velocity: *Alex worked at a fast rate and finished everything in one day.* **2** price, charge: *Phoning after six o'clock means you pay the cheap rate.* **3** proportion, ratio: *The rate of inflation is increasing.* *vb.* **1** price, value: *The dresses in this shop are rated too much over their cost.* **2** consider, regard; evaluate: *Jeanette is rated as one of the top students in the school.*

ration *n.* allowance, portion: *During the war, everyone was entitled to his ration of meat, butter, sugar, and other foods.* *vb.* apportion, parcel out, distribute: *The food was rationed out carefully among the marooned sailors.*

rational *adj.* **1** sensible, reasonable: *The only rational way for us to find a new leader is to elect one.* **2** sane, clearheaded, normal: *People who really believe that the moon is made of green cheese are not rational.* ANT. **(2)** irrational, insane, crazy.

rationalize *vb.* justify, defend, explain away, make allowances.

rattle *vb.* shake, clatter: *The collectors rattled their tins, wanting the passers-by to put some money in.* *n.* clatter, clack, click, shaking: *The rattle of the wooden wheels on the cobbles could be heard down the street.*

raucous *adj.* harsh, rough, gruff, loud.

ravage *vb.* damage, devastate, wreck.

rave *vb.* **1** rant, rage, storm: *The king raved on about how his generals were plotting against him.* **2** *Informal:* praise, laud:

Mrs. Johnston was raving about the new hairdresser in town.

raw *adj.* **1** uncooked, undone: *I love to eat raw carrots.* **2** unprocessed, untreated, rough, unrefined: *The factory takes raw materials and converts them into finished products.* **3** immature, untrained, new: *The raw recruits were ragged mercilessly.* ANT. (1) cooked. (2) processed, refined, finished. (3) experienced.

ray *n.* beam; gleam, flash.

reach *vb.* **1** arrive at, get to, come to: *We didn't reach home till after dark.* **2** stretch, extend: *I could just reach up to the top of the door.* *n.* extent, distance, range, scope: *The criminals fled to Brazil, beyond the reach of the law.*

react *vb.* respond, reply, answer.

reaction *n.* response, result, reply, answer.

readable *adj.* **1** legible, decipherable, clear: *My handwriting was once illegible, but now it's readable.* **2** interesting, exciting; enjoyable, pleasant, well-written: *The book I'm studying at the moment is very readable.*

readily *adv.* promptly, quickly; easily; willingly.

ready *adj.* **1** prepared, done; arranged, completed: *The roast joint will be ready in an hour.* **2** quick, prompt, skilful: *Whenever anyone said anything, the comedian was able to provide a ready wisecrack.*

real *adj.* true, actual, genuine, authentic. ANT. false, counterfeit, sham, bogus.

realistic *adj.* practical, pragmatic; real.

reality *n.* truth, actuality, fact; existence.

realize *vb.* **1** understand, be aware of, appreciate, recognize: *Do you fully realize whom you are speaking to?* **2** effect, complete, achieve, work out: *Plans are easy to think up but harder to realize.* **3** sell for, make: *The sale of work realized £25.*

really *adv.* actually, truly, honestly.

realm *n.* **1** kingdom, domain: *The queen's realm extended from one sea to the other.* **2** area, domain, sphere, province, department: *In the realm of surgery, Dr. Franklin has no equal.*

reap *vb.* harvest, cut, gather, mow, pick. ANT. sow, plant, seed.

rear[1] *n.* back; bottom, rump, posterior: *At the rear of the house stood an old car. Hugo was struck in the rear with the paddle.* *adj.* back: *The rear window of the car was misted up.* ANT. *n.* front.

rear[2] *vb.* **1** raise, bring up: *The little girl had been reared in a* *convent.* **2** lift, raise, elevate; rise: *The horse reared on its hind legs.* **3** put up, build, construct, erect: *The shed could be reared by two men in one afternoon.*

reason *n.* **1** purpose, motive, cause, object, objective, aim: *What was your reason for phoning me at midnight?* **2** explanation; excuse: *I have already given you two good reasons why you should study hard.* **3** judgment, understanding, intelligence, common sense: *The decision is a matter of reason, not of opinion.* **4** sanity: *The poor fellow painting the grass green seems to have lost his reason.* *vb.* **1** argue, justify: *You cannot reason with an angry man.* **2** conclude, suppose, assume, gather, infer: *I reasoned that the team that came first won the race.*

reasonable *adj.* **1** sensible, rational, logical: *As a reasonable person, you must know that no family can survive on that amount a week.* **2** moderate, bearable: *I think that £500 is a very reasonable price for that car, considering its condition.* ANT. **(1)** irrational, mad, crazy, insane. **(2)** outrageous.

reassure *vb.* comfort, console, encourage.

rebel *n.* revolutionary, mutineer, traitor: *The rebels attacked the president's palace last night.* *vb.* revolt, defy, overthrow: *The peasants rebelled when told that there wouldn't be enough to eat.*

rebellious *adj.* defiant, insubordinate, refractory.

rebuff *vb.* snub, reject, spurn, slight: *They rebuffed all my offers of help.* *n.* snub, rejection, repulse: *The rebuff of my plans came as a great surprise as I had thought they would have been accepted.*

rebuke *vb.* upbraid, chide, reproach, scold: *The teacher rebuked Peter for talking during an examination.* *n.* reprimand, reproach, scolding: *After the first rebuke from their parents, the children never again went near the cliff.* ANT. praise.

recall *vb.* **1** remember, recollect: *I recall having met you at last year's party.* **2** call in, withdraw: *The company recalled all cars of the model that had faulty brakes.* *n.* memory, recollection, remembrance: *Vincent has total recall and can remember everything that ever happened.*

recant *vb.* withdraw, retract, take back.

receive *vb.* **1** accept, get, acquire, come by, obtain: *I received my copy of the magazine today.* **2** entertain; greet, welcome: *The ambassador is receiving guests in the front hall.* ANT. **(1)** give, offer.

recent *adj.* late, up-to-date, new, novel. ANT. old, out-of-date, dated.

reception *n.* party, gathering.

recess *n.* 1 hollow, niche, dent, opening, cranny, nook: *The golden idol was concealed in a narrow recess in the cave.* 2 vacation, respite, rest, pause, break: *Parliament is now having a recess.*

recipe *n.* formula, directions, instructions.

reciprocal *adj.* mutual; interchangeable, exchangeable.

recite *vb.* repeat; report, list.

reckless *adj.* thoughtless, careless, rash, wild.

reckon *vb.* 1 calculate, compute; estimate, guess: *Counting the rows of seats, I reckoned that there were fifty-four people in the room.* 2 consider, regard: *I reckon your sister is very clever.* 3 think, suppose, believe: *It'll be fine tomorrow, I reckon.*

recognize *vb.* 1 recollect, recall, know: *I recognized the bank clerk as the man I had seen in the supermarket.* 2 acknowledge, admit: *I recognize your authority to order me about, but I don't like it.*

recoil *vb.* draw back, withdraw, shrink, wince, flinch.

recollect *vb.* remember, recall.

recommend *vb.* 1 commend, praise, approve: *I recommended Brad for the job.* 2 advise, counsel, suggest: *The board has recommended that a new school be built on the hill.* ANT. (1) disapprove, veto.

recompense *vb.* reward, repay, compensate.

reconcile *vb.* 1 unite, bring together, mediate: *The couple were reconciled after the misunderstanding.* 2 adjust, settle: *Leon and Debbie have reconciled their differences and are friends again.*

reconsider *vb.* think again, reevaluate, go back on.

record *vb.* write, enter, register: *The clerk recorded every transaction in the ledger.* *n.* 1 disc, recording: *I bought a lot of new records yesterday.* 2 document, register; archive, annal: *The records of births and deaths were destroyed in the fire.* 3 best place, top, first; highest attainment: *Mark broke the record for the long jump.* *adj.* unbeaten, top, best: *He completed the circuit in a new record time.*

recount *vb.* tell, narrate, describe; report.

recover *vb.* 1 regain, retrieve, redeem, salvage, recapture: *I recovered my balance after I tripped.* 2 improve, better; heal, mend, convalesce: *The economic situation is bound to* *recover by the end of the year. Father has recovered completely from his illness.*

recreation *n.* amusement, entertainment, leisure, diversion, enjoyment, fun.

recruit *n.* beginner, trainee; novice.

rectify *vb.* put right, correct, improve, remedy.

redress *n.* compensation, reparation, amends: *She sought redress for her injuries.* *vb.* compensate for; correct; put right: *Jake wanted to redress the distress caused to him by his opponents.*

reduce *vb.* 1 lessen, diminish, decrease: *I wish they would reduce the price on that dress I saw in the window.* 2 impoverish, lower, degrade: *Since Al's father lost his job, the family has been in reduced circumstances.* ANT. (1) increase, enlarge, swell. (2) promote, improve.

redundant *adj.* surplus, excessive; unnecessary, superfluous.

refer *vb.* 1 direct; recommend, commend: *At the town hall I was referred to the office which deals with education grants.* 2 concern, regard, deal with, relate: *The word "energy" refers to any kind of power.* 3 mention, suggest, touch on, hint at: *What do you suppose the doctor was referring to when he suggested I lose some weight?*

referee *n.* umpire, arbitrator; arbiter, judge: *The boxing referee took a very long time counting up to ten.* *vb.* umpire, arbitrate, judge: *On Saturdays, my father enjoys refereeing soccer games.*

reference *n.* 1 direction; allusion, mention: *Your mother made reference to my dirty shirt, so I'd better change for dinner.* 2 regard, concern, relation, respect: *"With reference to your letter of March 16, we would like to point out..." so the letter began.*

refine *vb.* 1 improve, clarify: *My summer job certainly refined my ideas on how restaurants are run.* 2 clean, purify: *Refined gold is almost 100% pure.*

refined *adj.* cultivated, polite, courteous, well-bred, civilized. ANT. rude, coarse, brutish.

reflect *vb.* 1 mirror; reproduce: *The strange face was reflected in the window of the shop.* 2 think, ponder, consider, deliberate, contemplate: *If you reflect on your experience a little, you'll realize that you are responsible for your own actions.*

reflection *n.* 1 image, appearance, likeness: *I could see my reflection in the highly polished table top.* 2 deliberation, consideration, study, meditation: *After some reflection, Len decided that he'd better go to the library after all.*

reflex *adj.* involuntary, automatic, unthinking, mechanical; spontaneous.

reform *n.* change, correction, improvement: *The new candidates campaigned on the promise to bring about reforms in government.* *vb.* change, improve, better, correct: *The criminal promised to reform, so he was released on parole.*

refrain[1] *vb.* stop, cease, desist, abstain: *The notice in the bus said, "Passengers are requested to refrain from talking to the driver while the vehicle is in motion."*

refrain[2] *n.* chorus; melody, theme: *You sing the refrain at the end of every verse of this song.*

refresh *vb.* renew, exhilarate, invigorate. ANT. tire, exhaust.

refreshment *n.* snack; food, drink.

refuge *n.* safety, shelter, protection.

refugee *n.* exile, fugitive, castaway; evacuce; runaway.

refund *n.* rebate, repayment, reimbursement: *When I returned the chipped cup to the shop, they gave me a refund.* *vb.* reimburse, pay back, repay, make good, recompense: *The garage refunded the customer £10 for their poor service.*

refuse[1] *vb.* turn down, deny, decline: *The teacher refused us permission to leave school early.* ANT. accept, allow.

refuse[2] *n.* waste, rubbish: *The refuse is collected on Mondays.*

regard *vb.* **1** look at *or* upon, consider, estimate: *Philip always regarded his brother as a better tennis player.* **2** attend, respect, honour, value: *I regard very highly your ability to get along well with so many people.* *n.* **1** reference, relation, concern: *With regard to your summer cottage, would you rent it to us this year?* **2** respect, concern, estimation, esteem: *I hold the English professor in very high regard.* **3** concern, thought, care: *Toby has no regard at all for his mother's feelings.*

regardless *adj.* despite, notwithstanding, aside (from); besides.

regime *n.* government, management, direction, administration.

regimented *adj.* orderly, ordered, rigid, controlled, disciplined. ANT. free, loose, unstructured.

region *n.* area, place, locale, territory.

regional *adj.* provincial, local, district.

register *n.* **1** record; catalogue: *All transactions were entered in the register daily.* **2** list, book, record, roll: *Every hotel guest* *must sign the register.* *vb.* enrol, record; enter, list, catalogue: *Please register for your classes before the beginning of the academic year.*

regret *vb.* lament, bemoan, feel sorry about, be sorry for: *I sincerely regret having hurt your feelings, but I didn't do it on purpose.* *n.* sorrow, concern, qualm, scruple, misgiving: *My regret at having to leave before the end of the summer was heartfelt.*

regular *adj.* 1 usual, customary, habitual, normal: *My regular routine gets me to the office at about eight-thirty in the morning.* 2 steady, uniform, even, systematic, orderly: *I could hear his regular breathing from the room next door.* ANT. (1) irregular, odd, unusual.

regulate *vb.* 1 govern, control, direct, manage, legislate: *The government doesn't regulate prices in a free economy like ours.* 2 adjust, set: *Please regulate the heat in this room so that we don't freeze and boil alternately.*

regulation *n.* law, rule, statute.

rehabilitate *vb.* restore, re-establish, improve.

rehearse *vb.* practise, repeat; train.

reign *n.* rule, dominion, sovereignty; power: *How long was the reign of Henry VIII?* *vb.* rule, govern: *Queen Elizabeth II is the reigning monarch of the United Kingdom.*

reimburse *see* **refund.**

reinforce *vb.* strengthen, support, back, assist.

reject *vb.* 1 refuse, deny; renounce: *I don't know why my application was rejected, unless I misspelled something.* 2 discard, expel, throw out *or* away: *The inspector rejected the radio as faulty.* ANT. accept.

rejoice *vb.* delight; celebrate, enjoy.

relapse *vb.* retrogress, backslide, degenerate. ANT. improve.

relate *vb.* 1 tell, report, narrate, recount, describe: *I shall relate to you everything that took place at the haunted house.* 2 connect, associate, compare: *How do the angles of a triangle relate to one another?*

relation *n.* 1 connection, association, relationship, similarity: *The relation between cause and effect is sometimes difficult to understand.* 2 relative, kinsman: *I spent last week visiting some relations in Bromley.*

relative *n.* relation, family, kinsman: *The orphan had no living relatives.* *adj.* corresponding, comparative, analogous: *The lecturer talked on the relative merits of different energy sources.*

relax *vb.* 1 loosen, slacken, let go: *The shark relaxed its hold* *on the raft, allowing it to drift away.* 2 repose, recline, unwind, rest: *When my father comes home from work, he likes to relax for a while, reading the newspaper.* ANT. (1) tighten, increase, intensify.

relaxation *n.* ease, comfort, rest.

release *vb.* 1 let go, relinquish, set loose, free, liberate, set free: *Stefanie released me from the promise I made not to tell anyone. I found a knife and cut through the ropes, releasing the prisoner.* 2 let out, publish, proclaim, announce: *The company finally released the story about the president's award.* *n.* 1 freedom, liberation: *After his release from prison, the ex-convict was able to find a decent job through the help of some friends.* 2 record; film: *The pop group's latest release soon became popular.*

relegate *vb.* demote, displace, remove, depose.

relentless *adj.* pitiless, unmerciful, implacable; inflexible.

relevant *adj.* pertinent, connected, appropriate, suitable.

reliable *adj.* trustworthy, dependable. ANT. unreliable, erratic, eccentric.

relic *n.* trace, vestige; token, remnant.

relief *n.* 1 ease, comfort: *The new medicine brought me some relief from the leg pains.* 2 aid, assistance, support, help: *The relief plans for the sick have not yet been approved.*

relieve *vb.* 1 ease, comfort, soothe, lessen: *That massage relieved the tension I felt.* 2 replace: *The new watchman relieved Bill at midnight so that he could go home early.*

religion *n.* faith, belief; creed, persuasion.

religious *adj.* 1 pious, devout, devoted, reverent, holy, faithful, godly: *Porter's family is very religious and goes to church every Sunday.* 2 strict, rigid, exacting, conscientious: *Religious observance of the rules will keep you out of trouble.* ANT. (1) irreligious, impious. (2) lax, slack, indifferent.

relinquish *vb.* give up, abandon, surrender, renounce.

relish *n.* 1 satisfaction, enjoyment, delight, appreciation, gusto: *Nicole ate the vegetables with such relish—yet I thought she didn't like them.* 2 condiment: *I like relish on my food.* *vb.* enjoy, like, appreciate: *Vincent relishes the idea of baking his own bread.* ANT. *n.* (1) distaste, disgust.

reluctant *adj.* unwilling, hesitant, disinclined, loath. ANT. ready, eager.

rely (on) *vb.* depend, trust, count.

remain *vb.* stay, continue, linger. ANT. depart, leave, go.

remainder *n.* residue, rest, remains.

remark *vb.* say, mention, comment, state, note, observe:

Imogene remarked that she liked Sophie's new dress. n. comment, statement, observation: *Your remark about Teddy's nose was really very unkind.*

remarkable *adj.* unusual, special, extraordinary, exceptional, noteworthy, uncommon. ANT. average, ordinary, commonplace.

remedial *adj.* corrective; restorative.

remedy *n.* cure, medicine, relief, medication: *In the old days, people thought that snake oil was a good remedy for almost any ailment.* *vb.* cure, correct, improve: *The town tried to remedy its financial problems by increasing the rates.*

remember *vb.* 1 recall, recollect: *I never can remember my cousin's telephone number.* 2 memorize, retain, know by heart, keep *or* bear in mind: *I remember every word of a poem I learned when I was ten years old.* ANT. forget.

remembrance *n.* 1 recollection, recall, memory: *My remembrance of the incident is nothing like yours.* 2 keepsake, souvenir, memento: *I keep the remembrances of my visit to Canada in a small brass box.*

remind *vb.* 1 bring back: *Strawberries remind me of the summer.* 2 prompt, jog, prod; advise: *I must remind my father to sign that letter.*

reminiscences *n.pl.* recollections, memories; account, story, anecdote.

remiss *adj.* negligent, careless, inattentive.

remit *vb.* 1 pay; send, forward: *Please remit £2 with your order.* 2 pardon, forgive, excuse, overlook: *The judge remitted the convict's sentence, and he was released.*

remittance *n.* payment, disbursement.

remnant *n.* remainder, remains, residue, rest.

remodel *vb.* reshape, remake, rebuild, renovate, redecorate; change, modify.

remorse *n.* regret, grief, contrition.

remote *adj.* 1 distant, far off *or* away: *Stanley went to a remote village in order to complete his book.* 2 slight, unlikely, inconsiderable: *You don't have even a remote chance of winning the lottery.* ANT. (1) near, nearby, close.

remove *vb.* 1 doff, take off: *Please remove your hat when you enter a building.* 2 transfer, dislodge, displace, take away, eliminate: *The rotten stump was removed from the garden, leaving a big hole.*

render *vb.* 1 make, cause to be *or* become: *Thirty families were rendered homeless by the flood.* 2 do, perform: *Norbert rendered us a great service by fetching the groceries from the* *market.* **3** present, submit, offer, give, deliver: *I rendered an account of the conference to my superiors.*

rendition *n.* version, interpretation, performance.

renew *vb.* refresh, revive; invigorate.

renounce *vb.* **1** give up, abandon, leave, abdicate, forsake, forgo: *The hermit renounced all worldly goods and went to live in a cave.* **2** disown, reject, deny: *When my aunt married a man her father didn't like, he renounced her.*

renovate *vb.* renew, restore, reconstruct.

renown *n.* fame, repute, reputation, glory, distinction, prestige. ANT. anonymity, obscurity.

rent *n.* rental, payment: *How much rent do they pay for the shop?* *vb.* lease, let, hire: *We don't rent our house, we own it.*

repair *vb.* mend, patch, restore, renew, adjust: *The painting was repaired so that you couldn't see the damage at all.* *n.* **1** patch: *I can see where the repair was made on your jacket.* **2** reconstruction, rehabilitation, rebuilding: *This old house is in need of repair.*

repay *vb.* pay back, reimburse, recompense; refund.

repeal *vb.* cancel, abolish, end: *The higher court repealed the action of the lower court.* *n.* cancellation, abolition, end: *The repeal of the act made some people happy and some unhappy.*

repeat *vb.* **1** reiterate, restate: *I've already told you three times, and I shall not repeat it again.* **2** redo, remake, reproduce: *Don't repeat your performance of last week—it was awful.* *n.* repetition, remake: *Many of the television programmes during the summer are repeats.*

repel *vb.* **1** repulse, check, rebuff: *The small force at the fort repelled the attacks all day long.* **2** refuse, reject, decline, discourage: *Frances repelled all friendly advances when she first came to town.* **3** revolt, offend, nauseate: *The smell of the marigold repels insects.* ANT. **(1, 3)** attract, lure.

replace *vb.* **1** supersede, take over, substitute, supplant: *Computers are replacing people in some jobs.* **2** put back, return, restore: *Please replace the books to where you found them.*

replica *n.* copy, reproduction, model, duplicate.

reply *n.* answer, response, rejoinder: *The reply to your request is still "No."* *vb.* answer, respond, rejoin: *"Are you feeling better now?" "Yes," I replied.*

report *n.* account, description, statement, record; outline: *Harold wrote a report of the meeting.* *vb.* account, describe, inform: *News teams try to report the news impartially.*

represent *vb.* **1** speak for, act for: *An MP represents his constituency in Parliament.* **2** render, describe, interpret: *The picture represents a wintry scene.*

repress *vb.* control, restrain, suppress.

reprimand *vb.* rebuke, criticize, admonish, censure.

reproach *n.* condemnation, blame, censure.

repudiate *vb.* disown, reject, deny, disavow.

repugnant *adj.* repellent, distasteful, offensive, disgusting.

repulsive *adj.* repellent, offensive, horrid.

reputation *n.* **1** repute, name, standing: *Your reputation as an expert on fossils is excellent. If you are unfriendly, you may get a bad reputation.* **2** fame, renown, distinction, prominence, prestige: *The doctor's reputation for success in treating arthritis has spread far and wide.*

request *n.* petition, question, appeal, entreaty: *Your request for a leave of absence has been approved.* *vb.* ask, appeal, petition, entreat, beseech: *We requested 500 towels for the gym, and they sent us 500 trowels!*

require *vb.* **1** need, want: *You will require petrol to run that car.* **2** demand, oblige; command, order: *Students are required to bring their textbooks to the lessons.*

requirement *n.* **1** need, demand, necessity: *What requirements should you provide for when you go camping?* **2** condition, prerequisite, provision: *There is no requirement that an applicant have experience for the job.*

rescue *vb.* save, set free, liberate, release, ransom, deliver: *The firemen rescued eight children from the burning building. The knight rescued the beautiful princess from the castle dungeon.* *n.* liberation, release, ransom, deliverance, recovery: *The mountain climbers survived the rescue.*

research *n.* study, scrutiny, investigation: *Research has shown that women live longer than men.* *vb.* study, scrutinize, investigate, examine: *Scientists are constantly researching the cause of major diseases.*

resemblance *n.* similarity, likeness.

resemble *vb.* take after, look like.

resentment *n.* bitterness, displeasure, indignation.

reserve *vb.* save, keep, hold, maintain. ANT. squander, waste.

reside *vb.* **1** abide, dwell, live, stay: *Where are you residing now?* **2** lie, abide: *Early scientists believed that the key to a person's health and personality resided in the fluids of the body.*

residence *n.* **1** home, abode, dwelling: *The residence down the road was sold last week to a young couple.* **2** stay, sojourn: *Because of my residence abroad, I don't have to pay any taxes here.*

resident *n.* inhabitant, native; householder; citizen.

resign *vb.* give up, abdicate, leave, abandon.

resist *vb.* stand firm, withstand, endure, tolerate; oppose. ANT. yield, give in, give way, surrender.

resolute *adj.* resolved, firm, determined, set, decided. ANT. wavering, irresolute, vacillating.

resolution *n.* **1** resolve, determination: *I thought that Jane had shown remarkable resolution in the performance of her work.* **2** statement, decision, recommendation, verdict, judgment: *The committee has approved the resolution that we allow women to join the club.*

resolve *vb.* **1** determine, settle, conclude, decide, confirm: *The students finally resolved to plan a picnic for the following Saturday.* **2** solve; explain: *Politicians have been unable to resolve the energy problem.* *n.* intention, purpose, resolution, determination: *Our firm resolve to return encouraged the downcast amongst the group.*

resort *n.* **1** holiday spot, rest-place: *We often go on holiday to the resorts on the East coast.* **2** relief, recourse, refuge: *Leaping across the chasm was the fugitive's only resort to avoid his pursuers.* *vb.* turn to, apply to, go to, use, employ: *Food was so scarce that the shipwrecked crew resorted to eating leaves and berries.*

resource *n.* reserve, store, supply, source.

respect *n.* **1** admiration, regard, honour, esteem, approval: *I have the greatest respect for your abilities.* **2** particular, regard, detail, point, feature: *In many respects, I find John the most suitable person for the job.* **3** reference, connection: *With respect to your wanting to go on the outing, you have our permission.* **4** concern, consideration: *You should have more respect for your elders.* *vb.* honour, esteem, revere: *I respect your opinion, even though I disagree with you.* ANT. *n.* (4) disrespect, disregard.

respectable *adj.* **1** acceptable, proper, decent, respected: *The manager of the bank ought to be a respectable citizen.* **2** fair, passable, presentable: *I think that coming second is a respectable showing in a national contest.* ANT. (1) disreputable.

respectful *adj.* polite, courteous, well-bred, well-behaved, well-mannered. ANT. rude, impertinent, flippant.

respite *n.* reprieve, interval, rest, pause.

respond *vb.* reply, answer; acknowledge; react.

response *n.* reply, answer, acknowledgment; response.

responsibility *n.* 1 obligation, duty, trust: *The responsibilities of a married man with six children are considerable.* 2 accountability, liability: *His sense of responsibility prevented him from giving in.*

responsible *adj.* 1 accountable, answerable: *Who is responsible for writing this on the blackboard?* 2 chargeable, culpable: *The man responsible for the accident has been identified.* 3 able, reliable, capable, trustworthy, upstanding, honest: *Do you consider yourself a responsible member of the community?*

rest[1] *n.* 1 repose, relaxation, inactivity, quiet, ease: *The doctor told my mother that she needed a rest after all that hard work this winter.* 2 immobility, standstill: *The wheel came to a rest on the number 17, and I had won £25.* *vb.* 1 relax, lounge: *I have a cousin who does everything backwards: he works for two weeks, then rests for the other 50.* 2 lie, lean, depend, hang: *Our decision on when to leave for home rests on the weather.*

rest[2] *n.* remainder, residue, surplus, excess: *After I have eaten everything I want, the rest goes to my dog.*

restaurant *n.* cafeteria, café.

restful *adj.* quiet, peaceful, calm, tranquil. ANT. disturbed, upsetting, tumultuous, agitated.

restless *adj.* nervous, fidgety, unquiet, restive. ANT. calm, tranquil, peaceful.

restore *vb.* 1 return, replace: *Please restore that book to the shelf where you found it.* 2 renew, repair, renovate, mend: *The antique clock has been restored to its original condition.* 3 reinstate, re-establish, reinstall: *After his military service, Len was restored to his old job at the press.*

restrain *vb.* control, check, hold, curb.

restraint *n.* control, self-control, reserve, constraint.

restrict *vb.* limit, confine, restrain.

result *n.* effect, outcome, consequence: *As a result of your misbehaviour, the entire class will have to remain after school.* *vb.* arise, happen, follow, issue: *The return of the watch resulted from the advertisement in the paper.* ANT. *n.* cause.

resume *vb.* continue, restart, recommence.

retain *vb.* 1 hold, keep: *Retain the ticket stub when you enter the theatre.* 2 remember, recall: *Can you retain facts easily?* 3 hire, employ, engage: *We retained a lawyer to look after our interests.* ANT. (1) free, release.

retaliate *vb*. take revenge, repay, return, avenge.

retard *vb*. delay, hold back, slow, hinder, check, obstruct. ANT. advance, speed.

retarded *adj*. backward, slow, behindhand; slow-witted, dull, stupid. ANT. advanced, quick.

retire *vb*. **1** leave, part, withdraw, retreat: *The knights retired from the battlefield in order to regroup their forces.* **2** resign, leave: *In our company, anyone who reaches the age of 70 must retire.* ANT. (**1**) advance, attack.

retiring *adj*. shy, withdrawn, modest, reserved. ANT. bold, impudent, forceful.

retort *vb*. reply, respond, snap back, answer, rejoin: *"You know what you can do with your cricket bat!" Tom retorted angrily.* *n*. reply, response, answer, rejoinder: *Don't be so rude and don't give me any of your nasty retorts!*

retract *vb*. withdraw, go back on, take back.

retreat *vb*. retire, leave, withdraw, depart: *Soundly defeated, the regiment retreated to the safety of the fort.* *n*. **1** departure, retirement, withdrawal: *In the face of the huge numbers of the enemy, the battalion's retreat was expected.* **2** rest; privacy, solitude, seclusion: *The church youth group went on a retreat for the weekend.* **3** shelter, refuge; sanctuary: *Our local authority has a retreat to help drug addicts.* ANT. *vb*. advance.

return *vb*. **1** go back, come back: *I returned home at midnight.* **2** bring *or* take back: *When will you return the lawnmower you borrowed last summer?*

reveal *vb*. disclose, communicate, tell, divulge, publish, announce, publicize, broadcast. ANT. conceal, hide.

revenge *n*. vengeance, reprisal, repayment, retaliation: *Steve will get his revenge for Don's taking his bike by letting the air out of the tyres.* *vb*. avenge, repay, retaliate: *We'll revenge the insults to our team by beating them in the championship.*

revenue *n*. income, take, profit, receipts, proceeds, return.

reverberate *vb*. resound, echo, reflect, rebound.

revere *vb*. venerate, respect, admire. ANT. despise.

reverence *n*. respect, homage, veneration.

reverent *adj*. respectful, deferential; solemn, worshipful. ANT. disrespectful, impious.

reverse *adj*. opposite, contrary: *Why are the handlebars of your bicycle in reverse position?* *n*. **1** opposite, contrary: *Bill said he would disapprove the action, but he did the reverse.* **2** back, rear: *The reverse of a tapestry looks untidy, but the front is regular.* **3** defeat, setback, misfortune, catastrophe: *The army suffered one reverse after another when fighting the enemy.*   vb. **1** invert, transpose, turn: *The middle letters of the sign were reversed, so it read "LAIDES," which means "ugly people" in French.* **2** repeal, revoke, overthrow: *The higher court reversed the lower court's ruling.*

review vb. **1** re-examine; study: *I reviewed the plans for the new theatre and made a few changes.* **2** criticize, survey, inspect: *The new novel was reviewed in last Sunday's newspaper.*   n. **1** examination, study: *The review of the college's courses is going on now.* **2** criticism, critique, judgment, opinion: *The film at the local cinema received a very bad review in the press.*

revise vb. alter, change, improve, amend, correct, update.

revive vb. **1** renew, refresh, reanimate, rejuvenate, reawaken: *The new book revived people's interest in the Civil War.* **2** recover, recuperate, pick up: *I revived after that 15-minute nap before dinner.*

revoke vb. repeal, rescind, withdraw.

revolt vb. **1** rebel, mutiny, rise up: *The peasants revolted in England in the 14th century.* **2** disgust, nauseate, repel, sicken: *The sight of the injured at the train wreck revolted me so much that I was unable to help.*   n. **1** revolution, rebellion, mutiny, uprising: *The revolt of the masses in Russia took place in 1917.* **2** disgust, revulsion, aversion, loathing: *What a feeling of revolt the sight of a dead animal gives me!*

revolution n. **1** revolt, rebellion, uprising, overthrow, mutiny: *The French Revolution followed soon after that in America.* **2** turn, cycle, rotation, spin, orbit: *The earth makes one revolution about the sun each year, and one revolution on its axis each 24 hours.*

revolve vb. turn, rotate, spin, cycle, circle.

revolver n. pistol, gun, rifle.

revulsion n. loathing, disgust, repugnance.

reward n. prize, award, recompense, pay: *As a reward for saving the dog from the river, Dirk received a medal from the society.*   vb. compensate, pay: *If you are good to people, you may be rewarded by their being good to you.*

rhyme n. **1** verse, poem, poetry: *Putting the lesson in rhymes made it easier to learn.* **2** similarity in sound: *Children are fascinated by stories told in rhyme, whether by Mother Goose or Dr. Seuss.*

rhythm n. beat, accent; metre.

rich adj. **1** wealthy, well-off, well-to-do, affluent: *The big house on the hill is owned by the richest man in town.* **2**

abundant, bountiful, plentiful, fruitful, fertile: *The farmers will have a rich harvest this year.* ANT. (1) impoverished, poor. (2) scarce, unproductive, scanty.

rid *vb.* clear, free, shed, eliminate: *It was the Pied Piper who rid the town of Hamelin of its rats.* *adj.* clear, free, delivered: *I'm happy to be rid of that awful cold I had last week.*

riddle *n.* problem, puzzle, question, mystery.

ride *vb.* **1** journey, tour, motor, drive: *We rode through the jungle on the back of an elephant.* **2** drive, manage, guide, control: *Don't ride your bicycle on the wrong side of the road.*

ridicule *vb.* mock, deride, taunt, tease: *Don't ever ridicule anyone because he's different—he may be much better, too.* *n.* mockery, derision, burlesque, satire: *The writers held the politicians up to ridicule until they resigned.* ANT. respect, praise.

ridiculous *adj.* nonsensical, farcical, absurd, laughable, ludicrous, comic, preposterous. ANT. sensible, sound.

right *adj.* **1** correct, factual, accurate, true: *The calculation is right, but you have the wrong answer.* **2** good, just, honest, upright, lawful, moral: *I know that you want to do what is right.* **3** proper, suitable, apt, correct: *Phoebe knows which is the right fork to use for her salad.* *n.* **1** justice, virtue, morality, goodness: *Right shall prevail and evil will be conquered.* **2** title, claim, privilege: *You have the right to think whatever you like.* *adv.* **1** properly, correctly, legally, honourably, fairly: *I believe that the reporter didn't get the story right.* **2** directly, straight, straightway: *I went right home after school.* ANT. *adj.* (1) wrong, incorrect, fallacious. (2) bad, dishonest. (3) unsuitable, inappropriate. *n.* (1) evil, wrong.

righteous *adj.* virtuous, moral, just, upright, honourable.

rigid *adj.* **1** stiff, unbending, unyielding, inflexible: *The leather belt was so rigid that I had to oil it in order to bend it.* **2** severe, strict, stern, inflexible, harsh: *Why must the headmaster be so rigid about the rules?*

rigorous *adj.* **1** severe, harsh, strict: *Some people think the country needs a return to rigorous discipline.* **2** scrupulous, meticulous, exact, precise: *His dissertation was written with a rigorous attention to detail.*

rim *n.* edge, lip, border, brim.

rind *n.* skin, shell, crust, peel.

ring[1] *n.* band, circlet, loop, circle: *The ring of mushrooms in the forest meant that fairies and elves had been dancing there.*

Why don't you wear your diamond ring tonight? *vb.* circle, surround, encircle: *The police ringed the street when the prisoners rioted.*

ring² *vb.* **1** peal, resound, sound, tinkle, jingle: *The doorbell just rang.* **2** summon; announce, proclaim: *Please ring this bell for service.* *n.* tinkle, jangle, peal, jingle: *To this day I can recall the ring of the old school bell.*

rinse *vb.* clean, wash.

riot *n.* disorder, disturbance, tumult, uproar, confusion: *When the police prevented the people from buying food, there was a riot in which 200 people were injured.* *vb.* rebel, revolt: *The prisoners rioted because there wasn't enough food and clean clothing.*

rip *vb.,n.* cut, tear, slit, slash: *The sword ripped through the drapery like a hot knife through butter. Nancy was embarrassed because there was a big rip in her dress.*

ripe *adj.* ready, mature, developed, grown, aged. ANT. immature, ungrown.

ripen *vb.* mature, age, develop, mellow.

ripple *vb.* ruffle, wave, roll, swell, flutter: *A light breeze rippled the surface of the pond.* *n.* wave; undulation: *Tim threw a pebble in the lake and watched the ripples spread from the centre.*

rise *vb.* **1** arise, get up; awake: *We rose at dawn to watch the animals drink at the watering place.* **2** ascend, mount, arise, climb: *The string broke and Dottie's balloon rose up into the summer sky.* **3** prosper, flourish, advance, thrive, succeed, progress: *After marrying the boss's daughter, Bill rose rapidly in the company.* *n.* **1** increase, addition, enlargement: *A rise in wages is soon followed by a rise in the cost of living.* **2** ascent, climb: *The rocket's rise from the launching pad was noisy but swift.*

risk *n.* peril, danger, hazard, chance: *I don't think that the glory of having climbed the mountain is worth the risk of getting killed trying.* *vb.* chance, hazard, endanger; gamble: *Would you risk your life running into a burning house to rescue a dog?*

risky *adj.* dangerous, chancy, perilous, hazardous, unsafe. ANT. safe, secure.

ritual *n.* ceremony, custom, formality, convention.

rival *n.* competitor, contestant, antagonist, opponent: *My rival in the boxing match is a lot heavier than I.* *vb.*

compete, contest, oppose: *Your beauty rivals that of the rose.*
adj. competing, opposing, opposed: *A rival suitor won the hand of the fair maiden.*

river *n.*   stream, brook, creek, tributary.

road *n.*   way, street, avenue, drive; motorway; by-pass, ring road.

roam *vb.*   wander, ramble, rove, range.

roar *vb.,n.*   bellow, cry, shout, yell, brawl: *When the tiger became caught in the net, it roared until the jungle seemed to shake. The roar of the crowd at the football stadium could be heard throughout the surrounding area.*

rob *vb.*   steal, pilfer, rifle; sack, pillage, plunder.

robber *n.*   thief, bandit, pilferer, swindler, criminal.

robbery *n.*   theft, burglary, larceny.

robust *adj.*   strong, firm, hardy.

rock[1] *n.*   stone, boulder; pebble: *The children collected stones off the beach and took them home.*

rock[2] *vb.*   sway, reel, totter: *The dinghy rocked to and fro in the heavy waves.*

rod *n.*   pole, bar, wand, staff, stick, baton.

rogue *n.*   rascal, criminal, outlaw, scoundrel, villain.

role *n.*   **1** part, character: *Theodora was selected for the leading role in the play.*   **2** function, task: *What role do temperature and dampness play in catching cold?*

roll *vb.*   **1** turn, revolve, spin, rotate, whirl: *A huge rock came rolling down the hill.*   **2** wind, tie, wrap: *Please roll up that cord so we can use it again.*   **3** flatten, press, level, smooth: *The baker rolled out the dough before cutting it to make biscuits.*   *n.* **1** bun; bread: *After eating two buttered rolls, I was no longer hungry.*   **2** list, register, roster: *Please read the roll so we can tell if everyone is here.*

romance *n.*   **1** love affair, affair, enchantment: *The entire court knew that the queen was carrying on a romance with the butler.*   **2** novel, story, tale: *Romances were always very popular reading.*

romantic *adj.*   **1** sentimental; idealized; fanciful: *Penny dreamt that she would meet a romantic lover one day.*   **2** visionary; impractical; idealistic, extravagant, exaggerated, fantastic, wild: *Your plans are always so romantic but they never quite come off.*   ANT. realistic, down-to-earth.

romp *vb.*   run, play, frolic, caper.

roof *n.*   cover, shelter, top.

room *n.* **1** chamber; accommodation: *We have an extra room if you'd like to stay a few days.* **2** space: *There was room for one more person in the lift.*

roost *vb.* perch, lodge, settle.

root *n.* cause, origin, basis, reason, source.

rope *n.* cord, thread; string.

rosy *adj.* **1** pink, reddish: *At dawn, the sky became rosy just before the sun came up.* **2** fresh, healthy, ruddy: *After a week at the seashore, we all returned home in rosy condition.* **3** cheerful, happy, bright, promising, optimistic: *Everything is beginning to look rosy again.*

rot *vb.* spoil, decompose, decay, mould, putrefy: *The fruit will begin to rot on the trees if it isn't picked soon.* *n.* decay, mould: *There was some rot in one of the planks of the boat, and we had to replace it.*

rotate *vb.* **1** turn, revolve, spin, orbit: *The tray rotates in the centre of the table and everyone can help himself to pickles and relishes.* **2** alternate, take turns: *Instead of your dealing the cards all evening, why don't we rotate?*

rotten *adj.* **1** mouldy, decayed, spoiled, decomposed, putrid, tainted: *Food kept without refrigeration soon becomes rotten.* **2** corrupt, immoral, dishonest, deceitful: *The government of some cities in the world has become rotten through bribery and greed.* ANT. (1) fresh.

rough *adj.* **1** uneven, unpolished, irregular, bumpy: *The rough surface of the furniture would have to be sandpapered before painting.* **2** coarse, impolite, unpolished, rude, crude, unrefined: *The farmer's rough manner made no difference to us because he was so kind.* **3** stormy, wild, violent, disorderly, turbulent: *The sea was beginning to get very rough, and we knew a storm was brewing.* **4** uncomfortable, inconvenient: *Life in earlier times was very rough.* **5** unfinished, hasty, crude, vague: *I saw a rough draft of the article before it was rewritten.* ANT. (1) smooth, sleek. (2) suave, sophisticated. (3) calm.

roughly *adv.* about, approximately, nearly.

round *adj.* **1** circular, curved, spherical: *That serving platter isn't round, it's oval.* **2** arched, bowed, rounded: *The top of the tree is round now that it has been trimmed.* **3** approximate, rough: *In round figures, I'd say 50 people came.* *adv.* circularly, around: *The merry-go-round went round and round.* *prep.* enclosing, encircling, circling: *The costume called for her to wear a heavy steel collar round her neck.* *n.* routine, series, succession, cycle, course: *The doctor makes* *his rounds in the hospital every day, visiting each patient in turn.*

roundabout *adj.* indirect, devious: *Why don't you come right out and say what you mean instead of talking in a roundabout way?* *n.* junction, intersection: *Take the third exit at the roundabout.* ANT. *adj.* direct, straightforward.

rouse *vb.* **1** awaken, waken, wake up: *I was roused at four o'clock in the morning to stand watch on the ship.* **2** stir up, excite, stimulate: *The band played a rousing march.*

rout *vb.* scatter, defeat, conquer, overcome: *The enemy was completely routed by the attack from all sides.* *n.* flight, defeat, retreat: *When reinforcements arrived from the fort, the attackers were put to rout.*

route *n.* track, way, course, road, path.

routine *n.* way, method, system, habit: *I generally follow the same routine every day, rising at seven and retiring by eleven.* *adj.* customary, usual: *I'm going to the dentist for a routine check-up.* ANT. *adj.* uncommon, rare, unusual.

row[1] *n.* series, rank, file, array, order: *The commanding officer marched past a long row of soldiers who stood at attention.*

row[2] *n.* quarrel, squabble, disturbance: *Whenever my sister threatened to move out of the house, there would be a big family row.*

royal *adj.* regal, majestic, noble, sovereign, ruling, imperial; kingly, queenly, princely.

rub *vb.* scour, scrape; shine, polish: *Rub the table surface with sandpaper till it's smooth.* *vb. phr.* **rub out** erase, delete, eradicate: *The teacher rubbed out the writing on the board.*

rubbish *n.* **1** waste, litter, debris, trash: *Please take the rubbish out when you leave.* **2** nonsense, drivel, balderdash: *If she thought before speaking, maybe Mabel wouldn't talk such rubbish.*

rude *adj.* impolite, crude, unmannerly, uncivil, coarse, impudent, impertinent. ANT. polite, courteous, polished, cultivated.

rudiments *n.pl.* basis, fundamentals; beginnings.

ruffle *vb.* disturb, disarrange, disorder, rumple: *The pages of the book were ruffled by so many children having read it.* *n.* frill, trimming: *There was an old-fashioned dress in the museum with white lace ruffles at the collar and cuffs.*

rug *n.* mat, carpet, floor-covering.

ruin *vb.* **1** spoil, destroy, demolish, wreck: *Barbie's hairdo was ruined in the rain.* **2** bankrupt, impoverish: *My grandfather* *was ruined when the company in which he had invested went bust.* n. **1** rubble, wreck: *The grass grew among the few walls of the ruin that still stood.* **2** destruction, devastation, decay, disintegration, dilapidation: *The ruin of the beautiful ancient Greek temples has deprived us of much architectural knowledge.*

rule n. **1** order, ruling, law, regulation, guide: *If you want to get along with a minimum of trouble, follow the rules.* **2** control, government, dominion, domination: *The islands off the coast don't come under the rule of the king.* vb. **1** govern, control, manage, lead, conduct, direct: *The king ruled the country with an iron hand.* **2** decree, decide, judge: *The judge ruled that the defendant was guilty.*

ruler n. **1** leader, governor, commander, chief: *The countries' rulers met for a summit conference.* **2** rule, tape measure, measure: *Put the ruler along this edge of the cabinet and tell me how long it is.*

ruling n. decision, decree, judgment.

rumble vb. drone, hum, whirr, resound.

rummage vb. search, hunt, ransack.

rumour n. gossip, hearsay, news; scandal.

rumpus n. uproar, commotion, tumult.

run vb. **1** speed, hurry, hasten, race: *The man just snatched my purse and ran.* **2** operate, function, work, go: *My car hasn't run properly since the accident.* **3** go, come, pass; ferry: *The train runs only once a day. The boat runs between here and the island all the time.* **4** stretch, lie, extend, reach: *This railway line runs from here right down the valley.* **5** flow, stream, pour: *The tears came running down Anne's cheeks.* **6** compete, contest, oppose: *Who will run for election next year?* n. **1** sprint, dash, rush: *After a ten-minute run, I finally caught the train.* **2** series, sequence; spell, period: *I've had a run of bad luck at cards lately.* vb. phr. **run away** escape, elope, flee: *The children ran away after breaking a window.* **run down** hunt, seize, catch: *The police dogs ran down the escaped convicts in a nearby swamp.* **run into 1** crash, collide: *The two cyclists ran into each other head on.* **2** meet, encounter: *Guess whom I ran into at the cinema last night.* **run out** use up, exhaust, consume; squander: *I ran out of petrol on the motorway.* **run up** incur: *I ran up a large phone bill last quarter.*

rupture n. break, burst.

rural adj. country, rustic, countrified, pastoral, farm, agricultural. ANT. urban, citified.

rush *vb.* run, hasten, speed, hurry, dash: *I rushed to the phone but it stopped ringing just as I got there.* *n.* haste, hurry: *Dick came into the house in a rush—he'd forgotten his keys.* ANT. *vb.* linger, tarry.

rustle *vb.,n.* stir, whisper, swish; scratch, crackle: *The leaves rustled in the wind. There was a great rustle of papers at the meeting.*

rut *n.* **1** groove, furrow, hollow, trench: *The ruts in the road are getting worse as they are not being repaired.* **2** routine, habit: *My life is in such a rut at the moment; how can I change?*

ruthless *adj.* pitiless, merciless, hardhearted.

S

sack *n.* bag, sac, pouch.

sacred *adj.* holy, hallowed, divine, consecrated. ANT. blasphemous, profane, sacrilegious.

sacrifice *n.* offering; atonement, propitiation: *In olden days, animals were offered as a sacrifice to God.* *vb.* surrender, give up, forgo: *We all have to sacrifice some things in life.*

sad *adj.* **1** unhappy, downhearted, sorrowful, depressed, dejected, melancholy, glum, downcast, gloomy, cheerless: *Mimi's kitten is lost—that's why she looks so sad.* **2** saddening, discouraging, dismal, tragic: *I was just sitting down to dinner when they phoned with the sad news about grandpa.* ANT. happy, joyous.

sadden *vb.* dishearten, cast down, deject.

sadism *n.* perversion, cruelty.

safe *adj.* **1** protected, secure: *I ran down the street and didn't feel safe till I'd locked the house door behind me.* **2** reliable, trustworthy, dependable: *Do you think that putting money in your firm might be a safe investment?* *n.* vault, strongbox, deposit box: *We don't keep important papers around the house but in the safe at the bank.* ANT. adj. (1) dangerous.

safeguard *n.* protection, guard, shield, defence.

safety *n.* security, protection, impregnability.

sag *vb.* droop, fail, weaken; hang down.

sail *n.* sheet, fabric, cloth: *The sails were hoisted on the ship.* *vb.* travel, navigate, voyage, cruise: *We sailed across the Channel.*

sailor *n.* mariner, seaman.

sake *n.* **1** reason, purpose, motive: *The lieutenant said he would carry the flag for the sake of the regiment.* **2** benefit, welfare, advantage: *I'll give some money for the sake of the elderly.*

salary *n.* wage, pay, compensation, payment.

sale *n.* **1** business, trade, commerce: *Sales were bad last year.* **2** transaction, deal; trading; auction: *The sale of the goods went well.* **3** clearance, reduction, auction: *The sales after Christmas bring in a lot of money.*

saloon *n.* bar, lounge.

salute *vb.* greet, welcome, receive: *When Lord Flimsy went to* *his club, his friends all saluted him with much respect.* n. greeting, welcome, celebration: *Great was the salute at the return of the celebrity to his home town.*

salvation *n.* 1 rescue, liberation, deliverance; release: *Grasping that root as I fell off the cliff proved to be my salvation.* 2 forgiveness, redemption; justification: *Christ died on the cross and rose again for our salvation.*

same *adj.* identical, equivalent, corresponding; alike.

sample *n.* example, specimen, token: *The company was giving away free samples of soap and cologne.* vb. test, taste; examine, inspect: *Would you care to sample some of this ham that I have just cooked?*

sanctify *vb.* consecrate, purify; set apart.

sanction *n.* 1 permission, authority, authorization, support, approval: *I give you my sanction to put on a musical festival at Christmas.* 2 ban, embargo, penalty, punishment: *Some nations declared sanctions against the countries that supported their enemies.* vb. approve, authorize, allow, permit, support: *Does your mother sanction that kind of behaviour in public?*

sane *adj.* rational, sound, normal, balanced, reasonable. ANT. insane, irrational, crazy.

sap *vb.* exhaust, weaken, drain.

sarcasm *n.* mockery, irony, satire, derision, scoffing.

satire *n.* ridicule, irony, mockery, parody.

satisfaction *n.* 1 pleasure, contentment, gratification, enjoyment: *My father got considerable satisfaction from my having been picked for the football team.* 2 payment, repayment, amends: *The refugees demanded satisfaction from the Germans after the war, and many of them got it in the form of pensions.*

satisfactory *adj.* sufficient, all right, adequate. ANT. unsatisfactory, poor.

satisfy *vb.* 1 fulfil, meet: *Will you be able to satisfy the camp's requirements for a swimming instructor?* 2 cheer, comfort, please: *Jane's mother wasn't satisfied till she heard that the children had arrived safely.*

saturate *vb.* overfill, soak, drench, steep.

saunter *vb.* amble, wander, stroll, walk.

savage *adj.* 1 wild, uncivilized, uncultivated, rough, rugged, crude, natural: *The savage wilderness had never seen man's footprints.* 2 cruel, heartless, fierce, ferocious: *The man was the victim of a savage attack on his way home that evening.* n. aborigine, cannibal, native, barbarian: *The painted savages* *had begun their dance at the fire.* ANT. *adj.* (1) tame, cultivated.

save *vb.* 1 rescue, free, liberate; preserve, salvage: *The fireman saved three people from the burning building.* 2 preserve, keep, reserve; hoard: *I managed to save £2 a week from the money I earned mowing lawns.*

savour *n.* scent, flavour, relish, tang.

say *vb.* speak, utter, remark, state, declare.

scald *vb.* burn, scorch, singe.

scale *n.* measure, graduation, range; ratio, proportion: *The people who do hard physical work are seldom paid on the same scale as office workers.* *vb.* climb, mount: *The two men scaled the prison wall and ran away.*

scan *vb.* 1 glance at *or* over: *I only scanned the material and I don't remember what it says.* 2 examine, study: *After scanning the data carefully, the analyst was ready with his report.*

scandal *n.* disgrace, disrepute, shame, dishonour.

scanty *adj.* sparse, scarce, meagre, inadequate, insufficient. ANT. plentiful, abundant.

scarce *adj.* rare, sparse, scanty, insufficient. ANT. common.

scarcely *adv.* hardly, barely.

scare *vb.* frighten, shock, startle.

scatter *vb.* spread, sprinkle, disperse. ANT. gather, collect, assemble.

scene *n.* view, display, exhibition, spectacle.

scent *n.* 1 odour, smell, fragrance, aroma, perfume: *The scent of roses filled the morning air.* 2 trail, spoor, track: *A bloodhound's sense of smell is so strong that he can follow a week-old scent.*

sceptical *adj.* cynical, suspicious, doubting.

schedule *n.* timetable, programme, plan, calendar: *We've a very tight schedule today and shall be busy.* *vb.* plan, programme; timetable: *My English class is scheduled for ten o'clock every morning.*

scheme *n.* 1 plan, plot, design, programme: *I have worked out a scheme that will allow me to have a library study period before my history class.* 2 plot, intrigue, conspiracy: *The secret service discovered a scheme to assassinate the cabinet minister.* *vb.* plan, plot, intrigue, contrive: *They're scheming how to get rid of him.*

schism *n.* division, split, faction.

scholar *n.* schoolboy, schoolgirl; student; academic, lecturer, professor.

scintillate *vb.* shine, sparkle, twinkle.

scoff *vb.* mock, belittle, deride, ridicule.

scold *vb.* reprove, berate, reprimand, criticize, censure, blame.

scope *n.* range, reach, extent.

scorch *vb.* char, burn, singe.

score *n.* **1** record, tally, reckoning: *According to the score, the home team is winning. The coach asked me to keep score.* **2** mark, total: *Dick received the highest score in the class.* **3** grievance, complaint, case: *I have a score to settle with Dorothy because of what she has been telling people about me.* *vb.* record, tabulate, count: *Brenda scored the highest of all the students in the maths test.*

scorn *n.* contempt: *Betty turned up her nose to show her scorn for anyone who cheated in an exam.* *vb.* **1** despise, hate: *All our friends scorned people who were dishonest.* **2** refuse, ignore, spurn, reject: *I scorned his offer to behave because I knew he'd do the same thing again.*

scour *vb.* scrub, clean, wash.

scourge *n.* **1** affliction, plague: *Lack of adequate food is the scourge of many countries.* **2** whip, lash: *The slave-driver lay about him with a leather scourge.* *vb.* punish, chastise, afflict; torment: *In the old days, criminals were scourged in public by beating with a cat o'nine tails.*

scowl *vb.,n.* glare, frown, glower: *The teacher scowled at anyone who gave a wrong answer. The old man looked unpleasant because of the scowl on his face.*

scramble *vb.* **1** mix, blend, combine: *I had scrambled eggs for breakfast.* **2** hasten, scurry; clamber, climb: *When the announcement came to abandon ship, the passengers scrambled into the lifeboats.*

scrap *n.* **1** piece, part, fragment, crumb: *Please pick up every scrap of paper you can find.* **2** waste: *Vincent's uncle is a dealer in metal scrap.* *vb.* discard, abandon: *I should have scrapped that car months ago—it's not safe to drive any more.*

scrape *vb.* scour, rub; rasp, scratch.

scratch *vb.,n.* scar, scrape: *I scratched my finger with that saw, so I'll put some ointment on it. My mother was angry when she saw the scratch on the table.* *n. phr.* **from scratch** *Informal:* from the beginning, from the outset: *You're better starting from scratch when rewriting your idea.*

scrawl *vb.* scribble, scratch.

scream *vb.,n.* shriek, cry, yell, screech: *We heard a woman scream so we called the police. When she saw that someone* *had walked on her flower bed, my aunt let out a scream.*

screech *vb.,n.* scream, shriek, yell, cry: *The owl screeched in the darkness, and we huddled together. When Anne saw us get off the plane, she gave a screech of joy and ran towards us.*

screen *n.* cover, protection, separation, partition: *An ornate screen divided the room in two.* *vb.* shield, conceal, hide; separate, partition: *The bookcase screened the other side of the room from my view.*

script *n.* **1** handwriting, hand, penmanship, writing: *The old man wrote his letters in a beautiful ornate script.* **2** copy, manuscript, lines, text: *Maureen didn't know her part because, she said, she'd lost her script on the bus.*

scrub *vb.* scour, wash, cleanse, clean.

scruple *n.* doubt, hesitation, qualm, compunction.

scrutinize *vb.* examine, study.

sea *n.* ocean, waters, waves.

search *vb.* explore, examine, investigate, scrutinize, inspect: *We searched everywhere but couldn't find a trace of the stolen coins.* *n.* exploration, examination, investigation; quest, hunt: *The search for the kidnapped heir goes on.*

seat *n.* **1** chair, stool, bench: *Please find a seat and sit down.* **2** situation, location, centre, place: *London is the seat of government in this country.*

secondary *adj.* subordinate, subsidiary, auxiliary. ANT. primary.

secret *adj.* hidden, concealed, unknown: *My brother and I used to talk together in a secret language.* *n.* confidence; mystery: *If you can keep a secret, I'll tell you where Ma has hidden the chocolate.* ANT. *adj.* open, public.

sect *n.* denomination; group, faction.

section *n.* part, segment, division, subdivision; share.

secure *adj.* **1** firm, tight, fast, fastened, stable, fixed: *"The lifeboats are all secure, Captain," reported the seaman.* **2** safe, protected, defended: *We felt secure, huddled in the warm room round the fire.* **3** assured, self-assured, confident, resolute: *I envy Barbie when she applies for a job—she always seems so secure.* *vb.* **1** fasten, fix, tighten: *Please secure the door when you go out.* **2** obtain, procure, acquire: *The officer ordered the seamen to secure a supply of diesel fuel for the launch.* **3** protect, defend, guard: *The fort will be secured from attack when the cavalry arrives.* ANT. *adj.* **(1)** loose, free. **(2)** endangered.

security *n.* **1** safety, protection, shelter: *The attic offered security to the weary refugees.* **2** guarantee, surety, pledge, promise: *I've some savings in the bank as a security against hardship.*

sediment *n.* dregs, lees, grounds, residue.

seduce *vb.* lead astray, allure, entice, tempt.

see *vb.* **1** observe, perceive, look at, regard, examine, study, view, eye, notice: *I can see a small red barn or boathouse across the river, but it's too far to see if anyone is near it.* **2** understand, comprehend, recognize, appreciate: *Yes, I see what you mean about Louis.* **3** learn, determine, find out, ascertain: *Please see who's at the door.* **4** experience, undergo, go through: *I've seen a lot of suffering these last few years.* **5** escort, attend, accompany: *I'll see you to your limousine, madam.* **6** think, deliberate, ponder: *I'll see about that matter at another time.*

seek *vb.* search for, look for.

seem *vb.* appear, look.

seep *vb.* ooze, leak, percolate.

seize *vb.* **1** grab, grasp, clutch: *The thief tried to seize the woman's handbag, but she held it tight and he ran off.* **2** capture, take: *After a siege of 40 days, the attackers finally seized the castle.* ANT. (1) release, loosen.

seldom *adv.* rarely, not often, infrequently, scarcely.

select *vb.* choose, pick, prefer: *In a supermarket you select the food you want by yourself.* *adj.* special, chosen, choice, preferred, selected, picked, elite: *The select troops became the king's personal bodyguard.*

self-control *n.* restraint, discipline.

selfish *adj.* self-centred, greedy, mean, miserly.

self-righteous *adj.* egoistical, sanctimonious, holier-than-thou.

sell *vb.* trade, barter, market, retail, merchandise.

send *vb.* post, dispatch, transmit, forward, convey, ship.

senior *adj.* older, elder; superior. ANT. junior, minor.

sensation *n.* **1** sense, feeling, sensibility, perception, sensitiveness: *The dentist gave me an injection when I had a filling, and I had no sensation in my lower lip.* **2** excitement, thrill, stimulation: *The new rock group was an overnight sensation.*

sensational *adj.* thrilling, startling, exciting, marvellous, superb, spectacular.

sense *n.* **1** sensation, feeling, perception: *The doctor asked me if I had any sense in my left leg.* **2** understanding, reasoning, intellect, judgment, wit, common sense, brains: *I don't know what's the matter with Sadie, but she hasn't the sense she was born with!* **3** awareness, consciousness: *Have you no sense of honour or of loyalty?* *vb.* perceive, feel, discern, appreciate: *I sensed someone near me, even though I had heard nothing and couldn't see in the darkness.*

sensible *adj.* reasonable, rational; thoughtful, judicious; responsible. ANT. foolish.

sensitive *adj.* **1** sore, tender, delicate: *The end of my finger is still sensitive where I burned it yesterday.* **2** touchy, tense, nervous: *Donald is still very sensitive about his exam results last year.* **3** perceptive, keen, receptive: *Bob has very sensitive hearing.*

sentiment *n.* **1** feeling, attitude, opinion: *Roger never let his sentiments be known about the loss of his aunt.* **2** tenderness, emotion: *The film was so full of sentiment that even the adults cried.*

separate *vb.* **1** divide, disconnect, split, break up: *We finally separated the two fighting dogs.* **2** isolate, segregate: *The boys and the girls are separated in our school.* *adj.* **1** apart, divided, detached: *We were able to keep the dogs and the cats separate.* **2** distinct, different: *Please sort the nuts and the bolts into separate containers.* **3** independent: *Victor's mother and father have decided to lead separate lives.*

sequel *n.* consequence, result, development.

sequence *n.* order, succession, series, arrangement.

serene *adj.* peaceful, quiet, calm, tranquil. ANT. agitated, turbulent, stormy.

series *n.* order, sequence, succession.

serious *adj.* **1** grave, earnest, sober, solemn: *I think you ought to have more fun and try to be less serious.* **2** important, critical: *Disobeying the school rules is a serious matter.* ANT. (1) frivolous, jocular, light.

sermon *n.* address, talk; lecture, discourse.

servant *n.* domestic, attendant; butler, valet, manservant, footman; maidservant, maid.

serve *vb.* **1** attend, wait on: *The waitress came over to our table and asked, "May I serve you?"* **2** assist, help, aid: *The solider re-enlisted in order to serve his country.*

service *n.* **1** help, aid, assistance: *Can I be of service to you?* **2** worship, ceremony, ordinance: *We went to the church service on Sunday morning.*

servile *adj.* menial, beggarly, submissive, obsequious, fawning.

session *n.* meeting, sitting, gathering.

set *vb.* **1** put, place, position: *You can set the armchair in the corner over there, please.* **2** assign, appoint, fix, settle, establish, determine: *If you will set a time when we are to* *meet, I shall be there.* **3** harden, solidify, thicken, congeal, gel: *The cement will set overnight.* **4** rate, price, value: *The discount at the sale was set at 20 per cent.* *vb. phr.* **set apart** separate, divide: *The children who refused to behave were set apart from the others.* **set aside** save, reserve: *The man in the shop has set aside a transistor radio for me till I have the money to pay for it.* **set back** slow, retard, hinder, delay: *Our original schedule was set back six weeks by a fire at the factory.* **set down** write, record: *Each student should set down his own ideas before starting to write.* **set forth** begin, start: *The explorers set forth on their journey from Plymouth.* **set free** liberate, release, free: *We took the fawn into the forest and set it free.* **set off** **1** detonate, touch off, explode: *The children are not allowed to set off the fireworks by themselves.* **2** embark, start out: *I like to set off on a car trip early in the morning.* **3** contrast, offset: *The red necktie sets off the pale pink shirt very well.* **set on** attack: *The stagecoach was set upon by robbers as soon as it left town.* **set out** begin, start, commence: *There were ten people at the inn who had set out from London that morning.* **set up** establish, found: *The children set up a business to sell lemonade during the hot summer.* *n.* **1** collection, assortment; kit: *The stamp collector has a complete set of first-day covers. Do you have a chemistry set?* **2** group, company, clique, circle: *I don't like the set that Margie is going with these days.* *adj.* settled, firm, unchanging: *Agnes's father is very set in his ways, isn't he?*

setback *n.* hindrance, disappointment, adversity, defeat.

settle *vb.* **1** agree upon, establish, decide: *I think we ought to be able to settle who is going to clean the stairs.* **2** pay, satisfy: *The insurance company settled the claim in two weeks.* **3** locate, lodge, reside, abide: *My ancestors settled in Sydney, Australia.* **4** sink, subside: *The ground under the new house settled, creating cracks in the walls.*

sever *vb.* cut; divide; split. ANT. join, connect.

several *adj.* a few, some, a couple, a handful.

severe *adj.* **1** cruel, strict, harsh, rigid, firm, unyielding: *The headmaster of our school is a severe disciplinarian.* **2** difficult, harsh, unpleasant: *An especially severe winter has made our fuel bill much higher.* **3** violent, dangerous: *The severe storm knocked down power lines all over the area.* ANT. (1) lenient, easygoing. (2) mild.

sew *vb.* stitch, seam, embroider; mend.

shabby *adj.* ragged, worn, threadbare.

shack *n.* hut, hovel, shed, shanty.

shade *n.* 1 shadow, darkness, gloom, dusk: *In the shade, I was unable to see who it was.* 2 tint, colour, hue: *That shade of blue goes with your eyes very well.* *vb.* 1 darken, blacken: *If you shade that part of the drawing, it will look more natural.* 2 screen, conceal, cover, block: *I shaded the sun from my eyes with my hand.*

shadow *n.* shade, darkness, umbra, gloom.

shaft *n.* 1 pole, rod, bar: *The natives held the shafts of the spears ready to hurl them onto the strangers.* 2 ray, beam, streak: *A shaft of light came in through the gap in the curtains.*

shaggy *adj.* woolly, hairy, uncombed, unkempt.

shake *vb.* 1 quiver, tremble, quake, shiver, shudder: *The tiny kitten was shaking with cold on our doorstep, so we took it inside.* 2 grasp, clasp, take: *I shook John's hand as I was introduced to him.*

shallow *adj.* slight, superficial, inconsiderable. ANT. deep, profound.

sham *n.* fake, fiction, pretence.

shame *n.* 1 embarrassment, humiliation: *A feeling of shame came over me when I realized that Suzie had overheard me talking about her sister.* 2 disgrace, dishonour: *The soldier's court martial brought shame to the entire platoon.* *vb.* 1 humiliate, humble, abash, mortify: *Tony was shamed into admitting that he had taken all the sweets out of the jar.* 2 disgrace, dishonour, humble: *Should a teacher be shamed by a student who misbehaves?* ANT. *n.* (2) pride, honour.

shameful *adj.* disgraceful, humiliating, dishonourable, scandalous.

shameless *adj.* unashamed, unembarrassed; bold, brazen, insolent, impudent.

shape *n.* 1 form, figure, outline; appearance: *That swimming pool is in the shape of a letter "C."* 2 mould, frame, form, pattern, cast: *The clay hardened into the shape of the container where it was kept.* *vb.* form, fashion, model; mould, cast: *Try to shape this block of wood to look like an apple.*

share *n.* portion, part, ration, allotment; helping: *You have already eaten your share of the pie.* *vb.* 1 participate, partake: *Everyone who does his work can share in the rewards.* 2 divide, distribute, apportion: *I think you ought to share the chocolates among you equally.*

sharp *adj.* keen, acute, cutting, fine. ANT. blunt, dull.

shatter *vb.* **1** smash, break, burst, split; destroy: *The ball went through Mrs. Maloney's window and shattered it.* **2** upset, shock: *The news that Andy had failed his exam shattered him.*

shave *vb.* cut, trim, clip, bare.

shawl *n.* scarf, stole.

shed *n.* hut, lean-to, shelter, outbuilding.

sheer *adj.* **1** utter, simple, absolute: *Your story about the frog turning into a prince is sheer nonsense.* **2** steep, abrupt: *We were faced with a sheer rocky cliff that no one could climb.* **3** fine, transparent, thin, clear: *The model was wearing sheer stockings.*

sheet *n.* **1** covering, cloth; bed-linen: *I'll change the sheets on the bed today.* **2** layer, leaf; film, coating: *Put a sheet of paper over the top of the jar before sealing it. There's a sheet of ice on the roads tonight, so be careful.*

shelf *n.* ledge, plank, rack.

shell *n.* crust, case, husk; covering, layer, outside.

shelter *n.* protection, haven, sanctuary: *We sought shelter from the storm by crouching in a cave.* *vb.* protect, shield, harbour, guard: *The farmer sheltered many fugitives who escaped from the gang.*

shield *n.* guard, defence, protection, shelter: *We had to plant a row of trees alongside the house as a shield from the winds.* *vb.* guard, defend, protect, shelter: *The man raised his arms to shield himself from the attack.*

shift *vb.* move, change, transfer: *The foreman shifted three men from the factory to the warehouse. The wind, which had been from the south, shifted to the north.* *n.* **1** move, change, transfer: *My shift to another job in the company meant I would earn more money.* **2** turn, spell, period: *I work the day shift but I used to work nights.*

shimmer *vb.* shine, glimmer, glisten, gleam.

shine *vb.* **1** gleam, beam, glisten, glimmer, shimmer, glow, radiate: *The sun shone every day of our holiday.* **2** polish, brush: *I shined my riding boots in preparation for the horse show competition.* *n.* gloss, lustre, radiance, polish: *My face was reflected in the shine of the chrome on the car.*

shiny *adj.* glossy, polished, bright, glistening. ANT. dull.

ship *n.* vessel, craft; tanker; liner; barge; tug; tanker; hover-craft.

shipshape *adj.* neat, clean, orderly. ANT. messy, sloppy.

shirk *vb.* evade, avoid, dodge.

shiver *vb.* quake, tremble, quiver, shudder, shake: *We stood*

on the corner, shivering in the cold, waiting for the school bus.
n. shudder, tremble: *A shiver ran down my spine when I*
thought of the way the kitten had been killed.

shock *n.* **1** blow, clash, collision, impact: *The shock of the huge*
lorry striking the wall broke all the windows in the house. **2**
disturbance, upset, agitation: *The shock at the news of her*
son's death was too much for the mother to bear. *vb.* **1**
surprise, stagger, astound, stun, startle, bewilder: *The*
parents were shocked when they saw the film. **2** horrify,
outrage, offend, revolt, appal: *The world was shocked to*
discover what had been going on in the Nazi concentration
camps.

shoe *n.* footwear, boot, sandal.

shoot *vb.* fire, explode, burst, discharge.

shop *n.* store, supermarket; department store; kiosk.

shore *n.* beach, coast, seaside, seacoast.

short *adj.* **1** brief, concise, abbreviated, condensed, curtailed,
terse, abridged: *The film is short—it lasts only 20 minutes.* **2**
slight, little, undersized: *The string is too short to go around*
the package even once. ANT. long, lengthy.

shorten *vb.* **1** cut, curtail, abbreviate, abridge: *The article is*
good, but it has to be shortened to fit into the space in our
magazine. **2** take in, lessen, reduce: *The dressmaker had to*
shorten my sister's skirt a little. ANT. lengthen.

shortsighted *adj.* **1** myopic: *The optician said that I was*
shortsighted and needed glasses. **2** thoughtless, unthinking,
unimaginative: *It was quite shortsighted of you not to have*
foreseen your mother's displeasure at the ink on the carpet.

shot *n.* blast, burst, discharge, volley, gunfire.

shout *vb.,n.* yell, roar, cry, bellow: *I shouted to my sister that*
she'd better hurry up. Jimmy gave a shout when I stepped on
his toe.

shove *vb.,n.* push, jostle: *Can you help me shove this heavy*
bookcase? If you give the cart a good shove, it will roll down
the hill.

shovel *n.* spade, scoop.

show *vb.* **1** display, present, exhibit: *I have already shown you*
all the books I have on gardening. **2** indicate, note, point:
Show me the way to go home. **3** explain, reveal, tell: *I wish*
you would show me how to do that trick with the disappearing
mouse. **4** prove, demonstrate: *If you expect me to believe*
your story about the purple banana, you'll have to show
me. **5** guide, usher, lead: *The man in the green uniform will*
show you to your seats. *vb. phr.* **show in** conduct, lead,

direct: *Please show Mr. Gilbert in.* **show off** brag, boast: *Every time the teacher looks at him, Oscar shows off.* **show up 1** arrive, appear, turn up, surface: *Ten o'clock is no time to show up for school!* **2** expose, belittle, discredit: *The experienced pianist did not like being shown up by his own pupil.* *n.* **1** presentation, exhibit, exhibition, display: *Mother and I went to a flower show yesterday.* **2** drama, play, musical: *Where shall we meet after the show?*

shred *n.* fragment, piece, bit, tatter: *After the fight, Jack's shirt was in shreds.* *vb.* cut, strip, tear: *I like shredded carrots in my salad.*

shrewd *adj.* **1** cunning, sly, crafty, tricky: *Putting a drawing pin on the teacher's chair was not a very shrewd move, Moriarty.* **2** clever, ingenious, intelligent, astute: *My father is a very shrewd investor, and many businessmen seek his advice.*

shriek *vb.,n.* scream, screech, yell, howl: *Mother shrieked when she saw the mouse run along the floor. We were very frightened when we heard a piercing shriek at midnight.*

shrill *adj.* sharp, piercing; high-pitched.

shrink *vb.* **1** contract, diminish, dwindle, shrivel: *If you wash that shirt in hot water, it will shrink.* **2** recoil, withdraw, flinch, retreat: *Dick shrinks from any responsibility you try to give him.* ANT. **(1)** swell.

shudder *vb.,n.* shiver, tremble, shake, quiver: *I shuddered at the thought of going out into the bitter cold. The dog gave a violent shudder, making the rain from his coat fly everywhere.*

shuffle *vb.* **1** scuffle, plod, crawl, falter: *The old man shuffled along the street.* **2** mix, jumble, disorder: *It's your turn to shuffle the cards.*

shun *vb.* avoid, evade, elude.

shut *vb.* close; lock, seal: *Please shut the door after you.* *vb. phr.* **shut up** *Informal:* be quiet, hush, still: *Oh do shut up, I'm getting so tired of hearing your voice.* ANT. *vb.* open.

shy *adj.* timid, bashful. ANT. bold, self-confident; brazen.

sick *adj.* ill, unwell, ailing, unhealthy, infirm. ANT. healthy, well.

side *n.* **1** face, surface: *A cube has six sides.* **2** opponent, foe, rival: *Which side are you for, the one in the green shirts or the one in white?* *adj.* secondary, indirect; unimportant: *The main issue is the kind of television programmes we want; for the moment the cost of the programmes is a side issue.* *vb.* join, support, associate: *Maggie sided with her husband in the argument.*

siege *n.* blockade, barrage.

sieve *n.* strainer, colander; screen, riddle.

sift *vb.* 1 sieve, separate, sort, filter: *Jean sifted the flour to remove the coarser grains.* 2 evaluate, examine, scrutinize: *The detectives sifted the evidence before them.*

sigh *vb.* breathe, cry, gasp, groan.

sight *n.* 1 vision, eyesight: *Bill's sight requires him to wear glasses.* 2 view, spectacle, scene, display: *The trained porpoises leaping through the air together are quite a sight.* 3 *Informal:* eyesore: *My mother told me that my room was a sight and that I must clean it up at once.*

sign *n.* 1 symbol, token, indication, suggestion, hint: *Those black clouds on the horizon are the sign of a coming storm.* 2 signal, clue: *The dog gave no sign that it would bite.* *vb.* authorize, approve, confirm: *Please sign the contract on the dotted line.*

signal *n.* sign, beacon, flag.

significance *n.* importance, consequence, weight, moment.

significant *adj.* important, meaningful, vital, crucial, critical. ANT. unimportant, insignificant, trivial.

signify *vb.* 1 indicate, show, signal, communicate: *The policeman signified his permission to cross the street by beckoning with his arm.* 2 mean: *What do you suppose those strange hand movements signify?*

silence *n.* 1 quiet, stillness, noiselessness, soundlessness, hush: *After the noise and bustle of the city, I really enjoy the silence and serenity of the country.* 2 muteness, speechlessness: *Silence is golden, but speech is silver.* ANT. (1) noisiness, clamour, racket.

silent *n.* 1 quiet, noiseless, soundless, still, hushed: *I dived down into the lake, into its silent depths.* 2 mute, speechless, uncommunicative: *My father was silent on the subject of where we were going for our holiday.* ANT. (1) noisy, clamorous. (2) talkative, communicative.

sill *n.* shelf, ledge; beam; threshold.

silly *adj.* senseless, foolish, stupid, ridiculous.

similar *adj.* like, resembling, alike. ANT. different, dissimilar.

similarity *n.* likeness, resemblance. ANT. dissimilarity, difference.

simmer *vb.* boil, stew, bubble: *This soup should simmer for 10 minutes.* *vb. phr.* **simmer down** *Informal:* calm down, quieten down: *Alfred got very angry for a while but he then simmered down.*

simple *adj.* 1 uncomplicated: *Addition and subtraction are parts of simple arithmetic.* 2 clear, understandable, plain: *I* *cannot give you a simple explanation of why plants are green.* **3** easy: *That was a simple history exam.* **4** unadorned, plain, unimaginative: *Sue liked to wear simple dresses.* ANT. (**1**) complicated, complex. (**2**) puzzling, abstruse. (**3**) difficult, demanding. (**4**) ornate, grand.

simulate *vb.* pretend, feign, imitate.

simultaneous *adj.* at the same time; concurrent, coincident, contemporaneous.

sin *n.* trespass, transgression, wickedness: *The seven deadly sins are pride, anger, covetousness, lust, gluttony, envy, and sloth.* *vb.* trespass, transgress: *Jonah sinned by not obeying what God told him to do.*

sincere *adj.* **1** honest, open, candid, trusty, trustworthy, faithful: *Don is a sincere friend.* **2** genuine, real, true: *Mabel shed sincere tears for her lost puppy.*

sincerity *n.* honesty, guilelessness; openness, frankness. ANT. guile, deceit, insincerity.

sing *vb.* chant, croon.

singe *vb.* burn, scorch, scald.

single *adj.* **1** one, lone, sole, solitary: *A single man stood on the beach, looking out towards the horizon.* **2** celibate, unmarried, unattached: *The party at the club next week will be for single people only.* **3** individual: *I reserved a single room at the hotel.*

singular *adj.* **1** remarkable, unusual, extraordinary, rare, uncommon, exceptional: *Climbing Mount Everest is certainly a singular feat.* **2** strange, odd, peculiar, queer, eccentric, curious: *The mating dance of certain birds is very singular.*

sinister *adj.* ominous, unfavourable, adverse.

sink *vb.* descend, fall, drop.

sip *vb.* taste, drink: *You should sip the hot lemonade slowly.* *n.* taste, swallow, drink: *May I have a sip of your sherry?*

siren *n.* alarm, horn, signal, tocsin; warning.

sit *vb.* rest, squat, crouch, perch: *Please sit on a chair.* *vb. phr.* **sit on** *Informal:* repress, suppress: *The government sat on the committee's report and did not make its findings public.*

site *n.* location, place, position.

situation *n.* **1** location, site, position: *The situation of the house gives it magnificent views in three directions.* **2** condition, state, circumstances: *In the present situation, it may not be easy to find a job after school.*

size *n.* dimension, measurement; extent, scope; largeness.

skeleton *n.* bone(s); frame, framework.

sketch *n.* drawing, picture: *Here is a rough sketch of my home.*

vb. draw, outline, represent: *In the art class, the students were asked to sketch a model of a monkey.*

skid *vb.* slide, slip, glide.

skilful *adj.* skilled, accomplished, expert, adept, proficient. ANT. inept, clumsy, awkward.

skill *n.* ability, talent, aptitude.

skim *vb.* scan, look through, (*informal*) flick through, browse.

skin *n.* covering, outside, peel, shell, rind: *This lemon has a thick skin.* *vb.* peel, pare; flay: *Skin these grapes for me, would you? The cruel pirate gave the man twenty lashes, almost skinning him alive.*

skinny *adj.* thin, scrawny, lean, gaunt, raw-boned. ANT. heavy, hefty, fat.

skip *vb.* jump, leap, spring, gambol, hop.

sky *n.* air, atmosphere; blue.

slack *adj.* 1 loose, lax, limp: *Let the skipping rope hang slack, so that it touches the ground in the middle.* 2 lazy: *Tim is very slack about getting his work done.* 3 slow, inactive, sluggish: *Summer is the slack period in our business.* ANT. (1) taut, stiff, rigid. (3) active, busy.

slam *vb.* bang, push, close, fasten.

slander *n.* defamation, calumny, gossip, lie.

slang *n.* vulgarism; argot, cant; dialect, jargon.

slant *vb.* lean, incline, slope, tilt: *Many roofs slant downwards.* *n.* 1 incline, slope, pitch: *We came to a steep slant in the road and the car would go no further.* 2 angle, approach: *I got a new slant on you when I heard you give that talk at the meeting.*

slap *vb.,n.* smack, blow, pat: *I slapped him on the cheek for being naughty. He gave his friend a gentle slap on the back.*

slash *vb.* 1 slit, cut, gash: *The recipe says to slash the roast in several places with a sharp knife and to insert garlic in the slits.* 2 reduce, lower, cut: *Prices on clothing were slashed after Christmas.* *n.* slit, cut, gash: *There were three slashes in my car tyre.*

slaughter *vb.* kill, butcher, massacre, slay: *The cattle were slaughtered to produce food.* *n.* killing, butchery, butchering, massacre: *We must do something to prevent the continued slaughter of wildlife.*

slave *n.* serf, vassal, captive.

sleep *vb.,n.* rest, repose, slumber, nap, snooze, doze: *If you sleep too little, you're tired the next day. I had only five hours' sleep last night.*

slender *adj.* slim, slight, thin. ANT. heavy, fat, overweight.

slide *vb.* slip, glide, skid, skim.

slight *adj.* **1** small, sparse, scanty, spare: *It takes only a very slight amount of insecticide to kill a fly.* **2** insignificant, unimportant, trivial: *Irena has a terrible temper and gets angry at the slightest thing.* *vb.* ignore, disregard, snub, scorn: *I felt slighted because I wasn't invited to the dance.* ANT. *adj.* (1) large, enormous, huge. (2) major, significant. *vb.* flatter, compliment.

slim *adj.* **1** slender, thin, slight; lank: *Sophie looks quite slim now that she has lost weight.* **2** small, unimportant, insignificant, weak, scanty, slight: *Ben stands a very slim chance of winning if he has to play chess with me.*

slime *n.* mire, ooze, mud, filth.

sling *n.* bandage, dressing: *Pete had his injured arm in a sling to help support it.* *vb.* hurl, throw, send: *He's slinging the disc into the air now; can you see him?*

slip *vb.* **1** slide, glide; shift: *I was about to slip off the edge of the cliff when a strong hand caught me and hauled me to safety.* **2** err, blunder: *I slipped when I gave away your secret.* *n.* error, mistake, blunder: *Your telling my father about where we went yesterday was an unfortunate slip.*

slit *vb.* cut, slash: *With one stroke, I slit open the fish.* *n.* cut, slash, slot, tear: *The slit in the evening dress started at the hem and went up above the knee.*

slogan *n.* motto, cry, catchword.

slope *vb.,n.* incline, slant: *The lawn behind my house slopes down to the river. The trees on that slope are all bent by the wind.*

slouch *vb.* droop, lounge, languish.

slow *adj.* **1** unhurried, gradual, leisurely: *The slow pace of life in the country is more to my liking than the hectic activity of the city.* **2** late, delayed, behindhand: *My watch is five minutes slow.* **3** dull, boring, tedious: *The play was very slow—I fell asleep.* *vb.* retard, hinder, obstruct, slacken: *We slowed down when we came to the bend.* ANT. *adj.* (1) fast, quick. (2) fast, ahead.

slump *n.* decline, descent, drop, fall; depression: *Business has hit a slump, I'm afraid.* *vb.* sink, decline, descend: *George slumped in his chair when Bob told him he couldn't go to the match with him.* ANT. *n.* boom.

slur *vb.* **1** blur, garble, swallow: *Whey does June slur her vowels?* **2** discredit, smear, (*slang*) knock: *And why does she slur you?*

sly *adj.* cunning, crafty, secretive, wily, foxy.

smack[1] *n.* smell, flavour: *There was a faint smack of lavender in the room.*

smack[2] *n.* slap, pat, spank: *Shut up, or I'll give you a smack on the face.* *vb.* hit, strike, slap: *Is it always good to smack a naughty child?*

small *adj.* **1** little, tiny, miniature: *The watch was so small I could hardly see the face.* **2** unimportant, insignificant, minor, trivial: *Whether you go to the theatre or not is a small matter to me.* ANT. (**1**) large, big, enormous.

smart *adj.* **1** modish, stylish; neat, tidy: *Alec looks very smart in his new suit, doesn't he?* **2** clever, intelligent, bright: *Donald was smart enough to get through all his exams.* *vb.* sting, hurt, burn: *That witch hazel smarts when you put it on an open cut.* ANT. (**1**) untidy; unfashionable; dowdy. **2** stupid, slow, dumb.

smash *vb.* break, crash, crush, demolish: *The car was badly smashed in the accident.* *n.* crash, shattering: *I heard the smash of a pane of glass and thought it was a burglar.*

smear *vb.* rub, spread, wipe.

smell *vb.* scent, sniff, detect: *I can smell turkey roasting, and it's making me hungry.* *n.* **1** scent, odour, aroma, bouquet: *The smell of orange blossoms filled the air.* **2** odour, stench, stink: *I can't stand the smell of dead fish.*

smile *vb.,n.* grin, beam, smirk: *Bill smiled when I handed him his birthday present. I can see the smile on your face when I start talking about ice creams.* ANT. scowl, frown.

smooth *adj.* even, level, flat, unwrinkled: *There was no wind, and the lake was as smooth as glass. After he shaves, my father's cheek is so smooth!* *vb.* level, even, flatten, iron: *Doris smoothed down the sheets on the bed before putting on the blankets.* ANT. *adj.* rough, uneven.

smother *vb.* stifle, asphyxiate, suffocate.

smug *adj.* self-satisfied, complacent. ANT. modest; shy.

snare *n.* trap, net: *We set snares for the fox that was eating our chickens.* *vb.* trap, catch, capture: *Dave built a large cage in which he hoped to snare a rabbit.*

snarl *vb.* growl, gnarl.

snatch *vb.* seize, grab, grasp.

sneak *vb.* slink, skulk, steal: *Roger sneaked in when no one was looking and stole a pie.* *n.* informer, (*slang*) rat, turncoat; coward: *Hugh was a sneak when he went and told teacher what I'd done.*

sneer *vb.* scorn, scoff, mock, jeer, taunt: *Don't sneer at my swimming records unless you can do better.* *n.* jeer; disdain:

With a sneer, Victor dismissed my attempt at drawing a plan for our new house.

snip *vb.* cut, clip, nip.

snore *vb.* snort, sleep, breathe, wheeze, pant.

snub *vb.* slight, insult; rebuke: *Mary was upset when her friends snubbed her at the party just because she had a shabby dress.* *n.* slight, insult, humiliation: *We all felt the snub when we weren't invited to dinner at the country club.*

snug *adj.* **1** cosy, sheltered, comfortable: *The children remained snug in bed while the storm raged outside.* **2** close-fitting, trim, tight: *Don't you think that those trousers are a little snug round the hips?*

soak *vb.* drench, wet, steep, saturate.

soar *vb.* fly, glide, tower.

sob *vb.* lament, cry, weep.

sober *adj.* **1** clearheaded, moderate: *Whenever my grandfather has to drive a car, he doesn't drink and stays sober.* **2** serious, solemn, grave: *The funeral service for the comedian was the only sober occasion he had ever been associated with.* ANT. **(1)** drunk, inebriated. **(2)** frivolous.

so-called *adj.* supposed, alleged.

sociable *adj.* social, friendly, affable.

social *adj.* group, human, common.

society *n.* **1** community, civilization, nation: *Society's problems, like having enough food for everyone, cannot be solved easily or quickly.* **2** club, organization, association, circle, group: *My mother is a member of two professional medical societies.*

soft *adj.* **1** flexible, pliable, pliant; elastic: *This clay is soft enough now for you to mould a figure out of it.* **2** smooth, velvety, satiny: *My kitten's fur is so soft!* **3** quiet, low, gentle: *The girl was singing in a soft voice.* ANT. **(1)** hard, rigid.

soften *vb.* moderate, mellow, weaken.

soil *n.* earth, loam, dirt: *You'll need more soil to plant that flower in such a large pot.* *vb.* dirty, stain, spot: *Badly soiled clothes should be allowed to soak for a while before washing.*

sole *adj.* single, only, exclusive.

solemn *adj.* **1** serious, sober, grave: *The partners make solemn promises in the marriage ceremony.* **2** formal, dignified, important: *The coronation of the monarch is a most solemn occasion.* ANT. **(1)** lighthearted, frivolous.

solicit *vb.* request, seek, pray, beg, beseech.

solid *adj.* 1 firm, compact, hard, dense: *The ball was made out of solid rubber.* 2 reliable, trustworthy; sensible: *I know that James is a solid type of person.*

solitary *adj.* isolated, lonely, deserted; sole, only, single.

solution *n.* answer, explanation.

solve *vb.* answer, unravel, explain.

sombre *adj.* 1 serious, sober, grave, gloomy, dismal: *The sun hasn't shone for so many days that I am in a very sombre mood.* 2 dismal, mournful, sad, melancholy: *The funeral was a sombre event.* ANT. (1) happy, cheerful.

sometimes *adv.* occasionally, now and then, at times. ANT. always, invariably.

soon *adv.* shortly, in a little while, before long.

soothe *vb.* calm, pacify, comfort, quiet. ANT. disquiet, upset, unnerve.

sordid *adj.* foul, dirty, filthy, unclean.

sore *adj.* aching, painful, hurting, tender, sensitive: *My finger is still sore where I caught it in the door yesterday.* *n.* cut, bruise, burn, wound, injury: *I have a sore on my knee where I scraped it playing games.*

sorrow *n.* sadness, grief, misery, anguish, depression.

sorrowful *adj.* sad, unhappy, melancholy, depressed.

sorry *adj.* 1 apologetic; remorseful, repentant: *I'm sorry if I hurt your feelings, for I didn't mean to.* 2 pitiful, wretched, poor, paltry; shabby: *She is in a sorry state having lost her husband.*

sort *n.* kind, variety, type: *What sort of a dog did you get for your birthday? a poodle? a spaniel?* *vb.* separate, classify, arrange, order: *Please sort these words into alphabetical order.*

soul *n.* spirit; intellect, will, emotions, heart.

sound¹ *n.* noise; din, racket: *The silence was so great that we could hear the sound of a pin drop.* *vb.* echo, resound: *The fire alarm sounded throughout the building.*

sound² *adj.* 1 secure, safe, uninjured, unharmed, whole, healthy: *We returned home during the storm, safe and sound.* 2 trustworthy, reliable; sensible: *I think we can rely on Philip's judgment to be sound.*

sour *adj.* 1 acid, tart: *Those lemon sweets are so sour they make my mouth pucker up.* 2 bad-tempered, unpleasant, cross: *That old man certainly has a sour disposition—he doesn't like anyone or anything.* ANT. (1) sweet. (2) good-natured, sunny, benevolent.

source *n.* origin, beginning.

souvenir *n.* memento, keepsake.

sovereign *n.* ruler, lord; monarch, king, queen, emperor, empress: *Queen Elizabeth II is the sovereign of Great Britain.* *adj.* supreme, chief, principal: *Freedom of speech is a sovereign right of our people.*

sow *vb.* scatter, plant, propagate.

space *n.* 1 area, location, room: *Please put the desk into the open space against that wall.* 2 cosmos, galaxy, outer space: *The Americans launched a further rocket into space.*

spacious *adj.* roomy, large. ANT. cramped, small, narrow, confined.

span *n.* extent, spread: *This history book covers a span of four centuries.* *vb.* extend, reach, cross: *The bridge spans the river about a kilometre north of here.*

spare *vb.* 1 save, set aside *or* apart, reserve: *The police detective was able to spare just 15 mintues to talk with our class.* 2 save; forgive; show mercy to: *Because the robber was a great musician, the king spared his life.* *adj.* extra, additional, unoccupied: *I think we can find a spare tennis racket that you can borrow for today.*

spark *n.* flash; glitter, sparkle.

sparkle *vb.* 1 shine, glisten, glitter, twinkle: *The sea sparkled in the bright sunlight.* 2 bubble, effervesce: *I like sparkling water with my dinner.* *n.* 1 shine, glitter, twinkle: *The sparkle of the glasses caught my eye.* 2 spirit, liveliness, brilliance: *Valerie's personality lent sparkle to the party.*

sparse *adj.* scanty, few, rare, scattered. ANT. dense.

spasm *n.* convulsion, fit, attack, seizure.

speak *vb.* say, talk, utter; address.

special *adj.* 1 exceptional, unusual, extraordinary, distinguished, different: *We have reserved this jewellery for our special customers only.* 2 particular, distinct, certain: *I have made special plans to spend this weekend in the country.* ANT. (1) average, ordinary.

specialist *n.* expert, authority.

specific *adj.* definite, particular, distinct, precise. ANT. general, non-specific.

specification *n.* description, designation, condition.

specify *vb.* designate, name, define.

specimen *n.* sample, example, model, type, pattern.

speck *n.* bit, spot; mite.

spectacle *n.* show, scene, exhibition, display.

spectator *n.* watcher, viewer, observer, onlooker. ANT. participant, player, contestant.

spectre *n.* ghost, phantom, apparition.

speculate *vb.* guess, consider, surmise, view, suppose, theorize.

speech *n.* 1 talk, address, oration, lecture, sermon: *The MP gave a speech on the steps of the town hall.* 2 utterance, articulation, diction, accent, pronunciation, enunciation: *From your speech I can tell that you come from Scotland.*

speed *n.* 1 rapidity, swiftness, haste: *I could see that the girl hadn't eaten for a long time by the speed with which she gulped her food.* 2 velocity: *The speed of the train decreased as it came into the station.*

spell *n.* 1 formula, incantation, enchantment: *The witch cast a spell on the poor little girl.* 2 period, time, term, stretch: *We had several spells of cold weather last winter.*

spend *vb.* 1 pay, expend, lay out: *I spent much too much money on that tie.* 2 use up, consume: *I wish you wouldn't spend so much time watching television.* ANT. (1) save, hoard.

sphere *n.* 1 ball, orb, globe: *In nature, many objects have the form of a sphere.* 2 area, field, environment, domain: *In my sphere of work, one must study for many years to become an expert.*

spice *n.* seasoning, condiment, flavouring, herb.

spike *n.* pin, nail, prong, point.

spill *vb.* scatter, drop; let go.

spin *vb.* 1 turn, revolve, whirl, rotate, twirl: *When we were children, we used to spin our tops and try to do tricks with them.* 2 narrate, tell, relate: *At night the old men would get together at the club to spin tales of long ago.*

spine *n.* backbone, spinal column.

spineless *adj.* weak, feeble, limp; cowardly. ANT. strong, brave, courageous.

spirit *n.* 1 mood, attitude, outlook, feeling: *Jim has been in very low spirits since his older brother went away to college.* 2 vitality, liveliness, energy: *It takes a lot of spirit for an invalid like Betsy to remain cheerful.* 3 angel, fairy, devil, elf, sprite, goblin, demon: *In the old days, many people blamed evil spirits for their own mistakes.* 4 ghost, phantom, spectre: *That house—the deserted one—is inhabited by spirits.* 5 meaning, intention, intent: *There is often a difference betwee the letter of the law and the spirit of the law.* 6 will; soul: *After your body dies, the spirit still exists.*

spirited *adj.* animated, excited, active, lively, energetic, vigorous. ANT. lazy, indolent, sleepy.

spiritual *adj.* 1 immaterial, intangible; otherworldly: *Spiritual beings are active in the world, although you cannot see them.* 2 religious, holy, consecrated: *Gerald is very spiritual: he follows God's will in every way.* ANT. (1) material, physical, tangible.

spite *n.* malice, contempt, resentment. ANT. goodwill, affection.

splash *vb.* spatter; dash, break.

splendid *adj.* 1 magnificent, brilliant, gorgeous, sumptuous, elegant, luxurious: *The king ordered the craftsmen to create splendid furnishings for the palace.* 2 excellent, superb, superior: *That's a splendid painting of the Grand Canal in Venice.*

splendour *n.* magnificence, grandeur, display, brilliance.

splinter *n.* sliver, chip, piece, fragment: *Be careful with that board or you'll get a splinter in your finger.* *vb.* split, shiver: *The glass splintered into a thousand pieces when it dropped on the floor.*

split *vb.* divide, break, separate: *Let's split the chocolate bar among the three of us. If you hammer a wedge into the crack in that log, it will split easily.* *n.* crack, opening: *The split in the wood was repaired by the carpenter.*

splutter *vb.* stutter, stammer.

spoil *vb.* 1 damage, ruin, destroy: *I left my painting out in the rain and it's completely spoiled.* 2 rot, go bad: *If you leave milk out of the refrigerator too long it will spoil.*

spokesman *n.* representative, agent; mouthpiece.

sponge *vb.* mop, wipe, swab.

sponsor *n.* patron, supporter, promotor.

spontaneous *adj.* natural, voluntary, unconscious, unplanned. ANT. studied, cautious.

sport *n.* 1 game, play, recreation: *I play football for sport.* 2 mockery, jest, joke ridicule: *You are making sport of me when you say I'm the greatest singer you've ever heard.*

sporting *adj.* fair, considerate, sportsmanlike.

spot *n.* 1 mark, blemish, blot, stain, flaw, speck: *I wouldn't go near Peter—he has spots all over his face.* 2 place, location, site: *We have built our new home in a beautiful spot right near the lake.* *vb.* 1 mark, stain, blot, spatter: *You've splashed tomato juice everywhere and have spotted the clean tablecloth.* 2 locate, find: *I spotted you in the school photograph even though it was taken years ago.*

spotless *adj.* immaculate, clean, unsullied. ANT. dirty, impure.

spout *vb.* squirt, spurt: *The lava could be seen spouting out of the volcano from far away.* *n.* nozzle, tube: *The water comes out of the green spout and the milk out of the white one.*

sprawl *vb.* lounge, relax, slouch, loll, sit, rest.

spray *n.* spatter; splash: *There was a fine spray of cologne from the top of the bottle.* *vb.* sprinkle, spatter, splash: *I sprayed the roses with a fluid that would keep off the bugs.*

spread *vb.* **1** distribute; disperse: *The icing must be spread evenly over the top of the cake before serving.* **2** open, unfurl, unroll, unfold: *I helped to spread the sails on the lawn so they could dry in the sun.* **3** scatter: *The news about the fire spread throughout the town.* *n.* **1** extent, range; diffusion: *The spread of nuclear weapons is terrifying.* **2** jam, jelly, preserve, conserve: *I like to put a spread on hot toast after it has been buttered.*

spring *vb.* **1** leap, bound, jump: *I sprang to my feet when the teacher entered the room.* **2** start, begin, arise, originate: *Dave's eagerness to help with the cooking springs from his wish to be closer to the food.* *n.* **1** leap, jump, bound: *With one leap the cat was out of the door and scurrying down the hall.* **2** source; origin: *This stream is fed by a spring in the mountains.*

sprinkle *vb.* scatter, spread, strew: *Sprinkle the pancake lightly with powdered sugar.* *n.* scattering, rain; drizzle: *We were getting wet in the sprinkle that came from the garden hose.*

sprint *vb.* dash, rush, race.

sprout *vb.* grow, germinate, develop.

spry *adj.* lively, nimble, quick, alert, agile, energetic. ANT. inactive, lethargic.

spur *n.* goad; stimulus: *The will to win is a spur to athletes to do their very best in competitive sports.* *vb.* goad, stimulate, urge: *The thought of a good meal and a warm fire spurred Nicholas on as he trudged home through the snow.*

spurious *adj.* unreal, fake, counterfeit. ANT. real, genuine.

spy *n.* informer, secret agent, agent: *The spies were shot as soon as they were caught, even without a trial.* *vb.* watch, observe, pry: *"Stop spying on me," John told his younger brother.*

squalid *adj.* filthy, dirty; foul.

squander *vb.* waste, throw away, lavish, fritter away.

squat *vb.* crouch, stoop: *The young children squatted on the floor.* *adj.* thickset, stubby, dumpy; compact: *Some modern squat chairs are not very comfortable.*

squeak *vb.,n.* cry, creak, squeal: *The hinges of the door squeaked and I knew someone was approaching. The squeak of the mouse frightened us all.*

squeeze *vb.* pinch, clasp, press.

stab *vb.* pierce, gore, stick, spear; knife, bayonet.

stable *adj.* steady, firm, robust, sturdy, steadfast, solid. ANT. unstable, shaky.

stack *n.* pile, mound, heap, mass: *There's a big stack of firewood if you want to make a fire.* *vb.* pile, heap, accumulate: *Please try to stack those stones more neatly next time.*

staff *n.* **1** stick, pole, club: *Little John always carried his staff with him and used it as a weapon.* **2** employees, personnel, help, crew: *The company has a skilled staff of 35 people.*

stage *n.* **1** theatre: *When I was younger, I wanted to go on the stage, but I couldn't act well enough, so now I'm a star on television.* **2** phase, step, period: *The project has reached a stage where we need more people right away.* *vb.* produce, direct; present, put on: *Our school staged the musical comedy* The Boy Friend *this year.*

stagger *vb.* **1** sway, totter, reel, falter: *Here comes Freddie, staggering down the street as if he'd been hit on the head.* **2** vary, alternate: *If you could stagger your working days and your days off, you could get some rest.*

stagnant *adj.* still, dead; foul, filthy.

stain *n.* **1** spot, blemish, blot, mark: *There's a big stain on your collar—it looks like blood.* **2** disgrace, smirch, blot: *It will take many weeks of very good behaviour, Roberto, to clear up that stain on your record.* *vb.* **1** spot, blot, mark: *You've stained the tablecloth with ketchup!* **2** tint, dye, colour: *The cabinet-maker stained the wood a very dark mahogany.*

stair *n.* stairway, flight of stairs, staircase, steps.

stake *n.* **1** post, stick, pole, pale, picket, rod: *The hunters tied the goat to a stake in the clearing to act as bait for the tiger.* **2** wager, bet: *The stakes are too high for me to play poker with those men.* **3** interest, concern: *I bought a stake in a silver mine but I lost everything.*

stale *adj.* **1** old, spoiled, dry; inedible: *We break up any stale bread we have and feed it to the birds.* **2** uninteresting, flat, dull, trite: *We had to sit through dinner listening politely and laughing whenever Bill told another of his stale jokes.* ANT. (1) fresh, new.

stalk[1] *vb.* follow, dog, pursue, shadow, track, hunt: *Have you* *ever stalked a tiger in the jungles of India?*

stalk² *n.* stem, shaft: *The stalks of the plants are now growing rapidly.*

stall *vb.* stop; hesitate, postpone, delay: *My car keeps stalling in the middle of traffic.* *n.* stand, booth, kiosk: *Sheila manned the cake stall at the fair.*

stammer *vb.* stutter; falter, hem and haw.

stamp *vb.* **1** trample, crush: *Our guests stamped all over our newly seeded lawn and ruined it completely.* **2** brand, mark, imprint: *Ellie stamped her name all over my shirt and I can't wash it out.* *n.* die, block, seal: *My father gave me a rubber stamp with my name and address on it.*

stand *vb.* **1** rise, arise, stand up: *Please stand when the band plays the national anthem.* **2** remain, stay: *My original instructions still stand.* **3** tolerate, endure, abide, bear: *I can't stand listening to rock 'n' roll all day long.* *vb. phr.* **stand down** resign: *When are you going to stand down so I can take over?* **stand for** represent: *This symbol stands for good quality.* **stand out** be prominent: *The high buildings stood out in the landscape.* *n.* **1** position, attitude, opinion: *His stand on the issue is that anyone who goes on strike ought to be fired.* **2** table, platform: *The vase was knocked off that wooden stand in the corner.* ANT. *vb.* (1) lie, recline, repose.

standard *n.* **1** measure, gauge, example, model, criterion: *Some people think that the standard for judging right and wrong depends on each situation.* **2** banner, pennant, flag, emblem, symbol: *In the ancient Roman army, the man who carried the legion's standard was very important.* *adj.* basic, typical, approved, official, regular: *Light bulbs are manufactured in a few standard sizes to fit sockets.* ANT. *adj.* unusual, irregular, special.

standpoint *n.* viewpoint, position, attitude.

staple *adj.* principal, main, chief, necessary, essential.

starch *n.* stiffening, size.

stare *vb.* gaze, watch; gape.

stark *adj.* **1** absolute, utter, complete, sheer: *The stark truth is that your son did chop down the cherry tree, Mrs. Washington.* **2** harsh, severe, rough, grim: *The stark countryside was uninviting during the winter.*

start *vb.* **1** begin, commence, initiate: *I wish you hand't started Grandpa off on his storytelling—now he'll never stop.* **2** jump, jerk; twitch: *Oh! You made me start! I didn't know anyone was here.* *n.* **1** beginning, commencement, outset, onset: *At the start of a race no-one knows who will win.* **2**

shock, surprise: *You gave me quite a start, peering in the window wearing that spooky mask!* **3** lead, head start, advantage: *I have a start on the rest of the class because I've already read this book.*

startle *vb.* surprise, shock, alarm.

starve *vb.* **1** die, famish: *Some of the refugees in the boat starved to death.* **2** *Informal:* be hungry: *I'm starving—is it time for lunch yet?*

state *n.* **1** nation, country: *What were once colonies in Africa have mostly all now become independent states.* **2** condition, status; situation: *The doctor told us that the state of the family's health is excellent.* *vb.* declare, say, assert, express; tell: *For the second time in one hour, Mornie stated why she had come to see the show.*

stately *adj.* grand, dignified, imposing, elegant, impressive, majestic, magnificent. ANT. mean, base, squalid.

statement *n.* **1** announcement, declaration, assertion: *The minister issued a statement to the press after his trip abroad.* **2** account, record: *The bank send me a statement regularly.*

statesman *n.* minister, parliamentarian.

station *n.* depot, post; stopping place: *The police station is open 24 hours a day. I got on the bus at the bus station.* *vb.* place, position, put, locate: *The colonel stationed eight men to stand guard duty last night.*

stationary *adj.* still, motionless, fixed. ANT. mobile.

statistics *n.pl.* data, figures, tables.

statue *n.* figure, bust, cast.

status *n.* rank, position, standing.

statute *n.* law, rule, ruling, ordinance.

staunch *adj.* firm, steadfast, loyal.

stay *vb.* **1** remain, rest, tarry, linger: *Please stay where you are for a moment.* **2** remain, continue: *Do you stay happy all the time?* **3** delay, check, hinder, halt, hold: *The judge stayed the execution of the convicted murderer because new evidence had been discovered.* *n.* **1** stop, hindrance, halt, delay: *On Christmas Eve, a stay of execution saved six men who were to die the following week.* **2** brace, support; rope, line: *When the stay snapped, the mast broke in two and we radioed for help.* ANT. *vb.* (1) go, leave, depart.

steady *adj.* **1** even, regular, stable, unremitting: *A steady rain fell throughout the day.* **2** firm, steadfast, reliable: *We need a steady hand at the helm if this boat is to sail across the Atlantic.* **3** firm, solid, stable: *That little table, the wobbly* *one, isn't quite steady enough for the typewriter.*

steal *vb.* **1** take, pilfer, rob, shoplift, embezzle: *Binks stole a dog biscuit and ran out into the yard to eat it.* **2** sneak, prowl: *Dressed in black from head to toe, the thief silently stole down the hall towards the strongroom.*

stealthy *adj.* secret, sly, furtive. ANT. open, direct, obvious.

steam *n.* vapour, condensation.

steep *adj.* sheer, perpendicular, abrupt, sudden.

steeple *n.* tower, turret, spire.

steer *vb.* guide, direct; navigate; drive.

stem *n.* trunk; stalk: *The stems of the plants were so thick I couldn't cut them.* *vb.* **1** arise, originate: *Some of the problems in schools stem from a shortage of money.* **2** stop, check, hinder, halt: *We must do something to stem the tide of crime in the area.*

step *n.* **1** pace, stride: *All those who want to go on the outing should take one step forward.* **2** action, move, measure: *It was essential that we take steps to make certain the bank was locked up.* **3** stage: *What's the next step in the process?* *vb.* walk, move, come, go: *Please step this way if you want to watch the sea lions being fed.* *vb. phr.* **step up** *Informal:* increase, accelerate: *You must step up your rate of work.*

sterile *adj.* infertile, impotent, barren. ANT. fertile.

stern *adj.* strict, severe, harsh, hard, rigid, unyielding. ANT. lenient, forgiving.

stew *n.* goulash, ragout: *Mother made lamb stew for dinner.* *vb.* simmer, seethe, boil: *You have to stew this kind of meat for three hours before you can chew it.*

stick *n.* twig, stalk, branch, staff, rod, pole: *I poked a wooden stick through a hole in the fence and something grabbed the other end of it.* *vb.* **1** stab, pierce, puncture, spear, gore: *Get a needle—Gary has a splinter stuck in his finger.* **2** catch, adhere, hold, cling: *Chewing gum was stuck to the bottom of my shoe.* **3** remain, abide, stay, persist; be faithful: *No matter what you say, I'll stick by you.*

stiff *adj.* **1** rigid, unbendable, inflexible, firm, solid, hard: *My mittens were frozen stiff, and I couldn't get them off.* **2** severe, harsh, strong: *Ten years is a very stiff sentence.* **3** difficult, arduous: *We had a very stiff exam at school today.* ANT. (1) limp, lax. (2) lenient. (3) easy, simple.

stiffen *vb.* thicken, harden.

stifle *vb.* smother, suffocate, strangle, choke.

stigma *n.* mark, stain, blot, blemish.

still *adj.* **1** motionless, stationary: *Please be still while I try to* *bandage your finger.* **2** tranquil, peaceful, calm, serene: *The room was so still you could hear a pin drop.* *conj.* but, nevertheless, however; besides: *I realize that you have a job; still, you ought to continue your studies.* *vb.* **1** silence, quiet, hush: *The crowd had to be stilled so that we could hear the speaker.* **2** calm, soothe, pacify: *My fears for Ruth's safety weren't stilled until I learned that she'd arrived home.* *n.* stillness, quiet, calm, hush: *Only a dog's barking broke the still of the night.* ANT. *adj.* (1) mobile. (2) noisy. *n.* noise.

stilted *adj.* forced, laboured, heavy.

stimulate *vb.* arouse, activate, excite, urge, animate; invigorate.

sting *vb.* tingle, prick; burn, smart.

stingy *adj.* miserly, mean, tightfisted, penny-pinching, selfish. ANT. generous, openhanded, giving.

stink *vb.* smell, reek: *A skunk stinks.* *n.* smell, stench, reek, odour: *The stink of the mouldy food filled the kitchen.*

stint *n.* job, work, task, assignment.

stir *vb.* **1** mix, beat, agitate: *Adele puts five spoons of sugar into her coffee and then doesn't stir it.* **2** arouse, rouse, stimulate; move: *The leader's patriotic speech really stirred his listeners.*

stitch *see* **sew.**

stock *n.* supply, store: *The shop bought an ample stock of decorations for sale before Christmas.* *vb.* store, supply, keep, carry: *The salesman told me that they didn't stock every size of shoe in that style.*

stone *n.* pebble, cobble; rock, boulder.

stool *n.* seat, pedestal, chair.

stoop *vb.* bend, lean, bow, crouch.

stop *vb.* **1** cease, conclude, end, finish: *I wish you'd stop calling me Bill: my name happens to be George.* **2** halt, stay, pause: *When I heard footsteps behind me I started running and didn't stop till I was safe at home.* **3** intercept, obstruct, hold: *Stop that man! He stole my purse!* *n.* **1** halt, end: *You must put a stop to copying your homework from others.* **2** stay, delay, halt: *The train makes a stop at Watford to let off passengers.*

stopgap *n.* substitute, makeshift, expedient.

store *n.* **1** shop, market: *If you go to the store, please buy some eggs.* **2** supply, reserve, stock, deposit: *There is a large store of food in the company's warehouse.* *vb.* keep, preserve, stock, save: *My aunt stores tins in her larder for years.*

storey n. level, floor.

storm n. tempest; gale, thunderstorm: *In the middle of the storm, all of the lights went out when the house was struck by lightning.* vb. **1** rage, rant: *Father went storming about the house because he couldn't find his slippers.* **2** attack, besiege, assault: *The army stormed the enemy camp by night.*

story n. **1** tale, narrative, anecdote: *Grandpa used to tell us funny stories at bedtime.* **2** lie, fabrication, fib: *You have to learn not to tell such stories or no one will believe you when you tell the truth.*

stout adj. **1** fat, obese, overweight, plump, heavy, portly: *If you make fun of someone who is stout, you might hurt his feelings.* **2** strong, sturdy: *They tied up the prisoners with some stout twine and then called the police.* ANT. **(1)** slim, thin, skinny, lean. **(2)** flimsy.

straight adj. **1** direct, uncurving: *Motorways have many straight sections.* **2** honest, upright, honourable, moral: *Alan is one of the straightest people I know.* **3** orderly, tidy: *Please try to keep your room straight.* adv. directly: *You must come straight home from school today for your piano lesson.* ANT. adj. **(1)** crooked, twisted.

strain vb. **1** stretch, tighten: *We strained the rope trying to pull the car out of the ditch.* **2** injure, harm, sprain: *Bend at the knees to lift something heavy or you'll strain your back.* **3** filter, screen, sift: *Strain the tea before serving it.*

strainer n. sieve, colander, filter.

strait n. **1** channel, passage: *Do you know where the Strait of Magellan is? I don't.* **2** difficulty, trouble, distress, crisis: *The family has been in dire straits since Peter's father lost his job.*

stranded adj. lost, abandoned, destitute, helpless.

strange adj. **1** odd, peculiar, unusual, curious, extraordinary, queer, bizarre: *A small man, wearing strange silvery clothes, stepped out of the spaceship.* **2** foreign, unfamiliar, exotic: *A strange odour lingered in the room after our mysterious visitor left.*

stranger n. foreigner, alien, outsider. ANT. friend, acquaintance.

strangle vb. throttle, choke, suffocate.

strap n. belt, strip, band, thong.

strategy n. technique, approach, tactics; plan, stratagem.

stray vb. wander, rove, roam: *The horse broke its tether and strayed off into the woods.* adj. lost, strayed: *The dog was trained to find and return stray sheep to the farm.*

stream n. **1** brook, run, creek, rivulet, river: *In the winter, the stream near our house froze over.* **2** flow, rush, torrent: *A stream of abuse from the audience greeted the discredited leader when he rose to speak.* vb. flow, rush, pour, gush: *Tears streamed down the girl's face.*

street n. road, way; avenue.

strength n. **1** power, vigour, might: *Sally's father showed off his strength by crushing a brick with his bare hands.* **2** durability, soundness: *For its weight aluminium has remarkable strength.* ANT. (1) weakness, frailty.

strengthen vb. reinforce, fortify; arm; confirm.

strenuous adj. energetic, forceful, vigorous, active, determined.

stress vb. emphasize, accent, accentuate: *The minister said that he couldn't stress the importance of honesty enough.* n. **1** emphasis, accent, weight, importance: *In my day, great stress was laid on a classical and literary education.* **2** pressure, strain: *The stress on the cable was too great and it gave way.*

stretch vb. **1** extend, elongate, lengthen: *The rope cannot be stretched to go around the package twice.* **2** expand, spread, extend: *I can't wear that sweater because it's stretched out of shape.* n. extent, range: *I had a long stretch in Germany—I was there for 20 years.* ANT. vb. contract, shrink.

strict adj. stern, unbending, inflexible, stiff, harsh. ANT. lenient, easygoing.

stride n. walk, step, pace, gait: *The major took large strides along the road.* vb. march; walk: *We strode over the fields at a steady pace.*

strife n. conflict, disagreement, discord, difference, quarrel, unrest. ANT. peace, tranquillity, concord.

strike vb. **1** hit, beat: *The detective knocked the man down by striking him on the jaw with his fist.* **2** attack, assault: *The commandos strike at dawn.* **3** impress, affect, overwhelm: *I was struck by the similarity between the two books.* n. walkout, sit-down: *The entire staff went out on strike for longer hours and less pay.*

stringent adj. rigorous, harsh, severe, uncompromising.

strip vb. **1** undress, disrobe: *The doctor's nurse told me to strip for the examination.* **2** uncover, peel, remove: *That test was as easy as stripping the skin from a banana.* n. band, piece, ribbon: *I cut a strip of cloth to use as a bandage.*

strive vb. try, attempt, endeavour.

stroke n. **1** blow, knock, tap, rap: *The huge man knocked down the tree with one stroke of his axe.* **2** achievement, accomplishment, feat: *Starting a restaurant in the country was a stroke of genius.* vb. touch, smooth, rub; caress, pet: *The vet stroked the dog to calm it.*

stroll vb.,n. walk, amble, ramble, saunter: *The robber casually strolled into the bank. We went for a stroll along the river before dinner.*

strong adj. **1** powerful, mighty; brawny, muscular: *The man in the circus is strong enough to pick up an elephant.* **2** solid, resistant, unbreakable: *The glass in the windscreen is almost strong enough to resist the blow of a hammer.* **3** sharp, spicy, hot; aromatic: *The flavour of this dish is strong enough—don't add any more pepper.* ANT. (1) feeble, weak. (2) fragile. (3) bland, tasteless.

structure n. framework, construction, arrangement.

struggle vb. fight, strive, oppose: *The two men struggled for possession of the gun.* n. **1** fight, encounter, clash, battle, conflict: *At the end of the struggle thousands lay wounded on the battlefield.* **2** effort, exertion: *It's a struggle getting up on time every day.*

stubborn adj. obstinate, unyielding, inflexible, rigid, unbending. ANT. yielding, complaisant.

student n. pupil; scholar; learner.

studio n. workshop, workroom.

study n. attention, examination, research: *The committee decided that much study must be given to the question of where the new airport was to be built.* vb. examine, investigate; consider, weigh: *We ought to study the problem before giving a reply.*

stuff n. **1** substance, material: *What kind of stuff do they make plastic out of?* **2** cloth, fabric, textile: *The king's throne room was hung with gold-embroidered stuffs.* vb. ram, fill, pack, cram: *I stuffed rags in the cracks to keep out the cold.*

stuffy adj. **1** close, sticky, unventilated, oppressive: *The air is very stuffy in this room—can you open a window?* **2** dull, staid, stodgy, conservative: *The old lecturer gave a very stuffy talk on the days of the Empire.*

stumble vb. trip; lurch, flounder, fall.

stun vb. **1** knock out: *I was temporarily stunned when the ball struck me on the head.* **2** astonish, surprise, shock, amaze, astound: *Ike was stunned when they told him that he'd won the gold medal.*

stupefy vb. **1** deaden, stun, numb: *Peter was stupefied with sorrow when he heard the news of the death of his sister.* **2** amaze, astound, confuse: *Rose was stupefied on hearing she* *had won a scholarship to go abroad to study music.*

stupendous *adj.* amazing, astounding, marvellous.

stupid *adj.* dull, half-witted, silly, idiotic. ANT. intelligent, smart, bright, quick.

stupor *n.* daze; torpor, inertness.

sturdy *adj.* firm, strong, well-built. ANT. frail, flimsy.

stutter *vb.* stammer, stumble, falter.

style *n.* 1 kind, sort, type: *What style of shoe were you looking for?* 2 elegance, chic, smartness: *Greta's mother has a great deal of style, no matter what she does or wears.*

suave *adj.* sophisticated, smooth, urbane.

subconscious *adj.* inner, inmost, mental, hidden.

subdue *vb.* 1 defeat, conquer, beat, overcome: *The people, without any defence, were quickly subdued by the advancing army.* 2 lower, reduce, soften, tone down: *The mourners talked in subdued voices at the funeral.*

subject *n.* 1 topic, theme: *On what subject should I write the essay for the English class?* 2 subordinate, dependant: *The people were considered subjects of the queen.* *adj.* 1 depending, dependent: *Subject to your approval, we'd like to plan a picnic for the class.* 2 subordinate, inferior: *The subject peoples of the world have come a long way towards independence.* *vb.* 1 dominate, influence, control, tame, subdue, suppress: *Because of you, we were caught and subjected to punishment.* 2 expose: *Why must I be subjected to constant abuse just because I have red hair?*

sublime *adj.* noble, exalted, lofty.

submerge *vb.* dip, sink, subside. ANT. rise, surface.

submit *vb.* 1 yield, surrender: *The few soldiers remaining finally submitted when the fort was bombed.* 2 offer, tender: *Our class submitted a plan to the headmaster for cleaning up the grounds.* ANT. (1) resist, fight.

subordinate *adj.* inferior, lower: *Ken was able to get only a job subordinate to the head of department.* *n.* worker, assistant, inferior: *Beth is a subordinate of Mrs. White's in the company.* *vb.* lower, demean, reduce: *You ought to learn to subordinate your desires to those of the entire group.* ANT. superior.

subscribe *vb.* 1 pay, contribute: *I want to subscribe to your magazine. How much does it cost a year?* 2 support, approve: *Great men subscribe to different theories about the origin of the universe.*

subsequent *adj.* following, later, succeeding. ANT. previous, preceding.

subside *vb.* sink, lower; diminish. ANT. erupt, arise.

subsidy *n.* grant, support, aid.

substance *n.* **1** material, matter, stuff: *This dress is made out of some strange synthetic substance.* **2** essence: *Tom presented the substance of his argument but no one agreed with him.*

substantial *adj.* **1** considerable, large, sizable: *The professor received a substantial fee for writing the introduction to the book.* **2** real, actual, tangible: *The police have substantial reason to believe that the fire was not accidental.* **3** wealthy, influential: *My uncle is a substantial member of this community, I'll have you know.* ANT. (1) trivial, unimportant.

substantiate *vb.* establish, prove, confirm.

substitute *n.* replacement, relief, stand-in: *I'm not good enough to be a regular player, but I'm a substitute.* *vb.* replace, exchange, displace: *Rick was sent in to substitute for Bill when Bill broke his leg.*

subtle *adj.* indirect; suggestive; implied. ANT. obvious, overt.

subtract *vb.* reduce, diminish, deduct, lessen. ANT. add.

subvert *vb.* overthrow; upset; corrupt.

succeed *vb.* **1** thrive, prosper, flourish: *Fred has succeeded very well in business.* **2** follow; ensue; replace: *We were having such a wonderful time that the succeeding days meant nothing. Mr. Kensington succeeded Mr. Kew as chairman of the garden committee.* ANT. (1) fail, (*slang*) flop. (2) precede.

success *n.* **1** prosperity, fortune; luck: *The headmaster of the school wished each student every success in the future.* **2** achievement, attainment, accomplishment: *Your success at work is evident. Well done!*

successful *adj.* lucky, fortunate, prosperous, triumphant, victorious, favourable.

succession *n.* series, course, sequence.

successive *adj.* consecutive, sequential, serial.

successor *n.* follower, heir; sequel.

succinct *adj.* concise, brief, terse.

succumb *vb.* give way, yield, submit, surrender.

suck *vb.* absorb, take in, swallow; engulf.

sudden *adj.* unexpected, swift, abrupt, unforeseen.

sue *vb.* prosecute, accuse.

suffer *vb.* undergo, experience, endure, go through.

sufficient *adj.* enough, adequate.

suffocate *vb.* choke, stifle, strangle.

suggest *vb.* **1** offer, propose, recommend, hint: *I suggested that they might try putting out the fire with sand, since water was* *unavailable in the desert.* 2 evoke, hint, imply: *The colours in the picture suggested a note of optimism.*

suggestion *n.* 1 plan, proposal, idea: *The teacher liked my suggestion that everyone in the class start his own project.* 2 hint, trace, touch: *There was a faint suggestion of garlic in the soup.*

suit *n.* costume, outfit: *I'm going to buy a new suit today.* *vb.* agree with, befit, fit: *The arrangements suit us nicely, thank you.*

suitable *adj.* fitting, apt, becoming, proper. ANT. inappropriate.

sulk *vb.* glower, scowl.

sullen *adj.* 1 silent, moody, bitter, sulky: *Try to say something to cheer up Bob this morning—he seems so sullen.* 2 dismal, sad, gloomy, sombre: *These sullen winter days are very depressing.* ANT. (1) cheerful, cheery, jovial.

sultry *adj.* hot, oppressive, close, stifling.

sum *n.* amount: *There is no need for you to keep on giving such small sums of money to me.* *vb. phr.* **sum up** summarize, review: *The lecturer summed up his main points in conclusion.*

summary *n.* outline, digest, synopsis, abstract, precis: *Please let me have a summary of the book in just 250 words.* *adj.* brief, concise, short, compact, condensed: *A summary report of what happened at the meeting should be on my desk now.*

summit *n.* top, peak, crown.

summon *vb.* call, request, send for, invite. ANT. dismiss.

sumptuous *adj.* lavish, extravagant; splendid, magnificent.

sundry *adj.* various, several, diverse, miscellaneous.

superb *adj.* wonderful, splendid, marvellous, extraordinary, superior, excellent, magnificent, fine.

superficial *adj.* shallow, trivial, slight, inconsiderable. ANT. deep.

superfluous *adj.* unnecessary, redundant, excessive.

superintendent *n.* supervisor, manager, director, overseer, administrator.

superior *adj.* better, greater, finer: *One can easily see that this painting is of superior workmanship.* *n.* boss, employer, supervisor: *Each worker must have his time sheet signed by his superior.* ANT. inferior.

supernatural *adj.* invisible, unknown, hidden, mysterious.

supersede *vb.* replace, succeed, supplant.

supervise *vb.* oversee, direct, manage.

supplement *n.* addition; complement; extension: *The railway authorities issue supplements with details of changes to the main timetable.* *vb.* add, extend, complement: *Tim supplements his pocket money by working in a shop after school.*

supply *vb.* provide, furnish, stock: *The dealer who supplies our grocer with vegetables raised his prices again.* *n.* store, stock, inventory, quantity: *Our supply of pencils is running low, so please order some more.*

support *vb.* **1** bear, hold up, sustain, prop: *That flimsy chair cannot support the weight of an adult.* **2** maintain, sustain, finance: *How can Oscar support his family on so little money?* **3** back, assist, aid, promote: *I shall support your desire to travel to the States with financial help.* **4** strengthen, corroborate, verify, substantiate: *The confession of the thief was supported by the evidence of his fingerprints at the scene.* *n.* **1** brace, prop, stay: *I hope that these supports will hold in a storm.* **2** help, aid, assistance: *We need all the support we can get in the fight against disease.*

suppose *vb.* **1** assume, presume: *Suppose you are walking down a lonely street in the middle of the night: would you be scared?* **2** believe, think; judge: *I suppose you're right about not trusting Philip to get here on time.*

suppress *vb.* subdue, overpower, crush; repress.

supreme *adj.* best, highest, greatest.

surcharge *n.* excess, supplement, extra.

sure *adj.* **1** certain, positive, confident, convinced: *Are you sure that Mary said to meet her here?* **2** reliable, steady, trustworthy, unfailing: *A sure way to make someone angry with you is to punch him on the nose.* **3** firm, stable, solid, safe: *My footing on the icy steps was far from sure, and I soon slipped and fell.*

surface *n.* exterior, outside, covering, cover.

surge *vb.* swell, heave, grow. ANT. ebb, wane, diminish.

surmise *vb.* think, judge, suppose, assume, believe, presume, suspect: *I surmised, from seeing your red face and from your jumping up and down, that you are excited about something.* *n.* guess, thought: *It was your surmise that the sun would rise within an hour.*

surmount *vb.* overcome, conquer; scale, climb.

surpass *vb.* exceed, pass, outdo, excel.

surplus *n.* excess, remainder: *There will be a surplus of wheat in this year's harvest.* *adj.* extra: *All surplus money will be added to the picnic fund.*

surprise *vb.* **1** amaze, astound, astonish, startle: *I was sur-*

prised to see Georgina wearing a green dress—she looks so much better in blue. **2** catch, startle: *The teacher surprised three students hiding in the cubicle.* *n.* amazement, shock: *The enemy took us by surprise and we surrendered.*

surrender *vb.* yield, submit, give up. ANT. resist.

surround *vb.* encircle, circle, girdle.

survey *vb.* examine, scan, view, inspect: *Before moving into the territory, we surveyed it carefully.* *n.* **1** examination, inspection: *A survey of the area yielded no information.* **2** poll: *In a recent survey, more people said they preferred butter to margarine.*

survive *vb.* remain, persist, live, continue. ANT. fail, die, succumb.

susceptible *adj.* sensitive, aware, responsive, capable.

suspect *vb.* **1** doubt, mistrust, distrust, disbelieve: *The police suspect the three men who were seen loitering near the bank.* **2** suppose, presume, assume: *I suspect that Bob may be late because his car won't start.* *n.* defendant: *The suspect was seen leaving the scene of the crime.* *adj.* suspicious, suspected, questionable, doubtful: *Spending large amounts of money after a robbery makes certain people suspect.* ANT. *vb.* (1) know, believe, trust.

suspend *vb.* **1** hang; dangle: *The flag was suspended from the rafters in the gymnasium.* **2** postpone, defer, withhold, delay, interrupt: *We suspended payments on the television when it stopped working.*

suspense *n.* uncertainty, insecurity, anxiety, excitement.

suspicion *n.* doubt, mistrust, misgiving, scepticism.

suspicious *adj.* **1** distrustful, suspecting, doubting, doubtful, dubious, suspect, questioning, sceptical: *I was suspicious of Anne when she said she had memorized the entire telephone directory.* **2** questionable, suspect, irregular, unusual: *There was a suspicious-looking person lurking near the back door.*

sustain *vb.* **1** support, bear, carry, uphold: *That flimsy pole cannot sustain the weight of the entire roof.* **2** support, maintain, keep: *Our hopes were sustained by the sounds of digging from the other side of the cave.* **3** undergo, endure, suffer; bear: *The injuries sustained in the accident were all minor, and everyone was sent home.* **4** support, ratify, approve: *The findings of the lower court were sustained by the higher court.*

swab *vb.* clean, wash, mop.

swallow *vb.* eat, gulp, gorge: *Jack was in a hurry and swallowed his dinner quickly.* *n.* gulp, mouthful: *Take a* *swallow of water to help you to stop coughing.*

swamp *n.* bog, quagmire, fen, marsh, morass: *Keep away from the swamp if you want to avoid a dangerous area.* *vb.* deluge, overcome, flood: *After Sadie's singing debut, she was swamped with requests to sing.*

swap *vb.* exchange, barter.

swarm *n.* horde, throng, mass, host: *A swarm of insects hovered over the picnic table.* *vb.* throng, crowd: *The fans swarmed around the football players after the game.*

sway *vb.* **1** wave, bend, swing: *The palm trees swayed gently in the tropical breeze.* **2** influence, persuade, impress: *The judge refused to be swayed by appeals to sympathy.*

swear *vb.* **1** vow, declare, state, assert, vouch, vouchsafe: *The prisoner swore that he had never seen that man before in his life.* **2** curse, blaspheme: *We don't allow students to swear in this school.*

sweat *vb.* perspire: *Physical labour under that hot sun makes you sweat.* *n.* perspiration: *The sweat ran down from my forehead into my eyes, stinging them.*

sweep *vb.* brush, clean, clear.

sweeping *adj.* general, comprehensive, broad, all-embracing, all-inclusive.

sweet *adj.* **1** sugary, honeyed: *That chocolate is too sweet for me.* **2** pleasant, melodious, tuneful, musical, harmonious, mellow: *Nicole has a very sweet singing voice.* **3** charming, agreeable, pleasant, attractive: *Our parrot has a sweet disposition and would never bite anyone.* ANT. (1) sour, bitter. (2) discordant, harsh. (3) irritable, nasty, irascible.

swell *vb.* grow, increase, enlarge, expand. ANT. shrink, diminish.

swerve *vb.* turn, swing, veer.

swift *adj.* fast, quick, rapid, speedy. ANT. slow, sluggish, laggardly.

swim *vb.* bathe, dip; paddle, wade; dive; float, drift.

swindle *vb.* cheat, defraud, trick, deceive, (*informal*) con: *I was once swindled out of £100.* *n.* fraud, deception, trickery: *The company's guarantee is nothing more than a swindle to sell you the car.*

swing *vb.* sway, rock, wave.

swirl *vb.* roll, whirl, spin, reel, flow.

switch *vb.* change, shift, turn.

swoop *vb.* dive, plummet, pounce.

symbol *n.* sign, token, figure, representation; design, logo.

sympathetic *adj.* compassionate, considerate, tender, kind. ANT. unsympathetic, intolerant, indifferent.

sympathize *vb.* feel for, commiserate, weep for, comfort.

sympathy *n.* feeling, sentiment, compassion, understanding.

symptom *n.* sign, indication, mark.

synthetic *adj.* manmade, manufactured; artificial. ANT. natural.

system *n.* procedure, arrangement, plan, order, scheme.

systematic *adj.* organized, orderly, regular, methodical. ANT. random, irregular.

t

tacit *adj.* implicit, assumed, inherent, implied.

tackle *n.* gear, equipment, rigging, apparatus: *What kind of tackle would be used to raise a car from a dock onto a ship?* *vb.* **1** seize, grab, down, catch, throw: *The player was tackled near the centre of the field.* **2** undertake, try: *If they pay him enough, Jack will tackle any assignment they give him.*

tact *n.* judgment, sense, diplomacy, prudence.

tactful *adj.* diplomatic, considerate, sensitive, skilful. ANT. tactless, unfeeling.

tactics *n.pl.* strategy, plan, approach.

tag *n.* label, sticker, ticket, tab.

taint *vb.* contaminate, spoil, pollute, corrupt.

take *vb.* **1** grasp, hold, catch, seize: *They took the puppy from us because we couldn't keep it in the passenger section.* **2** win, capture, seize, acquire: *After a two-hour battle, the pirates took the treasure ship. You take first prize.* **3** pick, choose, select; prefer: *Take any number from one to ten; double it; then add the original number.* **4** guide, conduct, lead, escort, bring: *Who is going to take the children to school today?* **5** remove, steal, shoplift, rob: *Somebody took my left shoe.* **6** record, note, write, register: *Have you hired a secretary who can take shorthand?* **7** require, need, demand: *But it doesn't take two hours to wash your hair!* **8** charm, attract, engage, bewitch: *I must admit that I am very much taken with Fiona.* **9** purchase, buy, pay for: *I'd like to take one dozen of the red ones and two dozen of the blue.* *vb. phr.* **take after** resemble: *You certainly take after your mother, Sophie.* **take away** deduct, subtract: *Take 6 away from 11 and you're left with 5.* **take back** **1** reclaim, recover, regain: *The French took back all the conquered land after the war.* **2** retract, recall, deny: *You had better take back those things you said!* **take down** lower, remove: *The teachers made us take down the poster from the wall.* **take for** mistake, misunderstand: *Sorry, I took you for your twin brother.* **take in** **1** include, embrace: *When you say "mammal," that doesn't take in birds and snakes.* **2** deceive, dupe, fool: *You certainly were taken in by that fellow who sold you a comb without teeth.* **3** welcome, shelter, receive, accept: *My mother won't let me take in every stray dog or cat.* **4** shorten, reduce, lessen: *The tailor took in all my clothes when I lost a lot of weight.* **5** understand, comprehend: *Marcia took in everything I said but didn't even smile.* **take it** **1** assume, understand, accept: *I take it that you don't like eating raw eggs.* **2** endure, survive: *I guess that Merrill just can't take it.* **take off** **1** remove: *You'll have to take off all your clothes if you expect to have a bath.* **2** deduct, subtract, take away: *The owner offered to take off another 10 per cent if I paid promptly.* **3** leave, depart, go: *The plane takes off at three o'clock.* **4** *Informal*: mimic, imitate: *Gerald can take off some politicians perfectly.* **take on** **1** employ, hire, engage: *We took on 23 more people at the plant last month.* **2** undertake, assume: *I think that with his job after school and on weekends, Peter has taken on more than he can handle.* **3** assume, acquire: *After not having seen another person for so long, Jim took on a lean mean look.* **take out** **1** extract, remove: *The dentist said he had to take out my last baby tooth.* **2** go out with: *Are you old enough to take out girls?* **take over** seize, capture: *A gang from the other side of town took over our clubhouse.* **take to** enjoy, like, favour: *My new watchdog takes to strangers in the friendliest way.* **take up** **1** start, begin, commence: *Don't you think that it's a little late to take up hang-gliding at the age of 83?* **2** occupy, consume: *All of my days are taken up with going to school or working afterwards.*

tale *n.* story, anecdote.

talent *n.* skill, ability, gift, aptitude.

talk *vb.* **1** speak; communicate: *Betty says she doesn't want to talk to you.* **2** confer, discuss, consult: *I think you ought to talk it over with someone before making a decision.* *n.* **1** conversation, chat, discussion: *We had our chat before dinner.* **2** lecture, address, speech: *At the meeting I gave a short talk on butterflies.*

tall *adj.* high, big, lofty, towering. ANT. short, low.

tame *adj.* **1** domesticated, docile, mild, broken: *Civilization began when man learned how to make animals tame.* **2** dull, uninteresting, unexciting, flat, empty, boring: *Life must be pretty tame for you now that the summer holidays are over.* *vb.* domesticate, break: *It takes a lot of patience to tame a wild animal.* ANT. *adj.* (1) wild.

tamper *vb.* mess around, meddle, tinker.

tang *n.* savour, flavour, zest.

tangible *adj.* material, physical, concrete. ANT. spiritual, insubstantial, intangible.

tangle *vb.* knot, twist, confuse, snarl: *You've tangled the kite string in the branches of the tree.* *n.* **1** knot, muddle: *The string was in a complete tangle in the tin.* **2** confusion: *Everything is in such a tangle in this office: we must clear things up sometime.*

tank *n.* container, cistern; basin, tub.

tap *vb.* rap, pat, strike, hit: *If you tap the ball gently, it will roll into the hole and you'll win.* *n.* rap, pat, blow: *A slight tap on the door or window and the dog will start barking.*

tape *n.* strip, ribbon: *Please let me have a piece of tape from that roll.* *vb.* **1** bind, tie, fasten; bandage: *I taped the sign onto the board.* **2** record: *Brad taped the entire show and now can play it back any time he wants to hear it.*

taper *n.* candle: *We lit a taper and the room sprang into light.* *vb.* decrease, narrow, lessen: *A cone has a circular base and its side tapers to a point.*

target *n.* goal, objective, object, aim.

tariff *n.* tax, levy, duty, rate.

tarnish *vb.* stain, soil, dirty.

tart *adj.* **1** acid, sour: *Lemons are very tart.* **2** sharp, biting, cutting: *Victoria's tart comment about my hat was not at all welcome.* ANT. (1) sweet, sugary.

task *n.* job, duty, chore, undertaking.

taste *vb.* **1** sip, try, savour, sample: *Have you tasted Mrs. O'Neill's apple pie?* **2** experience, undergo: *Only someone who has never tasted war could want to go into battle.* *n.* **1** flavour, savour: *I don't like the taste of orange juice in my milk.* **2** appreciation, discernment, discrimination, judgment: *That book is in very bad taste.*

taunt *vb.* tease, annoy, bother, pester; mock, jeer, ridicule, make fun of.

taut *adj.* tight, tense, stretched.

tawdry *adj.* cheap, poor, dull, shoddy.

tax *n.* tariff, levy, duty, rate: *Will the government increase taxes in the budget?* *vb.* **1** assess: *A government should not tax its citizens without giving them a voice in running the country.* **2** strain, burden, encumber, load, overload: *The work taxed her so much she fell ill.*

taxi *n.* taxicab, cab.

teach *vb.* instruct, train, educate, inform, tutor.

teacher *n.* instructor; tutor; lecturer, professor.

team *n.* group, organization, club; crew.

teamwork *n.* cooperation, collaboration, partnership.

tear[1] *vb.* rip, split, rend, divide: *My father is so strong that he can tear a telephone book in half.* *n.* rip, split, rent: *There's a tear in my coat that I have to sew up.*

tear[2] *n.* drop, teardrop: *A tear ran down Penny's cheek when she peeled the onion.* *vb.* water: *The pollution in the air makes my eyes tear.*

tease *vb.* irritate, annoy, pester, bother, vex, harass.

technical *adj.* technological, industrial, mechanical; specialized.

technique *n.* method, system, approach, routine, procedure.

tedious *adj.* tiring, tiresome, dull, boring, wearisome. ANT. interesting, engaging, exciting.

tedium *n.* boredom, monotony, dullness.

teem *vb.* swarm, abound, bristle.

teeter *vb.* wobble, totter, sway, waver.

telephone *n.* phone, receiver: *The first thing to do when making a call is to pick up the telephone.* *vb.* phone, ring (up), dial: *I don't like you telephoning me at work: it distracts me.*

tell *vb.* **1** relate, narrate: *Please tell us a bedtime story.* **2** inform, advise, explain: *Can't you tell me where you live?* **3** reveal, disclose, divulge, declare: *Doesn't Philip ever tell the truth?* **4** determine, discern, discover: *I can't tell whether the car is blue or green in this dim light.* **5** command, order, bid: *You tell Harvey that he'd better get to work on time or he won't have a job.* *vb. phr.* **tell off** scold, reprimand, rebuke: *Why does Peter have to keep telling his children off? Because they're always naughty.*

temper *n.* **1** mood, disposition, temperament; humour: *Ellie seems to be in a bad temper this morning.* **2** self-control, patience: *Edward loses his temper over very unimportant things.* *vb.* **1** moderate, soothe, soften, pacify: *If you want to get along with people, you must learn to temper your outbursts.* **2** toughen, anneal: *The first swords were made from tempered steel in Toledo, Spain.*

temperament *n.* disposition, nature, temper.

temperamental *adj.* moody, irritable, touchy, sensitive. ANT. calm, serene, unruffled.

temperate *adj.* moderate, controlled, restrained, cool, calm.

tempest *n.* storm; tumult, commotion, turmoil.

temporary *adj.* passing, short-lived, short, fleeting, momentary. ANT. permanent, everlasting, fixed.

tempt *vb.* lure, allure, entice, seduce, attract, invite.

tenable *adj.* defensible, reasonable, possible.

tend *vb.* 1 incline; lead, point: *Students tend to be more intelligent people.* 2 guard, look after, care for, take care of: *Who was left at home to tend Grandma?*

tendency *n.* inclination, trend, leaning, disposition.

tender[1] *adj.* 1 delicate, soft; fragile: *That's the most tender steak I've ever eaten.* 2 loving, gentle, affectionate, sympathetic: *I received a very tender note from a friend when I became ill.* 3 sensitive, sore, painful: *My arm is still tender where I banged it last week.* ANT. (1) tough, chewy. (2) unfeeling, cruel.

tender[2] *vb.* offer, proffer, present, propose: *The company tendered a bid of £50,000 to complete the road works.* *n.* offer, proposal: *A tender of £55,000 has already been rejected.*

tenderhearted *adj.* sympathetic, compassionate, softhearted, kind, merciful. ANT. hardhearted, cruel.

tense *adj.* 1 stretched, strained, tight: *My arm was tense from carrying so many books.* 2 excited, nervous, (*slang*) uptight, (*informal*) worked up: *Bill was tense from lack of sleep.* ANT. (1) loose, lax. (2) calm, composed, unruffled, (*informal*) unflappable.

tentative *adj.* provisional, experimental, trial.

term *n.* 1 word, expression, phrase, name: *The technical term for salt is sodium chloride.* 2 period, interval: *What is the term of your agreement?*

terminate *vb.* end, stop, cease, close, finish, conclude. ANT. begin, commence, start.

terrible *adj.* horrible, awful, horrifying, dreadful, terrifying.

territory *n.* area, region, province; section.

terror *n.* horror, dread, fear, fright, panic, alarm.

test *n.* trial, examination, exam, quiz: *We are going to have a French test tomorrow.* *vb.* question, examine; review, inspect: *Are we going to be tested on what was taught today?*

testify *vb.* warrant, declare, affirm, attest, state, witness.

textile *see* **cloth.**

texture *n.* surface, pattern, feel, fibre.

thank *vb.* show one's gratitude, appreciate, recognize.

thankful *adj.* grateful, obliged, appreciative.

thaw *vb.* melt, liquefy, dissolve. ANT. freeze, solidify.

theft *n.* robbery, thievery, stealing, larceny, burglary; pillage, plunder.

theme *n.* 1 subject, topic, thesis, argument, point: *The main* *theme that ran through the speech was that we must be good to each other.* **2** melody, tune, leitmotif: *The theme in that symphony is easy to recognize.*

theoretical *adj.* unproved, tentative; ideal, hypothetical.

theory *n.* explanation, opinion, hypothesis, guess, assumption.

therefore *adv.* consequently, thus, hence, so then, accordingly.

thick *adj.* **1** dense, solid: *The crowd was so thick that I was unable to get through.* **2** heavy, compact, syrupy, viscous: *The oil was quite thick and coated everything with a black goo.* ANT. **(1)** thin, slim. **(2)** watery.

thief *n.* robber, burglar, criminal.

thin *adj.* **1** narrow, slim, lean, slender; sparse, meagre, scanty: *Carolyn looks thin after losing weight. That's a pretty thin excuse for being late—you couldn't find a sock?* **2** watery, weak, light: *The soup is so thin here that they seem to make it by boiling a pot of water with only one noodle in it for flavour.*

thing *n.* object, article; device, gadget, instrument.

think *vb.* **1** consider, contemplate, reflect, meditate: *I have been thinking about going on holiday, but I cannot decide where.* **2** judge, deem: *Don't you think that Mr. Carson is an excellent teacher?* **3** suppose, assume, believe: *I think that you'll want to go to the football match when you find out who's playing.*

thirst *n.* desire, appetite, craving, longing.

thorn *n.* barb, nettle, spine, prickle, bramble.

thorough *adj.* complete, careful. ANT. careless, haphazard, slapdash.

thought *n.* **1** meditation, deliberation, contemplation, reasoning, cogitation: *I didn't want to disturb Irene because she was deep in thought.* **2** idea, belief: *It was Patrick's thought that taking a holiday in Greece might help him get a good rest.*

thoughtful *adj.* **1** kind, considerate, attentive, courteous, friendly: *Gerry is so thoughtful—he always brings wine when invited to dinner.* **2** absorbed, pensive, reflective: *When he heard about how difficult it was for uneducated people to get a job, Tom became very thoughtful.* ANT. **(1)** thoughtless.

thoughtless *adj.* inconsiderate, careless; imprudent, negligent. ANT. thoughtful, careful, kind.

thrash *vb.* beat, whip, flog, punish, defeat.

threat *n.* warning; menace, intimidation.

threaten *vb.* **1** warn, menace, caution, forewarn, intimidate:

The bully threatened Percy with a beating if he didn't give him the ball. **2** loom, advance, near, impend: *The black clouds threatened from the west.*

thresh *vb.* separate, winnow, sift, flail.

threshold *n.* **1** sill, door, entrance, gate: *It used to be customary for a husband to carry his bride over the threshold of their new home.* **2** edge, verge; beginning, start: *I was on the threshold of telling the secret when they stopped torturing me.*

thrift *n.* economy, saving; care, caution, prudence.

thrifty *adj.* frugal, sparing, parsimonious, economical, saving. ANT. spendthrift, prodigal.

thrill *n.* excitement, stimulation, tingle: *We all got a great thrill out of watching our team win the gold medal for swimming.* *vb.* excite, stimulate, rouse, arouse: *The star said that she was thrilled to receive the award.*

thrive *vb.* prosper, succeed, grow, flourish. ANT. languish, expire, die.

throng *n.* crowd, multitude, swarm, mass, horde: *A throng of people crowded round the plane to welcome the visitor from the distant land.* *vb.* crowd, swarm, teem: *Spurred on by favourable reviews, people thronged to the theatre to see the play.*

throttle *vb.* strangle, choke, stifle.

throughout *prep.* **1** everywhere, all through, all over: *We searched throughout the house but couldn't find the cat.* **2** during: *Throughout the last three days you have been nagging me constantly. Why?*

throw *vb.* toss, hurl, pitch, cast, fling, send: *Throw the ball to me and I'll run with it.* *n.* thrust, shove, toss, pitch: *That was a great throw from the boundary.*

thrust *vb.* push, shove; force: *You don't have to thrust the thing right into my face just because I didn't see it at first.* *n.* push, shove, drive: *With a single powerful thrust, the native's spear had killed the wild boar.*

thud *n.* plonk, plump, plop, bump.

thump *vb.,n.* whack, rap, wallop, beat: *I thumped her for being so horrid to me. She gave him a thump on the back in return.*

thwart *vb.* frustrate, obstruct, stop.

tick *n.* tap, click, rap.

ticket *n.* permit, pass; note, slip; voucher, certificate.

tickle *vb.* **1** rub, stroke, touch, titillate: *Tickling young* *children is fun.* **2** excite, delight, amuse, stimulate: *He was quite tickled to think he would shortly be in Africa!*

tide *n.* current, flow, ebb.

tidy *adj.* organized, neat, orderly.

tie *vb.* **1** bind, secure, fasten: *June is a little early to be tying up Christmas presents, isn't it?* **2** join, connect, knot, link, fasten: *The captive was tied to a stake and the natives danced about him, singing. If you tie these two pieces together, then the cord will be long enough to go round.* *n.* **1** link, bond, connection; constraint: *Harry has few ties: he has no family and his parents are both dead.* **2** cravat, bow tie, necktie: *You must wear a tie and jacket to eat in the dining room of the hotel.*

tight *adj.* **1** firm, taut, secure, strong, fast, fixed: *This knot was tied so tight that no one could open it.* **2** sealed, airtight, watertight, locked, fastened: *I can't open this jar because the cover was screwed on too tight.* **3** *Informal:* tipsy, high, drunk, intoxicated, inebriated: *Mother got a little tight from drinking champagne at her anniversary party.* **4** stingy, miserly, niggardly: *Old Jack is too tight to donate any money to charity.* ANT. (1) loose, slack. (3) sober.

till *vb.* cultivate, farm, work.

tilt *vb.* slope, incline, slant, lean, tip: *You tilted the table when you leaned on it, spilling my milk and biscuits onto the floor.* *n.* slope, angle, incline: *The plank was put at a tilt to help the workmen push their wheelbarrows up and down.*

time *n.* **1** period, interval, span, space, term: *The time between spring and autumn is called summer. Don't spend so much time talking on the phone, Mabel.* **2** rhythm, tempo, beat, measure: *The orchestra then played Beethoven's Eighth Symphony in fast time.* *vb.* regulate, gauge, adjust, measure: *The engineers are trying to time the number of pulses per second.*

timely *adj.* opportune, convenient; favourable, auspicious.

timetable *n.* calendar, schedule.

timid *adj.* shy, bashful, retiring, coy, fainthearted, diffident, fearful. ANT. bold, forward, self-confident.

tinge *vb.,n.* tint, colour, dye, stain: *We tinged our T-shirts a pale shade of blue. There's a slight tinge of pink in the sky at sunset.*

tingle *vb.* prickle, itch, sting; thrill.

tinkle *vb.* ring, jingle, chime.

tint *vb.,n.* tinge, colour, dye, stain: *Some older people with white hair tint it bluish. These walls need a warm tint in order to set off the colour of the carpet.*

tiny *adj.* small, wee, little, miniature.   ANT. large, huge, enormous.

tip[1] *n.* end, point, peak, top: *That huge mountain is just the tip of the iceberg—most of it is under water.*

tip[2] *vb.* tilt, upset, knock over: *The canoe tipped, and we both fell into the cold water.*

tip[3] *n.* **1** gratuity, gift, reward: *My father gave the waiter a good tip because the service had been so good.* **2** hint, clue, inkling, suggestion: *The man in the green suit just gave me a tip on which horse would win the race.*

tire *vb.* weary, weaken, fatigue, exhaust.   ANT. exhilarate, invigorate, refresh.

tired *adj.* exhausted, weary, run-down, fatigued, sleepy.

tireless *adj.* energetic, active, strenuous, enthusiastic.

title *n.* **1** name, heading, designation: *What is the title of that book?* **2** ownership, deed, right, claim: *The title to that property is held jointly by my mother and father.*   *vb.* name, designate, entitle, call: *I have titled my latest book: "The Birth of an Iceberg."*

toil *vb.* work, slave, sweat: *Think about all those people toiling in the fields to harvest the food that you take for granted.*   *n.* work, labour, drudgery, effort, exertion: *After ten hours of toil, I just want to eat and go to sleep.*   ANT. *vb.* relax, loll.

token *n.* sign, mark, sample.

tolerant *adj.* considerate, patient, liberal, impartial.   ANT. intolerant, biased, bigoted, prejudiced.

tolerate *vb.* permit, allow, authorize, stand, condone.

tomb *n.* grave, vault, sepulchre.

tone *n.* **1** sound, noise: *The tone of the clarinet is soft and mellow.* **2** manner, mood, expression: *Sheldon's voice reflected the angry tone of the argument.*

tonic *n.* stimulant, refresher, pick-me-up; preparation.

tool *n.* utensil, implement, instrument, device.

top *n.* **1** peak, summit, tip, pinnacle: *From the top of that mountain you can see far into the distance.* **2** cap, cover, lid: *I've lost the top of the toothpaste tube.*   *vb.* excel, surpass, outdo, exceed, beat, better: *Ted topped his earlier performance in this week's swimming match by five seconds.*   ANT. *n.* (1) bottom, base.

topic *n.* subject, issue, theme.

topical *adj.* current, modern, contemporary; recent.

topsy-turvy *adj.* confused, muddled; disorganized, untidy.

torch *n.* light, lamp.

torment *vb.* annoy, vex, pester, harass, torture, distress: *Peter was tormented by the worry that he'd miss the train if he waited for the message to come through.* *n.* torture, agony, anguish, misery: *I can't describe the torment I went through until I learned you were safe.*

torrent *n.* downpour, flood, deluge.

torture *n.* torment, anguish, misery, pain, cruelty: *The soldiers used torture to make the captive tell where the guns were hidden.* *vb.* torment, abuse; annoy, irritate: *Stop torturing me any longer—did you pass your driving test or not?*

toss *vb.* 1 throw, pitch, hurl, cast: *Larry tossed the paper into the wastepaper basket across the room.* 2 turn, stir, move, tumble: *I tossed all night and couldn't have slept more than one hour.*

total *adj.* entire, whole, complete, full: *The total number of students who volunteered to help clean up was six.* *n.* sum; entirety: *What is the total of this column of figures?* *vb.* add: *Would you please total the number of times you were late or absent?*

totter *vb.* reel, stagger, falter.

touch *vb.* 1 feel, handle, finger: *Please do not touch the paintings.* 2 affect, move, concern: *We were all touched by the story of the orphan who had found a home.* 3 mention, refer to, treat, discuss: *The speaker touched on the subject of cheating in exams and Alan looked nervous.* *n.* 1 contact; stroke: *The very touch of her hand makes me tingle all over.* 2 hint, trace, suggestion: *This soup needs a touch more pepper.* 3 skill, knack, ability, talent: *That clock cabinet shows the touch of a master craftsman.*

touching *adj.* moving, effective, tender.

touchy *adj.* sensitive, jumpy, nervous, short-tempered, irritable. ANT. calm, collected.

tough *adj.* 1 strong, hard: *This shoeleather is so tough it will last forever.* 2 leathery, inedible, sinewy: *This steak is as tough as leather.* ANT. (1) weak, vulnerable. (2) tender.

tour *vb.* travel, visit: *Our whole family will be touring the country this summer in our new car.* *n.* trip, excursion, voyage, journey: *I once took a tour of all the sights of London.*

tourist *n.* sightseer, holiday-maker, visitor, day-tripper.

tournament *n.* contest, match, competition.

tow *vb.* pull, drag, draw, haul.

towel *n.* cloth, sheet.

tower *n.* spire, steeple: *The tower on the parish church is in need of restoration.* *vb.* overlook, look over, soar, rise above; exceed, transcend: *The new office block towers over the rest of the town centre.*

town *n.* borough, city, municipality.

toy *n.* plaything, game: *It's time to put away your toys and come in to have dinner.* *vb.* play, trifle: *Sadie was just toying with my emotions: she really loved Arthur.*

trace *n.* sign, mark, hint, suggestion, vestige: *You can taste just a trace of rust in this water. I couldn't find the slightest trace of her in the entire building.* *vb.* track, hunt, pursue, follow: *The detective traced the thief's movements on the night of the robbery.*

track *n.* 1 mark, sign, trail, trace: *The tracks of the dog were plainly visible in the snow.* 2 trail, path, road, route, way: *We went far from the beaten track to find these blueberries.* *vb.* trail, pursue, trace, hunt, follow: *The police tracked the fugitive through the wilderness till they caught him.*

tract *n.* region, area, district, territory.

trade *n.* 1 commerce, business, dealing, traffic: *Trade between the countries has become competitive.* 2 occupation, livelihood, craft, profession: *Where do you think Phil learned the harness-making trade?* *vb.* barter, exchange, swap: *I'll trade my bat for your football.*

tradition *n.* customs, conventions, practices.

traditional *adj.* usual, customary, established, conventional; conservative.

traffic *n.* 1 movement, flow, travel, passage: *The traffic is very heavy in the rush hour.* 2 trade, business, dealings: *The drugs traffic is increasing yearly.*

tragedy *n.* disaster, calamity, catastrophe.

tragic *adj.* sad, unfortunate, miserable, depressing, mournful, melancholy. ANT. comic.

trail *vb.* 1 drag, draw: *Phoebe came in, trailing her fur coat on the floor just to show off.* 2 pursue, track, trace, follow: *The dogs trailed the fox to the woods and then lost the scent.* *n.* 1 track, smell, scent: *The dogs picked up the trail of the escaped convict and began to howl.* 2 path, way: *Let's follow the trail through the woods to the village.*

train *vb.* teach, guide, drill.

trait *n.* feature, quality, characteristic.

traitor *n.* betrayer, turncoat, spy.

tramp *vb.* march, stamp, trample, stomp, trudge: *Vickie came* *into the house quite angry and tramped up the stairs to her room.* n. vagabond, vagrant, hobo: *The tramps wandered around town, looking very sad.*

trample vb. stomp, crush, squash.

tranquil adj. peaceful, calm, undisturbed, quiet. ANT. disturbed, upset, agitated.

transaction n. negotiation, deal, settlement.

transcend vb. go beyond, exceed, rise above.

transfer vb. 1 shift, move, transport: *All of these boxes must be transferred to another warehouse today.* 2 assign, reassign, change: *The author has transferred all his rights to the book to his wife.* n. change, move, shift: *The transfer of ownership of the boat will be completed when we receive payment.*

transform vb. change, convert, turn into.

transgress vb. break, violate, infringe.

transient adj. passing, transitory, temporary.

translate vb. render, put into.

translation n. rendering, equivalent, version.

transmit vb. send, dispatch, transfer, pass; broadcast.

transparent adj. 1 clear, limpid: *If you can see everything through it, it's transparent, but if it's frosted, we call that translucent.* 2 clear, obvious, evident, plain: *The meaning of this sentence is quite transparent—it can only mean one thing.* ANT. opaque.

transport vb. carry, transfer, move, shift: *The ore is transported from the mine to the processing plant by ship.* n. transportation, transit, carriage: *The transport systems of this country are very complex.*

trap n. snare, pitfall, net, deadfall: *We set a trap to catch the animal that has been stealing our corn.* vb. ensnare, entrap, net, bag: *In some places, hunters used to trap beavers for their fur.*

trauma n. shock; ordeal, crisis.

travel vb. journey, voyage, cruise, roam: *After travelling all over the United States, we finally returned home, exhausted.* n. travelling, touring: *Travel to foreign countries can be very educational.*

treacherous adj. 1 dangerous, deceptive, misleading: *The icy conditions look treacherous to me.* 2 unfaithful, false, traitorous: *The soldiers were found guilty of treacherous behaviour.* ANT. (2) loyal, faithful.

treachery n. betrayal, disloyalty, treason. ANT. loyalty, steadfastness.

tread vb. walk, step; trample, tramp: *Tread lightly over this* *broken glass.* n. step, walk: *We sneaked along with catlike tread.*

treason n. treachery, betrayal, disloyalty.

treasure n. riches, wealth, abundance: *The pirates were said to have buried their treasure on this beach, but no one has yet found it.* vb. guard, prize, value: *Martin told me that he treasures our friendship above anything else.*

treat vb. **1** handle, deal with, manage, negotiate: *How do you plan to treat the problem of increased student absences?* **2** administer, attend, tend, heal: *A doctor knows best how to treat the condition you complain of.* **3** approach, discuss, regard: *Scientists treat UFO sightings with very little respect.* **4** indulge, pay for: *May I treat you to an ice cream cone?* n. **1** present, gift: *Dinner tonight is to be a treat for you, so you needn't pay for anything* **2** surprise; fun, amusement: *We're having a trip to the fair, as a treat for Robin's birthday.*

treatment n. **1** care, cure, remedy, assistance: *The doctor talked with Rosemary about treatment for her asthma.* **2** handling, dealing, manner: *The treatment of the subject in your essay was excellent.*

tremble vb. quiver, shake, quake, shiver, shudder.

tremendous adj. huge, enormous, gigantic, colossal, great, large: *Looming above us, disappearing into the clouds, was a tremendous beanstalk.* **2** *Informal:* excellent, fantastic; unusual, remarkable: *That tea was really tremendous, Mum.*

trench n. ditch, gully, moat, gorge.

trend n. tendency, inclination, course, drift.

trepidation n. fear, anxiety, shock, dread; quaking.

trial n. **1** test, examination, proof, analysis: *The race that was run yesterday was just a trial to see which cars would qualify.* **2** suit, lawsuit, hearing, case, contest: *The defendant is on trial for murder.* **3** ordeal, suffering, difficulty: *Since her husband died, Mrs. Davies has been through a terrible trial.*

tribe n. clan, race.

tribute n. praise, admiration, recognition, acknowledgment.

trick n. **1** deception, trickery, stratagem, wile: *Throwing that pebble against the window was just a trick to make the teacher look the other way.* **2** joke, jest, prank: *The children's putting salt in the coffee was just a trick—they meant no harm.* vb. dupe, fool, bamboozle, cheat, swindle, defraud: *The swindlers tricked me out of £2000.*

trickle vb. dribble, drop, drip, seep, leak.

tricky *adj.* difficult, complicated; delicate.

trifle *n.* frivolity, knickknack: *Squandering your pocket money on trifles is useless.* *vb.* toy, dally: *It is not good to trifle with other people's feelings.*

trifling *adj.* unimportant, trivial, insignificant, petty.

trim *vb.* **1** clip, prune, shave, cut, shear: *The gardener trims the hedge about three times a year.* **2** decorate, adorn, ornament: *Let's trim the Christmas tree tonight.* *adj.* neat, compact, tidy: *Susan does not have what I would call a trim appearance.*

trip[1] *vb.* **1** stumble: *Marla tripped over the rug and sprawled on the floor.* **2** err, bungle, blunder, slip: *I tripped on the last five questions and failed the exam.*

trip[2] *n.* voyage, cruise, excursion, journey, tour: *The fortune-teller told me that I would soon take a long trip.*

trite *adj.* commonplace, hackneyed, dull.

triumph *n.* conquest, victory, success: *After winning the golf match, the champion had another triumph to add to his list.* *vb.* win, prevail, succeed: *Justice and goodness always triumph over evil in the end, but I can't always wait till the end.* ANT. *n.* defeat, failure. ANT. *vb.* lose; fail.

triumphant *adj.* victorious, successful, conquering. ANT. defeated, beaten.

trivial *adj.* trifling, unimportant, insignificant, petty, paltry.

trophy *n.* prize, award, reward; medal, cup, badge.

trot *vb.* canter; jog, amble.

trouble *vb.* **1** distress, disturb, worry, concern, upset, confuse: *As you can imagine, my mother was a little troubled to learn that I had failed my exam.* **2** bother, inconvenience: *You needn't trouble to go to the door: I can let myself out.* *n.* **1** misfortune, difficulty, concern: *Sometimes I think that our watchdog is more trouble than he's worth.* **2** pains, inconvenience, exertion, effort: *Please don't go to any trouble to make anything special—sausages and mashed potato will be fine.*

trouble-maker *n.* rascal, mischief-maker, nuisance.

troublesome *adj.* annoying, irritating.

true *adj.* **1** correct, accurate, valid: *That is a true account of what happened.* **2** genuine, real, actual, valid, legitimate: *Can you prove that you are the true and rightful heir to the fortune?* **3** faithful, trusty, steady, staunch, loyal, dependable, sincere: *If you were a true friend of mine, you would come to the rescue at once.*

trust *n.* **1** confidence, reliance, dependence, faith: *I have* *always put my trust in my equipment, which is why I haven't had an accident yet.* **2** hope, faith: *I shall accept your story on trust.* *vb.* rely on, have confidence in, depend on: *Whenever someone says to me, earnestly, "You can trust me," I don't.*

trusted *adj.* reliable, trustworthy, dependable, true, loyal, devoted, staunch. ANT. untrustworthy.

truth *n.* **1** truthfulness, correctness, veracity, accuracy; reality: *The truth about something is not always what one sees at first glance.* **2** fact(s), the case: *Please tell me the truth; what really happened?*

truthful *adj.* honest; frank, open. ANT. dishonest, lying.

try *vb.* **1** attempt, endeavour, strive: *I am trying to tell you, but you keep interrupting.* **2** test, examine, analyse, investigate, prove: *Let's try this new kind of washing powder.* *n.* attempt, endeavour, effort: *If you give it a try, I'm sure you'll succeed.*

trying *adj.* difficult, annoying, troublesome, bothersome.

tube *n.* pipe, channel, conduit.

tuck (in) *vb.* **1** put in, insert; put to bed: *Mother tucked the children in and kissed them goodnight.* **2** *Informal:* eat up: *Here's your meal: now tuck in!*

tug *vb.* yank, pull, jerk.

tumble *vb.* fall; trip, stumble.

tumble-down *adj.* decrepit, ramshackle, dilapidated, broken-down, rickety.

tumbler *n.* beaker, glass, cup, mug.

tumult *n.* to-do, ado, confusion, disturbance, commotion, disorder, uproar. ANT. peacefulness, tranquillity.

tune *n.* melody, song, air, strain.

tuneful *adj.* melodious, harmonious, sweet-sounding.

tunnel *n.* excavation, hole; shaft, passage.

turbulent *adj.* stormy, violent, raging, uncontrolled, restless, agitated. ANT. calm, quiet, peaceful.

turn *vb.* **1** spin, revolve, rotate: *The wheel continued to turn long after the motor had stopped.* **2** reverse, change: *Turn to face the wall.* **3** become, change, transform: *The bitter cold turned the pond to ice overnight.* **4** send, drive: *They turned me away at the door, saying I was too young.* **5** sour, spoil, ferment: *The milk has turned, so you'll have to drink your coffee black.* *vb. phr.* **turn against** rebel against, defy, oppose: *Why do some people turn against their friends?* **turn aside** divert, deflect: *The heavy armour turned aside the spears and arrows.* **turn down** **1** lower, decrease: *Please* *turn down the volume of that stereo.* **2** refuse, deny, reject: *They turned down my application for a promotion.* **turn in 1** deliver, offer, give: *I turned in my report early this week.* **2** retire, rest: *I think I'll turn in, as it's past my bedtime.* **turn into** change into, become: *You can't make a frog turn into a prince by kissing it, you fool!* **turn loose** free, liberate, unchain, release: *I don't want to be around when they turn that leopard loose.* **turn off** stop; close: *Please turn off the machine before you leave.* **turn on** start; open: *Turn on the lights.* **turn out 1** switch off: *Please turn out the lights.* **2** dismiss, discharge, evict: *The landlord turned us out for not paying the rent.* **turn up 1** appear, arrive, surface: *Judy turned up late for the party.* **2** be found, come to light: *The lost coins turned up in the cupboard.* **3** increase, raise: *Don't turn that radio up any further; I can hear it perfectly well.* *n.* **1** revolution, rotation, cycle, round: *Let's watch the merry-go-round do one more complete turn.* **2** change, alteration, turning: *Make a right turn at the corner.* **3** opportunity, chance, stint: *Why can't I have a turn at shooting the gun?*

tussle *vb.,n.* fight, scuffle, struggle: *The ruffians tussled in the street. There was a tussle as to who would control the project.*

tutor *n.* teacher, instructor: *Fred was doing badly in maths, so his parents paid for a tutor to help him.* *vb.* teach, instruct, coach, train, guide: *I used to tutor French students when I was at college.*

twilight *n.* dusk, nightfall.

twinkle *vb.* scintillate, sparkle, shine.

twirl *vb.* spin, rotate, whirl.

twist *vb.* **1** intertwine, interweave, braid: *These wires are so twisted I'll never get them apart.* **2** contort, distort, warp: *The steel girders of the bridge were twisted out of shape by the fire. Why do you always twist everything that I say?* *n.* curve, bend, turn: *The road had too many twists and turns for safety.*

twitch *vb.,n.* jerk, shudder: *The dying snake lay there twitching in the sand. With a sudden twitch, the dog had released himself from the collar.*

type *n.* **1** kind, sort, variety: *What type of person would want to kill birds?* **2** sample, example, model: *Is this the type of car you would like?*

typical *adj.* representative, characteristic. ANT. atypical, odd.

tyranny *n.* despotism, oppression; injustice.

tyrant *n.* dictator, despot, autocrat.

u

ugly *adj.* **1** unsightly, hideous, repulsive: *If you want to see something really ugly, take a look at a Gila monster at the zoo.* **2** unpleasant, nasty, vicious, wicked, evil: *There's an ugly rumour going around that Penny was seen going out with Charlie.*

ulterior *adj.* concealed, hidden, implied. ANT. evident, revealed.

ultimate *adj.* final, last, decisive, extreme.

umpire *n.* referee, arbitrator, judge: *After playing cricket for 20 years, Roger got a job as an umpire.* *vb.* referee, arbitrate, judge: *Can we get your father to umpire the game this Saturday?*

unanimity *n.* agreement, unity, accord.

unassuming *adj.* modest, humble, retiring. ANT. vain, showy, pompous, arrogant.

unaware (of) *adj.* unmindful, ignorant, oblivious. ANT. aware, informed.

unbroken *adj.* continuous, complete, whole, uninterrupted.

uncertain *adj.* unsure, doubtful, dubious, questionable, indefinite, vague. ANT. certain, positive, unmistakable.

uncommon *adj.* rare, unusual, scarce, odd, peculiar, strange, queer, remarkable, exceptional. ANT. usual, ordinary.

unconditional *adj.* total, absolute, complete, unqualified, unlimited. ANT. partial, conditional.

unconscious *adj.* **1** insensible; faint, dead, out, (*slang*) cold: *The man lay unconscious on the street.* **2** unaware, unmindful: *Martha seemed unconscious of the fact that she could help her mother.*

uncouth *adj.* vulgar, rude, ill-mannered, discourteous, impolite. ANT. polite, courteous; civilized, cultivated, cultured.

under *prep.* **1** beneath, below, underneath: *We crawled under the ledge of the rock and were safe till the storm stopped.* **2** following, below, in accordance with, subject to: *Under the law you cannot kill other people.* ANT. (**1**) above, over.

undercover *adj.* secret, hidden.

undergo *vb.* experience, endure, tolerate, suffer, go through.

underhand *adj.* secret, sly, crafty, sneaky, stealthy, secretive. ANT. open, honest, direct.

understand *vb.* **1** see, comprehend, grasp, realize: *I under-*

stand what you're saying but I can't see why you'd want to squeeze oranges for a living. **2** hear, learn: *I understand that some children have been playing with fireworks.*

undertake *vb.* try, attempt, venture.

underwrite *vb.* support, guarantee, finance.

undesirable *adj.* objectionable, displeasing, unwanted.

undress *vb.* strip, divest, disrobe.

unearth *vb.* find, discover, bring to light.

unearthly *adj.* strange, foreign, weird, eerie, supernatural, ghostly.

uneasy *adj.* anxious, apprehensive, worried, restless.

unemployed *adj.* jobless, idle, inactive, unoccupied.

unexpected *adj.* surprising, sudden, abrupt, startling, unforeseen. ANT. expected, predicted, anticipated.

unfair *adj.* unjust, impartial, biased; dishonest. ANT. fair, objective.

unfeeling *adj.* callous, hard, unsympathetic.

unfortunate *adj.* unlucky, unhappy, sad, unsuccessful. ANT. lucky.

unfriendly *adj.* hostile, antagonistic; gruff. ANT. friendly, kind; outgoing.

ungrateful *adj.* forgetful; selfish, self-centred; grumbling, dissatisfied.

unhappy *adj.* miserable, sad, melancholy, wretched, distressed. ANT. happy, joyful, joyous.

unhealthy *adj.* sick, infirm, diseased, ill. ANT. healthy, well.

uniform *adj.* unvarying, regular, unchanging: *All laws are not uniform throughout the Common Market.* *n.* outfit, costume: *Policemen wear uniforms.*

unimportant *adj.* trivial, trifling, petty, paltry, insignificant.

uninteresting *adj.* dull, boring, tiresome, tedious, dreary, monotonous.

union *n.* combination, alliance; association, society.

unique *adj.* single, sole, solitary; incomparable, unparalleled; unprecedented. ANT. common, ordinary, commonplace.

unit *n.* entity, whole; system; part.

unite *vb.* join, combine, connect, link, associate. ANT. divide, separate, sever.

universal *adj.* general, prevailing, prevalent, common. ANT. local, regional.

universe *n.* world, cosmos, creation.

unjust *adj.* biased, unfair, partial. ANT. just, impartial.

unkind *adj.* unsympathetic, unfeeling, cruel, unpleasant, harsh.

unlawful *adj.* illegal, illegitimate, illicit.

unlike *adj.* different, dissimilar.

unlikely *adj.* improbable, implausible. ANT. likely, probable.

unload *vb.* remove, discharge, unpack, unburden, relieve.

unlucky *see* **unfortunate.**

unnecessary *adj.* needless, purposeless, pointless, superfluous.

unoccupied *adj.* vacant, empty, uninhabited.

unparalleled *adj.* unequalled, peerless, unique, rare, unmatched.

unpleasant *adj.* disagreeable, offensive, obnoxious, repulsive, unpleasing.

unqualified *adj.* **1** unfit, incompetent, incapable: *Unless you can offer a year's experience, you would be unqualified for this job.* **2** absolute, unquestioned, utter: *After insulting me, you can expect an unqualified "No!" to your request for a good reference.*

unreal *adj.* imaginary, fanciful, fantastic; visionary, ideal.

unreasonable *adj.* **1** excessive, immoderate, extreme, exorbitant, inordinate: *The trade unions made unreasonable demands in their wage claims.* **2** silly, thoughtless; irrational: *Your unreasonable behaviour shows your immaturity.*

unrest *n.* disquiet, turmoil, trouble; tension.

unruly *adj.* unmanageable, disobedient, disorderly, undisciplined. ANT. orderly.

unsightly *adj.* unattractive, ugly, hideous.

unsound *adj.* **1** weak, flimsy, feeble, fragile: *The foundations of the house are unsound and it will collapse in a few months.* **2** unstable, diseased, sick, impaired, unhealthy: *I am sorry to say that we consider your brother to be of unsound mind.* **3** faulty, invalid, false: *The reasoning in your argument is unsound if you think that people will eat insects.*

unsuitable *adj.* inappropriate, unfit, improper.

untidy *adj.* unkempt, disorderly; unorganized; sloppy, messy, slovenly. ANT. tidy, neat.

unusual *adj.* uncommon, exceptional, strange, remarkable, extraordinary, peculiar, queer, odd.

unwieldy *adj.* bulky, awkward, clumsy.

uphold *vb.* support, maintain, back.

upkeep *n.* maintenance, support, sustenance.

upright *adj.* **1** erect, vertical, perpendicular: *We gradually raised the flagpole till it was upright.* **2** just, honest, honourable, true: *Bill is one of the most upright members of our* *community*. *n*. pole, support, prop, column: *Slip that upright under the board while I hold it up in the air.*

uprising *n*. revolt, revolution, rebellion, mutiny.

uproar *n*. commotion, disturbance, tumult, disorder, noise.

upset *vb*. **1** overturn, capsize, topple: *The rowing boat upset in the middle of the lake and we almost drowned.* **2** disturb, agitate, fluster, bother: *I was upset by the news that you were moving so far away.* *adj*. disturbed, unsettled: *I had an upset stomach all night from eating a lot of chocolate.*

up-to-date *adj*. current, new, modern.

urban *adj*. civic, municipal, city, metropolitan.

urge *vb*. **1** force, push, drive, press, prod: *Unless you had urged me, I never would have run for office.* **2** plead, persuade, beg, implore: *I urge you to finish your homework first.* **3** advise, recommend: *The doctor urged that everyone stop smoking.* *n*. impulse: *I suddenly got the urge to phone my sister in South America.* ANT. *vb*. dissuade, discourage.

urgent *adj*. **1** pressing, immediate: *There is urgent business that prevents my mother from leaving work this week.* **2** insistent, persistent, demanding: *The urgent ringing of the doorbell finally woke me, and I ran to see who it was.*

usage *n*. **1** treatment; use: *This puppy has been subjected to bad usage.* **2** custom, habit, practice, convention, tradition: *Usage has it that men hold doors open for women.*

use *vb*. **1** employ, utilize: *I use green nail polish only on Tuesdays.* **2** exhaust, spend, expend, consume: *Why use your energy to do housework?* **3** exercise, work: *I use my left hand less than my right.* *n*. **1** employment, utilization: *The use of certain dyes has been found unsafe for human consumption.* **2** advantage, profit, point, benefit: *It's no use trying to convince you that the earth is flat.*

useful *adj*. helpful, beneficial, advantageous.

useless *adj*. worthless, ineffective, unusable.

usher *n*. guide, escort.

usual *adj*. customary, ordinary, normal, regular, habitual, accustomed, common.

usurp *vb*. seize, lay hold of, take over, appropriate, assume.

utensil *n*. tool, appliance, implement, instrument.

utmost *adj*. furthest, greatest; ultimate.

utter[1] *vb*. say, speak, pronounce, express: *Nicole uttered her first words at the age of nine months (and hasn't been quiet since).*

utter[2] *adj*. absolute, complete, total, unqualified: *Anyone who would try to cross a motorway on foot is an utter fool.*

V

vacant *adj.* **1** unoccupied, empty; uninhabited: *The flat will not be vacant till the end of the month.* **2** thoughtless, vapid, vacuous, stupid: *In reply to my question, all I got was a vacant stare.* ANT. **(1)** filled, occupied. **(2)** bright, alert, intelligent.

vaccinate *vb.* inoculate, immunize.

vague *adj.* uncertain, indefinite, unsure, obscure. ANT. specific, unequivocal.

vain *adj.* **1** useless, worthless, idle, trivial, unfruitful, unsuccessful: *I made a vain attempt to catch the paddle, but it had floated out of reach.* **2** proud, conceited, self-important, arrogant: *Tim is a vain man who will never admit to being wrong.* ANT. **(1)** successful. **(2)** humble.

valiant *adj.* brave, bold, courageous, heroic, intrepid, dauntless, unafraid, fearless. ANT. cowardly, afraid, fearful.

valid *adj.* **1** sound, logical, well-founded: *Your argument is valid, but I just disagree with you.* **2** genuine, real, true, actual, authentic, trustworthy: *This painted bowl is a valid example of Etruscan art.* ANT. **(1)** invalid, illogical. **(2)** fake, counterfeit.

valour *n.* bravery, boldness, courage, intrepidity, heroism, fearlessness.

valuable *adj.* **1** important, worthy: *I have valuable information that I am ready to sell to the highest bidder.* **2** costly, high-priced: *This necklace is very valuable, even though you bought it at a jumble sale.* ANT. **(2)** worthless.

value *n.* **1** importance, worth, merit, benefit: *Anyone who has had any experience has learned the value of an education.* **2** cost, price: *I asked the salesman about the value of the diamond necklace.* *vb.* **1** rate, price, appraise, evaluate: *This Persian carpet has been valued at more than £25,000.* **2** esteem, prize, appreciate: *I value your friendship much more highly than I do the winning of the contest.*

vanish *vb.* disappear, evaporate, dissolve. ANT. appear.

vanity *n.* pride, conceit, smugness. ANT. humility.

vanquish *vb.* conquer, defeat, beat, overcome, subdue.

vapour *n.* mist, fog, steam; haze.

variable *adj.* changeable, shifting, unsteady. ANT. constant, unwavering.

variety n.   **1** change, diversity: *For variety, why not have an egg for breakfast instead of just cereal?*   **2** sort, kind, form, class, type: *I am not familiar with this variety of gateau, but it's delicious.*

various adj.   several, diverse, sundry, different.

vary vb.   change, alter, diversify.

vast adj.   extensive, huge, enormous, immense, measureless, unlimited.

vault[1] vb.   leap, jump, spring: *The runner easily vaulted over the high wall and eluded his pursuers.*

vault[2] n.   **1** tomb, sepulchre, crypt, grave, catacomb: *The archaeologists unsealed the vault of the Pharaoh, who had died 3000 years before.*   **2** safe, safety-deposit box: *We keep our valuable papers in a vault at the bank.*

veer vb.   swing, turn, deflect, deviate, swerve.

vehicle n.   conveyance.

veil n.   gauze, mask, film, web: *The mysterious lady wore a dark veil and we couldn't see her features.*   vb. conceal, hide, cover: *Your veiled threats don't frighten me.*

velocity n.   speed, swiftness, quickness, rapidity.

vengeance n.   revenge, retaliation.

venom n.   **1** poison, toxin: *The spitting cobra can shoot its venom into the eyes at a great distance.*   **2** spite, bitterness, hate: *The prisoner spoke of his accomplices with such venom that the police were afraid to release him on bail.*

vent vb.   release, let out, discharge: *Harold vented his anger on the first person he met.*   n. opening, ventilator, hole: *Can you open a vent? It's so stuffy in here.*

ventilate vb.   air, freshen, aerate, refresh.

venture n.   attempt, risk, chance, test: *The investor wouldn't put his money in a venture like yours.*   vb. risk, dare, gamble, hazard: *I'd venture to say that we ought to leave before the fight starts. Don't try to venture out in the storm.*

verbal adj.   spoken, oral, unwritten.   ANT. written, printed.

verbose adj.   wordy, lengthy, long-winded, prosaic.

verdict n.   decision, judgment, opinion, finding.

verge n.   edge, rim, lip, margin, brim, brink.

verify vb.   confirm, prove, substantiate, affirm, corroborate.

versatile adj.   adaptable, all-round; many-sided.

version n.   rendering, interpretation, rendition, account.

vertical adj.   upright, perpendicular, erect.   ANT. horizontal.

very adv.   extremely, greatly, exceedingly, considerably.

vessel n.   **1** ship, boat, craft: *How many vessels pass through the Suez Canal in a year?*   **2** container, receptacle, holder:

Certain acids that attack glass are stored in wax vessels.

vestige *n.*   trace, hint, suggestion, token.

veteran *n.*   old hand, master; expert.

veto *n.*   denial, refusal: *The chairman's veto was overridden by a unanimous vote of the committee.*   *vb.* deny, refuse, negate, prohibit, forbid: *The college wanted to increase its staff, but the local council vetoed their decision.*   ANT. *n.* approval.   *vb.* approve.

vex *vb.*   bother, pester, annoy, irritate, anger, plague.

vibrate *vb.*   tremble, shake, quake, quiver.

vice[1] *n.*   evil, wickedness, sin, corruption, depravity: *Of his many vices, drinking and smoking were so mild as to be like virtues.*

vice[2] *adj.*   deputy, subordinate; acting: *The vice-chairman chairs a meeting when the chairman is away.*

vicinity *n.*   neighbourhood, area, proximity; nearness.

vicious *adj.*   **1** wicked, evil, bad, sinful, corrupt: *Blackmail is a vicious crime.*   **2** savage, dangerous, cruel: *There's a vicious killer on the loose in Cairo.*

victim *n.*   sufferer, prey, scapegoat; target, butt; dupe, fool.

victimize *vb.*   swindle, dupe, cheat, take advantage of, deceive.

victor *n.*   winner, champion, conqueror.   ANT. loser.

victory *n.*   conquest, success, triumph.   ANT. defeat.

view *n.*   **1** sight, vision: *Suddenly the figure of a huge toad came into view up the road, and we ran.*   **2** vista, prospect, look: *There's a lovely view of the town from this window.*   **3** thought, opinion, belief, judgment, impression: *Please let me have your views on the subject before tomorrow.*   *vb.* see, look at, examine, regard, inspect: *The entire class was invited to view the model of the city at the museum.*

viewpoint *n.*   opinion, attitude, standpoint; aspect; stance.

vigilant *adj.*   watchful, alert, attentive, observant.   ANT. negligent, careless.

vigorous *adj.*   energetic, strong, active, forceful, powerful.

vigour *n.*   energy, vitality, liveliness, strength.

vile *adj.*   **1** wicked, sinful, base, bad, wretched, evil: *How could you have done such a vile thing as to feed the goldfish to the cat?*   **2** offensive, objectionable, disgusting, revolting, obnoxious: *Simon has some exceedingly vile habits of which failing to have a bath is the least.*

villain *n.*   scoundrel, brute, rascal, rogue, scamp.

vindicate *vb.*   **1** acquit, free, absolve: *The statement issued by the authorities vindicated him and said that he had acted properly in the circumstances.*   **2** justify, prove: *His success at*

college vindicates my encouraging him to study further.
vindictive *adj.* resentful, revengeful, retaliatory.
violate *vb.* break, infringe, transgress.
violent *adj.* **1** powerful, forceful, strong, forcible: *A violent wind tore the sail to shreds and we were at the mercy of the waves.* **2** furious, angry, savage, fierce; passionate: *My mother and father have never had a violent argument since they were married.* ANT. (1) gentle.
virgin *n.* maiden, maid: *The young virgins danced around the maypole in the rites of spring.* *adj.* untouched, pure, unused, chaste: *That district is virgin territory that remains to be explored.*
virile *adj.* manly, masculine; beefy, solid. ANT. female; effeminate.
virtual *adj.* potential; possible.
virtually *adv.* nearly, almost, practically; in effect.
virtue *n.* **1** goodness, morality, righteousness, honour: *A man of virtue would never treat anyone badly.* **2** distinction, quality, characteristic: *This machine has the virtue of never needing any oil as it has no moving parts.*
visible *adj.* perceptible, apparent; evident, obvious. ANT. invisible, hidden.
vision *n.* **1** sight, eyesight: *The optician told me that these glasses would improve my vision.* **2** illusion, fantasy, apparition, spectre, phantom, ghost, spook: *Coming down the old creaking dusty stairs was a vision of ugliness that gave me nightmares for years.* **3** farsightedness, imagination, foresight: *The council had the vision, 20 years ago, to see this town as a great yachting centre.*
visit *vb.* call on, look in on, drop in on: *Sometimes I visit my friends in the evenings.* *n.* appointment; call: *I had a visit from your aunt last night.*
visitor *n.* guest, caller.
vital *adj.* essential, critical, life-and-death.
vivid *adj.* clear, strong, bright.
vocal *adj.* **1** spoken, said, oral, uttered: *A vocal insult isn't ever as deeply felt as one in writing.* **2** outspoken, definite, specific: *If Laura weren't so vocal in her criticism of others, she might be better liked.*
vocation *n.* career, profession, occupation, calling, employment.
vogue *n.* fashion, style, practice, custom.
voice *n.* speech, sound, utterance, cry.
void *adj.* **1** meaningless, useless, invalid, worthless: *This*

document is void unless both husband and wife sign it. **2** empty, vacant, unoccupied: *The light was switched on and we saw that the room was completely void.* *n.* space, emptiness: *I haven't eaten since breakfast, and I feel a great void where my stomach is.* ANT. *adj.* (1) valid. (2) full.

volatile *adj.* **1** fickle, changeable, capricious: *Why are some women so volatile?* **2** light, vaporous: *Petrol is a volatile substance.* ANT. (1) constant, steady. (2) heavy, dense.

volume *n.* **1** book, work; tome: *The first volume of the encyclopedia is free.* **2** capacity, dimensions: *The volume of the lorry was large enough to hold a car.* **3** quantity, mass, bulk, amount: *We received a huge volume of orders for the fences.*

voluntary *adj.* spontaneous, optional, free. ANT. compulsory, required, forced.

volunteer *vb.* come forward, offer oneself.

voluptuous *adj.* excessive, extravagant, indulgent, luxurious.

vomit *vb.* be sick, (*informal*) throw up.

vote *n.* **1** election; ballot; choice: *The vote for the new parish council takes place next month.* **2** suffrage, franchise: *When did women get the vote?* *vb.* elect, ballot; choose, decide: *We vote for a new MP in a general election.*

vouch *vb.* guarantee, affirm, confirm.

voucher *n.* certificate, document; receipt; slip.

vow *n.* pledge, promise, oath: *I took a vow that I would get to school on time from now on.* *vb.* **1** pledge, promise, swear: *The men vowed their allegiance to the new leader.* **2** declare, state, assert: *Imogene vowed that she would never see Eustace again after the way he had behaved.*

voyage *n.* cruise; journey, trip, tour, excursion.

vulgar *adj.* rude, crude, bad-mannered, unrefined, coarse. ANT. polite, refined.

W

wad *n.* **1** block, bundle; gathering: *Can you get me a wad of scrap paper from the office?* **2** material; stuffing, packing: *Wads of cotton wool protected the fragile vase in the case.*

wage *vb.* carry on, pursue, conduct, make: *The two countries waged continuous war for almost a century.* *n.* **wages** pay, compensation, salary, rate, earnings: *Your wages will be doubled because you have saved the company so much money.*

wail *vb.* moan, cry; mourn, bewail, lament: *Stop that wailing, here's your teddy bear back.* *n.* moan, cry: *I heard a low wail coming from the cupboard.*

wait *vb.* stay, remain, tarry, linger: *Please wait a few minutes; the doctor will be right with you.* *n.* delay, postponement, pause: *There will be a 20-minute wait while the engine is changed.*

waiter *n.* steward, attendant, servant.

waive *vb.* forgo, renounce, relinquish.

wake (up) *vb.* rouse, arouse; awaken, waken. ANT. sleep, doze.

walk *vb.* amble, stroll, saunter, step, march, hike: *The usher told me, "Walk this way."* *n.* **1** stroll, march, amble: *We had a very nice walk in the garden with Grandpa.* **2** path, lane, passage; promenade: *We met on the walk by the beach.*

wallow *vb.* flounder, grovel, immerse; indulge.

wander *vb.* **1** rove, roam, ramble: *This poor dog has been wandering all over the neighbourhood looking for his master.* **2** err, digress: *Don't wander so much and try to keep to the point of what you're saying.*

want *vb.* desire, need, require, wish, crave: *Don't you want to grow up to be a big strong man? What do you want for dinner?* *n.* need, requirement, desire: *The fund has been set up for those wants that people are unable to fulfil.*

war *n.* hostilities, combat, battle: *Now that we have won the war, let's see if we can win the peace.* *vb.* battle, fight: *The two warring families have hated one another for three generations.*

warble *vb.* sing, trill, whistle, pipe.

ward *n.* **1** district, division: *The town is divided into wards for* *elections.* **2** child, dependant, foster child, orphan: *The parents and their ward, Joy, came to tea.* **3** room: *Which ward in the hospital is Alison in?*

warden *n.* guardian, custodian, keeper, guard; jailer.

wardrobe *n.* **1** cupboard, closet: *Michael keeps all his suits and jackets hanging in the wardrobe.* **2** clothes, clothing: *Sandra will buy a completely new wardrobe for the summer.*

warehouse *n.* depot, depository; stockroom, storeroom.

warfare *n.* battle, conflict, strife.

warm *adj.* **1** heated, temperate; tepid, lukewarm: *The water was warm but not hot enough for tea.* **2** eager, enthusiastic, sympathetic: *The teacher was not very warm to the suggestion that we go home early.* *vb.* heat: *Warm the milk before adding the chocolate.* ANT. *adj.* (1) cool, cold, brisk. (2) indifferent, cool.

warmhearted *adj.* friendly, kind, loving, kindhearted.

warn *vb.* caution, admonish, advise.

warning *n.* caution, intimation, sign, advice.

warrant *n.* authorization, sanction; warranty, pledge, guarantee, assurance: *The financial executive of the bank has given the broker warrants to purchase 10 000 shares.* *vb.* guarantee, declare; authorize, approve: *I warrant that with his record for lateness, no one will want to hire him.*

warrior *n.* fighter, soldier, combatant.

wash *vb.* **1** clean, cleanse, scrub, rub, launder: *The clothes and the dishes are all washed, and now I need a bath.* **2** touch, border, reach: *The waves began to wash the bottom of the sea wall as the storm became more severe.*

waste *vb.* **1** squander, misspend, dissipate; spend, consume: *Don't waste your money on gambling because you won't win in the long run.* **2** decay, dwindle, decrease, wear, wither: *Bob has wasted away to a shadow of his former self.* *n.* **1** consumption, loss, dissipation: *The waste of money last year will be difficult to make up for.* **2** rubbish, refuse; effluent: *The waste from the factory is being dumped directly into the river, polluting it.* *adj.* unused, useless, extra: *We take the waste paper and have it recycled.*

wasteful *adj.* extravagant, careless, reckless, prodigal, imprudent. ANT. thrifty; cautious.

watch *vb.* **1** observe, look (at), note, regard, notice: *Watch the way that porpoise leaps out of the water!* **2** look after, guard, attend, tend, protect: *Will you please watch the baby while I run out to buy some milk?* *n.* **1** timepiece, chronometer:

No, I don't have a watch that speaks the time—I have to look at it. **2** vigil, patrol, shift, duty: *When we sailed from Bermuda, each of us took turns standing three-hour watches.* **3** guard, sentinel, sentry, watchman: *The midnight watch approached us and demanded the password, which I had forgotten.*

watchful *adj.* attentive, alert, vigilant, careful, cautious, wary.

waterfall *n.* cataract, cascade.

wave *n.* **1** undulation, ripple, breaker, whitecap, surf, sea: *The waves on that coastline are very good for surfing.* **2** surge, swell, flow, tide, stream: *A wave of protest followed the prime minister's announcement about imports.* *vb.* **1** flutter, stream, flap: *The flag waved in the slightest breeze.* **2** gesture, signal, beckon, motion: *When I saw my son coming, we both waved at each other.*

waver *vb.* **1** flicker: *The light wavered and we could hardly see.* **2** hesitate, deliberate: *Why do you waver over a decision as important as the one you must make?*

way *n.* **1** manner, method, approach, style, technique; fashion, mode; means, system, procedure: *Which way would you suggest as the best for getting good work out of a student?* **2** road, path, trail: *A narrow way leads to the stable at the back.* *n. phr.* **by the way** incidentally: *By the way, did you remember to bring your walking shoes?* **by way of** through, via: *You can get to Aston by way of Birmingham.* **under way** going, proceeding, moving, leaving, departing: *We have to be under way before dark.*

wayward *adj.* contrary, stubborn, obstinate, headstrong, disobedient, naughty. ANT. obedient, submissive.

weak *adj.* **1** feeble, frail, fragile, delicate: *The legs of the table are too weak to support your standing on the top.* **2** diluted, watery: *This drink is a little too weak for me.* **3** undecided, irresolute, unsteady, wavering: *That poor fellow is so weak that he lets his wife tell him when he's hungry and thirsty.* ANT. (1) strong, powerful.

wealth *n.* **1** riches, fortune, property, means, money: *The Grindles' wealth comes from a factory they own.* **2** quantity, abundance, profession: *There's a wealth of mineral resources at the bottom of the sea if we could only find some economical way to get at it.*

wealthy *adj.* rich, well-to-do, prosperous, affluent. ANT. poor, destitute, impoverished, poverty-stricken.

weapon *n.* arms, munitions, armament.

wear *vb.* have on, be dressed in.

weary *adj.* **1** tired, exhausted, fatigued: *I'm so weary from that hike that I could sleep for a week.* **2** bored; tiresome, tedious: *Mara was just doing the same old weary tasks.* *vb.* tire, exhaust, fatigue: *The same old routine, day after day, just wearies me.*

weave *vb.* plait, braid, intertwine, interlace, lace, knit.

web *n.* cobweb, netting, net, network.

wed *vb.* marry, take; espouse.

weep *vb.* cry, sob, lament; mourn, bemoan.

weigh *vb.* **1** measure, balance, poise: *We weighed the ingredients for the cake.* **2** consider, deliberate, ponder, study: *You really have to weigh the advantages of having the extra money against working for a company like that one.*

weight *n.* **1** heaviness; pressure; mass, bulk: *The weight of the suitcase on the roof rack was almost too much for the car.* **2** importance, significance, influence: *Your opinion will carry a lot of weight with the other members of the committee.*

weird *adj.* strange, peculiar, odd, unnatural, eerie.

welcome *n.* greeting, reception: *We always give Dad a warm welcome when he comes home from work.* *vb.* greet, receive: *There is a very attractive young lady to welcome you at the door of the restaurant.*

welfare *n.* well-being, good, prosperity; happiness.

well *adv.* **1** satisfactorily, adequately, competently: *I think that Joe does his job very well.* **2** fully, completely, thoroughly: *You are well rid of that unpleasant friend of yours.* **3** surely, certainly, undoubtedly: *After the experience, they well know not to try doing such a thing again.* **4** personally, intimately: *Of course, I know that lady very well: she's my mother.* *adj.* healthy, sound, fit, trim, robust: *Are you sure you're feeling well enough to go out?*

well-behaved *adj.* polite, courteous, good. ANT. misbehaved.

well-known *adj.* famous, celebrated, renowned. ANT. unknown.

wet *adj.* soaked, drenched; moist, damp, dank: *I am wet to the skin from walking in the rain. In this weather, the washing stays wet for days.* *vb.* soak, drench; moisten, dampen: *Don't try to wet the stamp too much, or it won't stick.* ANT. *adj.* dry, arid, parched.

whack *n.* **1** blow, strike, crack: *There was a whack as the wood struck the waves suddenly.* **2** *Informal:* attempt, try: *Let me have a whack at opening that jam jar.* *vb.* strike, rap, crack, slap: *The man whacked his son with a stick.*

wharf *n.* dock, pier.

whine *vb.* moan, cry; whimper; complain.

whip *vb.* thrash, beat, scourge; flog: *The cruel man whipped his dog just to be mean.* *n.* scourge, cat o' nine tails, lash: *The man struck the horses with his whip.*

whirl *vb.* spin, rotate, revolve, twirl, reel.

whisper *vb.* speak softly, mutter, murmur: *The girls whispered in the dormitory so that the prefects wouldn't hear them.* *n.* undertone, rustle, hum; murmur, mutter: *The whispers of crickets in the grass is delightful.*

whistle *vb.* **1** trill, howl, warble: *The bird's whistling in the spring is music to my ears.* **2** call, signal: *The referee whistled to mark the end of the game.* *n.* **1** blast, shriek, piping: *The whistle of the wind could be heard across the valley.* **2** pipe: *The old man loved to play tunes on his whistle.*

whole *adj.* **1** entire, complete, undivided, total: *I can't believe that you ate that whole apple pie by yourself.* **2** unbroken, undamaged, entire, intact: *If only I could make a wish and make the window I broke whole again!* ANT. (1) part, partial.

wholesome *adj.* healthy, nourishing, good, nutritious.

wicked *adj.* evil, bad; sinful, immoral, ungodly, profane, blasphemous.

wide *adj.* broad; extensive; expansive, spacious. ANT. narrow, thin.

width *n.* breadth, extensiveness, wideness.

wield *vb.* brandish, handle, flourish, manipulate.

wild *adj.* **1** uncontrolled, unrestrained, unruly: *Some of those boys are very wild because they aren't being disciplined by their parents.* **2** primitive, savage: *There was a wild animal at the zoo who they said came from far away.* **3** silly, impetuous, crazy, foolish: *Going over Niagara Falls in a barrel is the wildest stunt I've ever heard of.* **4** untamed, ferocious, undomesticated: *It's against the rules to keep a wild animal as a pet in this hostel.* ANT. (1) restrained. (4) tame.

will *vb.* wish, desire: *Do what you will with the sausages, but please don't ruin the eggs.* *n.* **1** decision, resolution, resoluteness, determination: *Jo has a strong will, and I doubt that you'll convince her to diet.* **2** choice, volition: *I have come here of my own free will.*

willing *adj.* agreeing, agreeable; energetic, eager, enthusiastic.

wilt *vb.* droop, sag; weaken.

win *vb.* **1** succeed, gain: *If they win this game, we have no chance of the trophy.* **2** obtain, gain, acquire, get, earn: *If you knock over all the milk bottles with this ball, you'll win a doll.* ANT. lose, forfeit; fail.

wind¹ *n.* **1** air, breeze, breath, gust, draught, flurry, puff, blow; gale, hurricane, cyclone, typhoon, tornado: *A man by the name of Beaufort devised a scale for winds from calm to hurricane force.* **2** hint, suggestion, clue, rumour: *We got wind of what they were planning to do, so we locked every door and window.*

wind² *vb.* **1** crank; coil, screw: *Wind up my clock, please. Wind the tinsel round the Christmas tree.* **2** wander, meander, weave, twist: *The stream winds round and round before coming to the river.*

wing *n.* **1** pinion, feathers: *The albatross has very big wings.* **2** annexe: *The main part of the hotel was full, so we were put in the wing.*

wink *vb.* blink; twinkle.

wipe *vb.* clean, dry, rub, mop: *We wiped the dishes after dinner.* *vb. phr.* **wipe out** eradicate, remove, destroy: *The population was almost entirely wiped out during the plague.*

wire *n.* cable, filament, line.

wise *adj.* **1** intelligent, sensible, reasonable, sage, judicious: *You would be very wise to keep as far away as possible from that shark.* **2** learned, knowledgeable, sage; smart: *A wise old man once told me that I should never fail to be loyal to someone and to some idea.* ANT. **(1)** foolish, foolhardy.

wish *vb.* **1** desire, want, long for, crave: *I wish to have you near me always. Betty said to tell you that she wishes you all the best.* **2** bid, express, tell: *Gentlemen, I wish you a good evening.* *n.* **1** desire, want, longing, craving, yearning: *I hope that your wish to visit Russia is granted.* **2** order, command, request: *In keeping with your wishes, I shall be home by ten o'clock, but I'll miss half the party.*

wit *n.* **1** humour, wittiness, drollery: *Della's wit in placing the drawing pin on Vera's chair was what made everyone laugh.* **3** humorist, comedian, wag: *Now, ladies and gentlemen, I have pleasure in introducing one of our greatest wits—Cosmo!*

witch *n.* sorcerer, sorceress, magician, enchanter, enchantress, warlock.

withdraw *vb.* **1** remove, retract, recall: *I wish you would withdraw my nomination for being chairman.* **2** retreat, retire, depart, go; secede: *When the troops saw how hopeless their position was, they decided to withdraw.* ANT. **(1)** place, enter. **(2)** advance.

withdrawn *adj.* shy, reserved, introverted, isolated.

wither *vb.* fade, dry, shrivel, decay.

withhold vb.   check, repress, keep back, hold back.

withstand vb.   resist, oppose.

witness n.   eyewitness, spectator, observer, onlooker: *There were only two witnesses to the events that took place in that locked room.*   vb. see, observe, watch, perceive, notice: *Did you witness the defendant remove his gun from the holster?*

witty adj.   keen, quick-witted, humorous.

wizard n.   sorcerer, magician, miracle-worker, conjuror.

wobble vb.   sway, rock, quake, tremble, quiver, dodder.

woe n.   grief, sadness, misery, distress, suffering, sorrow, anguish.

woman n.   lady; female; girl.

wonder vb.   1 question, conjecture: *I wonder if Tim will ever make the hockey team.*   2 marvel: *All the people wondered at how the escape artist could get out of his chains.*   n. amazement, astonishment, surprise: *The children watched the elephant ballet in wide-eyed wonder.*

wonderful adj.   marvellous, extraordinary, amazing, astonishing, astounding, remarkable.

woo vb.   court, make advances; seek.

wood n.   1 log, timber; firewood, stick: *Please put some more wood on the fire.*   2 woodland; forest; spinney, copse: *We went for a walk in the wood.*

word n.   term, expression; phrase, utterance: *I just can't find the words to tell you how happy I am to have won the competition.*   vb. term, express, phrase, articulate: *The speech by the headmaster was very carefully worded to make sure that all the students understood.*

work n.   1 effort, exertion, labour: *It's too much work to write an essay for school three times a week.*   2 employment, occupation, job: *Some people have been looking for work for more than six months.*   3 output, product; achievement, accomplishment: *An enormous amount of work is turned out by this factory in the course of a week.*   vb. 1 labour, toil: *I wish you didn't have to work so hard to make a living.*   2 operate, run; function, perform: *Does your old car still work as well as it did?*   vb. phr.   **work out** 1 solve, calculate: *Let's work out the answer to this problem together.*   2 plan, devise: *We spent the evening working out where we were going on holiday.*

workman n.   labourer; craftsman, artisan; engineer, mechanic, operator.

world *n.* earth, globe; universe.

worldly *adj.* earthly, secular; worldly-minded, materialistic. ANT. spiritual.

worry *vb.* **1** fret, bother; grieve, agonize: *Don't worry about me; I'll be all right.* **2** bother, annoy, pester, disturb: *Not knowing where the children are is worrying me.* *n.* anxiety, concern, uneasiness: *Now that Martin is safe in bed I have one less worry.*

worsen *vb.* **1** degenerate, deteriorate: *The state of morals in this country is worsening.* **2** exacerbate; increase, deepen: *The cold weather worsened our problems.* ANT. improve.

worship *vb.* **1** revere, reverence, venerate, respect, glorify, honour: *Each of us is to worship God.* **2** adore; idolize: *All of the girls worship that new rock singer.* *n.* reverence, respect, honour: *The worship of God is a very personal thing with most people.*

worth *n.* value, importance, merit: *Can an expert estimate the worth of this diamond?* *adj.* deserving, meriting: *I must say that I don't think that film is worth going to see.*

worthless *adj.* useless, ineffective, unprofitable, insignificant.

worthy *adj.* worthwhile, deserving, meriting, earning; good.

wound *vb.* injure, harm, hurt, damage: *Abbie came home wounded from the fight.* *n.* injury, damage, hurt, harm: *Isaac has a wound in his leg from where he was shot by the thief he was chasing.*

wrap *vb.* cover; enclose, surround, envelop.

wrath *n.* anger, fury, rage.

wreck *vb.* ruin, damage, destroy: *The car was wrecked in the accident. The discovery that there was money missing wrecked the young man's career.* *n.* destruction, ruin, devastation: *The ship had struck a rock, and the wreck could now be seen, stranded on the reef.*

wrench *n.,vb.* twist, jerk, tug: *I gave it a strong wrench, and the handle came off. With a sharp movement, Charlie wrenched the gun from the man's hand.*

wrestle *vb.* grapple, tussle; fight.

wretched *adj.* pitiful, miserable, sorrowful.

wriggle *vb.* worm, twist, squirm, wiggle.

wring *vb.* extract, twist.

wrinkle *n.* ridge, crease, furrow: *My grandfather has many wrinkles on his face.* *vb.* crease, crumple; twist: *The cloth began to wrinkle with age.*

write *vb.* record, put down, communicate.

writer see **author.**

writhe *vb.* squirm, twist.

wrong *adj.* **1** incorrect, inaccurate, false: *If you had fewer wrong answers in your exam, you would have passed.* **2** bad, naughty, improper: *That was the wrong thing to do, and Morris knew that he'd be punished for it.* **3** improper, inappropriate, unsuitable: *You're wearing your shoes on the wrong feet, you silly boy!* **4** out of order, amiss: *The thing that was wrong with my watch is that it was overwound.* *adv.* improperly, incorrectly: *You've put your sweater on wrong.* *n.* **1** evil, wickedness, sin: *People often remember the wrong that a person has done rather than the right.* **2** impropriety, incorrectness: *That poor fellow doesn't seem to know right from wrong.* *vb.* injure, harm, abuse, hurt: *The officer was unjustly accused and he felt he had been wronged.* ANT. *adj.* **(1)** right, correct, accurate. **(2)** good, proper.

y, z

yacht *n.*   boat, pleasure craft, sailing boat, cruiser.
yard *n.*   court, square, precinct, quadrangle, enclosure; playground.
yarn *n.*   **1** thread; fibre: *You are using pink yarn to darn my blue socks!* **2** *Informal:* tale, story, anecdote: *The old man had many yarns he used to tell us when we sat around the stove in the workshop.*
yawn *vb.*   **1** gape: *If you had slept last night, you wouldn't be yawning so much today.* **2** gape, open: *A huge bottomless chasm yawned before us, and Rebecca almost fell in.*
yearn *vb.*   desire, want, crave, long for.
yell *vb.,n.*   shout, scream, roar: *Don't yell at me, I'm doing the best I can. Give Bruce a yell and ask him to join us in a game of volleyball.*
yield *vb.*   **1** produce, bear, supply: *This year's crop will not yield as much as last year's.* **2** give way, surrender, cede, submit, give up: *The strikers yielded in their demands after long negotiations.*   *n.* harvest, return, fruits, produce, crop: *The yield from our investment has been very poor this year. This area has a huge annual yield of strawberries.*
young *adj.*   **1** youthful, immature: *You are too young to see an X-film.* **2** undeveloped, underdeveloped: *This crop is still too young to be harvested.*   ANT. (1) old, mature, grown.
youth *n.*   teenager; lad, youngster, child.   ANT. adult, grown-up.
zeal *n.*   eagerness, enthusiasm, fervour, passion.
zealous *adj.*   ardent, eager, enthusiastic.   ANT. indifferent, apathetic.
zero *n.*   nothing, nought.
zest *n.*   spice, relish, tang, gusto.
zone *n.*   area, region, district, section.